A Conspiracy
Against Obamacare

IV

A Conspiracy
Against Obamacare

The Volokh Conspiracy
and the Health Care Case

Randy E. Barnett
Jonathan H. Adler
David E. Bernstein
Orin S. Kerr
David B. Kopel
Ilya Somin

Edited by Trevor Burrus

A CONSPIRACY AGAINST OBAMACARE

Copyright © Randy E. Barnett, Jonathan H. Adler, David E. Bernstein, Orin S. Kerr, David B. Kopel, Ilya Somin, and Trevor Burrus, 2013.

First published in 2013 by PALGRAVE MACMILLAN® in the United States—a division of St. Martin's Press LLC, 175 Fifth Avenue, New York, NY 10010.

Where this book is distributed in the UK, Europe and the rest of the world, this is by Palgrave Macmillan, a division of Macmillan Publishers Limited, registered in England, company number 785998, of Houndmills, Basingstoke, Hampshire RG21 6XS.

Palgrave Macmillan is the global academic imprint of the above companies and has companies and representatives throughout the world.

Palgrave® and Macmillan® are registered trademarks in the United States, the United Kingdom, Europe and other countries.

ISBN: 978-1-137-36374-9 (paperback)
ISBN: 978-1-137-36073-1 (hardcover)

Library of Congress Cataloging-in-Publication Data is available from the Library of Congress.

A catalogue record of the book is available from the British Library.

Design by Scribe Inc.

First edition: November 2013

10 9 8 7 6 5 4 3 2 1

Contents

Foreword by Paul D. Clement   vii

Acknowledgments   xi

Introduction   1

1   In the Beginning   9

2   The Law Is Passed   25

3   The First Decisions   59

4   More Decisions   79

5   Moving Up the Ladder   117

6   The Big Show   157

7   Argument   179

8   Decision Time and Aftermath   221

Postscript and Concluding Thoughts   257

About the Contributors   279

Index   283

Some posts in this volume have been slightly altered from their original form in order to avoid redundancy, increase clarity, and address issues with hyperlinks. Most of the original hyperlinks have been turned into endnotes.

Foreword

Paul D. Clement

The challenge to the Affordable Care Act (ACA) was a constitutional case like no other. That was true in many respects, but for purposes of this remarkable volume, four are particularly relevant.

First, the arc of the health care case that took it to the Supreme Court was quite unusual. Many great constitutional disputes involving congressional statutes present themselves as such from the very beginning. Take, for example, the constitutional challenge to the McCain-Feingold campaign finance statute, which culminated in the Supreme Court's decision in *McConnell v. FEC*.[1] In that case, the congressional debates were constitutional debates about the meaning, scope, and contemporary relevance of the First Amendment. First Amendment objections—and related policy and political arguments framed in First Amendment terms—had prevented earlier campaign finance proposals from becoming law. And when McCain-Feingold finally passed, First Amendment arguments before Congress transitioned almost seamlessly into First Amendment litigation before the courts. Indeed, the statute itself recognized the reality of imminent First Amendment litigation by including a provision for expedited Supreme Court review. Perhaps as a result, the First Amendment litigation over McCain-Feingold was taken very seriously from the outset.

Not so when it came to the constitutional challenge to the Affordable Care Act. The trajectory of the health care cases was entirely different. While the health care legislation was actively debated in Congress, it was a political and policy debate, not a constitutional one. Legislators hotly contested the wisdom of the individual mandate, but constitutional concerns about the mandate were not raised until the very end of deliberations and were neither central to the debate nor taken particularly seriously.

Thus, when a number of challengers—most prominently a number of states with Republican attorneys general—filed suit and attacked the law as unconstitutional, the challenges were near universally dismissed as frivolous. The suits were seen more as a continuation of the policy debate and derided as political stunts with little realistic prospects of success. Two things changed that: the decisions of two federal district courts and the contributions collected in this volume.

The official game changers were the decisions issued in rapid succession by Judges Henry Hudson of Virginia and Roger Vinson of Florida. Judge Hudson first issued an opinion striking down the individual mandate as unconstitutional.[2] Then in relatively short order, Judge Vinson did Judge Hudson one better and struck down the health care law in its entirety.[3] Once these Article III judges accepted the arguments against the health care statute, and in one case invalidated it in toto, the challenges could no longer simply be dismissed as frivolous.

But there was an important caveat. While Judges Hudson and Vinson had embraced constitutional challenges to the law, other district court judges rejected similar challenges.[4] And commentators could not help but notice that the judges striking down the statute as unconstitutional were appointed by Republican presidents, while those upholding the law were appointed by Democratic presidents. This disparity received considerable media attention and fueled the perception that the constitutional challenge against the Affordable Care Act was more a matter of politics than a serious constitutional theory.

Enter the *Volokh Conspiracy* (VC). Founded by my friend Eugene Volokh, who clerked for Justice Sandra Day O'Connor the same year I clerked for Justice Antonin Scalia, the *Volokh Conspiracy* had long (at least in Internet terms) been a clearinghouse for serious constitutional analysis of contemporary issues with a particular focus on libertarian and conservative views. But if ever a legal blog and a constitutional moment were meant for each other, it was the *Volokh Conspiracy* and the challenge to the Affordable Care Act. Precisely because the constitutional challenge to the law came in like a lamb and not a lion and precisely because many were eager to dismiss the challenge as a political device rather than the manifestation of a serious constitutional theory, there was a need for pointed constitutional analysis and for voices ready to counter the cacophony of skepticism. And this need arose over and again.

Thus, the second distinguishing aspect of the health care case was the intensity and duration of the media focus. Unlike some of the contributors to the *Volokh Conspiracy*, I was not present at the creation of the case. I did not become involved until Judge Vinson's decision reached the court of appeals. By then, the challenge had grown to include over half the states in the Union. In the interview with members of the steering committee, I mentioned that I had experience with earlier high-profile cases involving everything from campaign finance to the war on terror to issues of race. Little did I know that the coverage of the health care case would eclipse all those other high-profile matters.

In many ways, the health care case was the perfect storm for media coverage. The impact on the economy in general and the health care sector in particular were undeniable. As a consequence, the press corps covering medicine, health care, and business issues were fully engaged in the case. In addition, for the talented corps of reporters who cover the Supreme Court, the health care case was a temporary reversal of fortune. In most outlets, Supreme Court reporters generally seem to have to fight for a few column inches to cover momentous cases. With the health care case, by contrast, editors seemed to have an almost insatiable appetite for stories exploring any angle. And, finally, there were the political reporters fascinated by the dynamic of the president's signature legislative accomplishment being evaluated by the Supreme Court in the midst of a reelection campaign.

This continual attention on the case from a still mostly skeptical media corps created an unprecedented need for continuing constitutional commentary. In most cases, the constitutional debate is confined to the briefs and perhaps a few blog entries. And generally speaking, even a substantial constitutional case engenders coverage at the time of argument and the time of decision, and that is it. But with the health care case, every decision by multiple courts as the issue made its way to the Supreme Court, and every filing in the Supreme Court, engendered substantial commentary, criticism, and rebuttal. And the most penetrating of that continuing commentary is collected in this volume.

Third and relatedly, the health care case captured the public imagination like no other case in recent memory. Whether because of the saturation coverage, the political dynamic, the practical impact, or something else, many people who had never paid significant attention to a constitutional case were riveted by this one. As a result, the stakes could not have been higher. The case went beyond the precise issues before the Court to implicate the general public's confidence in the legal system as a whole.

Thus, the attention placed on the party of the president appointing the district court judges deciding the health care cases created the real prospect of the public viewing constitutional adjudication as nothing more than politics by other means. The seriousness and timeliness of the constitutional analysis collected here helped provide an antidote to that, as did the courts of appeals, where the results necessitated a more nuanced narrative. A number of prominent appellate court judges appointed by Republican presidents, such as Laurence Silberman of the D.C. Circuit and Jeffrey Sutton of the Sixth Circuit, voted to uphold the statute. But at roughly the same time, Judge Frank Hull, an appointee of President Clinton, was one of two Eleventh Circuit judges to strike down the law in the challenge brought by Florida and a growing number of states. The *Volokh Conspiracy* was there to discuss all of these developments in virtually real time and to emphasize that this more complicated pattern of judicial decisions both underscored the seriousness of the challenge and demanded a more nuanced discussion of the relationship between judicial philosophy and the political party of an appointing president.

Finally, the constitutional stakes in the health care case were and remain critically important. Much of the focus in the immediate aftermath of the decision understandably emphasized the chief justice's analysis of the taxing power and the practical reality that, although there were four votes to do so, the Court's majority did not invalidate the law in toto. But that should not obscure the reality that there are five votes to invalidate the mandate as exceeding Congress's power under the Commerce and Necessary and Proper Clauses, and a remarkable seven votes holding that the Medicaid expansion exceeded Congress's spending power.

When the case began, there were confident predictions that there would be seven or eight votes against the Commerce Clause challenge. Even on the eve of argument, seasoned commentators were still insisting that the constitutional challenge was frivolous. And these predictions were not merely wishful thinking. It was far from obvious that the new appointees of President George W. Bush would have the same enthusiasm for federalism as the justices they replaced. While former Chief Justice William Rehnquist and especially Justice O'Connor cut their teeth in the state courts and in state politics, both Chief Justice John Roberts and Justice Samuel Alito had their formative experiences in the executive branch of the federal government. There was a palpable sense in some circles that the health care case could be the swan song for the federalism revival—marking the end of one of the signal doctrinal achievements of the Rehnquist Court.

Thus, the Court's decision was an important constitutional moment because it underscored the Court's continued willingness to pursue its ongoing project of identifying judicially enforceable limits on Congress's power. The comments collected in this volume are critically important to understanding that constitutional moment—in terms of both why it happened and what it means. The Constitution had its Federalist Papers, and the challenge to the Affordable Care Act had the *Volokh Conspiracy*.

Paul D. Clement
Partner, Bancroft PLLC,
43rd Solicitor General of the United States,
Counsel to 26 states in the challenge to the Affordable Care Act

Notes

1. McConnell v. FEC, 540 U.S. 93 (2003).
2. Virginia v. Sebelius, 728 F. Supp. 2d 768 (E.D. Va. 2010).
3. Florida v. U.S. Dep't. of Health & Human Servs., 780 F. Supp. 2d 1256 (N.D. Fla. 2011).
4. See, e.g., Liberty Univ. v. Geithner, 753 F. Supp. 2d 611 (W.D. Va. 2010); Thomas More Law Ctr. v. Obama, 720 F. Supp. 2d 882 (E.D. Mich. 2010).

Acknowledgments

The contributors to this volume give special thanks to Eugene Volokh, creator of the *Volokh Conspiracy*, for inviting them to join that special community. We'd also like to thank the readers and commenters at the *Volokh Conspiracy*, without whom we would have little incentive to keep blogging.

Additionally, we'd like to thank Paul Clement for both contributing to this volume and for masterfully bringing the case to the Supreme Court. Paul and his team, as well as Mike Carvin and those at Jones Day, could not have done a better job in bringing *NFIB v. Sebelius* to the Court.

We'd also like to thank Brian O'Connor and Scarlet Neath at Palgrave Macmillan for believing in this project and effectively seeing it through.

Ilya Somin would like to thank the Washington Legal Foundation (WLF) for giving him the opportunity to write amicus briefs in several of the health care cases on their behalf and that of a group of well-known constitutional law scholars and members of Congress. He also thanks Cory Andrews of the WLF for his invaluable assistance with the briefs. In addition to VC bloggers, several scholars gave helpful advice about the briefs or other writings he did on these cases, including Steve Calabresi, Brad Joondeph, Gary Lawson, and Neil Siegel.

Trevor Burrus thanks Matt Gilliam for help gathering material, and Ilya Shapiro and Roger Pilon for giving him time to work on the project. Additional thanks go to Roger for offering him a job at the Cato Institute right as the Obamacare litigation was gaining momentum.

Introduction

The constitutional challenge to the Affordable Care Act (a.k.a. Obamacare; ACA) was the biggest Supreme Court case in decades. In the beginning, however, it was just the "little case that could," chugging along to get up a steep legal hill. Legal academics derided the challenge as hopeless. Pundits called it political posturing. At the *Volokh Conspiracy*, however, a group of legal academics were taking the case very seriously.

As you will see in the pages that follow, the bloggers at the *Volokh Conspiracy* helped popularize and refine the arguments behind the challenge. More important, they also influenced the arguments submitted to the courts—and eventually the Supreme Court. Never before had a legal academic *blog* influenced historic Supreme Court litigation.

For over a century, law reviews have been at the center of legal scholarship. During the early to mid-twentieth century, law professors were more likely to publish articles that helped practitioners, perhaps by clarifying difficult issues, explaining how new laws could be advantageously used, or advocating for coherently restructuring laws. The American Law Institute focused on clarifying the common law through the restatements and proposals such as the Model Penal Code. Treatises were written to help practitioners understand complex legal subjects. While these works were certainly not free of ideology, assisting the bar was still seen as one of law professors' paramount duties. Professor John H. Langbein wrote that American legal education in the 1960s "was distinctively practical and rigorous, reflecting its orientation on training and writing for the needs of practicing lawyers and judges."[1] Now, writes Langbein, "This vision of the mission of the national law school has largely vanished."[2] Or, in the words of Chief Justice John Roberts (a man who will play a prominent role in the narrative that follows), "Pick up a copy of any law review that you see, and the first article is likely to be, you know, the influence of Immanuel Kant on evidentiary approaches in 18th Century Bulgaria, or something, which I'm sure was of great interest to the academic that wrote it, but isn't of much help to the bar."[3]

The new medium of blogging, because of its current-events focus and ability to dynamically respond to events as they happen, can be more relevant to current legal issues than law review articles. The *Volokh Conspiracy* contributors' discussions on Obamacare were the bellwether for an emerging trend in legal scholarship.

This book collects those discussions over the course of the Obamacare saga, both before the law was passed and through the Supreme Court's fateful verdict. Its narrative arc plays out in real time as arguments get refined, modified, and discarded.

* * *

After months of intense debate, President Barack Obama signed the Affordable Care Act into law on March 23, 2010, radically transforming American health care for the worse.

Some argue that the inefficiencies of America's pre-ACA system demonstrated that free-market mechanisms do not work for health care. This is an odd thing to say about a system that essentially lacked two of the most important qualities of a market: meaningful prices and fluid consumer choice. Call your doctor and ask for the price of a basic procedure. At best, you'll wait a few hours, if not days, and then only get a vague and probably inaccurate answer. More likely, however, is that the receptionist will ask if you're serious. The predominance of the insurance model of health care, as well as the growth of Medicare and Medicaid, helped create a literally "priceless" system.[4]

The ACA took the dysfunctional parts of our former system—particularly the persistent, incorrect, and damaging belief that health insurance is the same as health care—and made them worse. The act tries to create the functional equivalent of a single-payer system—mandatory coverage for the sick at no extra cost to them with the extra funding coming from healthier citizens—and wrap it in the patina of a market. By using the trappings of a market, lawmakers got many bonuses. Not only were they able to sidestep the criticism of a "government takeover of health care," but they were able to hide the true cost of the ACA, an enormous political win.

The ACA rests on three pillars: (1) "community rating" price controls that force insurers to sell coverage to those with preexisting medical conditions at the same premiums they charge healthy people of the same age, (2) an "individual mandate" requiring essentially everyone purchase a qualifying health insurance plan, and (3) subsidies to keep people of modest means from walking away from the overpriced insurance the individual mandate forces them to buy. The second and third pillars are necessary to prop up the market under the weight of the first. Many people outside of the insurance market are younger, healthier, and do not consume much health care. To offset the cost increases from the first pillar, the individual mandate forces healthy people to buy coverage at much higher premiums than they would pay in a competitive market. By mandating that individuals make those payments to private insurance companies, and again by subsidizing insurers directly, Congress hoped to get insurers the needed funds to cover people with preexisting conditions.

The law's passage brought immediate lawsuits. Two cases were the most prominent. One was spearheaded by Virginia's Attorney General Ken Cuccinelli II. The other was led by the National Federation of Independent Business (NFIB); Pam Bondi, the attorney general of Florida; and 25 other states. The Florida/NFIB case eventually reached the Supreme Court.

The legal challenges mostly focused on the individual mandate, particularly whether Congress has the power, pursuant to the Commerce Clause and the Necessary and Proper Clause, to compel people to enter into commerce. A few academics argued that the taxing power justified the mandate, but that was a sideshow to the commerce power argument. This, of course, would come back to haunt the challengers when Chief Justice John Roberts unexpectedly upheld the mandate's penalty as a "tax." The provision that induced states to drastically expand their Medicaid programs or risk losing federal funding for all Medicaid programs was also challenged.

Volokh Conspiracy bloggers were involved in the challenge to the Affordable Care Act from the beginning. Before he joined the NFIB's legal team, Randy Barnett joined the Cato Institute on amicus briefs filed in lower federal courts. Ilya Somin authored briefs on behalf of the Washington Legal Foundation, as did David B. Kopel on behalf of the Independence Institute. Very few people engaged with the challenge to the Affordable Care Act more than the bloggers featured in this book.

* * *

For many of the public, and for most legal academics, the case against the individual mandate seemed too clever by half. The arguments often focused on subtle distinctions and minute differences in wording in order to distinguish the individual mandate from the broad scope of Congress's commerce power.

But the case against the mandate was always more clear to me than those nuanced discussions. Effective lawyering requires careful language and subtle distinctions, but only because lawyers must play the hand the Court dealt us.

For me, the argument was, and is, simple: A pure "effects-based" theory of the commerce power has no limits. Congress's power must be limited by kind, not degree.

The Court accepted that argument in *United States v. Lopez*[5] and *United States v. Morrison.*[6] In those landmark cases, Chief Justice William Rehnquist decided that enough was enough. Since the New Deal, the government had won every challenge to the scope of Congress's commerce power, mostly with the argument that "everything affects everything else." Such limitless expansion of federal power had to stop. Chief Justice Rehnquist believed that if a limited national government is more than a forgotten lesson from civics class, that if the federal government is to be actually rather than theoretically limited, then the commerce power must not be a blank check based on Rube Goldberg–like connections to commerce. Thus, he ruled that having a gun in a school zone (*Lopez*) or committing violence against women (*Morrison*) were not the kind of quintessentially economic activities that fall under scope of the Commerce Clause and the Necessary and Proper Clause, regardless of their effects on interstate commerce. With the individual mandate, the government believed they could avoid running afoul of *Lopez* and *Morrison* by arguing that decisions not to purchase a product were economic in a way guns in school zones and violence against women are not.

But all purchases and nonpurchases, as well as all actions and nonactions, obviously affect commerce, and this would have been obvious to any Framer. If you walked into the Pennsylvania State House during the convention (or, better yet, joined the equally important after-hours discussions at the Indian Queen Tavern or at Benjamin Franklin's house), and argued that the inchoate Commerce Clause could lead to "everything-affects-everything-else" reasoning, the Framers would've looked at you quizzically. Someone, perhaps Edmund Randolph, would've said, "Yeah, it *could* allow that, but who would make such a spurious argument, and why would the states ever accept such tenuous reasoning? They would revolt at such a usurpation, and rightly so. 'Commerce' is a *type of thing* we're giving Congress the power to regulate, not a zone of effects. If that were the nature of Congress's commerce power, why would we spend time listing any other powers?"

Some may chastise me for invoking the illegitimate specter of "Framer's intent," which was rightfully discarded from the most prominent theory of originalism decades ago. Yet I do not need to peer into the heads of the Framers to make my central point: Whatever "commerce" means, and whatever interpretive method you use to fill in that meaning, it must be a "type of thing" rather than a zone of effects. If "commerce" is merely a zone of effects without de minimis exceptions, then the Constitution ultimately fails in one of its central purposes: to ensure that the federal government does not have limitless power. Granting Congress limitless power violates any legitimate theory of constitutional interpretation.

Perhaps, to make my point clearer, it would be helpful to put the Constitution and the Framers' discussions into a modern context. The Founding Generation seems remote, and our post–Civil War, post–New Deal nation looks very different from the early United States.

Let's look at the European Union. The EU was mostly created to facilitate an economic union—that is, a free trade zone between the member states. The core powers of the EU are related to facilitating the free flow of people, goods, services, and capital across sovereign boundaries. Questions about manufacturing regulation, local agriculture, and other internal economic practices are largely left to the sovereign members under the correct theory that Germany, France, and the others are better situated, fully capable, and authorized to take care of local issues within their borders. If Brussels took jurisdiction over those local concerns, the member states would be rightly upset.

But what is truly "local?" The Netherlands's lax drug laws certainly affect the other nations, particularly those sharing its borders. Germany's labor laws and manufacturing regulations affect interstate commerce. France's limits on weekly working hours affect the economic intercourse with other nations.

The Netherlands, Germany, and France cannot dispute those effects. Instead, they must rely on the principle that drug laws, labor laws, and manufacturing regulations are not the type of thing the EU has power over. That will be the only useful argument if and when the centralizing forces in Brussels start to view local laws as impediments to their well-crafted schemes.

When that time comes to Europe, and in some subjects it already has, the issues will be the same as they were, and are, in America. Defenders of the sovereign powers of the member states will say that "manufacturing" is a type of thing that is not commerce, despite its obvious effects on commerce. Advocates of centralization will say that the distinction is arbitrary and that an "effects test" is necessary for Brussels to accomplish its goals. When they look to America for guidance, the defenders of limited government must say, "Don't give in. Give them an inch, they'll take a mile."

For us, the individual mandate was the last mile in a marathon we've been running since the New Deal.

Although I'm not here to remind you of lessons from high school civics, it might be worthwhile to keep these abstract concepts in mind as you read the pages that follow. The discussions between contributors to this volume may seem esoteric, but at the core they are talking about drawing lines—even if they're arguably arbitrary lines that only partially map onto our interconnected world. The Supreme Court once asked whether there is a meaningful line between "manufacturing" and "commerce" and decided that there wasn't. With the Affordable Care Act, we looked for a meaningful line between "action" and "inaction." Sure, these distinctions are nuanced, but should the lack of easily discernible lines make us throw up our hands and abandon our federal system altogether?

Even national borders are powerless against a pure, effects-based jurisdictional test. Yet if the United Nations began asserting jurisdiction over U.S. manufacturing laws based on the theory that the effects of our laws are not contained within our borders, we would boldly and confidently assert that our laws are none of their business. Our manufacturing laws certainly have extraterritorial effects, but they are not the type of thing the UN has power over.

Obviously the UN is a poor analog to our integrated federal system. Yet many of the reasons we don't want the UN running our health care also apply to reposing those personal choices in Washington, D.C.

Nevertheless, some regard these attitudes as philistine. For many, the course of human progress requires centralization, and those who stand in the way of Congress's attempts to solve problems of a national scale are reactionaries holding on to unenlightened theories no longer relevant to modern nations.

To this I say that it is hardly enlightened to require every group with deep convictions about health care—from Catholics to Jehovah's Witnesses to those who simply don't believe in Western medicine—to create lobbying organizations in Washington so they can defend their convictions in a tribal, yet dapper, Hobbesian war over what our "national health care plan" looks like.

Because of the synergistic effects of constitutional interpretation, the only way to resist such centralizing force is to stand against an illegitimate proposal *even if you think it is a good idea*. If you believe that the Constitution authorizes all good ideas, then you do not really believe in the Constitution—you just believe in good ideas.

With the legalization of marijuana in Colorado and Washington and the legal quagmires that have emerged due to the quirky fact that marijuana is simultaneously legal and illegal in those states, perhaps some champions of centralization are realizing the costs of an expansive federal government. The untenable situation in Washington and Colorado is a good indicator that the federal government has overstepped its constitutional boundaries. After all, whereas Congress once believed it lacked the power to prohibit alcohol without a constitutional amendment, they now prohibit drugs by statute. They do this based on the same Supreme Court cases—for example *Wickard v. Filburn*,[7] *NLRB v. Jones & Laughlin Steel Corp.*,[8] *United States v. Darby*[9]—that were the basis for the argument that Congress can force inactive people to purchase health insurance.

Much of this kvetching about ships that have long sailed and discussions of rudimentary constitutional analysis may seem simplistic and mostly irrelevant. Yet the purpose, structure, and principles of our Constitution have been forgotten by many. Most disturbingly, many people have forgotten the most important rule about power: every time you consider granting a new power to government you must first imagine that power in the hands of your most feared political opponents.

Due to the chief justice's unpredictable opinion, we are now likely stuck with a law that I fear will seriously damage the health of Americans. What's more, attempts to further centralize power will not stop at the individual mandate. When the law fails, as I predict it will, it will be said that the federal government lacked enough power to make it work. The chief justice's opinion gives people a real choice whether to comply with the requirement to purchase insurance or pay a "tax." Many people will not, and as the price of insurance goes up, more and more people will choose to remain uninsured. This will certainly be called a "loophole." Similarly, the Court also gave states a choice about whether to comply with the Affordable Care Act's Medicaid expansion. Another "loophole." Finally, the states that don't create health care exchanges will also throw wrenches in the law's overall scheme. "Loopholes" all around. Having freedom of choice in deeply personal health care decisions, however, is not a loophole.

When the time comes to revisit the Affordable Care Act, those choices by free, sovereign entities (citizens and states) will be blamed for the law's dysfunctions. To paraphrase philosopher Robert Nozick, liberty disrupts patterns. Free choice inevitably upsets the carefully crafted plans of Washington.

As a solution to the law's problems, more power will be proposed. A few voices, such as many who write for the *Volokh Conspiracy* and those of us at the Cato Institute, will strenuously argue that the problem is not a lack of power but a lack of freedom. I am not optimistic, however, that very many entrenched bureaucrats and politicians will locate the problem in the mirror rather than in the freedoms of the American people.

* * *

I am deeply grateful that Randy, Ilya, Dave K., Dave B., Orin, and Jonathan asked me to be a part of this exciting project. The conversations recorded here are truly historic, and I hope that this volume will be a valuable and novel contribution to Supreme Court history.

Trevor Burrus
Research Fellow
Cato Institute Center for Constitutional Studies

Notes

1. John H. Langbein, "Scholarly and Professional Objectives in Legal Education: American Trends and English Comparisons," in *Pressing Problems in the Law, Volume 2: What Are Law Schools For?*, ed. Peter Birks (New York: Oxford University Press, 1996), 3.

2. *Id.* at 5.
3. "Annual Fourth Circuit Court of Appeals Conference," CSPAN, http://www.c-span .org/Events/Annual-Fourth-Circuit-Court-of-Appeals-Conference/10737422476–1.
4. For more on this theory, see John C. Goodman, *Priceless: Curing the Health Care Crisis* (Oakland, CA: Independent Institute, 2012), and David Goldhilll, *Catastrophic Care: How American Health Care Killed My Father—and How We Can Fix It* (New York: Knopf, 2013).
5. United States v. Lopez, 514 U.S. 549 (1995).
6. United States v. Morrison, 529 U.S. 598 (2000).
7. Wickard v. Filburn, 317 U.S. 111 (1942).
8. NLRB v. Jones & Laughlin Steel Corp., 301 U.S. 1 (1937).
9. United States v. Darby Lumber Co., 312 U.S. 100 (1941).

1

In the Beginning

From the moment he took office, President Barack Obama saw health care reform as one of his administration's top priorities. In February 2009, President Obama announced to a joint session of Congress that discussions on reforming American health care would move forward as a priority. Meetings were held with industry leaders, lobbyists, and influential senators and members of Congress over the next many months.

The discussions in this chapter occurred prior to the signing of the final version of the Affordable Care Act (ACA). As Congress, pundits, and average Americans debated health care reform, so too did the *Volokh Conspiracy* (VC) bloggers.

On November 7, 2009, the House of Representatives passed the "Affordable Health Care for America Act" by a 220–215 vote, with 39 Democrat votes against and 1 Republican vote in favor.

In the Senate, the road was more difficult. Senate Republicans vowed to filibuster, so any bill needed a filibuster-proof 60 votes. Having only 58 votes at the time (before Senator Al Franken (D-MN) won his recount and before Arlen Spector switched parties), Senate Democrats had to appease their more centrist colleagues. The Democrats were further stymied when, in late August, before the bill could come up for a vote, Senator Ted Kennedy (D-MA) succumbed to brain cancer.

Senate Democrats focused on getting the votes of their moderate colleagues, particularly Connecticut's Joe Lieberman and Nebraska's Ben Nelson. Lieberman would not support any bill that had a "public option"—that is, a government-run insurance program that competes with private insurers. In exchange for Lieberman agreeing to support the bill, Senate Majority Leader Harry Reid permanently shelved the public option provision, much to the anger of many Democrats and liberal pundits.

That left Nelson. During late-night negotiations, Reid approved several of Nelson's "concerns," the most famous being higher federal Medicaid payments to Nebraska, which would become known as the "Cornhusker Kickback." Whatever name people wanted to call it, Reid got Nelson's vote.

Early in the morning on December 24, 2009, Reid called the vote and the bill passed 60–39. All Democrats and two independents voted for; all Republicans voted against, with one abstention (Jim Bunning of Kentucky).

In January 2010, Republican Scott Brown was surprisingly elected to Ted Kennedy's seat. Senate Democrats had lost their filibuster-proof voting bloc, but they still had the bill that was passed on Christmas Eve. It became clear that the most viable method to pass health care reform was for the House to abandon the "Affordable Health Care for America Act" and try to pass the Senate bill. Although House Majority Leader Nancy Pelosi got resistance from pro-life Democrats, on March 21, 2010, the House passed the Senate bill 219–212 despite opposition from all 178 Republicans and 34 Democrats. On March 23, 2010, President Obama signed the Patient Protection and Affordable Care Act.

The act is long and complex and, as is par for the course in modern legislation, contains many extraneous provisions. The core of the act, however, tries to expand quality health care to millions of Americans.

Insurance companies must now have a policy of "guaranteed issue," meaning that all who want health insurance can get it regardless of preexisting medical conditions. And insurance cannot be more expensive for someone because he or she has cancer, a chronic condition, or some other expensive malady. Under the "community rating" provision insurers can only vary the price based on a few limited criteria, for example age, geographic location, and tobacco use.

To support the increased costs that will come from the guaranteed issue and community rating provisions, the law includes a constellation of subsidies, mandates, and tax credits. The most important one is the "individual mandate," which requires essentially all Americans to purchase and maintain a qualifying health insurance plan. The mandate is backed up by a fine that is enforced by the IRS. That fact will ultimately be crucial to the outcome of this saga.

The individual mandate is a central character in this book, arguably the star. Although other aspects of the law were challenged, are being challenged, and will continue to be challenged, no challenged provision caught the public's attention like the individual mandate. Not only is it easy to understand and directly relevant to every American's life—"You mean I have to buy insurance even if I don't want it?"—but it also gnaws at the limited government sensibilities that are a constant part of American political culture.

As our story begins, the individual mandate takes center stage.

* * *

Is Obamacare Constitutional?

David B. Kopel
August 17, 2009

Independence Institute Senior Fellow (and University of Montana constitutional law professor) Rob Natelson suggests not.[1]

Natelson puts aside the question of whether it is constitutional under originalism (for which the answer is "obviously not"), and instead points to four problems under modern constitutional doctrine:

1. It is not based on any enumerated power of Congress, not even on a very expansive reading of the power to regulate interstate commerce.

2. It relies on excessive delegation of the type held unconstitutional in *Schechter Poultry Corp. v. United States*.[2]
3. It violates substantive due process and interferes with doctor-patient medical decisions to a vastly greater extent than did the laws declared unconstitutional in *Roe v. Wade*.[3]
4. It violates the Tenth Amendment by commandeering state governments.

There are a couple caveats: It's a blog post, not a law review article, so it just sketches out the previous points briefly. It's obviously written in the spirit of starting a public ~~dialogue~~ conversation. In the spirit of constructive dialogue, we promise not to say that we "don't want the folks who created the mess to do a lot of talking." (By "created the mess," I mean the people who created the legislation with little apparent consideration for constitutionality and who appear to have operated from the presumption that Congress can exercise powers that are not enumerated.)

Is Obamacare Unconstitutional?

Jonathan H. Adler
August 22, 2009

David Rivkin and Lee Casey argue that a federal mandate requiring all individuals to obtain health insurance would lie beyond the scope of Congress's enumerated powers.[4] Specifically, they argue that neither the power to "regulate commerce among the several states" nor the taxing and spending power could support such an all-encompassing mandate. Here is a taste of their argument:

> Although the Supreme Court has interpreted Congress's commerce power expansively, this type of mandate would not pass muster even under the most aggressive commerce clause cases. In *Wickard v. Filburn* (1942), the Court upheld a federal law regulating the national wheat markets. The law was drawn so broadly that wheat grown for consumption on individual farms also was regulated. Even though this rule reached purely local (rather than interstate) activity, the Court reasoned that the consumption of homegrown wheat by individual farms would, in the aggregate, have a substantial economic effect on interstate commerce, and so was within Congress's reach.
>
> The Court reaffirmed this rationale in 2005 in *Gonzales v. Raich*, when it validated Congress's authority to regulate the home cultivation of marijuana for personal use. In doing so, however, the justices emphasized that—as in the wheat case—"the activities regulated by the [Controlled Substances Act] are quintessentially economic." That simply would not be true with regard to an individual health insurance mandate.
>
> The otherwise uninsured would be required to buy coverage, not because they were even tangentially engaged in the "production, distribution or consumption of commodities," but for no other reason than that people without health insurance exist. The federal government does not have the power to regulate Americans simply because they are there. Significantly, in two key cases, *United States v. Lopez* (1995)

and *United States v. Morrison* (2000), the Supreme Court specifically rejected the proposition that the Commerce Clause allowed Congress to regulate noneconomic activities merely because, through a chain of causal effects, they might have an economic impact. These decisions reflect judicial recognition that the Commerce Clause is not infinitely elastic and that, by enumerating its powers, the framers denied Congress the type of general police power that is freely exercised by the states.

As much as I oppose the various health care reforms promoted by the Obama administration and current congressional leadership (and as much as I would like to see a more restrictive Commerce Clause jurisprudence), I do not find this argument particularly convincing. While I agree that the recent Commerce Clause cases hold that Congress may not regulate noneconomic activity, as such, they also state that Congress may reach otherwise unregulated conduct as part of an overarching regulatory scheme, where the regulation of such conduct is necessary and proper to the success of such scheme. In this case, the overall scheme would involve the regulation of "commerce" as the Supreme Court has defined it for several decades, as it would involve the regulation of health care markets. And the success of such a regulatory scheme would depend upon requiring all to participate. (Among other things, if health care reform requires insurers to issue insurance to all comers and prohibits refusals for preexisting conditions, then a mandate is necessary to prevent opportunistic behavior by individuals who simply wait to purchase insurance until they get sick.)

Jack Balkin is similarly unconvinced.[5] I generally agree with his bottom line but would question some of his argument as well. First, he chides Rivkin and Casey for making an argument that would effectively invalidate the New Deal. I am not sure this is true. While some post-1937 programs might be at risk, one might also distinguish *Wickard* on the grounds that it involved a commodity sold in interstate commerce (wheat), whereas health insurance is a service. One might also argue that there is a difference between seeking to control the conditions of any commodity sale (its price, quantity, etc.) and mandating that a sale take place. This line would be similar to that embraced in some New Deal Commerce Clause cases that upheld federal regulations setting conditions on the manufacture of goods sold in interstate commerce while ostensibly leaving the manufacture of goods not sold in interstate markets untouched. If I recall correctly, this line was maintained until *Maryland v. Wirtz*[6] in 1968. So while The Rivkin-Casey argument is aggressive, I don't think it would completely overturn the New Deal.

Balkin also chides Rivkin and Casey for citing *Bailey v. Drexel Furniture*,[7] "a case from the *Lochner* Era,"[8] to make their case. Well, like it or not, *Bailey* has never been expressly overturned, and I think there's a good reason for that. In *Bailey*, the Court held that Congress could not use the taxing power to regulate behavior that would otherwise lie beyond the scope of the federal government's other enumerated powers. This may well be true. The problem with *Bailey*, then, is not its view of the taxing power but rather the *Bailey* court's restrained view of the federal commerce power. What makes *Bailey* and other cases largely irrelevant today is that there is so little that the federal government seeks to tax that it cannot otherwise regulate. I'd also note that it is not as if the Court is averse to relying upon other cases with *Lochner v. New York*–era pedigrees. Indeed, *Meyer v. Nebraska*[9] and *Pierce v. Society of Sisters*[10] are still good law, and each is closer kin to *Lochner* than *Bailey*, as they relied upon *Lochner*'s substantive due process rationale.

Speaking of substantive due process, there may be other constitutional problems arising from national health care reform—but not of the enumerated powers variety. While the federal government may be able to require national health insurance coverage, could it require all individuals to purchase plans that cover certain procedures? What if the guidelines for acceptable plans include contraception, abortion, and certain types of end-of-life care? Could the federal government require devout Catholics to purchase such plans for themselves? Insofar as a new federal entitlement and regulatory scheme severely limits the ability of individuals to make fundamental health-related choices for themselves without undue federal interference, might it also run up against *Griswold v. Connecticut*,[11] *Cruzan v. Director, Missouri Department of Health*,[12] and other cases recognizing a right to privacy that extends to health-related matters? So long as individuals retain a choice of health care providers such concerns may be quite marginal, but were a "public plan" to become a de facto single-payer plan, the constitutional issue could grow. If limitations on abortion procedures must contain a health exception in order to be constitutional under *Planned Parenthood v. Casey*,[13] would this complicate efforts to control costs by excluding some potentially life-saving treatments under a single-payer system? Of course, these sorts of arguments are more likely to come from libertarians than conservatives, as the latter may be uncomfortable with expanding the scope of the Court's fundamental rights jurisprudence.

Is Obamacare Unconstitutional?: Part Deux

Jonathan H. Adler
September 18, 2009

David Rivkin and Lee Casey are back on the *Wall Street Journal* editorial page, arguing once again that current health care proposals are unconstitutional.[14] Specifically, they argue that an "individual mandate" would exceed the scope of congressional power under current precedent. Further, they argue that this limitation cannot be avoided by using the taxing power to impose a tax on those who fail to purchase a qualifying health care plan.

As with their last effort in this vein, I am unconvinced. I agree with them that an individual mandate would, in many respects, "expand the federal government's authority over individual Americans to an unprecedented degree," but I disagree that such a mandate would be unconstitutional under current precedent, particularly if adopted as part of a comprehensive health care reform plan.

There is a strong temptation to believe that every onerous or oppressive government policy is unconstitutional. Were it only so. Even were the federal government confined to those powers expressly enumerated in the text, it would retain ample ability to enact many bad ideas into law, and current precedent is far more permissive. Opponents of current health care reform proposals should defeat them the old fashioned way, through the political process, and not depend upon salvation from the courts.

Is Mandatory Health Insurance Unconstitutional?

Randy E. Barnett
September 18, 2009

In *Politico's Arena*, we are debating Rivkin and Casey's *Wall Street Journal* op-ed piece,[15] which Jonathan notes previously. While my take on this issue differs somewhat from his, in my contribution, I respond to a rather catty post by Washington and Lee law professor Timothy Stoltzfus Jost. This is what I wrote:

OK, let's be old fashioned and start with what the Constitution says. After the Preamble, the very first sentence of the Constitution says "All legislative powers *herein granted* shall be vested in a Congress of the United States. . . ." And again the Necessary and Proper Clause gives Congress the power "To make all laws which shall be necessary and proper for carrying into execution *the foregoing powers*, and all other powers *vested by this Constitution* in the government of the United States, or in any department or officer thereof." The Tenth Amendment is not required to see that Congressional power must be found somewhere in the document. ("Tenthers"? What's next? "Firsters"? "Necessary and Proper Clausers"? Enough with the derogatory labels, already.) So where in the document is the power to mandate that individuals buy health insurance?

The power "to regulate commerce . . . among the several states"? This clause was designed to deprive states of their powers under the Articles to erect trade barriers to commerce among the several states. It accomplished this by giving Congress the exclusive power over interstate sales and transport of goods (subject to the requirement that its regulations be both "necessary and proper"). It did not reach activities that were neither commerce, nor interstate. The business of providing health insurance is now an entirely intrastate activity.

The "spending power"? There is no such enumerated power. There is only the enumerated power to tax. Laws spending tax revenues are authorized, again, if they are "necessary and proper for carrying into execution *the foregoing powers*." So we return to the previous issue: what enumerated end or object is Congress spending money to accomplish?

But following the text of the Constitution is so Eighteenth Century. Professor Jost tells us that "a basic principle of our constitutional system for the last two centuries has been that the Supreme Court is the ultimate authority on the Constitution, and the *Constitution the Court now recognizes* would permit Congress to adopt health care reform." So the Supreme Court gets to rewrite the written Constitution as we go along.

Never mind *Dred Scott*, *Plessy*, *Korematsu* and other not-so-famous Supreme Court "mistakes." *The Constitution* was what the Supreme Court said it was—until it changed its mind. And the Supreme Court has certainly not limited either the enumerated commerce power or the implied spending power to the original meaning of the text.

Fine. But has the Constitution of the Supreme Court been extended to include mandating that individuals buy insurance? Professor Jost admits "the absence of a clear precedent." Really! So what has the Supreme Court's Constitution told us about the Commerce Clause power? Professor Jost cites the medical marijuana case of *Gonzales v. Raich*.

As Angel Raich's lawyer, who argued the case in the Supreme Court, I think the Court erred (6–3) in reading the interstate commerce power broadly enough to allow Congress to prohibit you from growing a plant in your back yard for your own consumption. By all accounts, however, this is the most far reaching interpretation of the commerce power ever adopted by a majority, exceeding the reach of the past champion, *Wickard v. Filburn*. But even the six Justices in the majority did not say that Congress had the power to mandate you grow a plant in your back yard. Do you think a majority would find that power today?

Perhaps. But under Professor Jost's approach to constitutional law, we must await the Supreme Court's ruling before we know what "the Constitution" requires or prohibits. Until then, the Supreme Court's First Amendment still gives even "two former Bush officials" the right to publish their opinion that the written Constitution delegates to Congress no such power, provided of course they are not trying to influence the outcome of a federal election. Maybe a bare majority will decide this matter by reviewing the text. Stranger things have happened. After all, without any precedent standing in their way, a majority of the Supreme Court decided to follow the original meaning of the text of the Second Amendment in *District of Columbia v. Heller*.

And when we are done examining Congress's power to mandate that you buy a particular service—or pay a fine, er "tax"—we can then consider its power to restrict the exercise of a person's fundamental right to preserve his or her life.[16]

Does a Federal Mandate Requiring the Purchase of Health Insurance Exceed Congress's Powers under the Commerce Clause?

Ilya Somin
September 20, 2009

I come late to the debate over whether a federal law requiring people to purchase health insurance exceeds Congress's powers under the Commerce Clause. In my view, the answer under current precedent is clearly "no." At the same time, I do think that such a law would be unconstitutional under the correct interpretation of the Commerce Clause—or any interpretation that takes the constitutional text seriously.

I. The Health Insurance Mandate under Current Supreme Court Precedent

Current Supreme Court precedent allows Congress to regulate virtually anything that has even a remote connection to interstate commerce so long as it has a "substantial effect" on it. The most recent major precedent in this field is *Gonzales v. Raich*, where the Court held that Congress's power to regulate interstate commerce was broad enough to uphold a ban on the use of medical marijuana that was never sold in any market and never left the confines of the state where it was grown. This regulation was upheld under the "substantial effects" rule noted previously. As I describe in great detail elsewhere,[17] *Raich* renders Congress's power under the substantial effects test virtually unlimited in three different ways:

1. *Raich* holds that Congress can regulate virtually any "economic activity," and adopts an extraordinarily broad definition of "economic," which according to the Court encompasses anything that involves the "production, distribution, and consumption of commodities."
2. *Raich* makes it easy for Congress to impose controls on even "noneconomic" activity by claiming that it is part of a broader regulatory scheme aimed at something economic.
3. *Raich* adopts a so-called rational basis test as the standard for Commerce Clause cases, holding that "[w]e need not determine whether [the] activities [being regulated], taken in the aggregate, substantially affect interstate commerce in fact, but only whether a rational basis exists for so concluding." In legal jargon, a "rational basis" can be almost any noncompletely moronic reason for believing that a particular claim might be true.

Any of these three holdings could easily justify a federal requirement forcing people to purchase health insurance. The decision to purchase or not purchase health insurance is probably "economic activity," as *Raich* defines it, since it involves the distribution and consumption of commodities such as medicine. When you buy health insurance, you are contracting with the insurance company to provide you with medicine and other needed commodities should you get sick.

Even if the purchase of health insurance is "noneconomic" in nature, it could easily be upheld as part of a broader regulatory scheme aimed at economic activity—in this case regulation of the health care industry. As I discuss on pages 516–18 of my article on *Raich*, the Court makes it very easy to prove that virtually any regulation can be considered part of a broader regulatory scheme by not requiring any proof that the regulation in question really is needed to make the broader scheme work. Finally, even if a court concludes that the government was wrong to assume that the decision to buy health insurance is "economic activity" under *Raich*'s broad definition and wrong to believe that the mandatory purchase requirement was part of a broader regulatory scheme, the requirement could still be upheld because there was a "rational basis" for these ultimately mistaken beliefs.

II. Why Current Doctrine Is Wrong

For reasons laid out in my article, I think that *Raich* and other decisions interpreting the Commerce Clause very broadly were wrongly decided. I also agree with most of Randy Barnett's arguments to that effect in [his previous post]. Looking at the text of the Constitution, the Commerce Clause merely grants Congress the power to regulate "Commerce . . . among the several states." Choosing to purchase (or not purchase) health insurance is not interstate commerce, if only because nearly all insurance purchases are conducted within the confines of a single state. Obviously, the decision to purchase health insurance may well have an impact on interstate commerce, and modern doctrine, even before *Raich*, allowed congressional regulation of any activities that have such a "substantial effect." However, this "effects" test is badly misguided. If the Commerce Clause really gave Congress the power to regulate any activity that merely affects interstate commerce, most of Congress's other powers listed in Article I of the Constitution would be redundant. For example, the very same phrase that enumerates Congress's power to regulate interstate commerce also gives it the power to regulate "Commerce with foreign Nations" and "with the Indian tribes." Foreign trade and trade with Indian tribes (which was a much more important part of the economy at the time of the founding than today) clearly have major effects on interstate trade. Yet these two powers are separately enumerated, which strongly suggests that the power to regulate interstate commerce doesn't give Congress the power to regulate any activity that merely has an effect—substantial or otherwise—on that commerce.

Be that as it may, it is highly unlikely that the Supreme Court would invalidate a major provision of the health care bill, should it pass Congress. In addition to requiring the overruling of *Raich* and considerable revision of other precedents, such a decision would lead to a major confrontation with Congress and the president. The Court is unlikely to pick a massive fight with a still-popular president backed by a large congressional majority. Of course, it is still possible that the Court could invalidate some minor portion of the bill on Commerce Clause grounds. But even that is unlikely so long as the majority of justices remain committed to *Raich*. Five of the six justices who voted with the majority in that case are still on the Court. The only exception—Justice David Souter—has been replaced by a liberal justice who is unlikely to be any more willing to impose meaningful limits on congressional power than Souter was.

Gonzales v. Raich and the Individual Mandate

Ilya Somin
October 5, 2010

The Supreme Court's 2005 decision in *Gonzales v. Raich* ruled that Congress's power to regulate interstate commerce gives it the power to ban the possession of medical marijuana that had never crossed state lines or been sold in any market anywhere. It was easily the broadest-ever Supreme Court interpretation of the Commerce Clause. When I first considered the question, I thought that *Raich*'s reasoning was expansive enough to justify the individual mandate. I still believed that the mandate was unconstitutional (primarily because I have always argued that *Raich* was a horrible decision). But I thought that it could probably go through under *Raich*. And the government has in fact relied heavily on *Raich* in its brief in the Virginia case challenging the mandate.

A closer look at *Raich*, however, led me to reconsider my initial view. I presented my revised position in the amicus brief (pp. 6–10) I recently wrote on behalf of the Washington Legal Foundation and a group of constitutional law scholars.[18] As I explain in my 2006 article on *Raich* and my September 2009 post on the individual mandate, *Raich* gives Congress extremely broad power in three separate ways.[19] A closer look reveals that none of them actually requires lower courts to uphold the mandate.

I. The Court's Definition of "Economic Activity"

The Court's definition of economic activity in *Raich* is extremely broad, even ridiculously so. For example, it gives Congress the power to regulate your decision to eat dinner at home, since that decision entails the "consumption" of commodities such as food. Expansive as this definition may be, the mere status of being uninsured doesn't qualify. Choosing not to purchase health insurance involves neither production, nor distribution, nor consumption of commodities. Indeed, an individual who chooses not to purchase insurance has chosen *not* to consume or distribute the commodity in question. And, obviously, he or she is also not "producing" any commodity by refusing to purchase insurance. By contrast, the *Raich* defendants were engaged in "economic activity" since they were both producing and consuming marijuana.

II. The Broader Regulatory Scheme Rule

This rule too is very broad in the way it allows Congress to regulate even "non-economic" activity so long as there is even a remote connection to some sort of regulation of commerce. However, the power outlined by the Court applies only to the regulation of "*activity*." The Court itself repeatedly uses the term "activity" to describe the object of regulation. It does not cover regulation of inactivity or the refusal to engage in economic transactions. Angel Raich and Diane Monsen had not been inactive or merely refused to engage in some transaction. To the contrary, they were actively involved in the production and consumption of homegrown medical marijuana. The Court's logic *could* be extended to cover regulation of inactivity. But *Raich* itself doesn't do this.

III. The Rational Basis Test

This part of the Court's reasoning is harder to interpret than the two issues described previously. Still, it cannot be the case that the rational basis test is triggered by the mere invocation of the Commerce Clause by the government. If it were, then the Court would have had to overrule cases such as *United States v. Lopez* and *United States v. Morrison*, both of which failed to apply the rational basis test. Moreover, such an approach would give the federal government a virtual blank check for unlimited power, since all the government would have to do to get near-total judicial difference is claim that they were operating under the Commerce Clause. For these and other reasons, it is reasonable to conclude that the rational basis test applies only to regulations of activity rather than inactivity. I cover this admittedly more complex aspect of the case in greater detail in my brief.[20]

What changed my mind about *Raich's* relevance? Partly, it was coblogger Randy Barnett's insightful analysis of the issue in a December 2009 paper coauthored with Todd Gaziano and Nathaniel Stewart.[21] But even more important was the simple experience of carefully rereading *Raich* with this issue in mind. Once you look closely at the text of the Court's opinion, it's hard to avoid the conclusion that it simply doesn't address the possibility that Congress might try to regulate inactivity or force ordinary citizens to engage in economic transactions. Cynics will claim that I changed my mind because I dislike the Obama plan on policy grounds. Maybe so. But I was just as opposed to the plan when I held a different view on the relevance of *Raich*. What changed was not my view of Obamacare (which was always negative), but my view of the relevant legal doctrine.

Obviously, a court could try to extend *Raich* to cover forced economic transactions. If Congress has virtually unlimited power to regulate activity, why not regulate inactivity? Perhaps the Supreme Court will eventually do just that. But *Raich* itself doesn't compel any such result. To the contrary, the wording of the Court's opinion and the way in which it interacts with previous decisions such as *Lopez* and *Morrison* suggests that its logic is confined to regulation of activity. And, as I explain in the brief,[22] what is true of *Raich* is even more true of the Court's less expansive pre-*Raich* Commerce Clause decisions. If the government can't win the Commerce Clause issue using *Raich*, it can't win it under any other existing precedent either.

Could an Individual Mandate Violate Article I, Section 9?

Jonathan H. Adler
November 19, 2009

Most discussions about the constitutionality of an individual mandate in health care reform proposals have focused on whether such a mandate could be justified under the federal government's enumerated powers in Article I, Section 8. Some (including me) have opined that, under existing case law, an individual mandate would probably pass muster. For example, under existing precedent I think it likely that the Court would see an individual mandate as a necessary and proper incident of comprehensive regulation of health care markets, as a mandate is necessary to prevent other aspects of health care reform (such as a ban on refusing to cover preexisting conditions) from driving up health care markets. (Of course, were the Court to apply the original public meaning of the relevant provisions, an individual mandate would be out of bounds.) But in focusing on Article I, Section 8, I wonder whether we've ignored another potential constitutional problem with provisions of Article I, Section 9.

As I understand the current proposals, the individual mandate would operate as follows: a tax would be imposed on all individuals, and the tax would be offset by a credit for those who purchase or are otherwise covered by qualifying plans. The constitutional problem would arise if this tax is considered a "direct tax." Why? Because Article I, Section 9 provides, "No capitation, or other direct, Tax shall be laid, unless in Proportion to the Census or Enumeration herein before directed to be taken." So if the mandate is imposed through the tax code, and the provision operates as a "capitation" or "other Direct tax," it would have to be apportioned.

Do the respective individual mandate provisions constitute direct taxes? I'm not sure. "Indirect" or so-called event taxes are not subject to apportionment under Article I, Section 9, and income taxes were exempted from the apportionment requirement under the Sixteenth Amendment. So the question would be whether any tax imposed on those who fail to purchase qualifying health plans would constitute a "direct" tax or whether they could be properly characterized as indirect or income taxes. From what I understand, the tax in the House bill is, at least for some individuals, based upon income up to a set threshold. This might be enough to avoid the Article I, Section 9 problem. I have not yet had a chance to look at how the mandate provisions are written in the Senate bill. I would be curious to read what others think about whether an individual mandate imposed through the tax code could run afoul of Article I, Section 9.

The Constitutionality of an Individual Mandate: A Reply to Senator Max Baucus

Jonathan H. Adler
December 23, 2009

Yesterday, on the Senate floor, Senator Max Baucus quoted my August 22 VC post on the constitutionality of an individual mandate.[23] Specifically, he quoted the following passage:

> In this case, the overall scheme would involve the regulation of "commerce" as the Supreme Court has defined it for several decades, as it would involve the regulation of health care markets. And the success of such a regulatory scheme would depend upon requiring all to participate.

This quote was part of a longer speech in which Senator Baucus sought to show that many "prominent legal scholars" believe that "Congress has the constitutional authority to impose a requirement on individuals to maintain health coverage."

While Senator Baucus quoted me correctly, I think he left out some important context and, as a consequence, may have created a mistaken impression of my views.

My August 22 post was a comment on an op-ed by David Rivkin and Lee Casey.[24] In response to their claim that an individual mandate was unconstitutional under current law, I argued:

> While I agree that the recent Commerce Clause cases hold that Congress may not regulate noneconomic activity, as such, they also state that Congress may reach otherwise unregulated conduct as part of an overarching regulatory scheme, where the regulation of such conduct is necessary and proper to the success of such scheme.

What I did not mention in that post, but have written repeatedly elsewhere, is that I believe that some of these "recent Commerce Clause cases," most notably *Gonzales v. Raich*, were wrongly decided and adopted an excessively expansive view of federal power under the Commerce and Necessary and Proper Clauses. Under these cases, I believe that it is difficult to argue that an individual mandate exceeds congressional authority. Under a more constrained reading of the Commerce Clause, however, I don't think the argument is so difficult.

In my view, the biggest problem with the argument for the constitutionality of an individual mandate is that it is an argument without limit. Basically, the argument is that if Congress can regulate economic activity X, then it can also mandate that each and every American engage in economic activity X. If this is true for health care, there is no reason why it is not also true for Christmas trees, savings bonds, or GM cars. In short, Congress could mandate universal participation in any economic activity and mandate the purchase of any product or service it chooses so long as it does so as part of a broader regulatory scheme.

While some of the language in the majority opinion and Justice Antonin Scalia's concurrence in *Raich* implies Congress has such power, this approach would create a commerce power without limit; an outcome that both *Lopez* and *Morrison* said was incompatible with the concept of enumerated powers. So to embrace this view, as I argued elsewhere,[25] is to eviscerate their holdings. As I believe *Lopez* and *Morrison* are more consistent with the text of the Commerce Clause and the principles of enumerated powers, I would prefer that the Supreme Court uphold these decisions and overturn or severely limit *Gonzales v. Raich*, *Wickard v. Filburn*, and a few others.

So, while Senator Baucus correctly quoted my belief that an individual mandate is likely constitutional under existing precedent, he omitted my belief that existing precedent is unduly expansive. So while I would expect a lower court judge to uphold the mandate as against a constitutional challenge, I do not think the Supreme Court is required to do so. Indeed, I believe the Court could distinguish *Raich* and hold the mandate out of bounds.

I should also note that I do not believe that members of Congress should base their decisions on whether to support proposed legislation based upon their prediction of how federal courts are likely to rule. Every member of Congress takes an oath to uphold the Constitution. I am old fashioned enough to believe this oath obligates each and every member of Congress to consider the constitutionality of proposed legislation for themselves and refuse to vote in favor of legislation they conclude is out of bounds, even if they think the legislation would be a good idea. So Senator Baucus should spend less time quoting the assessment of folks like me about what current precedent means for proposed legislation and more time explaining why he finds this and other legislative proposals to be consistent with the text, structure, and history of the Constitution he took an oath to uphold.

The Myth of an Expert Consensus on the Constitutionality of an Individual Health Insurance Mandate

Ilya Somin
December 23, 2009

In an important recent speech, Senator Max Baucus claims that there is a broad consensus among legal scholars that the individual mandate is constitutional. He claims that "those who study constitutional law as a line of work have drawn th[e] same conclusion" as congressional Democrats. Similar assertions have been made in parts of the liberal blogosphere. For example, Think Progress denounces Republican Senators John Ensign and Jim DeMint for citing only "right-wing think tanks" in support of their claims that the mandate is unconstitutional and chides them for supposedly being unable to cite "a single judge, justice or reputable constitutional scholar who believes that health reform is unconstitutional."[26]

There certainly are prominent constitutional law scholars who agree with Baucus. But the claim that there is an overwhelming expert consensus on the subject is simply false. As coblogger Jonathan Adler points out, Baucus mistakenly cited him as a scholar who agrees with the Democrats' conclusions even though he actually believes that the mandate is *not* constitutional. The "right-wing think tank" study cited by Ensign and DeMint was actually coauthored by coblogger Randy Barnett, one of the nation's most prominent constitutional law scholars and an expert on the original meaning of the Commerce Clause (the provision usually cited as authorizing Congress to impose the mandate). Richard Epstein of New York University and the University of Chicago is another prominent legal scholar (one of the ten most cited in the country) who believes that the mandate is unconstitutional.

I certainly wouldn't put myself on the same plane as Jonathan, Randy, or Richard Epstein. But I'm a professional constitutional law academic, federalism and the Commerce Clause are among my areas of expertise, and I think the mandate is unconstitutional too.

It probably is true that more constitutional law scholars believe that the mandate is constitutional than believe the opposite. But this simply reflects the fact that most constitutional law professors, like most other academics, are overwhelmingly left of center. There are many controversial constitutional issues that split experts along ideological lines. In such cases, it is misleading to claim that there is an expert consensus merely because there are more experts on one side of a broader ideological divide than the other. Moreover, it's worth noting that most of those left of center constitutional law scholars who believe that the mandate is constitutional hold that view in large part because they believe that there are essentially no limits whatsoever to Congress's ability to use its power to regulate "Commerce . . . among the several states" to control anything that has even a remote potential effect on commercial activity. If you believe that congressional power is basically unlimited (except by constitutional individual rights), then the mandate becomes an easy case. That view, however, is seriously at odds with the text and original meaning of the Commerce Clause, for reasons that I discussed in my earlier post on the subject of the constitutionality of the individual mandate[27] and in "*Gonzalez v. Raich:* Federalism as a Casualty in the War on Drugs."[28]

Notes

1. Rob Natelson, "Obama Care's Dubious Constitutionality," *The Cauldron* (blog), August 17, 2009, http://www.joncaldara.com/2009/08/17/obamacares-dubious-constitutionality.
2. Schechter Poultry Corp. v. United States, 295 U.S. 495 (1935).
3. Roe v. Wade, 410 U.S. 113 (1973).
4. David B. Rivkin Jr. and Lee Casey, "Constitutionality of the Health Insurance Mandate Questioned," *Washington Post*, August 22, 2009, http://www.washingtonpost.com/wp-dyn/content/article/2009/08/21/AR2009082103033.html?sub=AR.
5. Jack Balkin, "The Inevitable Conservative Argument against Obamacare," *Balkinization* (blog), August 22, 2009, http://balkin.blogspot.com/2009/08/inevitable-conservative-argument-that.html.
6. Maryland v. Wirtz, 392 U.S. 183 (1968).
7. Bailey v. Drexel Furniture Co., 259 U.S. 20 (1922) (holding that the Child Labor Tax Act of 1919 was an unconstitutional use of Congress's tax power).
8. Lochner v. New York, 198 U.S. 45 (1905) (overturning New York's maximum work-hours law for bakers as a violation of the Due Process Clause of the Fourteenth Amendment).
9. Meyer v. Nebraska, 262 U.S. 390 (1923) (overturning a Nebraska law forbidding foreign-language education as a violation of the Due Process Clause of the Fourteenth Amendment).
10. Pierce v. Society of Sisters, 268 U.S. 510 (1925) (overturning Oregon's law requiring compulsory public school attendance as a violation of the Due Process Clause of the Fourteenth Amendment).
11. Griswold v. Connecticut, 381 U.S. 479 (1965) (overturning Connecticut's ban on using contraceptives).
12. Cruzan v. Dir., Mo. Dep't of Health, 497 U.S. 261 (1990) (holding that a state can require "clear and convincing evidence" before allowing parents to remove a daughter from life support).
13. Planned Parenthood v. Casey, 505 U.S. 833 (1992).
14. David B. Rivkin Jr. and Lee Casey, "Mandatory Insurance Is Unconstitutional," *Wall Street Journal*, September 18, 2009, http://online.wsj.com/article/SB100014240529702 04518504574416623109362480.html.
15. *Id.*
16. Randy E. Barnett, "Health Care: Is 'Mandatory Insurance' Unconstitutional?," *Politico Arena*, last modified September 18, 2009, http://www.politico.com/arena/perm/Randy_Barnett_8256A4EF-01E6–4207-B4E8-C761F2FDB5BF.html.
17. Ilya Somin, "*Gonzales v. Raich*: Federalism as a Casualty in the War on Drugs," *Cornell Journal of Law and Public Policy* 15, no. 3 (2006): 507.
18. Brief for the Washington Legal Foundation and Constitutional Law Scholars as Amici Curiae in Support of Plaintiff's Motion for Summary Judgment, Virginia v. Sebelius, 728 F. Supp. 2d 768 (E.D. Va. 2010) (No. 3:10-CV-188).
19. Ilya Somin, "Does a Federal Mandate Requiring the Purchase of Health Insurance Exceed Congress's Powers under the Commerce Clause?," *supra.*
20. Brief for the Washington Legal Foundation, *Sebelius*, 728 F. Supp. 2d 768 at 9–10.

21. Randy Barnett, Nathaniel Stewart, and Todd F. Gaziano, "Legal Memorandum 49: Why the Personal Mandate to Buy Health Insurance Is Unprecedented and Unconstitutional," Heritage Foundation, last modified December 9, 2009, http://www.heritage .org/research/reports/2009/12/why-the-personal-mandate-to-buy-health-insurance -is-unprecedented-and-unconstitutional.

22. Brief for the Washington Legal Foundation, *Sebelius*, 728 F. Supp. 2d 768 at 11–14.

23. Jonathan H. Adler, "Is Obamacare Unconstitutional?," *supra*.

24. David B. Rivkin Jr. and Lee Casey, "Constitutionality of the Health Insurance Mandate Questioned," *Washington Post*, August 22, 2009, http://www.washingtonpost.com/ wp-dyn/content/article/2009/08/21/AR2009082103033.html?sub=AR.

25. Jonathan H. Adler, "Is Morrison Dead? Assessing a Supreme Drug (Law) Overdose," *Lewis and Clark Law Review* 9 (2005): 751.

26. Ian Milhiser, "DeMint and Ensign Look to Right-Wing Think Tanks Rather than Judges to Interpret the Constitution," ThinkProgress.com, last modified December 23, 2009, http://thinkprogress.org/politics/2009/12/23/74940/demint-tenther.

27. Ilya Somin, "Does a Federal Mandate Requiring the Purchase of Health Insurance Exceed Congress's Powers under the Commerce Clause?" *supra*.

28. Somin, *Gonzalez v. Raich*, 507.

2

The Law Is Passed

Two days before President Barack Obama signed the Patient Protection and Affordable Care Act, Randy Barnett wrote this op-ed (abridged here) for the *Washington Post*. Barnett would eventually find himself on the legal team that challenged the law in the Supreme Court. At this time, however, there were just less-refined arguments and the hope that some court would take those arguments seriously.

Now the bill had become law and America was stuck with Obamacare, like it or lump it. At the *Volokh Conspiracy*, the conversations on the blog picked up steam.

* * *

Is Health Care Reform Constitutional?

Randy E. Barnett
Washington Post, March 21, 2010

With the House set to vote on health care legislation, the congressional debate on the issue seems to be nearing its conclusion. But if the bill does become law, the battle over federal control of health care will inevitably shift to the courts. Virginia's attorney general, Ken Cuccinelli II, has said he will file a legal challenge to the bill, arguing in a column this month that reform legislation "violate[s] the plain text of both the Ninth and Tenth Amendments." On Friday, South Carolina Attorney General Henry McMaster and Florida Attorney General Bill McCollum announced that they will file a federal lawsuit if health care reform legislation passes.

Will these cases get anywhere? . . . [T]he smart money says there won't be five votes to thwart the popular will to enact comprehensive health insurance reform.

But what if five justices think the legislation was carried bleeding across the finish line on a party-line vote over widespread bipartisan opposition? What if control of one or both houses of Congress flips parties while lawsuits are pending? Then there might just be five votes against regulating inactivity by compelling citizens to enter into a contract with a private company. This legislation won't go into effect tomorrow. In the interim, it is far more vulnerable than if some citizens had already started to rely upon its benefits.

If this sounds farfetched, consider another recent case in which the smart money doubted there were five votes to intervene in a politicized controversy involving technical procedures, a case in which five justices may have perceived that long-established rules were being gamed for purely partisan advantage.

You might have heard of it: *Bush v. Gore.*

Is the Tax Power Infinite?

David B. Kopel
March 22, 2010

One source of the impending constitutional challenge to the individual mandate is that it exceeds the enumerated powers granted to Congress under Article I, Section 8—for example, that the people's grant to power to Congress to regulate commerce among the several states does not include the power to compel people to engage in commerce. Jack Balkin, writing in the *New England Journal of Medicine*,[1] has two responses: (1) Yes it does because of *Wickard* and *Raich*, since people without insurance will eventually get sick and then buy health services, and allowing these people to buy health services outside the congressional system would undermine the congressional regulation. (2) The mandate is structured as a tax.

For the moment, let's put aside the question of whether the Obamacare tax is an Article I tax, or a Sixteenth Amendment income tax. Does Congress have the infinite power to control people's behavior (such as by ordering them to engage in commercial transactions) via the tax power? I suggest not. When the Bill of Rights was being debated in front of Congress, the skeptical Representative Theodore Sedgwick of Massachusetts asked if there should also be an enumeration that "declared that a man should have a right to wear his hat if he pleased; that he might get up when he pleased, and go to bed when he thought proper."[2] Sedgwick's point was that national laws about bedtimes and hat wearing were self-evidently beyond the authority of Congress.

However, if the tax power means that Congress can order citizens to buy something they don't want to buy, why does Congress not have the power to assess taxes on people who get too little sleep, or too much sleep, and thereby harm their own health and the public fisc; or who wear hats so little that they increase their risk of skin cancer; or who wear hats so often that they dangerously reduce their levels of vitamin D? In *Sonzinsky v. United States*,[3] the Supreme Court declared that it would not inquire into hidden regulatory motives that might have motivated a tax. But in *Sonzinsky*, the underlying activity (running a for-profit commercial business selling machine guns) was unquestionably within the scope of commercial activities that might be subject to an excise tax.

In contrast, *not* buying health insurance is not in its nature a commercial taxable activity, neither is wearing a hat, or getting up when you please, or going to bed when you think it proper.

Sonzinsky is deferential to congressional motives, but it does nothing to support the claim that noncommercial activity may be taxed. Construing the tax power as less than infinite—as not encompassing the power to tax bedtimes or the decision not purchase a product—is strongly supported by the Ninth Amendment. This is so whether one agrees with Randy Barnett's view of the Ninth Amendment (as an enforceable guarantee of natural rights)[4] or with Kurt Lash's (as a rule that enumerated powers should be narrowly construed so as not to violate natural rights, including the right of self-government in the states).[5]

Finally, as Jack Balkin has ably argued, "Constitutional change occurs because Americans persuade each other about the best meaning of constitutional text and principle in their own time. These debates and political struggles help generate Americans' investment in the Constitution as their Constitution and they create a platform for the possibility—but not the certainty—of its redemption in history."[6]

Americans today are not bound to meekly accept the most far-ranging assertions of congressional power based on large extrapolations from Supreme Court cases that themselves come from a short period (the late 1930s and early 1940s) when the Court was more supine and submissive to claims about centralized power than was any other Supreme Court before or after in our history. American citizens, in the political process and in their personal lives, will ultimately have the final word on the Constitution.

A large and permanent majority of the American people immediately accepted Social Security as a constitutional solution to poverty among the elderly and to massive unemployment (since Social Security would open up jobs by encouraging people to retire sooner). The American people have not accepted Obamacare as a constitutional solution to health insurance problems. If the American people believe that there is a "crisis" about the high cost of health insurance, then the American people can also believe that the solution is not to punish people for refusing to buy overpriced insurance that they don't want. The American people can reject the notion that our Constitution should be contorted and distorted to accommodate such a destructive and intrusive scheme.

It is eminently within the authority of "We the People" to act politically on our constitutional beliefs that the congressional power to regulate interstate commerce does not extend to forcing people to buy a product that Congress has forbidden to be sold across state lines, that the power to regulate interstate commerce is not the power to compel a person to participate in intrastate commerce, and that the power to levy income or excise taxes does not include the power to impose punishment in the form of punitive taxes on persons who choose not to buy something—or who choose whether to wear hats and when to sleep.

Legal Action and Political Action as a Two-Track Strategy for Opposing Obamacare

Ilya Somin
March 22, 2010

In a recent post, I suggested that Obamacare will be almost impossible to repeal through political action.[7] History shows that it is extremely difficult to eliminate entitlements. In addition, repeal would require Republican congressional majorities and a Republican president; I doubt we will get both simultaneously for years to come. Although various state governments and conservative and libertarian activists are planning to file legal challenges to the bill, I also doubt that lawsuits alone can achieve that goal. The Supreme Court is reluctant to take on the political branches of government on major issues that are a high priority for Congress and the president. When it has done so in the past (as in the 1930s), it has usually lost.

But while neither legal nor political action is likely succeed by itself, a two-track strategy combining the two stands a better chance. Unlike most high-profile policy initiatives enacted with strong presidential and congressional support, Obamacare is generally unpopular. Polls show substantial opposition to it, with opponents outnumbering supporters by ten to twenty points. If majority opinion continues to oppose the bill and Republicans make big gains in November as a result, the courts might be less hesitant to strike it down. They will not face any political retribution if they strike down a bill that most of the public and a new congressional majority actually opposes. Indeed, their public standing might even increase if they did so. As coblogger Randy Barnett puts it:

> [I]f this legislation is popular, they are unlikely to strike it down. But if it is deeply unpopular, and one or both houses of Congress flip parties as a result, then the legislation is much more vulnerable. Assuming the Supreme Court follows the election returns, as "realists" claim.

We should also remember that litigation is likely to center on the bill's mandate requiring individuals to purchase health insurance even if they prefer not to. This is one of the least popular elements of the bill, a fact that would give the courts further political cover. Eliminating the individual mandate might eventually destabilize other parts of the bill. Without the mandate, insurance companies might start lobbying for repeal of other elements of the plan (since the bill would no longer be a huge bonanza that gives them many additional customers). If the ban on excluding coverage of preexisting conditions is maintained, the elimination of the mandate would incentivize citizens to wait until they get sick to purchase insurance. It's unlikely that such a system could persist for long.

In my view, the individual mandate is unconstitutional because it exceeds Congress's powers under both the Commerce Clause and the Tax and Spending Clause. I believe that courts should strike it down regardless of the political situation.

As a practical reality, however, courts are unlikely to strike down major legislation if doing so will produce a massive backlash from the other branches of government. Thus, a strong political effort is probably necessary for litigation to succeed. Such two-track efforts have a long history. For example, The NAACP coupled its litigation strategy against segregation with a long-term political effort designed to win greater support for racial equality among white voters. *Brown v. Board of Education* and later decisions could never have happened without complementary political changes.

Even a successful political strategy doesn't necessarily guarantee victory in court. The conservative majority on the Supreme Court is a narrow one (5–4), and it's certainly possible that one or more conservative justices will refuse to strike down the individual mandate even if the political winds are favorable. And the political battle itself will be far from easy. It's likely that voters will take a more favorable view of the Obama administration and its policies as the economy begins to improve over the next several years.

If I had to guess, I would say that Obamacare is more likely to survive than not, for reasons I summarized previously. But a two-track strategy that combines litigation with political action has a much better chance of success than either taken alone.

What Are the Chances That the Courts Will Strike Down the Individual Mandate?

Orin S. Kerr
March 22, 2010

With all this blogging here at the VC about whether the courts will invalidate the individual mandate as exceeding Congress's Article I authority, I thought I would add my two cents by estimating the odds of that happening. In my view, there is a less than 1 percent chance that courts will invalidate the individual mandate as exceeding Congress's Article I power. I tend to doubt the issue will get to the Supreme Court: The circuits will be splitless, I expect, and the Supreme Court will decline to hear the case. In the unlikely event a split arises and the Court does take it, I would expect a 9–0 (or possibly 8–1) vote to uphold the individual mandate.

Blogging about such issues tends to bring out some unhappy responses, so let me be clear about a few things: (a) I don't like the individual mandate; (b) if I were a legislator, I wouldn't have voted for it; (c) I don't like modern Commerce Clause doctrine; (d) if I were magically made a Supreme Court justice in the mid-twentieth century, I wouldn't have supported the expansion of the Commerce Clause so that it covers, well, pretty much everything; (e) I agree that the individual mandate exceeds an originalist understanding of the Commerce Clause; and (f) I agree that legislators and the public are free to interpret the Constitution differently than the courts and to vote against (or ask their legislator to vote against) the legislation on that basis.

But with all of these caveats, I'll stand by my prediction. I just don't see lower courts finding these issues difficult, and I don't see the Supreme Court likely to take the case. I recognize there's always the theoretical possibility of the Supreme Court doing something totally unexpected—a *Bush v. Gore* moment, if you will—but I think the realistic possibility of that happening is less than 1 percent.

What Will Courts Do with the Individual Mandate?

Jonathan H. Adler
March 23, 2010

Like Orin, were I forced to make a prediction, I would predict that the individual mandate will survive judicial review. Federal courts have been quite reluctant to strike down federal statutes on enumerated powers grounds for quite some time, and the individual mandate is a larger and more consequential piece of legislation than those invalidated by the Rehnquist Court. But while I think judicial rejection of the mandate is unlikely, I hardly think the chances are as remote as Orin suggests.

Recall the history of *United States v. Lopez*. Academics and legal commentators were shocked when a panel of the U.S. Court of Appeals for the Fifth Circuit struck down the Gun-Free School Zones Act in 1993. Reversal in the Supreme Court was a foregone conclusion. No serious academic believed the decision would stand. And yet the Supreme Court confounded expectations and affirmed the Fifth Circuit, in part because the government was incapable of offering a theory upon which the statute could be upheld without obliterating what little was left of the limits on Congress's commerce power.

Lopez did not change much in the lower courts. Over the next five years, there were many Commerce Clause challenges to federal statutes and yet only one appellate court, in one case, struck down a federal law for exceeding the scope of the Commerce Clause. Federal appellate courts were completely uninterested in enforcing any limits on the Commerce Clause, largely because few took the Court's *Lopez* decision all that seriously. The one exception was the U.S. Court of Appeals for the Fourth Circuit, which struck down a provision of the Violence Against Women Act. That case went up to the Supreme Court and, in *United States v. Morrison*, the Court again confounded expectations and affirmed the lower court. In both cases, the prevailing academic wisdom was that the Commerce Clause arguments had no chance, and yet in both cases, the challenges prevailed.

The individual mandate is certainly a far more consequential provision than was at issue in either *Lopez* or *Morrison*. This would seem to reinforce the argument that the Court is likely to reject any legal challenges. It is much easier for a court to invalidate a small piece of symbolic legislation than a major social reform. And yet the Court has, at times, been willing to cut wide swaths through the federal code or confront the political branches. Dozens of statutory provisions were invalidated by *INS v. Chadha*,[8] and the Court's aggressive review of the political branches' wartime policy decisions in *Boumediene v. Bush*[9] were unprecedented, so it's not as if the Court has not flexed its muscles in the recent past.

It is also worth speculating on the politics of the individual mandate by the time any legal challenges reach the Court. If, as many believe, the Court is somewhat responsive to political pressures and popular sentiment, this could influence how the Court evaluates arguments that Congress has gone too far. If recent polls are to be believed, a substantial majority of Americans oppose the health care reforms passed by Congress, and those who strongly oppose the reforms outnumber those who strongly support them by about two to one. Striking down a popular health care provision would be a risky course for the Court. But what if unhappiness with health care reform were to fester and grow? What if the only thing preventing repeal were to be the same supermajority requirements that almost killed health care reform in the first place? Were this the case, the Court would not be picking a fight with the political branches so much as it would be reaffirming the popular will. In such a case, a Court decision against Obamacare would not provoke howls of protest so much as sighs of relief.

In closing, let me also stress that the arguments against the individual mandate are anything but frivolous. For reasons I explained previously,[10] it would be difficult to strike down the mandate without limiting (if not overturning) the rationale of *Gonzales v. Raich*, but it would also be difficult to uphold the mandate without eviscerating what little is left of *Lopez* and *Morrison*. And while it's a relatively safe bet to predict the Court will reaffirm federal power if pressed, the Court has confounded such expectations before—and there's a nontrivial chance it could do so again.

Was the Individual Mandate a "Republican Idea"?

Jonathan H. Adler
March 29, 2010

Many commentators have noted that the individual mandate is an idea that some Republican politicians and right-of-center thinkers used to support. Over the weekend the Associated Press reported that many on the right once championed an individual mandate as part of a broader health care overhaul. Not only does the Massachusetts health care reform championed by Mitt Romney include an individual mandate, but back in the 1990s, the Heritage Foundation and many Republican office holders called for an individual mandate as part of a GOP alternative to the Clinton administration's proposed health care reforms. In 1993, for example, Heritage's Stuart Butler testified before Congress in support of a new, "more rational" social contract under which government would provide greater assistance to those lacking health care in return for greater individual responsibility. Butler explains as follows:

> This translates into a requirement on individuals to enroll themselves and their dependents in at least a basic health plan—one that at the minimum should protect the rest of society from large and unexpected medical costs incurred by the family. And as any social contract, there would also be an obligation on society. To the extent that the family cannot reasonably afford reasonable basic coverage, the rest of society, via government, should take responsibility for financing that minimum coverage.

It's certainly true that many conservatives and Republicans championed an individual mandate as part of a broader package of reforms (such as ending preferential tax treatment of employer-provided insurance). But others on the Right have always been opposed. So, for instance, when some congressional Republicans introduced health reform legislation based upon the Heritage Foundation's proposal, the Cato Institute published a paper by Tom Miller (now a health care analyst at the American Enterprise Institute) attacking the idea. Working in D.C. at the time (as one of Tom Miller's colleagues), I recall that many conservatives and libertarians believed those who had embraced the Heritage approach were engaging in preemptive compromise, proposing bad ideas in an effort to forestall worse ones. It was only after conservatives revolted that Republicans in Congress sought to defeat health care reform outright. The Cato Institute, among other groups, has also been extremely critical of Romneycare.

Even so, why were so many on the Right willing to embrace an idea that conservatives attack as unconstitutional today? How can the Heritage Foundation's legal scholars attack an idea once championed by its health care analysts? One possibility is that the Heritage Foundation is simply more conservative, or more free market, than it used to be. Another is that the legal environment has changed dramatically. In 1994 it had been over fifty years since the Supreme Court had invalidated a federal law for exceeding the scope of the Commerce Clause. The Supreme Court's decision in *United States v. Lopez*, striking down the Gun-Free School Zones Act, was not until 1995—after the Clinton health care plan had been defeated and after the Republicans had retaken Congress, effectively ending the debate over health care reform. Prior to *Lopez*, it was simply assumed there were no meaningful limits on the federal government's regulatory powers. After *Lopez* (and *United States v. Morrison* in 2000), that all changed. While the argument that the individual mandate exceeds the scope of federal power *as interpreted by the courts* is still difficult to make, it is no longer as implausible as it was in 1994 (particularly for those of us who believe *Gonzales v. Raich* was wrongly decided).

Of course it's also fair to argue that many Republican office holders and partisans are simply opportunistic, opposing ideas today they supported before merely to oppose the president. In many cases, I am sure this is true, just witness Republican efforts to transform themselves into champions of Medicare, opposing any and all spending cuts. But just because this may be true of partisans and politicians, it does not mean it's true of those in the broader conservative and libertarian movements. Many conservative and libertarian voices were no less critical of the individual mandate when proposed by the Heritage Foundation or Mitt Romney than they are today.

Inaccurate Legal Claim from the Democratic Governors Association

David B. Kopel
April 12, 2010

Today Nathan Daschle, executive director of the Democratic Governors Association, emailed me, as he does once every week or two. This week, his topic was urging me to sign a petition against the state lawsuits filed against Obamacare. (By the way, "Obamacare" is a standard part of political discourse, used by, *inter alia*, Michael Barone, one of America's foremost political reporters. It is similar to "Reaganomics," which was used to describe President Ronald Reagan's economic policies, or "Hillarycare," which was used to describe the health policy proposals promoted by the then–First Lady.) The letter from Daschle states: "Legal scholars are unanimous: these lawsuits have no merit." The text of the petition itself has only four sentences, one of which is "[l]egal scholars are unanimous in their opinion that these suits have no merit."

The statements are indisputably false. Among the legal scholars who contend that Obamacare is unconstitutional are Randy Barnett and Michael McConnell, both of them among the most important constitutional scholars of our time. Their views about Obamacare have appeared in widely read publications such as the *Wall Street Journal, Washington Post,* and *Washington Times.*

Accordingly, Republican governors who receive the DGA petitions demanding that the lawsuits be terminated might take them with a grain of salt, in that a plainly false claim was used to help induce the petitioners to sign.

An Act for the Relief of Sick and Disabled Seamen

David B. Kopel
April 2, 2010

This 1798 statute[11] is currently making the blogospheric rounds as purported proof that the 2010 congressional mandate to purchase health insurance from a private company is based on long-established practice. Incorrect.

Sections 1 and 2 of the act impose a 20 cent per month tax on seamen's wages, to be withheld by the employer.

Section 3 requires that all the withheld taxes be turned over to the U.S. Treasury on a quarterly basis and that the revenue shall be expended in the district where it was collected. The revenue shall be spent to support sick and injured seamen.

So the act is totally dissimilar to the Obamacare mandate. In the 1798 act, the government imposes a tax, collects all the tax revenue, and spends the revenue as it chooses. This is a good precedent for programs in which the government imposes a tax and then spends the money on medical programs (e.g., Medicare), but it has nothing to do with mandating that individuals purchase a private product.

Under Section 4, if there is a surplus in a district, the surplus shall be spent in the construction of marine hospitals; the executive may combine the tax revenue with voluntary private donations of land or money for hospital construction. The president may also receive voluntary private donations for relief of the seamen or for operation of the hospitals.

Section 5 instructs the president to select the directors of the marine hospitals. The directors shall make quarterly reports to the secretary of the Treasury. The directors will be reimbursed for expenses but will not receive other compensation.

Today the 1798 act is viewed as the beginning of the creation of the U.S. Public Health Service.

The act is very strong precedent for the federal government imposing taxes and dedicating the tax revenue to medical care for the taxed class. Further, the government may provide the medical care directly or may cooperate with private individuals for the providing of that care. The 1798 act thus shows that Medicare, while vastly broader in scope than anything from the early republic, is generally consistent with constitutional practice of that period.

The act certainly did not order seamen to purchase any form of private insurance nor did it order them to purchase any other type of private good. The act is a solid precedent for federal involvement in health care and no precedent at all for a federal mandate to purchase private products.

A Better Question

Orin S. Kerr
April 2, 2010

In light of David Kopel's and Ilya's posts on the constitutionality of the health care mandate, let me propose a better question to ask. It's a little more complicated, but I think it will be more illuminating. Here's the idea. Instead of asking experts, "Is the health care mandate constitutional?," we should ask experts this question:

In your view, which of the following federal programs or agencies are constitutional?

a. Social Security
b. The Federal Trade Commission
c. Medicare/Medicaid
d. The Securities and Exchange Commission
e. The new health care mandate

I think this would be a helpful question because it would it would distinguish those scholars who think most of the federal government is constitutionally OK, but that the health care mandate is different, from those scholars who think most of the federal government is unconstitutional, and the health care mandate is just one more unconstitutional part along with the rest. (And while I can't fairly put Ilya and David Kopel on the spot, I admit I would be kind of interested in their answers to the previous question.)

Destroying the Constitution's Structure Is Not Constitutional

David B. Kopel
April 2, 2010

Thus far, the argument among law professors over the constitutionality of Obamacare has been well represented by scholars who have made pro and con arguments over particular clauses in the Constitution, such as the Interstate Commerce Clause, or the tax power. In this post, I would like to examine an insight by Jonathan Turley, which points the way to strong, recent, and repeated precedent suggesting that Obamacare is unconstitutional.

Let's begin by getting rid of the red herring that questioning the constitutionality of Obamacare requires denying the constitutionality of the New Deal and the Great Society. Orin asks,

In your view, which of the following federal programs or agencies are constitutional?

a. Social Security
b. The Federal Trade Commission
c. Medicare/Medicaid
d. The Securities and Exchange Commission
e. The new Health Care mandate

In my view, (a), (b), (c), and (d) are constitutional, but (e) is not. My answer is based on using "constitutional" in the normal sense of the word as it appears in most modern public dialogue. That is, "Should a judge who accurately applies existing precedents, and other sources of legal authority, find the law to be constitutional?" This is the question that federal district judges and circuit courts of appeals judges will have to answer, since they have no authority to reject Supreme Court precedent. The Supreme Court can change its own precedents, but for the purpose of argument, I am presuming that the Supreme Court would not overrule any precedents.

As Jack Balkin, Sandy Levinson, and others have ably pointed out, "constitutional" can be used in a different way, in that people express aspirations about what the Constitution *should* mean, even if that meaning is contrary to current precedents. For example, a person in 1946 might say, "discrimination against women is unconstitutional." That person would not be describing the current state of the law but would be making an argument that constitutional interpretation should be changed. Often, these aspirational statements *do* become constitutional law, especially when they win the hearts and minds of the public. Some of the 1930s decisions upholding parts of the New Deal or its state analogues are examples of the success of this aspirational constitutional rhetoric. For example, the statement in 1890 that "mortgage relief laws are constitutional and do not violate the Contract Clause" would have been incorrect in regard to Supreme Court precedent and was utterly contrary to the original meaning of the Contract Clause. Nevertheless, the Supreme Court later changed its interpretation of the Contract Clause so that the aspirational statement became an accurate description of the law.

People are free to argue all they want, on the basis of aspiration, original meaning, or anything else, that items (a) through (d) on Orin's list are unconstitutional. If these people persuade enough of their fellow Americans, perhaps the Court might eventually narrow or overturn some of the precedents that uphold (a) through (d). However, my argument is based on the law as it actually exists today, and it presumes the continuing validity of all the New Deal and Great Society precedents.

Some parts of Obamacare, such as the calorie labeling requirement for restaurant chains, appear to be solidly within the scope of existing precedents. (At least based on the discussion I've heard thus far.)

In contrast, the individual mandate to purchase health insurance is not. It "is unprecedented in our jurisprudence."[12] It is possible to make arguments for extensions of cases such as *Wickard*, *Raich*, and *Sonzinsky* in support of the mandate. However, such arguments are a plea for *extending* those cases, not for merely applying them. For example, an *application* of *Wickard/Raich* might be a law against a person manufacturing her own medicine at home rather than purchasing the medicine through the federally controlled market.

No prior case stands for the proposition that Congress may use the interstate commerce power to order persons to buy a particular product, or may use the tax power to punish people for choosing not to purchase a particular product. I can imagine a judicial opinion that builds on the foundation of *Wickard*, *Raich*, and *Sonzinsky*, and extends those cases much further, in order to uphold the mandate. The Court might do so, but the Court would be doing much more than merely applying precedent.

At this stage in the debate, the only cited instance of Congress ever forcing people to buy particular products have come under the congressional exercise of the enumerated militia powers in Article I, Section 8, Clause 16, "To provide for organizing, arming, and disciplining, the Militia." Here, the congressional power to mandate is provided in the text itself. Further, the original understanding of the militia was that the militiamen "were expected to appear bearing arms supplied by themselves and of the kind in common use at the time."[13] The congressional power to provide for arming the militia straightforwardly includes the power to tell militiamen what kind of arms to bring to duty.

The federal militia powers come from the state militia powers, which (by enacting the Constitution) the people and the states chose to give (at least concurrently) to Congress. No one could possibly dispute that state militia powers included the power to require militiamen to bring certain types of arms to duty and thus to require the purchase of such arms if necessary. The federal power to regulate commerce among the several states was likewise granted to Congress from the powers that were then possessed by the states and by the people. There was certainly no understanding in 1789 that *state* power to regulate interstate commerce (e.g., by inspecting goods at ports of entry) included the power to compel individuals to purchase goods in commerce.

So neither the Militia Arming Clause nor any cases provide precedent for the unprecedented mandate to purchase insurance. At best, the mandate is in a constitutional gray zone. To resolve the gray zone question, we are not limited to wondering whether to greatly extend some prior cases on the Interstate Commerce Clause or the tax power. In addition, we can consider the structure of the Constitution itself.

As Jonathan Turley has written, allowing the individual mandate to stand "could amount to a 'do not resuscitate' order for federalism."[14] If judges find this argument (in the greatly elaborated form that will eventually be presented to the courts) to be persuasive, then the Supreme Court precedent is very clear. Several recent cases have demonstrated the Court's persistent determination to defend state sovereign immunity.[15] Some of these cases involved the Eleventh Amendment, and some involved the Fourteenth (Congress's powers under Section 5). In one case (*Nevada Department of Human Resources v. Hibbs*), the federal abrogation of sovereign immunity was upheld, partly because the federal law involved a state practice (sex discrimination) that was already unconstitutional.

These decisions have been heavily criticized by the academic left, and the critics have pointed out that these decisions have much less to do with the constitutional text, or with original meaning of the text, than they do with the Court's broad view of constitutional structure: the essential nature of state sovereignty and one of the attributes of sovereignty—namely sovereign immunity.

According to the Court, a congressional statute making it easier for states to be sued for patent infringement is such a serious violation of federalism that it must be held unconstitutional.[16] In terms of the practical harm to state sovereignty, the congressional law on patent suits is to Obamacare as a house cat is to a lion.

The extensive line of recent cases on state sovereignty is complemented by the Ninth Amendment. The Ninth Amendment may be read to create a presumption of liberty.[17] Or it may be read as a requirement that enumerated federal powers be narrowly construed so that they do not violate the retained natural rights of the people, including the people's right of self-government in the states.[18] Either reading raises further doubts about the constitutionality of the insurance mandate.

As the joint complaint of the 13 attorneys general has argued, Obamacare constitutes an immense assault on federalism. If Obamacare is upheld, the states may be well on the way to becoming like the Roman Senate in 100 AD: formerly an essential component of republican sovereignty but now a hollowed remnant, possessing the forms of the old republic but really functioning as a mere puppet of the Leviathan.

"[F]ederalism was the unique contribution of the Framers to political science and political theory," wrote Justice Anthony Kennedy in *United States v. Lopez*.[19] To declare Obamacare to be unconstitutional, the Court may take into account the importance of preserving the unique contribution of "our federalism." In doing so, the Court need not overrule a single precedent nor does the Court need to cast into doubt any of the creations of the New Deal or the Great Society. Instead, the Court may simply choose not to invent unprecedented extensions of the interstate commerce power and the tax power.

From federal district court to the Supreme Court, the judges and justices who decide to leave constitutional doctrine exactly as it is today will decline to validate the unprecedented exercise of power in Obamacare. The last 14 years of the Supreme Court's determination to defend our precious constitutional system of dual sovereignty gives reason to hope that the courts will apply the existing law rather than make up new law and that the insurance mandate will be declared unconstitutional.

The more than two thousand pages of laws certainly contain items (e.g., restaurant menu labeling, tanning taxes) that theoretically could have been enacted separately from the mandate and might be considered severable. But the main provision of Obamacare—turning private insurance companies into ultraregulated public utilities—makes no sense without the individual mandate; the rest of the act would not have been enacted without the mandate, and it is not severable.

In What Sense Is the Personal Health Insurance Mandate "Unconstitutional"?

Randy E. Barnett
April 16, 2010

When discussing the "constitutionality" of a governmental action, one must distinguish between three senses of "constitutionality": (1) what the Constitution says and means; (2) what the Supreme Court has said and meant; and (3) whether there are five votes on the Supreme Court to uphold or invalidate the action. Because of my well-known view that the text of the Constitution has a meaning that is independent of the opinions of the Supreme Court—a meaning that must remain the same until properly changed—as well as my exchanges with Orin on this blog, readers may be forgiven if they think my constitutional objections to the individual health insurance mandate are based on the original meaning of the Constitution—or what Orin calls the Constitution as it "ought to be." But I have been very clear in my publications and media statements that I am not offering an originalist objection to the individual health insurance mandate. Under the original meaning of the Constitution, for example, Congress would have no power to regulate the health insurance business since insurance contracts—like the practice of medicine—are not "commerce," which is why both activities have traditionally been regulated by the states. But I have not made anything like this objection and neither have the attorneys general in their lawsuit.

Instead, I have objected that the mandate that individuals purchase health insurance from a private company is unconstitutional under existing Supreme Court doctrine—the second of the three senses of unconstitutionality. And, in response to confident predictions that the Supreme Court will uphold the mandate, I have suggested that they may be less inclined to do so if the bill continues to be unpopular, one or both houses of Congress flip parties, a serious repeal effort is blocked by a presidential veto or filibuster in the Senate, and the "benefits" promised by the bill have yet to be implemented. Everyone should know I think this last type of analysis should have nothing to do with whether a measure is or is not "constitutional," but I do not deny these factors are relevant to whether the Supreme Court will uphold or invalidate an act of Congress. My point is that those who confidently predict that the Supreme Court will uphold this bill are not taking these sorts of factors adequately into account.

Part of my constitutional assessment (in the second sense) involves the unprecedented nature of this claim of power by Congress. (The other part is analysis of what the Supreme Court *has* said about the commerce power since the New Deal.) Having made this observation back in December in my coauthored paper for the Heritage Foundation,[20] my confidence in its accuracy has been increased by two developments. The first is the change of subject to the taxing power of Congress. Think about it. If the claim that this legislation was as clearly authorized by post–New Deal Commerce Clause doctrine as so many law professors seem to assume, then why almost immediately change the subject to the power of Congress to tax? This switch telegraphs a fundamental weakness of the Commerce Clause claim.

The second development is the inability of supporters of the bill to generate any examples of when the Commerce Clause power has been exercised in the past to mandate individuals engage in economic activity by entering a contract with a private company. True, the early Militia Act mandated militia members provide their own private arms, but this was not an exercise of the commerce power. And we have been treated to the discovery of an early statute taxing sailors and spending the money on hospitals for their care. Of course, this is very much akin to how Medicare works (which is clearly "constitutional" in the second and third senses), and the regulation of navigation is squarely within the original meaning of the Commerce Clause (as I have shown in *Restoring the Lost Constitution: The Presumption of Liberty*[21]), so this provision seems "constitutional" in the first sense as well.

The only examples currently bandied by law professors concern tax credits for certain activities—like buying a home—within the income tax code. How to distinguish between a mandate coupled with a fine or penalty and a general income tax that allows for credits for certain activity is an interesting conceptual question. But our intuitions run strongly against this equivalence. Indeed, the president publicly denied this was a tax—which would break his no taxes on persons making less than $200,000 promise—and the bill itself refers to the provision as a "requirement" backed by a "penalty." No, I am not claiming that the Court is bound by how the bill is worded, but this wording—and the president's defense of the mandate—reflects an underlying reality, as well as a deep intuition that a monetary fine for violating a mandate is not the same as the failure to receive a tax credit. Indeed, the express rationale for the measure in the bill itself rests on the commerce not the tax power:

> The requirement regulates activity that is commercial and economic in nature: economic and financial decisions about how and when health care is paid for, and when health insurance is purchased.[22]

Indeed the bill provides for refundable "tax credits" for qualified insurance plans in a different section than the "individual responsibility" section containing the mandate.

Consider this: if Congress had ever done anything like this before, we would all be able to think of countless things we are mandated to do by the federal government upon pain of a monetary penalty enforced by the IRS. Yet, apart from registering for the draft, I cannot think of anything the federal government mandates of people simply because they are alive, much less mandate pursuant to its Commerce Clause power. Of course there are a host of federal regulations that tell you how you must engage in particular economic activities should you choose to do so. Laws against discriminating with respect to employment or public accommodations come immediately to mind, but there are lots of others as well.

But regulating HOW one engages in economic activity (or prohibiting an activity) and mandating THAT one engage in economic activity are not the same thing. It is the latter that is unprecedented. To uphold such a claim of power, the Supreme Court would have to go beyond its existing precedents—and well beyond them. Of course, the smart money says the justices will do just that—but this is a reference to the third sense of constitutionality described previously: counting to five votes.

In light of all this, I am genuinely intrigued by this comment Orin posted on *PrawfsBlawg* (in which he is partially defending me from a criticism there):

> I should add that I don't buy Randy's argument: He is trying to take one issue (factually, whether the federal government has done this precise thing before) and treat it as if it answered a quite different issue (legally, the doctrine of stare decisis).[23]

This comment raises two questions of great interest to me.

First, what are the Commerce Clause precedents that Orin thinks cover the personal health insurance mandate and why? I think I am pretty familiar with the post–New Deal Commerce Clause cases on which my own analysis relies, so I would be very interested to learn which of these cases cover this type of mandate. Second, what theory of stare decisis is Orin employing here? Of course all law professors know that any two situations can be "factually" distinguished if only by the time and place. So a simple difference in facts does not necessarily take a case out of a "precedent." But I do not believe we are talking about this type of factual difference. We are talking about the difference between telling people engaged in economic behavior HOW they must act and telling people who are doing nothing at all THAT they must engage in economic behavior. This "factual" difference seems to be really germane—as germane as the traditional and intuitive (though sometimes problematic) act-omission distinction in private law.

So putting the tax power issue to one side, I am very curious to know on what basis Orin thinks this personal mandate is governed by Supreme Court Commerce Clause precedents. I ask this in all sincerity, as I would greatly benefit from Orin's considered explanation of how he thinks the doctrine of stare decisis applies here and decides this issue. Of course, Orin is under no obligation to post any reply to this query. However, since he seems to have a view on this, I am most curious as to what it may be.

One final thought: if, for some reason, we are not supposed to carefully consider what exactly the Supreme Court HAS said about the Commerce Clause power in its decisions—along with what it has NOT said in those decisions—and we are also not supposed to take seriously the independent meaning of the text of the Constitution itself, then ALL "constitutionality" means is a prediction of what the justices will do (sense three). And this would seem to be the epitome of the rule of men, as opposed to the rule of law. It is certainly nothing that any nominee to the Supreme Court could claim and still be confirmed.

A Quick Response to Randy on the Use of "Unprecedented"

Orin S. Kerr
April 16, 2010

My coblogger Randy asks for my explanation of part of a blog comment I left over at *PrawfsBlawg* on his use of "unprecedented." To fill in readers, I was responding to a post that began:

> Randy Barnett is not just a great scholar; he's also a great lawyer. Maybe someone else beat him to it, but I credit him with the now-popular claim that health care reform's "mandate" to buy insurance is "unprecedented" in American history, that never before has the government forced anyone to enter into a contract with another party for insurance. Fantastic rhetorical move. Not really accurate, though. People who refuse to buy insurance have been paying a penalty for almost seventy years now.[24]

My response in the thread suggested that the post misunderstood Randy's claim and then added (perhaps unartfully!) the caveat that I had difficulties with the suggestion in Randy's usage that I think makes it such a powerful rhetorical move—the suggestion being, it seems to me, that if a law is "unprecedented," then legal "precedents" do not answer whether it is constitutional.

To elaborate, my sense of the rhetorical power of the use of the term "unprecedented" in this debate owes in part to its mixing up two meanings of the term "precedent." One meaning is the popular use of the term "unprecedented," which generally means whether the same thing, however precisely defined, has happened before. ("The Houston Astros winning the World Series? That would be unprecedented!") The other is the technical legal usage of the term "precedent," the extent to which the reasoning of prior related judicial decisions direct or suggest an answer within the framework of existing case law. My point was just that these two meanings are conceptually different and shouldn't be blurred. Whether a new law is "unprecedented" is a distinct question from whether "precedents" address the constitutionality of that law.

Of course, it's entirely possible that Randy did not mean to equate these things, in which case I will apologize to Randy and thank him for the clarification of his view. But that's what I had in mind with my comment over at *PrawfsBlawg*.

In What Sense Is the Personal Health Insurance Mandate "Unconstitutional"? UPDATE

Randy E. Barnett
April 16, 2010

Thanks to Orin for his clarification. I take it from his response that he is not claiming that the personal insurance mandate is authorized by previous Supreme Court Commerce Clause cases. No apology is needed. I have been using "unprecedented" in both senses. But the fact this sort of thing has never been done before does figure into there being no judicial precedent for it—provided that it differs from what has been done before in a legally relevant way. That regulating HOW one engages in economic activity differs from mandating THAT you engage in economic activity is relevantly different is intuitively obvious, and I believe will be obvious to at least some judges. It takes a pretty counterintuitive comparison with tax credits against a general tax—or a highly counterintuitive denial of the act-omission distinction—to equate a mandate with a regulation or prohibition. While these counterintuitive moves can be understood by law professors and intellectual types, I think they are not an easy sell for a variety of reasons—including the fact that they would so greatly expand federal power beyond where it has ever been extended before. When this practical implication is combined with what the Supreme Court actually said in *NLRB v. Jones & Laughlin*, *Lopez*, *Morrison*, and *Raich*, I think the argument that a personal mandate is unconstitutional (in the second sense) is highly plausible, and the breezy assertion by some professors and pundits that the mandate is constitutional under existing doctrine is not supported by a close reading of these opinions—or so I claimed in my Heritage paper last December—if, that is, the Supreme Court follows its reasoning in previous cases when this issue comes before it, which returns us to issue three [whether there are five votes on the Supreme Court to uphold or invalidate the action].

Drawing Lines in the Commerce Clause Debate on Health Care Reform

Orin S. Kerr
April 26, 2010

I've generally stayed at the periphery on the debate over the constitutionality of health care reform, mostly because it's not something that I particularly enjoy blogging about. As I see it, a lot of the blogging about the legal issues are a weird mix of actual legal analysis and efforts to influence the broader political and legal culture. That mix isn't really my cup of tea. But I do have a question for those who believe that the individual mandate exceeds Congress's Commerce Clause power under existing law: how much of a statutory nexus to interstate commerce would Congress have to add in order to change your mind?

I ask that because Congress often adds some sort of statutory "hook" when it is regulating at the edges of the Commerce Clause. The hook adds an explicit requirement of some connection to interstate commerce, even though it is understood by everyone that the hook is there just to make sure the statute is constitutional rather than out of a genuine interest in regulating interstate commerce. For those who think the individual mandate exceeds the Commerce Clause power, my question is, "How much of a hook would be needed to make the mandate constitutional?"

An example might be helpful. In 2006 Congress enacted the Sex Offender Registration and Notification Act ("SORNA"), codified at 18 U.S.C. 2250(a). Congress's goal was to punish individuals for failure to register as sex offenders. But failure to register as a sex offender based on a state law conviction doesn't seem to have any connection at all to interstate commerce: not only is it regulating inaction rather than action—a distinction Randy might point out—but it also addresses something without any connection to commerce. So Congress added a hook: if you have to register as a sex offender based on a state criminal conviction, the regulation applies to you only if you cross state lines or enter, leave, or reside in Indian country. So formally, it's traveling across state lines without having registered as a sex offender that is punished. The circuit courts have held unanimously (at least so far) that this prohibition is within the power of Congress to regulate interstate commerce.[25]

So my question is, "What is the minimum statutory hook that would make the individual mandate constitutional?" Presumably under the SORNA line of cases, it would be within Congress's Commerce Clause power to punish crossing state lines after failing to purchase health care insurance. But what about some narrower hook like failing to purchase health care insurance while having crossed state lines at some point in the past or failure to purchase health care insurance while traveling on interstate roads? Such a prohibition might look odd, obviously, but my point is only to get a sense of where readers who object to the constitutionality of the individual mandate see the constitutional line. In your view, what would be the minimum statutory hook to save the constitutionality of the statute?

Deference and the Constitutionality of Health Care Reform

David E. Bernstein
August 22, 2010

As constitutional challenges to the new health care law work their way up the courts, proponents of the law's constitutionality will inevitably argue that the Supreme Court should defer to Congress's understanding of its own constitutional powers, especially when it comes to such significant legislation. As early as 1922, the Supreme Court wrote, "Whatever amounts to more or less constant practice, and threatens to obstruct or unduly to burden the freedom of interstate commerce is within the regulatory power of Congress under the commerce clause and it is **primarily for Congress** to consider and decide the fact of the danger and meet it."[26] This message was reiterated with greater force in the late 1930s, when the Supreme Court gradually abandoned policing the limits of the commerce power.

As a matter of constitutional construction, I think there is a lot to be said for the courts adopting a general posture of deference to the elected branches on constitutional matters but *only* if a reasonable observer would be satisfied that Congress and the executive took their duty to ensure the constitutionality of the legislation they passed seriously. An example of where the Court could have exhibited more deference than it did was *United States v. Morrison*, where Congress collected substantial (though not incontrovertible) evidence that the Violence Against Women Act was a proper exercise of Congress's Section 5 power under the Fourteenth Amendment to guarantee equal protection of the laws.

From what I can tell, though, Congress and the Obama administration treated the idea that the health care law needed to be within Congress's enumerated powers with thinly veiled contempt. Most famously when Speaker Nancy Pelosi was asked last fall where the Constitution gives Congress the power to enact an "individual mandate," she replied with a mocking "[A]re you serious? Are you serious?"

I didn't follow the health care debate extremely closely, but I seem to remember reading that other congressmen, and some administration officials, also acted befuddled, bewildered, or with contempt when constituents or journalists asked them about the constitutionality of the health care legislation. Not to mention the refrain that no one will know what's in the bill until its final passage, which hardly inspires confidence that its constitutionality was properly considered, and the shifting rationales that have been used to justify the individual mandate's constitutionality.

UPDATE: Many commenters are confusing the issue of whether the Court should defer to Congress's assertion of the scope of its own authority with the issue of whether the Court should ultimately uphold the health care law, on which I've expressed no opinion. I could explain this in detail, but instead I'll just point out what seems to me to be obvious: the Court could decide that it shouldn't defer to Congress, that is, it should not *presume* that Congress was acting within its enumerated powers but still ultimately conclude that Congress was indeed acting constitutionally. But I think there is no valid reason to defer to Congress's (or the executive's) purported constitutional judgment if the relevant actors didn't, in fact, spend much if any mental energy thinking about it.

The Individual Mandate Is Unprecedented? So What?

Randy E. Barnett
August 25, 2010

Over on Concurring Opinions, Gerard Magliocca is bothered by my persistent claim that the health insurance mandate is "unprecedented":

> Folks like Randy Barnett rely heavily on the idea that congressional regulation of inactivity (or commercial coercion) is unprecedented under the Commerce and Taxing Clauses. But isn't it equally unprecedented to establish a "private action" limitation on congressional authority pursuant to those provisions. Where does that doctrine come from? There's no case law to support the concept, for example. Thus, each side in the litigation wants courts to do something new—either by upholding or invalidating the individual mandate. It's a jurisprudential wash.[27]

Magliocca is a thoughtful guy and, in an important sense, I agree with him here. For months now I have been affirmatively saying that the bare fact that this exercise of power by Congress is unprecedented does not in and of itself make it unconstitutional. Here is how that point is made in my *Wall Street Journal* interview a few weeks ago:

Such a mandate is unprecedented: "This is the first time in American history that Congress has claimed to use its power over interstate commerce to mandate, or require, that every person enter into a commercial relationship with a private company," Mr. Barnett notes. "As a judicial matter, it's also unprecedented. There's never been a court case which said Congress can do this." **That doesn't establish that Congress *can't* do it**, but the high court could reach that conclusion without undoing existing law.[28]

Although the passage in bold is the interviewer's words, he was getting that point from me. In the balance of the interview, I explain why I think the mandate is not only unprecedented; it is also unconstitutional.

Having said this, I think the unprecedented nature of the individual mandate is highly significant for a number of reasons that the mandate's supporters would rather not discuss. First, it destroys their constructed narrative that any constitutional challenge to the individual mandate is "frivolous" or, as Washington and Lee law professor Tim Jost put it on *Politico's Arena* back on September of 2009, "[T]his is not a serious legal issue. The claim that health reform is unconstitutional was apparently adopted as a talking point at last week's Republican briefing on health care reform . . . it is not, however, an argument taken seriously by constitutional scholars."[29] Several of the Republican state attorneys general were criticized by home state Democrats for wasting tax payer money pursuing a "ridiculous enterprise," a "specious claim," or, yes, a "frivolous" lawsuit. Professor Magliocca's contention that "[it]'s a jurisprudential wash"—like Tim Jost's latest reference on *Politico* to "the closeness of the case"—is a major concession that the constitutional challenges are serious. Indeed, for some judge-centric law professors, these concessions are probably driven by Judge Henry Hudson's denial of the government's motion to dismiss the Virginia attorney general's lawsuit. Judge Hudson's opinion, while not a ruling on the merits, was an express ruling on the *seriousness* of the challenge. Frivolous challenges get dismissed. As a commenter on Concurring Opinion observes, "Well, since Randy is mainly trying to combat those who say his argument is a dead loser, going from 'sure loser' to 'jurisprudential wash' is a pretty big advance."

Second, whoever has the formal burden of proof in a lawsuit challenging the mandate's constitutionality, it is the government who must somehow justify its claim that Congress has the power to impose the mandate. This is an implication of the federal government being a government of limited and enumerated powers. If the issue is really a "wash," then such a claim is currently not authorized by prior precedents of the Supreme Court and the appropriate stance of an inferior court would be to strike down the mandate until the Supreme Court decides to extend Congress's power beyond where it has gone before. While the Supreme Court is, of course, free to do this, it is not at all clear that a district court judge should be devising a new and unprecedented doctrine extending federal power. In other words, unless the government can justify this exercise of power on the basis of precedent, a lower court should sustain the challenge and leave the creation of new doctrine to the Supreme Court.

Third, due to the now concededly unprecedented nature of this claim of power, ANY constitutional theory adopted by the Supreme Court will be a novel one. Any doctrine UPHOLDING Congress's power to impose a mandate either as an exercise of its commerce power or as a necessary and proper means to regulating interstate commerce will be new. For this reason, defenders of the mandate cannot complain about the novelty of a theory opposing the constitutionality of the mandate because ALL theories about so unprecedented an exercise of power will necessarily be new and novel. For example, the doctrine that it is "improper" for Congress to exercise its Commerce Clause power to "commandeer" or mandate state legislatures or executive branch officials was novel when it was adopted by the Supreme Court in the 1990s because imposing such mandates on states was until then unprecedented. So too with the individual mandate that, for the first time in American history, attempts to commandeer the American people because it is deemed by Congress to be convenient to the regulation of interstate commerce. In sum, due to the unprecedented nature of the mandate, that a constitutional objection to it is novel provides no objection to the objection. As Professor Magliocca implicitly acknowledges, any and all theories in this case will be novel.

So that should bring us to the merits of the claim that the individual mandate is not justified as an exercise of the commerce or tax powers nor as a necessary and proper means to the end of regulating interstate commerce. Professor Magliocca is entirely correct that the unprecedented nature of the mandate does not supply the analysis of why it is unconstitutional.

Some Tentative Thoughts on the Constitutionality of the Individual Mandate under Current Supreme Court Doctrine

Orin S. Kerr
October 6, 2010

I haven't blogged any detailed thoughts on the constitutionality of the individual mandate, as I'm not an expert in the Commerce Clause or the Necessary and Proper Clause. But I've been pondering some of the issues, and I have some tentative thoughts on the constitutionality of the mandate based on current Supreme Court doctrine that I wanted to put out there for responses. So let me put out the tentative argument, and then readers can then feel free to throw tomatoes, claim "fraud!," cite Bingham [John Bingham, principal framer of the Fourteenth Amendment], allege bad faith, and make all the other helpful contributions we see in VC comment threads. I'll make the argument in two parts: first, the constitutionality of the ends of the legislation and second, the constitutionality of the means of the legislation.

First, the ends. Health care accounts for about 17 percent of the entire United States economy, and the purpose of health care reform was to regulate that market in various ways to expand coverage, lower costs, and so on. Thus, whether the new health care reform is a good idea or a bad idea, smart or dumb, it is legislation designed to regulate a large chunk of the United States economy. That large chunk of the United States economy is a complex and sprawling web of interstate commerce. Thus, the goal of the health care reform package—not the means, at this stage, but the goal—was to regulate interstate commerce as permitted under Article I, Section 8. And that's true of the individual mandate specifically: love it or hate it, the goal of it is to influence decisions about buying health care services that are in interstate commerce.

Second, the means. The next question is whether Congress's choice of the individual mandate counts as "necessary and proper for carrying into Execution the foregoing Power" to regulate interstate commerce, such that Congress's means of carrying out its power is constitutionally legitimate. This is governed by cases such as last term's decision in *United States v. Comstock*,[30] the recent decision in *Sabri v. United States*,[31] and *McCulloch v. Maryland*.[32] Under these cases, as summarized earlier this year in *Comstock*, "in determining whether the Necessary and Proper Clause grants Congress the legislative authority to enact a particular federal statute, we look to see whether the statute constitutes a means that is rationally related to the implementation of a constitutionally enumerated power. . . . [T]he relevant inquiry is simply whether the means chosen are reasonably adapted to the attainment of a legitimate end under the commerce power." That's a very deferential standard, for better or worse. As the Supreme Court stated just a few months ago in *Comstock*,

> We have . . . recognized that the Constitution addresses the choice of means [of carrying out enumerated powers] primarily to the judgment of Congress. If it can be seen that the means adopted are really calculated to attain the end, the degree of their necessity, the extent to which they conduce to the end, the closeness of the relationship between the means adopted and the end to be attained, are matters for congressional determination alone.[33]

Thus, under current Supreme Court doctrine, the constitutional issue raised by the individual mandate is only whether an individual mandate for health insurance is "really calculated" to regulate interstate commerce—not whether the actual conduct prohibited by the mandate is *itself* interstate commerce.

As I've blogged before, I don't happen to support the individual mandate as a policy matter. But if I'm right that this is the standard, it seems to me that the individual mandate was "really calculated" to regulate interstate commerce. As I understand it, the basic idea was to stop people from burdening the health care system with the costs of emergency care that resulted when people opted out of health insurance. Whether that was wise or not, it's a genuine effort to regulate interstate commerce. It therefore would seem to be constitutional under the deferential standard of current Supreme Court doctrine on the Necessary and Proper Clause.

That's the tentative argument, anyway. What's wrong with it? Please note that I am asking for answers of what is wrong with this analysis under current Supreme Court doctrine, not the doctrine that once existed or should have existed. Many thanks.

Necessary and Proper Clause Doctrine and the Individual Mandate

Ilya Somin
October 6, 2010

In a recent post, coblogger Orin Kerr outlines what has become the standard argument that the Obama health care plan's individual mandate is authorized by the Necessary and Proper Clause. The claim is that the goal of the legislation is to regulate commerce in health insurance (which, under current doctrine, is a permissible end under the Commerce Clause) and the individual mandate is a "necessary and proper" means even if it isn't one that comes under one of Congress's enumerated powers by itself.

I think this is probably the government's best argument. But it's not nearly as much of a slam dunk—even under current doctrine—as Orin and others imagine. I explain why in greater detail in my recent amicus brief on behalf of the Washington Legal Foundation and a group of constitutional law scholars.[34] To summarize, there are two major problems with the argument: the mandate flunks the five-part test outlined in the Supreme Court's recent decision in *United States v. Comstock*, and it is not "proper." The Court has (wrongly in my view) adopted a highly permissive definition of what counts as "necessary." But proving "necessity" is not enough for the government to win its case.

I. The Comstock Five-Part Test

Comstock outlines a five-part test that applies to assertions of power under the Necessary and Proper Clause. As I explain in "Taking Stock of Comstock: The Necessary and Proper Clause and the Limits of Federal Power,"[35] and in the brief, the mandate flunks at least three of the five prongs and is questionable under a fourth:

> [The Court] lists five factors that determined the outcome [in *Comstock*]:
> We take these five considerations together. They include: (1) the breadth of the Necessary and Proper Clause, (2) the long history of federal involvement in this arena, (3) the sound reasons for the statute's enactment in light of the Government's custodial interest in safeguarding the public from dangers posed by those in federal custody, (4) the statute's accommodation of state interests, and (5) the statute's narrow scope. *Taken together*, these considerations lead us to conclude that the statute is a "necessary and proper" means of exercising the federal authority that permits Congress to create federal criminal laws, to punish their violation, to imprison violators, to provide appropriately for those imprisoned, and to maintain the security of those who are not imprisoned but who may be affected by the federal imprisonment of others. (emphasis added)
>
> [T]he Obamacare individual health care mandate, is certainly not "narrow in scope" (it forces millions of people to buy a product they may not want), does not "accommodate state interests" to the extent the Court claims the *Comstock* legislation does (that legislation allowed states to opt out essentially at will), and may lack a comparable "long history of federal involvement" (the federal government has often regulated health care, but never by forcing individuals to purchase products) [federal

insurance regulation of any kind was forbidden by Supreme Court precedent until 1944, and health insurance regulation did not become common until well into the post-WWII era; in *Comstock*, the Court pointed to a 155-year history of relevant federal regulation].

In the article and the brief, I also explain why the mandate's status under prong two (the "sound reasons" for its enactment) is at least questionable. Prong one—the breadth of the Necessary and Proper Clause—does not vary from case to case and therefore cannot justify upholding a statute by itself. If it did, then the other four prongs would be superfluous.

I'm no fan of the *Comstock* five-prong test. I think it's vague, confusing, and flawed in various other ways as well. I would much rather the Court junks the test and strike down the mandate on textualist and originalist grounds. But the test is clearly part of current doctrine, and the individual mandate doesn't do very well under it.

II. The Proper Meaning of "Proper"

The second doctrinal problem with the necessary and proper rationale for the mandate is that, under the clause, legislation must not only be "necessary," it also has to be "proper." The Supreme Court has recognized this at least since *McCulloch v. Maryland*. But it has said very little about what "proper" actually means. Under the text and original meaning of the Constitution (which the Court is more likely to resort to in cases where there is little or no relevant precedent), "proper" at the very least means that the federal government cannot claim virtually unlimited power. Otherwise, it would render all or most of Congress's other enumerated powers completely superfluous, making a hash of the text.

And the logic of the government's position does indeed lead to virtually unlimited federal power. Just about any mandate the government might care to impose is "rationally related" to some possible effort to affect commerce. If Congress were to mandate that every American citizen wake up by 7 a.m. and exercise for half an hour before leaving for work, that might be considered "rationally related" to the purpose of increasing worker health and productivity, which in turn would increase interstate commerce.

In addition to these two major points, there are also some other holes in the government's Necessary and Proper Clause case. For example, Orin, like the government, claims that the "end" of the legislation is to regulate interstate commerce. However, under current law, virtually all purchases of health insurance are purely *intrastate* commerce. Buying health insurance across state lines is actually forbidden by law. This doesn't completely defeat the government's argument under current doctrine (though I think it should be a deal breaker under the constitutional text). But it certainly weakens it further by attenuating the connection between the mandate and any actual regulation of interstate commerce. As the Court explained in *United States v. Lopez*, the government is not permitted to enact regulations that rely on rationales that "pile inference upon inference in a manner that would bid fair to convert congressional authority under the Commerce Clause to a general police power of the sort retained by the States."[36] What is true for the Commerce Clause is also true for the Necessary and Proper Clause.

III. The Bottom Line

There is a strong argument against the health care mandate under current Supreme Court Necessary and Proper Clause doctrine. At the very least, there is no precedent that clearly decides the issue in favor of the government. And the recently announced *Comstock* five-part test is potentially a major millstone around the government's neck.

I don't claim that the doctrine definitively resolves the issue *against* the mandate. Much of the relevant precedent is vague. It's hard to predict how the Court will apply the five-part test in the future and even harder to foresee what it might do with the meaning of "proper." But there is no doctrinal slam dunk here for the government. If the Court wants to uphold the mandate under the Necessary and Proper Clause, it can do so. But it will have to make some new law to get there.

More on the Constitutionality of the Individual Mandate

Orin S. Kerr
October 6, 2010

I appreciate Ilya's reply to my post on the constitutionality of the individual mandate. Three points in response:

1. Ilya suggests that the Supreme Court has never answered what makes legislation "proper," and he suggests a first-principles argument for why there may be limits on what is "proper" that would permit the Supreme Court to say that the individual mandate is unconstitutional because the justices do not see it as "proper." He writes,

   [The Supreme Court] has said very little about what "proper" actually means. Under the text and original meaning of the Constitution (which the Court is more likely to resort to in cases where there is little or no relevant precedent), "proper" at the very least means that the federal government cannot claim virtually unlimited power. Otherwise it would render all or most of Congress's other enumerated powers completely superfluous, making a hash of the text. And the logic of the government's position does indeed lead to virtually unlimited federal power.

   But of course the Supreme Court has said a lot about what kind of power is permitted under the Necessary and Proper Clause—that's the point of *McCulloch v. Maryland, Sabri v. United States, Comstock,* and the like. And those cases seem to reject Ilya's approach. Just a few months ago in *Comstock,* the Supreme Court quoted this passage from *Burroughs v. United States*, as the correct statement of the law:

> If it can be seen that the means adopted are really calculated to attain the end, the degree of their necessity, the extent to which they conduce to the end, the closeness of the relationship between the means adopted and the end to be attained, are matters for congressional determination alone.[37]

If the Supreme Court has said that "the extent to which [statutes] conduce to the [constitutional] end, [and] the closeness of the relationship between the means adopted and the end to be attained, are matters for congressional determination alone," what room is there under current Supreme Court precedent to start from scratch with a first-principles conceptualization of the meaning of "proper"?

2. I don't find myself persuaded by Ilya's reading of *Comstock*. It's true that *Comstock* held that the relevant program questioned in that case was constitutional after considering five factors. But I don't think the opinion is best read as holding that the constitutionality of federal programs is henceforth answered by applying a five-factor test. To see why, I think it's helpful to realize how far divorced was the law in *Comstock* from any actual enumerated power in the Constitution. *Comstock* considered a federal civil-commitment statute that authorized the federal government to detain a mentally ill, sexually dangerous federal prisoner beyond the date the prisoner would otherwise be released. The Supreme Court held that this was a "necessary and proper" law within the power of Congress:

> [T]he statute is a "necessary and proper" means of exercising the federal authority that permits Congress to create federal criminal laws, to punish their violation, to imprison violators, to provide appropriately for those imprisoned, and to maintain the security of those who are not imprisoned but who may be affected by the federal imprisonment of others. The Constitution consequently authorizes Congress to enact the statute.[38]

Notably, the *Comstock* opinion didn't even bother to link the means with an actual enumerated power, such as regulating interstate commerce. Rather, the civil-commitment law was "necessary and proper" because under the five factors it was a necessary and proper part of the federal criminal justice system as a whole—and the federal criminal justice system as a whole was itself an unquestioned part of the means of enforcing the actual enumerated powers in the Constitution. It's in that context that the Court looked to the five factors.

If I'm right about that, then no such gymnastics such as the five-factor analysis would seem to be needed when assessing whether the individual mandate is "necessary and proper" to carry out an actual enumerated power in the Constitution. The connection between a law requiring persons to purchase health insurance and regulating interstate commerce is much more direct than the connection between a law requiring the civil commitment of sexual predators who have finished a federal prison term and regulating interstate commerce.

3. Finally, much of Ilya's reply is addressed to whether my tentative view is a "slam dunk." But that's not the question I'm considering. I'm only trying to identify the most faithful application of current doctrine, not classify that faithful application as merely "right" versus a "slam dunk." To use a sports betting metaphor, I'm trying to figure out which team should win rather than debate the spread.

More on the Necessary and Proper Clause and the Health Care Mandate

Ilya Somin
October 6, 2010

Orin makes three points that I will briefly answer. First Orin suggests that current Supreme Court doctrine gives a broad interpretation of the word "proper" in the clause. However, all the cases he cites are in fact interpretations of the word "necessary," not "proper." As I said in my original post, the Court has interpreted "necessary" very broadly. But it has not done the same with "proper." The main textual argument against the mandate focuses on the latter.

Second, Orin suggests that the five-part test outlined in *United States v. Comstock* does not apply going forward and only applies to the unusual circumstances of *Comstock* itself. However, the Court spent a great deal of time and space outlining and applying the five-factor test. Nothing in the opinion suggests that it applies only to *Comstock* itself or some narrow range of similar cases. If that were the Court's intention, surely they would not have omitted this extremely important qualification to their reasoning. After all, a big part of the justices' job is to provide guidance for lower courts on how to decide future cases, and they are well aware of that responsibility.

Moreover, Orin's interpretation of current doctrine is that anything flies so long as it is "rationally related" to the enforcement of an enumerated power. If that were so, the Court need not have applied the five-factor test even in *Comstock* itself. After all, as I explained in one of my earliest posts on *Comstock*,[39] the statute upheld in that case was "rationally related" to the regulation of interstate commerce as that power was defined by the Court in cases such as *Gonzales v. Raich*. Confining prisoners beyond the period of their term prevents them from traveling interstate and perhaps also from committing future crimes that might affect interstate commerce. That's enough for a rational relationship under the extremely deferential definition that the Court applies in "rational basis" cases. The fact that the Court *didn't* rely on this kind of argument suggests that the five-part test has at least some bite. I would also note that Chief Justice John Roberts was in the majority in *Comstock* (the one who cast the decisive fifth vote for the majority opinion as four other justices either dissented or rejected the majority's reasoning). I find it unlikely that he would sign on to an opinion that turns the Necessary and Proper Clause into a virtual blank check for Congress.

Finally, Orin says that he doesn't mean to suggest that current doctrine makes the case a "slam dunk" for the government, only to "figure out which team should win rather than debate the spread." I appreciate the clarification. For reasons I explained in my earlier post, current Necessary and Proper Clause doctrine simply does not squarely cover the main issues raised by the mandate case. To the extent that the doctrine is tangentially relevant, it gives considerable ammunition to the opponents of the mandate; but defenders are not without resources of their own. Therefore, even a heavily precedent-oriented judge won't be able to decide the case going by precedent alone. Ultimately, you can't figure out which team should win this game simply by looking to see who won the last one.

If It's Necessary and Proper, then It's Proper: A Reply to Ilya

Orin S. Kerr
October 6, 2010

I've enjoyed my exchange with Ilya on the health care mandate, although I find myself in the exchange becoming increasingly of the view that this isn't a difficult issue under current Supreme Court case law. Here's one more round to try to sharpen the debate between us.

The crux of the disagreement between Ilya and me boils down to the Necessary and Proper Clause. The Supreme Court has often entered decisions on the scope of the Necessary and Proper Clause, construing the clause quite broadly and upholding statutes on the ground that it did not violate the clause. In my view, those cases pretty much end the matter—for better or worse, those cases are so deferential that they point pretty clearly to the view that the individual mandate satisfies the standard.

In contrast, Ilya sees the Supreme Court cases on the Necessary and Proper Clause as answering when legislation is "necessary" but not reaching what is "proper." Thus, as I understand Ilya's view, the cases on what satisfies the Necessary and Proper Clause are not particularly helpful because they do not expressly reach a conclusion—apparently because challengers forgot to raise the issue—on what is proper. Ilya thus concludes that there is no significant case law on what is "proper," and lower courts must construe the meaning of "proper" using text and original meaning unburdened by precedent.

I disagree with Ilya because the cases themselves—and the briefs for that matter—expressly and consistently articulate the question they decide as being whether the challenged laws are permitted under requirements of the Necessary and Proper Clause as a whole. The doctrine generally treats "necessary" and "proper" together, and litigants either brief them together or in some cases argue the "proper" issue separately. Just to pick one example, in *United States v. Comstock*, the challenger's brief expressly argued that the law was not proper. And here is how the Supreme Court articulated its holding in the first paragraph of the majority opinion:

> Here we ask whether the Federal Government has the authority under Article I of the Constitution to enact this federal civil-commitment program or whether its doing so falls beyond the reach of a government "of enumerated powers." *McCulloch v. Maryland*, 4 Wheat. 316, 405 (1819). We conclude that the Constitution grants Congress the authority to enact §4248 as "necessary and proper for carrying into Execution" the powers "vested by" the "Constitution in the Government of the United States." Art. I, §8, cl. 18.[40]

There are other examples, but I think you get the idea. The significance is that if a law satisfies the Necessary and Proper Clause, then it must be both necessary and proper. And as a result, logically it must be "proper." In my view, this means that the cases sustaining laws challenged under the Necessary and Proper Clause—and the cases articulating the very deferential standard of the Necessary and Proper Clause—do not give any room for an argument that what is "proper" is an open legal question permitting judges to insert a degree of scrutiny not found in the Supreme Court's cases. Just based on current Supreme Court doctrine, we're stuck with the very deferential standard found in the Supreme Court's cases on the Necessary and Proper Clause. So it seems to me, at least.

That Which Is "Necessary" Isn't Necessarily Proper

Ilya Somin
October 6, 2010

In his previous post in our debate over the Necessary and Proper Clause, Orin argues that Supreme Court precedent has resolved the issue of what counts as "proper" as well as what is "necessary." That, however, simply is not so. None of the cases Orin cites say anything about the meaning of "proper." They all focus on whether the measure in question was "necessary."

In the rare instances where the Court has given separate consideration to the meaning of "proper," the Court has made clear that it is a separate and distinct issue from what is necessary and that it is not subject to broad judicial deference. For example in *Printz v. United States*, the Court concluded that a federal law requiring state officials to perform background checks on gun purchasers was "improper" because it invaded state sovereignty even though it was clearly "necessary" for implementing the government's regulatory purposes (in the broad sense of "useful" or "convenient" adopted by the Court). As Justice Antonin Scalia's majority opinion in that case put it:

> What destroys the dissent's Necessary and Proper Clause argument . . . is . . . the Necessary and Proper Clause itself. When a "La[w] . . . for carrying into Execution" the Commerce Clause violates the principle of state sovereignty reflected in the various constitutional provisions we mentioned earlier. . . . "proper for carrying into Execution

the Commerce Clause," and is thus, in the words of The Federalist, "merely [an] ac[t] of usurpation" which "deserve[s] to be treated as such." (The Federalist No. 33)[41]

The Court did not apply broad deference to the government's position and did not conflate necessity with propriety. Notice also that Scalia doesn't deny that the background check provision is "necessary" for implementing the government's Commerce Clause–based purposes. Unfortunately, neither *Printz* nor any other case gives us anything approaching a complete definition of what counts as "proper" under the clause, so I don't claim that the current precedent proves that the individual mandate is "improper." But it is clear that propriety and necessity are two separate issues and that the Court is not especially deferential to the government when it comes to the former.

Orin also contends that the issue of what is "proper" was raised by the respondents in *Comstock*. Unfortunately Orin here conflates two separate questions: whether the statute serves a constitutionally permissible end and whether it uses "proper" means to do so. The respondents did not argue that the relevant statute was an "improper" means to a constitutionally permissible end. Rather the relevant section of their brief claims that the statute did not promote a purpose that is within Congress's enumerated powers. The title of the section makes this clear: "Police and Parens Patriae Powers Are Not Proper 'Ends' for Federal Government Regulation."[42]

The main point at issue in *Comstock* was whether a statute allowing the federal government to detain "sexually dangerous" federal prisoners after they had finished their sentences advanced an end that was connected to some enumerated power. That is a separate question from the issue of whether a statute that *does* promote a permissible end under current doctrine uses "proper" means to do so. The respondents' brief unnecessarily confused matters by claiming that a statute that doesn't pursue a permissible end is not "proper." In reality, whether it is "proper" is irrelevant because such a statute wouldn't pass muster anyway because it does not "carry into execution" one of the federal government's other enumerated powers, as the text of the clause requires. I discuss this distinction at greater length in my article on *Comstock*,[43] where I criticize the Court's expansive interpretation of legitimate ends but also explain how it says nothing about the issue of the propriety of means.

In any event, regardless of what the respondents said, the Court nowhere defines "proper" in *Comstock*. Neither does it overrule *Printz* and other previous cases holding that propriety and necessity are distinct issues.[44]

Notes

1. Jack M. Balkin, "The Constitutionality of the Individual Mandate for Health Insurance," *New England Journal of Medicine*, January 13, 2010.
2. 1 Annals of Cong. 759–60 (1789).
3. Sonzinsky v. United States, 300 U.S. 506 (1937).
4. Randy E. Barnett, "The Ninth Amendment: It Means What It Says," *Texas Law Review* 85 (2006): 1.

5. Kurt T. Lash, "The Lost Original Meaning of the Ninth Amendment," *Texas Law Review* 83 (2004): 331.

6. Jack M. Balkin, "Original Meaning & Constitutional Redemption," *Constitutional Commentary* 24 (2007): 427.

7. Ilya Somin, "Crisis, the Health Care Bill, and the Growth of Government," Volokh Conspiracy (blog), March 21, 2010, http://www.volokh.com/2010/03/21/crisis-the-health-care-bill-and-the-growth-of-government/.

8. INS v. Chadha, 462 U.S. 919 (1983) (ruling that a one-house legislative veto violates the doctrine of separation of powers).

9. Boumediene v. Bush, 553 U.S. 723 (2008) (extending the right of habeas corpus to enemy combatants detained in Guantanamo Bay).

10. Jonathan H. Adler, "The Constitutionality of an Individual Mandate—A Reply to Senator Max Baucus," *supra*.

11. An act for the relief of sick and disabled seamen, 1 Stat. 605 (1798).

12. Romer v. Evans, 517 U.S. 620, 633 (1996).

13. United States v. Miller, 307 U.S. 174, 179 (1939).

14. Jonathan Turley, "Is Health-Care Mandate Unconstitutional?," *USA Today*, March 31, 2010, http://usatoday30.usatoday.com/news/opinion/forum/2010-03-31-column31_ST_N.htm?csp=34.

15. Seminole Tribe of Fla. v. Florida, 517 U.S. 44 (1996); Alden v. Maine, 527 U.S. 706 (1999); City of Boerne v. Flores, 521 U.S. 507 (1997); United States v. Morrison, 529 U.S. 598 (2000); Bd. of Trustees of Univ. of Ala. v. Garrett, 531 U.S. 356 (2001); and Nev. Dep't of Human Res. v. Hibbs, 538 U.S. 721 (2003).

16. College Savings Bank v. Fla. Prepaid Postsecondary Educ. Expense Bd., 527 U.S. 666 (1999).

17. Randy E. Barnett, *Restoring the Lost Constitution: The Presumption of Liberty* (Princeton, NJ: Princeton University Press, 2004).

18. Kurt T. Lash, *The Lost History of the Ninth Amendment* (New York: Oxford University Press, 2009).

19. 514 U.S. 549, 575 (1995).

20. Randy Barnett, Nathaniel Stewart, and Todd F. Gaziano, "Legal Memorandum 49: Why the Personal Mandate to Buy Health Insurance Is Unprecedented and Unconstitutional," Heritage Foundation, last modified December 9, 2009, http://www.heritage.org/research/reports/2009/12/why-the-personal-mandate-to-buy-health-insurance-is-unprecedented-and-unconstitutional.

21. Barnett, *Restoring the Lost Constitution*.

22. Patient Protection & Affordable Care Act (PPACA), § 1501 (2)(A); 42 U.S.C. § 18091(2)(a).

23. Orin Kerr, comment, "Penalties on the Uninsured Are Thoroughly Precedented," *Prawfs Blawg* (blog), April 14, 2010, http://prawfsblawg.blogs.com/prawfsblawg/2010/04/are-tax-penalties-on-the-uninsured-unprecedented-in-a-word-no.html.

24. *Id.*

25. See, e.g., United States v. Guzman, 591 F. 3d 83 (2d Cir. 2010); United States v. George, 579 F. 3d 962, 966–67 (9th Cir. 2009); United States v. Whaley, 577 F. 3d 254, 258 (5th Cir. 2009); United States v. Gould, 568 F. 3d 459, 470–72 (4th Cir. 2009); United States v. Ambert, 561 F. 3d 1202, 1210–11 (11th Cir. 2009); United States v. Hinckley, 550 F. 3d 926, 940 (10th Cir. 2008); United States v. May, 535 F. 3d 912, 921–22 (8th Cir. 2008).

26. Stafford v. Wallace, 258 U.S. 495, 521 (1922).

27. Gerard Magliocca, "The Private Action Requirement," Concurring Opinions, last modified August 20, 2010, http://www.concurringopinions.com/archives/2010/08/the-private-action-requirement.html.

28. James Taranto, "'A Commandeering of the People': One of America's Leading Libertarian Legal Scholars Handicaps Whether the Supreme Court Will Find ObamaCare's Insurance Mandate Constitutional," *Wall Street Journal*, July 23, 2010, http://online.wsj.com/article/NA_WSJ_PUB:SB10001424052748703467304575383702986874016.html.

29. Id.

30. United States v. Comstock, 130 S. Ct. 1949 (2010).

31. Sabri v. United States, 541 U.S. 600 (2004).

32. McCulloch v. Maryland, 17 U.S. (4 Wheat.) 316 (1819).

33. *Comstock*, 130 S. Ct. at 1956 (quoting Burroughs v. United States, 290 U.S. 534, 547–48 [1934])

34. Brief for the Washington Legal Foundation, *Sebelius*, 728 F. Supp. 2d 768, *supra*.

35. Ilya Somin, "Taking Stock of Comstock: The Necessary and Proper Clause and the Limits of Federal Power," *2009–2010 Cato Supreme Court Review* (2010), 239.

36. *Lopez*, 514 U.S. at 567.

37. Burroughs v. United States, 290 U.S. 534, 547–48 (1934).

38. *Comstock*, 130 S. Ct. 1949 (2010).

39. Ilya Somin, "The *Comstock* Case, *Gonzales v. Raich*, and the Limits of Federal Power," *Volokh Conspiracy* (blog), January 8, 2009, http://www.volokh.com/archives/archive_2009_01_04–2009_01_10.shtml#1231464543.

40. 130 S. Ct. at 1949.

41. Printz v. United States, 521 U.S. 898, 923–24 (1997).

42. Brief for Respondents at 37, United States v. Comstock, 130 S. Ct. 1949 (2010) (08-1224).

43. Somin, "Taking Stock of Comstock."

44. UPDATE: I should acknowledge that the respondents' brief in Comstock does at one point suggest that the means used may be "improper" because they infringe on state prerogatives (35–36). I should have noted this in the main post, and I apologize for the oversight. However, the Court's opinion seems to ignore this argument. Alternatively, maybe the majority thought they had addressed this issue when they concluded that the statute "accommodated" state interests because it essentially allows states to opt out at will by choosing to take custody of the relevant prisoners themselves and then releasing them if they prefer. There is, of course, no such accommodation in the individual mandate.

Be that as it may, what matters in *Comstock* (or any case) is not what the litigants say but what the Court decides. And *Comstock* nowhere defines "proper." Neither does it overrule previous precedents holding that "necessary" and "proper" are separate issues.

3

The First Decisions

When a lawsuit challenges the constitutionality of a statute, the first step for the government is usually to file a "motion to dismiss," which is an argument that a case should be thrown out because the plaintiffs' arguments are simply not good enough to hold the court's attention. A successful motion to dismiss can kill a case before it even gets off the ground. Many legal academics predicted that the challenge to Obamacare would not even survive a motion to dismiss, which is an almost sneering way of indicating how bad they thought the arguments against the law were.

In early August 2010, United States District Judge Henry E. Hudson of the Eastern District of Virginia denied the government's motion to dismiss (previously mentioned by Randy in his post from August 26). But surviving a motion to dismiss does not mean that you have won a case—far from it. Instead, it merely means that you have enough of an argument to not get kicked out of court. A low standard indeed but one that many pundits believed the Affordable Care Act (ACA) challenge could not reach. The ACA's challengers felt that Judge Hudson's decision proved the arguments were not frivolous, while many defenders of the law thought the decision demonstrated the partisanship of Hudson, who was appointed by President George W. Bush.

On October 7, 2010, Judge George C. Steeh III of the United States District Court for the Eastern District of Michigan dismissed the Thomas More Law Center's challenge to the mandate. Yet on October 14, 2010, Judge Roger Vinson of the United States District Court for the Northern District of Florida also denied the government's motion to dismiss in *Florida v. U.S. Department of Health and Human Services*, the case that would eventually reach the Supreme Court. Six weeks later, another motion to dismiss would be granted in *Liberty University v. Geithner*.

At the *Volokh Conspiracy*, the conversation continued . . .

***

Michigan District Court Upholds Individual Mandate against Challenge by the Thomas More Law Center

Ilya Somin
October 7, 2010

The decision[1] upholds the mandate under the Commerce Clause alone. It does not address the government's arguments claiming that the mandate is authorized by the Taxing and Spending Clause and the Necessary and Proper Clause, except to say that Congress may use a monetary penalty to enforce a legitimate Commerce Clause regulation (which I think is correct).

The main point of the court's Commerce Clause argument is that not having health insurance counts as an "activity" rather than inactivity:

> Far from "inactivity," by choosing to forgo insurance plaintiffs are making an economic decision to try to pay for health care services later, out of pocket, rather than now through the purchase of insurance, . . . collectively shifting billions of dollars, $43 billion in 2008, onto other market participants.[2]

Because not being insured therefore turns out to be an activity rather than inactivity, it is covered by Supreme Court Commerce Clause cases such as *Gonzales v. Raich.*

The problem with this reasoning is that those who choose not to buy health insurance aren't necessarily therefore going to buy the same services in other ways later. Some will, but some won't. It depends on whether they get sick; how severe and how treatable their illnesses are; whether if they do get sick, they can get assistance from charity; and many other factors. In addition, some people might be able to maintain their health simply by buying services that aren't usually covered by insurance anyway, such as numerous low-cost medicines available in drug stores and the like. In such cases, they aren't really participating in the same market as insurance purchasers.

Of course, many people will buy the same service later, and for some the probability of doing so is quite high. But the individual mandate makes no distinctions on any such basis. It sweeps in nearly everyone. If the mere possibility that you might purchase a similar service somewhere else is enough to count as "activity" and therefore regulable under the Commerce Clause, then almost any regulatory mandate would be permissible. For example, a requirement that each citizen purchase a gym club membership and exercise for one hour per day could be defended on the basis that, otherwise, people will be less healthy, which will make it more likely they will spend more money on medical care, health insurance, and perhaps other forms of exercise.

The opinion also claims that the Commerce Clause covers "economic decisions" as well as "economic activity." "Economic decisions," by this reasoning, include decisions not to engage in economic activity. That, however, would allow the Commerce Clause to cover virtually any decision of any kind. Pretty much any decision to do anything is necessarily a decision not to use the same time and effort to engage in "economic activity." If I choose to spend an hour sleeping, I necessarily choose not to spend that time working or buying products of some kind.

Another noteworthy aspect of the Michigan decision is that it ruled that the Thomas More plaintiffs had standing and that the case was ripe. In this respect, it was similar to the earlier Virginia ruling, which also came down against the government on these points. It looks like standing and ripeness issues will be less of a problem for the antimandate plaintiffs than I first thought.

Finally, there is no question that the ruling is a setback for the antimandate cause. As a predictive matter, I have always thought that the government is ultimately more likely to prevail in the mandate litigation than lose it. This decision reinforces that impression.

At the same time, the ultimate outcome here is far from certain. The Michigan court's decision doesn't bind the Virginia and Florida district courts currently considering the two biggest challenges to the mandate (those brought by 21 states and the National Federation of Independent Business). Moreover, Judge Steeh's conclusion that this case is fairly easily covered by existing Commerce Clause precedent is at odds with the Virginia judge's earlier ruling concluding that no previous precedent covers this case. It therefore seems to me unlikely that the latter will follow the Michigan reasoning in his own eventual decision (though he could of course uphold the mandate on other grounds). And of course both this ruling and those that will be eventually issued by the other district courts are subject to review by the U.S. courts of appeals, and ultimately the Supreme Court.

Michigan District Judge Decides "Issue of First Impression" by Creating an "Economic Decisions" Doctrine

Randy E. Barnett
October 7, 2010

As Ilya notes previously, District Court Judge Steeh today dismissed a claim that the Patient Protection and Affordable Care Act exceeds Congress authority under the Commerce Clause. I agree with his assessment of the opinion, with one exception. I do not believe Judge Steeh relied upon existing Supreme Court doctrine because of his claim that this was a case "of first impression" and therefore not covered by that doctrine. This presents a new debate: Has the Supreme Court covered the field with its current Commerce and Necessary and Proper Clause analysis, in which case lower courts are bound to hold the act as unconstitutional because it extends beyond this doctrine? Or does the unprecedented nature of the individual mandate render this a case "of first impression" requiring new doctrine that lower courts are free to invent?

In the course of dismissing the plaintiff's Commerce Clause challenge, Judge Steeh has vindicated an important element of all such pending challenges: this claim of power by the government is without any precedent in experience or in law. In Judge Steeh's words,

The Court has never needed to address the activity/inactivity distinction advanced by plaintiffs because **in every Commerce Clause case presented thus far, there has been some sort of activity**. In this regard, the Health Care Reform Act arguably presents **an issue of first impression**.[3]

Never before in American history has the U.S. government imposed an economic mandate commanding that persons engage in economic activity. Given that there is no current Supreme Court doctrine recognizing such power in Congress, the appropriate stance of a district court judge is to follow Supreme Court precedent and deny this claim of power until the Supreme Court decides in due course to expand its doctrine.

Instead, Judge Steeh accepted the government's expansion of congressional power beyond regulating economic activity to regulating economic "decisions":

> While plaintiffs describe the Commerce Clause power as reaching **economic activity**, the government's characterization of the Commerce Clause reaching **economic decisions** is more accurate.[4]

But this was not the "plaintiff's description." It was how **the Supreme Court itself** described its own doctrine in each and every Commerce Clause case that allowed Congress to reach wholly intrastate activity because it was necessary and proper to the regulation of interstate commerce.

By inventing a **new "economic decisions" doctrine**, Judge Steeh has gone beyond the Commerce Clause and Necessary and Proper Clause doctrines established by the Supreme Court. Only the Supreme Court is authorized to expand its own interpretation of the scope of congressional power.

Of course, judges in other challenges will have their opportunity to opine on whether Congress has the power to regulate any "economic decision" that may substantially affect interstate commerce, the "economic decision" not to buy a car, the "economic decision" not to buy or sell your home, or even the "economic decision" not to have a physical exam. For make no mistake, if the Supreme Court ever accepts the government's "economic decision" theory, then there is nothing it cannot mandate in the future in the name of regulating "commerce . . . among the several states." Congress will then have the general police power that both the Constitution and the Supreme Court has always denied it.

The Individual Mandate and Applying versus Inventing Doctrine

Orin S. Kerr
October 8, 2010

I have a very different view of Judge Steeh's opinion than my coblogger Randy. As I read it, it offers an application of existing Supreme Court doctrine. Randy states that Judge Steeh claimed that this was a case of first impression and therefore not covered by Supreme Court doctrine. But I don't think that's what Judge Steeh said. First, Steeh wrote,

> The Court has never needed to address the activity/inactivity distinction advanced by plaintiffs because in every Commerce Clause case presented thus far, there has been some sort of activity. In this regard, the Health Care Reform Act arguably presents an issue of first impression.[5]

So according to Judge Steeh, the activity-inactivity distinction "arguably" is an issue of first impression. But a few pages later, Judge Steeh concludes that it's actually not a new issue at all, citing and quoting Supreme Court precedent:

> The Supreme Court has consistently rejected claims that individuals who choose not to engage in commerce thereby place themselves beyond the reach of the Commerce Clause. See, e.g., *Raich*, 545 U.S. at 30 (rejecting the argument that plaintiffs' home-grown marijuana was "entirely separated from the market"); *Wickard*, 317 U.S. at 127, 128 (home-grown wheat "competes with wheat in commerce" and "may forestall resort to the market"); *Heart of Atlanta Motel v. United States*, 379 U.S. 241 (1964) (Commerce Clause allows Congress to regulate decisions not to engage in transactions with persons with whom plaintiff did not wish to deal).[6]

Thus, on its own terms, Judge Steeh's opinion seems to me to be relying on existing Supreme Court doctrine. Now, of course you could argue that it's relying *incorrectly* on that precedent. But it seems to me that the opinion on its terms is applying Supreme Court precedent, not inventing a new doctrine.

I should add that, in my view, what district courts do with the individual mandate is essentially irrelevant for all but political purposes. The issue in this case is legal, not factual, and an appeal is guaranteed. This means all the district court decisions are just for show, and the real issue is whether any circuit court panels will get a majority to vote against the mandate, survive an en banc challenge, and therefore create a split that prompts Supreme Court review. I personally doubt they will, and I would guess that the Supreme Court won't review the issue without a split. If the Supreme Court does take the case it seems like a likely 8–1 to me, with Justice Clarence Thomas dissenting. But I'm not sure it's going to get there, so the key for now is to watch for a split that survives en banc review in the circuit courts.

On the political side, incidentally, I think it's quite different. In the political realm, district court decisions on the mandate are hugely important. A district court decision striking down the mandate would give added fuel to GOP efforts to repeal the mandate after the midterm election if Republicans take over the House and (maybe) Senate. This is all the more true if the opinion includes lots of majestic prose about overreaching government—"It's so un-American it's been struck down as unconstitutional!," the reasoning would run, with long excerpts of stirring rhetoric featured prominently on Fox News. But that's a political issue, not a legal one.

Some Additional Thoughts on the Michigan Decision
Upholding the Individual Mandate

Randy E. Barnett
October 8, 2010

Judge Steeh's decision yesterday dismissing the Commerce and Necessary and Proper Clause challenge to the individual mandate was certainly not welcome news to those of us who believe the mandate to be unconstitutional. But his remarkably thin opinion brings to the fore the revolutionary implications of upholding the individual mandate without addressing them.

First, that some, perhaps all, federal district judges considering these challenges would uphold the statute was foreseeable. When these challenges were brought, no one believed that all constitutional challenges would be upheld by every district court judge who would consider them. Few believed that any district court judge would have the fortitude to strike down the mandate, regardless of how the Supreme Court might ultimately rule. Heck, many doubt that the Supreme Court has the fortitude to strike down so major a piece of legislation.

Second, as I mentioned yesterday, calling this an "issue of first impression," as Judge Steeh did, highlights the unprecedented nature of this claim of power. It expressly undercuts any claim that the mandate is constitutional under existing Supreme Court Commerce and Necessary and Proper Clause doctrine. Indeed it was necessary for the judge to claim that there was no existing Supreme Court doctrine applicable to the mandate to justify his adopting the government's novel "economic decisions" theory.

Third, by simply adopting the government's "economic decisions" theory, and rejecting "economic activity" as an existing limiting doctrine, Judge Steeh's opinion clearly exposes the expansionary nature of this claim of power. At the same time, he failed to seriously address any objections to this theory. Judge Steeh provided the other district judges considering the challenges of the attorneys general in Virginia and Florida with no reasons to uphold the mandate beyond those already provided to them by the government in its briefs. So other than the fact that another federal judge found the government's argument persuasive, Judge Steeh's decision provided no additional reasons for upholding the mandate that they did not already know.

Fourth, and most important, **Judge Steeh offers no limiting principle to the "economic decisions" theory.** His acceptance of the government's argument that the health insurance market is "unique" is window dressing. Allowing Congress to regulate all "economic decisions" in the country because Congress has a rational basis for thinking such mandates are essential to its regulation of interstate commerce cannot and will not be limited to the sort of public goods argument offered in support of this mandate. Given that his decision, on his own account, is expanding federal power beyond existing Supreme Court doctrine, was it not incumbent upon him to deal with the slippery slope issues raised by his newly minted "economic decisions" doctrine?

Yet like the government, Judge Steeh is silent on the radical implications of accepting this new doctrine. Imagine all the slippery slope questions in oral argument when the "economic decisions" doctrine is more seriously considered than it was by Judge Steeh. Conversely, there are zero slippery slope objections to striking down all economic mandates that reach inactivity. Why? Because the individual insurance requirement is the only such economic mandate ever enacted. So it is the only law that would be unconstitutional if the Supreme Court concludes that Congress has no such power to impose economic mandates under the Commerce and Necessary and Proper Clauses.

For all these reasons, Judge Steeh's opinion yesterday serves to highlight for other judges, and justices, the truly revolutionary implication of upholding this mandate without even attempting to deal with these implications. In this way, it actually contributes to the constitutional case against the individual mandate.

UPDATE: I do not disagree with the "politics" point made by Orin. When Judge Hudson denied the government's motion to dismiss the Virginia attorney general's challenge, it greatly bolstered the credibility of the challenges, as well as the political opposition to the mandate. It ended all talk about the challenges being "frivolous." Likewise, the government must feel greatly relieved by this victory, though I believe law professors are now sufficiently chastened and aware of the substance of this issue that they won't now revert to their previous view that the constitutional challenges are frivolous. Without a doubt, it would be much better for the challengers that either Judge Hudson or Judge Vinson find the mandate to be unconstitutional. But, while winning is always better than losing, it was never realistic for opponents of the act to count on success at the district court level.

I also agree with Orin that a circuit split makes a Supreme Court decision far more likely. Indeed, because one circuit would have had to strike down the act, a circuit split *guarantees* a Supreme Court decision doesn't it? However, given the high profile of this act among the American people, I think it would be hard for the Court to duck the issue even if the courts of appeals all uphold the act. If the act continues to be unpopular, would that not be widely perceived by the public as an abrogation of the Court's responsibility? Indeed, would the justices not reasonably fear that it would undermine the popular legitimacy of the "Supreme" Court to refuse to decide so highly publicized a constitutional controversy about which so much depends?

Finally, I disagree with Orin's prediction of how the Supreme Court would split on the merits. I now think the most favorable vote for upholding the act would be 6–3 (the same margin as *Raich*), and 5–4 is much more likely. And if there are four likely votes to strike down the act, then this makes a cert grant more likely even if the four cannot be confident of a fifth vote. Conversely should the Court strike down the mandate, a margin greater than a 5–4 margin (the margin of *Lopez* and *Morrison*) would be unlikely.

The End of All Lines around Congressional Powers?

Randy E. Barnett
October 17, 2010

Orin claims that "[t]he challenge to the constitutionality of the individual mandate tries to engage in just the kind of line-drawing that the justices have concluded they can't do. It tries to carve out a zone of economic regulation that Congress is forbidden to enact. But exactly what is the zone? Where exactly is the line?"[7] Yet it is easy to distinguish regulating and prohibiting voluntary economic activity on the one hand from requiring such activity on the other. The justices never had to make this distinction before because Congress never before attempted to impose an economic mandate on the citizenry at large. And only one law will be in jeopardy if the Supreme Court declines to extend its current doctrine from activity to inactivity.

As to *why* the line should be drawn here, there are many powerful reasons, some of which I identify in my paper. But the ability to draw a principled line is easy: it is the difference between acts and omissions. Of course, Orin (like Justice Breyer) may think that the *rationale* for regulating economic activity may extend to inactivity, and he is entirely free to argue why the Supreme Court *ought* to recognize such a power in Congress. Indeed that issue will be debated seriously from now until the end of this litigation. But that is not a "line-drawing problem." That is a substantive legal debate requiring a substantive analysis.

I did not have Orin in mind when I wrote the following in my paper *Commandeering the People: Why the Individual Health Insurance Mandate is Unconstitutional*,[8] but I think it may well describe how he is approaching this issue:

> Until 1995, law professors believed that, beginning in 1937 with cases such as *NLRB v. Jones & Laughlin Steel*, *United States v. Darby*, and *Wickard v. Filburn*, the Supreme Court had so expanded the scope of the commerce power of Congress that Congress could do anything it wanted provided it was not violating some other constitutional constraint, like say the First Amendment.
>
> So law professors were shocked when the Supreme Court in 1995 held in *United States v. Lopez* that the Gun Free School Zone Act unconstitutionally exceeded the commerce power of Congress. They interpreted this case as an aberration. By 1995, Congress had become so complacent about the scope of its powers that it did not even bother to make findings about why the act was within its commerce power. Most law professors were confident that, in the future, the Court would uphold any law if Congress made adequate findings that the activity it sought to regulate had a substantial effect on interstate commerce.
>
> So law professors were, once again, surprised when the Supreme Court in 2000 held in *United States v. Morrison* that the Violence Against Women Act was unconstitutional—notwithstanding extensive hearings and findings about the substantial effects of violence against women on interstate commerce. In the wake of *Morrison*, law professors started to believe that the Court just might be serious about drawing a line between what is national and what is local, and lower courts started to be more receptive to Commerce Clause challenges.

In one such case I helped bring on behalf of Angel Raich and Diane Monson, the Ninth Circuit held that the Controlled Substances Act was unconstitutional as applied to marijuana grown at home for medical use as authorized by state law. When the Supreme Court in *Gonzales v. Raich* turned away this challenge, however, law professors breathed a sigh of relief that they had been right all along. **They reverted to their pre-*Lopez* understanding that Congress can do pretty much whatever it wants under its commerce power.**

Indeed, the new conventional wisdom is that, so long as Congress establishes a sweeping and ambitious regulatory scheme, it can reach any activity—whether economic or not—that it deems to be essential to that scheme. In other words, the more grandiose the claim of power by Congress, the stronger is its claim of constitutionality.

Hence some law professors have breezily asserted that Congress may, for the first time in American history, use its commerce power to mandate that all individuals in the United States engage in economic activity. After all, this mandate is essential to Congress's grandiose new scheme regulating private insurance companies. So under *Raich*, it must be constitutional.

The rest of my paper explains why I believe this conventional wisdom is an inaccurate understanding of existing doctrine governing "necessity" in the context of the commerce power and also why the Court should not expand beyond existing doctrine.

Given that Orin quotes from Justice Kennedy's concurring opinion in *Lopez*, we ought also to note Justice Kennedy's concurring opinion in *Comstock* where he insisted that,

The operative constitutional provision in this case is the Necessary and Proper Clause. This Court has not held that the *Lee Optical* test, asking if "it might be thought that the particular legislative measure was a rational way to correct" an evil, is the proper test in this context. Rather, under the Necessary and Proper Clause, application of a "rational basis" test should be at least as exacting as it has been in the Commerce Clause cases, if not more so . . .

I had thought it a basic principle that the powers reserved to the States consist of the whole, undefined residuum of power remaining after taking account of powers granted to the National Government. The Constitution delegates limited powers to the National Government and then reserves the remainder for the States (or the people), not the other way around, as the Court's analysis suggests. And the powers reserved to the States are so broad that they remain undefined. Residual power, sometimes referred to (perhaps imperfectly) as the police power, belongs to the States and the States alone.

It is correct in one sense to say that if the National Government has the power to act under the Necessary and Proper Clause then that power is not one reserved to the States. But the precepts of federalism embodied in the Constitution inform which powers are properly exercised by the National Government in the first place. See *Lopez*, 514 U.S., at 580–81 (Kennedy, J., concurring); see also *McCulloch*, supra, at 421 (powers "consist[ent] with the letter and spirit of the constitution, are constitutional"). It is of fundamental importance to consider whether essential attributes of state sovereignty are compromised by the assertion of federal power under the Necessary and Proper Clause; if so, that is a factor suggesting that the power is not one properly within the reach of federal power.

> The opinion of the Court should not be interpreted to hold that the only, or even the principal, constraints on the exercise of congressional power are the Constitution's express prohibitions. The Court's discussion of the Tenth Amendment invites the inference that restrictions flowing from the federal system are of no import when defining the limits of the National Government's power, as it proceeds by first asking whether the power is within the National Government's reach, and if so it discards federalism concerns entirely.
>
> These remarks explain why the Court ignores important limitations stemming from federalism principles. Those principles are essential to an understanding of the function and province of the States in our constitutional structure.[9]

True, Justice Kennedy expresses his concern here with compromising state sovereignty rather than categorical distinctions like the difference between "economic" and "noneconomic" activity, or activity and inactivity. (Recall that Justice Kennedy did join the majority opinion in *Lopez* that drew the line between "economic" and "noneconomic" activity while also concurring.) But the issue of Congress's power to impose economic mandates was not before him in *Comstock*. And this passage does not sound to me like a justice willing to overthrow the traditional effort to draw a line between the enumerated power of Congress and powers "reserved to the states respectively or to the people."

Of course, if Orin is right that a majority of the justices have indeed given up on all efforts to draw a "line" around Congress's power to reach any activity—or inactivity—it deems convenient to its regulation of interstate commerce, then the challenge to the mandate will surely fail—as will the scheme of limited and enumerated powers. That would be breaking new ground indeed. I wonder if the time is ripe for that sort of judicial declaration.

Adding an "Act" to Overcome the Proposed Act/ Omission Limitation on Federal Power

Orin S. Kerr
October 18, 2010

If the constitutional line is between acts and omissions, as Randy suggests, then I gather Randy would agree that Congress could circumvent this restriction by prohibiting an affirmative act together with failure to buy health insurance. That's what Congress did when it wanted to require sex offenders to register, for example. Under that recent law, a person who is supposed to register as a sex offender is guilty of a federal crime if he crosses a state line and has failed to register. The "act" is the crossing of state lines, even though the real goal is to require sex offenders to register. The circuit courts have so far unanimously upheld this prohibition as being within Congress's power.

Given that, I'd be interested in Randy's view of what "acts" Congress could legitimately use to overcome the proposed act/omission distinction in the case of the individual mandate. Here are four possibilities:

a. Congress prohibits the affirmative act of crossing state lines after having failed to purchase health insurance.
b. Congress prohibits the affirmative act of using a means of interstate commerce, such as the Internet or the telephone system, after having failed to purchase health insurance.
c. Congress prohibits the affirmative act of using the postal service after having failed to purchase health insurance.
d. Congress prohibits the affirmative act of purchasing any item in interstate commerce after having failed to purchase health insurance.

If the Supreme Court were to adopt the proposed act/omission distinction, which of these laws would be constitutional because they are punishing "acts" rather than "omissions"? All of them? None of them?

An Act/Omission Limitation on Federal Power over States?

Jonathan H. Adler
October 18, 2010

Orin is concerned about the ability of the Supreme Court to draw a line between the federal government's authority to regulate or prohibit conduct on the one hand and its ability to mandate conduct on the other. Drawing a line of this sort may be difficult, but it is hardly unprecedented.

Consider some of the Court's decisions regarding state sovereignty, which adopt a limitation on federal power that is similar to (though not completely analogous to) the act/omission limitation Orin and Randy have been discussing. The federal government may prohibit states from engaging in certain conduct, regulate particular conduct, and even place conditions on certain types of conduct, but the federal government may not mandate that states regulate private conduct. This sort of "commandeering" is prohibited under *New York v. United States*[10] and *Printz v. United States*.[11] The federal government may push against this line, such as by attaching conditions to the receipt of federal funds or regulating states in other ways so as to induce their cooperation, but the underlying limitation remains.

The rule against commandeering can be viewed as a limitation very similar to that which Randy has been defending, as the federal government can regulate state conduct (and prohibit it) but not mandate that states engage in conduct in the first instance. So, for instance, the federal government can say to states that if they hire employees, they must follow all sorts of rules (e.g. wage, hour, and nondiscrimination rules), but the federal government cannot mandate that states hire individuals in the first place. The federal government may require state governments to undertake steps to mitigate environmental impacts when building roads or other infrastructure, but it can neither require a state to construct infrastructure nor take affirmative conservation measures independently of some other activity subject to federal regulatory authority. The federal government may also condition the receipt of federal monies on compliance with all sorts of conditions on how the money will be spent and even require recipient states to adopt various programs, but it could not simply mandate that states create the programs in isolation. This may not perfectly track the act/omission distinction Randy and Orin have been debating, but I think it's close enough to demonstrate that the Court has engaged in the sort of line-drawing Randy is seeking to encourage here.

Again, my point in raising this is not to say that line-drawing of this sort is easy. I concede that it is not. Even lines that appear clear from a distance can be difficult to apply in particular cases. My point here is simply that the line-drawing the Court would be asked to undertake in the context of the individual mandate does not strike me as any more difficult than the line-drawing the Court has readily undertaken elsewhere, including in the context of the proper balance between federal and state power.

More on the Proposed Act/Omission Distinction and What It Means to "Mandate" an Act

Orin S. Kerr
October 18, 2010

I appreciate Jonathan Adler's response on the nature of Randy Barnett's proposed act/omission distinction on the scope of federal power. Given that this is a proposed distinction, not one presently recognized in the case law, my real interest at this stage is just getting a sense of how such a distinction is supposed to work—not, as Jonathan has focused on, the degree to which the general category of distinction would be "precedented" or "unprecedented."

In particular, I'm just trying to understand if the proposed test is that Congress can regulate it so long as there is *some affirmative act* included in the prohibition or rather if the proposed test is some kind of more complicated test that either includes some nexus requirement between the act or omission or else has some other requirement beyond an act. In the comment thread, Jonathan says that he assumes there is some sort of nexus requirement. But I don't know if that is what Randy has in mind.

While we're on the topic, I'd also be interested to know more on the meaning of "mandate" in the proposed distinction between regulating acts and regulating omissions by "mandating" conduct. What exactly does it mean to "mandate" action? For example, does the government "mandate" an act if a person has the choice of paying a fine instead of acting? What if the fine is very low, like, say, $400? $100? $1? Does it depend on the mechanism for collecting the fine? It seems to me that the difficulty is that the law often encourages people to take a certain act through economic incentives. For example, Congress might pass a tax break for people who do something that Congress wants people to do. Where exactly is the line between a (presumably) permitted *incentive* to act and an illegitimate *mandating* of conduct?

District Court Upholds Individual Mandate against
Challenge Filed by Liberty University

Ilya Somin
December 1, 2010

Yesterday, Federal District Judge Norman Moon of the Western District of Virginia upheld the Obamacare individual mandate against a constitutional challenge filed by Liberty University and several private plaintiffs.[12] For the most part, Judge Moon's reasoning closely follows that of Michigan District Judge George Caram Steeh in the recent *Thomas More Law Center* decision.[13] Both judges upheld the mandate under the Constitution's Commerce Clause alone on the grounds that failure to purchase health insurance, even if it doesn't qualify as "economic activity," is an "economic decision" that has substantial effects on interstate commerce. I've previously outlined my objections to Judge Steeh's reasoning and will not repeat them in detail in this post. Here is the most important flaw:

> "Economic decisions," [Steeh reasoned], include decisions not to engage in economic activity. This approach would allow the Commerce Clause to cover virtually any choice of any kind. Any decision to do anything is necessarily a decision not to use the same time and effort to engage in "economic activity." If I choose to spend an hour sleeping, I necessarily choose not to spend that time working or buying products. Under Judge Steeh's logic, the Commerce Clause authorizes Congress to force workers to get up earlier in the morning so that they would spend more time on the job.

Judge Moon also contends that the mandate should be upheld under *Gonzales v. Raich* and *Wickard v. Filburn*. In reasoning thus, he simply ignores the various ways in which *Raich* does not in fact cover the mandate case. To briefly summarize, *Raich* gave Congress the power to regulate virtually any kind of "economic activity" and a wide range of "noneconomic" activities but said absolutely nothing about regulation of inactivity, which is what the mandate does. His reliance on *Wickard* is even more dubious, since *Wickard* involved regulation of economic activity narrowly defined (commercial farming); I discuss this point in more detail in my amicus brief on behalf of the Washington Legal Foundation and a group of constitutional law scholars submitted in the antimandate case filed by the state of Virginia.[14]

Interestingly, Judge Moon follows Florida District Judge Roger Vinson in ruling that "the better characterization of the exactions imposed under the Act for violations of the employer and individual coverage provisions is that of regulatory penalties, not taxes."[15] This rejects the federal government's claim that the mandate should be upheld because it is a tax that Congress has the power to impose under the Taxing and Spending Clause.

Finally, Moon ruled that both Liberty University and some of the individual plaintiffs have standing. This contributes to an increasing trend under which every judge who has considered the case has ruled that plaintiffs have standing so long as they are state governments, private individuals who do not have health insurance, or employers who do not provide their employees the kind of health insurance benefits that the law requires.

Between this decision and the Michigan case, antimandate plaintiffs have now lost the first two district court rulings that addressed the merits of the mandate litigation. However, it is highly likely that they will win at least one and probably both of the next two decisions: those in the cases brought by the Commonwealth of Virginia and a coalition of twenty state governments and the National Federation of Independent Business. Both the Virginia and Florida judges have issued preliminary rulings expressing strong skepticism about the federal government's arguments. The *New York Times* reports that the Obama administration expects that there is a high probability that they will lose one or both of these cases at the district level.

As should by now be obvious, no district court is going to resolve this issue definitively. All these cases will next be addressed by federal courts of appeals. And there is a high likelihood that the matter will ultimately be resolved by the Supreme Court (a virtual certainty if even one federal appellate court strikes down the mandate). If the plaintiffs lose all the district court decisions, it could create momentum for the federal government that will be difficult to overcome. Courts of appeals judges might hesitate to upset what would seem like an emerging judicial consensus. Such an outcome is, however, highly unlikely given the situation in the two cases filed by state governments.

I continue to believe that the Supreme Court is more likely to uphold the mandate than strike it down. But the course of the litigation so far shows that there is no consensus on the issue among judges and other experts and that the plaintiffs have a much better chance of winning than many commentators (myself included) initially thought.

Why Going without Health Insurance Isn't an "Activity"

Ilya Somin
December 2, 2010

Current U.S. Supreme Court Commerce Clause precedent holds that Congress can regulate almost any "economic activity" and most "noneconomic activities" as well. The Obamacare individual mandate, however, seems to regulate inactivity—*not* purchasing a product. Both Judge Steeh in the *Thomas More Law Center* decision and Judge Moon in the recent *Liberty University* ruling argue that, contrary to appearances, not having health insurance really is an "activity." I have previously criticized parts of this argument, but it would be helpful to address it more thoroughly.

The argument comes in two forms: a broad version claiming that any "economic decision" qualifies as an economic activity and a narrow one focusing on supposedly unique characteristics of the health care market. Both versions fail for similar reasons: they end up giving Congress unconstrained power to mandate virtually anything, something the Supreme Court has repeatedly said is impermissible.

I. The Broad Version

The broad version of the argument claims that any decision with economic effects qualifies as an economic activity. Consider Judge Moon's statement of this argument:

> [D]ecisions to pay for health care without insurance are economic activities . . . [because] Plaintiffs' preference for paying for health care needs out of pocket rather than purchasing insurance on the market is much like the preference of the plaintiff farmer in *Wickard* for fulfilling his demand for wheat by growing his own rather than by purchasing it. . . . Because of the nature of supply and demand, Plaintiffs' choices directly affect the price of insurance in the market, which Congress set out in the Act to control.[16]

The flaw in this argument is obvious. Because "of the nature of supply and demand," any decision to do or not do *anything* will directly affect the price of some good or other. If I choose not to purchase a car, that will affect the price of cars. If I choose to sleep for an hour rather than work, I will earn less money, which in turn means that I will engage in less consumer spending and/or investment, which will affect the prices of various goods. By this analysis, Congress could not only force people to purchase any product of any kind, it could also force them to engage in just about any other kind of activity that affects the price of some good or other that "Congress set out . . . to control."

As I have previously pointed out, Judge Moon's citation of *Wickard* does not help his case because *Wickard* involved regulation of economic activity narrowly defined: commercial farming. Nothing in *Wickard* suggests that Congress has the power to force ordinary people to purchase wheat merely by virtue of their being residents of the United States.

II. The "Health Care Is Special" Version

In addition to arguing that Congress can regulate virtually any "economic decision," Steeh and Moon also contend that the individual mandate regulates an activity because of the special nature of the health care market. As Judge Steeh puts it, "[t]he health care market is unlike other markets. No one can guarantee his or her health, or ensure that he or she will never participate in the health care market. Indeed, the opposite is nearly always true."[17] For this reason, he contends, "The plaintiffs have not opted out of the health care services market because, as living, breathing beings, who do not oppose medical services on religious grounds, they cannot opt out of this market."[18] Since everyone participates in the health care market, the argument goes, choosing not to buy health insurance does not qualify as inactivity. It's just a decision to get health care some other way.

In reality, it is not quite true that everyone purchases health care. Some people rely on charity or home remedies or simply never get sick enough to require medical treatment before they die. Still, it's certainly true that the overwhelming majority of people participate in the health care market in some way.

This, however, doesn't differentiate health care from almost any other market of any significance. If you define the relevant "market" broadly enough, you can characterize any decision not to purchase a good or service exactly the same way. Notice that Steeh and Moon do not argue that everyone will inevitably use health *insurance*. Instead, they define the relevant market as "health *care*." The same sleight of hand works for virtually any other mandate Congress might care to impose.

Consider the case of a mandate requiring everyone to purchase General Motors cars in order to help the auto industry. Sure, there are many people who don't participate in the market for cars. But just about everyone participates in the market for "transportation." As Judge Steeh might put it, "No one can guarantee . . . [that he] will never participate in the [transportation] market." We all move from place to place in some way. If we don't do so by purchasing cars, we will have to pay for some other mode of transportation, such as planes, buses, or trains. Even people who walk everywhere they go will have to buy shoes to do so. Buying cars, planes, trains, buses and shoes are just different ways of paying for transportation.

How about a mandate requiring everyone to see the most recent Harry Potter movie? Sure, there are many people who don't watch movies. But just about everyone participates in the market for *entertainment*. If you don't go to the movies, that's just a decision to pay for some other form of entertainment somewhere else. Even ascetic monks who get their entertainment solely from meditation still have to use resources to pay for the space in which they meditate.

Finally, consider a mandate requiring everyone to pay to establish a blog and write in it every day. True, many people don't participate in the blogosphere in any way. But everyone participates in the market for *information*. You can't live without it! And blogging is just one way to convey information about yourself and your views to others. If you don't blog, that means you will be sending out information in some other way: email, snail mail, telephones, smoke signals . . . And of course all these modes of communication have to be paid for. No "living, breathing being . . . can . . . opt out of this market."

I won't bore readers with the details. But it's easy to apply the same analysis to just about any mandate to do anything.

Perhaps the real "specialness" of health care resides in the fact that it is such an important good. It is indeed very important (though the same can be said for transportation, information, and various other goods without which modern society would collapse). But that does not make not having health insurance any more an "economic activity" than it would be otherwise. In that legally relevant respect, health care turns out to not be special at all.

How Do We Know What Is an "Activity" for Commerce Clause Purposes?

Orin S. Kerr
December 2, 2010

I appreciate Ilya's post on the meaning of "activity" in Commerce Clause jurisprudence, and I wanted to add two brief observations:

1. If I understand Ilya's argument, he begins with an assumption as to how much power Congress has, and he then reasons backwards to infer the meaning of "activity" in order to make that assumption correct. A conscious decision not to do something cannot be an "activity," the thinking goes, because that would give Congress more power than a fair reading of the Commerce Clause would permit. Perhaps, but it seems to me that this argument largely assumes its conclusion. It uses the fact that Congress must have significant limits on its power to show that "activity" has a narrow meaning, which then is used to prove that Congress has significant limits on its power that the individual mandate exceeds. If you start with a different assumption, however, the argument doesn't work. For example, if you start with the assumption about the scope of the Commerce Clause that Justice Kennedy articulates in his *Lopez* concurrence, then you can get a different meaning of "activity."

    I suspect some readers will object to this argument on the ground that they share Ilya's assumption: because Ilya's assumption is correct, the argument works. That's a fair point within the group that shares the assumption. The problem is that others don't share the assumption, and starting with it won't go very far in persuading *them*. That doesn't necessarily mean Ilya is right or wrong. But I do think it means that this argument is likely not to have a lot of force among the people not already inclined to agree with it.

2. More broadly, I still think that the easiest path to resolving the constitutionality of the individual mandate is that it is a "necessary and proper" means of trying to regulate the massive interstate market in health care that is around one-seventh of the United States economy. As I have blogged before, I think that's a very strong argument based on Supreme Court case law on the meaning of "necessary and proper." I realize that Ilya thinks that the Supreme Court precedents on the meaning of "necessary and proper" have not actually addressed what is "proper" and thus that there is a still yet unarticulated limitation on the scope of federal power that remains to be developed—and that should be read as adding a level of scrutiny that the individual mandate fails to satisfy. But I don't think the cases can be fairly read in that way, so it seems to me that the Necessary and Proper Clause case law leads to the conclusion that the mandate should be upheld without getting into what counts as an "activity."

Assumptions and "Activities" in Commerce Clause Jurisprudence

Ilya Somin
December 2, 2010

In his response to my post on why going without health insurance doesn't qualify as an "activity" that Congress can regulate under the Commerce Clause, Orin Kerr claims that my reasoning "begins with an assumption as to how much power Congress has, and he then reasons backwards to infer the meaning of 'activity' in order to make that assumption correct." Therefore, Orin believes that the argument won't persuade anyone who isn't already inclined to agree with it.

What Orin ignores is that the relevant "assumption"—that Congress doesn't have unlimited authority to use the Commerce Clause to regulate anything and everything—is not idiosyncratic to me. It has been repeatedly reaffirmed by the Supreme Court, even in those cases where it has interpreted Congress's powers most broadly, including even *Gonzales v. Raich*, which distinguished the statute it upheld from those that don't regulate "economic activity" defined as the production, consumption, or distribution of a commodity; the state of not having health insurance doesn't qualify under any of these three counts.

As the Court explained in *United States v. Lopez*, "[t]he Constitution . . . withhold[s] from Congress a plenary police power that would authorize enactment of every type of legislation."[19] Orin is fond of citing Justice Kennedy's views. So it's worth noting that Justice Kennedy recently wrote an opinion in *United States v. Comstock* that emphasized the need to enforce the federalism "principles that control the limited nature of our National Government."[20] In his *Lopez* concurrence, cited in Orin's post, Kennedy also noted that "[i]n a sense any conduct in this interdependent world of ours has an ultimate commercial origin or consequence, but we have not yet said the commerce power may reach so far."[21] That seems to squarely reject the argument that the individual mandate is constitutional merely because not having health insurance has some kind of economic motive or has an impact on markets. And of course that claim is precisely what the lower court judges who have upheld the mandate rely on, especially in what I dubbed the "broad version" of their argument.

If my analysis in the previous post is correct, the Commerce Clause rationale for the individual mandate can't be squared with the principles endorsed by the Court and Justice Kennedy because it would give Congress virtually unlimited authority to mandate anything it wants, so long as the mandate has some effect on prices within some market (which is true of virtually any requirement).

If I were basing the analysis on my own view of the correct interpretation of the Commerce Clause, I would simply rely on the powerful arguments suggesting that *Raich* and many other modern Commerce Clause cases can't be squared with the text, structure, and original meaning of the Constitution. Under an originalist or textualist approach, the case against the individual mandate is easy to make, and indeed overwhelming. My point in the previous post, however, was to explain why the mandate can't be squared even with the much weaker limits on congressional Commerce Clause power endorsed by current Supreme Court precedent.

Finally, Orin reiterates his previous argument that the mandate can be upheld under the Necessary and Proper Clause. That, however, is a different claim from the one I was addressing, which is the argument that not having health insurance is an "activity" that Congress can regulate using its powers under the Commerce Clause alone. That's the theory adopted by both of the two district judges who have upheld the mandate so far.

UPDATE: It's also worth noting that Orin doesn't seem to dispute my argument that the same logic used to justify the individual mandate under the Commerce

Clause would also justify federal mandates requiring people to purchase GM cars, go to the movies, or even establish and operate a blog (though perhaps that may not seem onerous to a blogger as active as Orin), indeed virtually any mandate Congress might care to impose. I recognize that it's difficult to persuade people who have already formed strong opinions on an issue as contentious as this one. But, fine points of legal doctrine aside, I suspect that the sweeping nature of this kind of power might give pause to at least some people who haven't yet reached a firm conclusion on the question.

"Not Unlimited" Is Not the Same as "Significantly Limited": A Reply to Ilya

Orin S. Kerr
December 2, 2010

Just a quick reply to Ilya's response on the scope of the Commerce Clause. In my view the basic problem with Ilya's argument is that it mixes up two different claims:

1. Congress does not have unlimited power.
2. Congress has significantly limited power.

The Supreme Court has said (1). But it has *not* said (2), and the Court's precedents for the last 75 years or so seem pretty clearly inconsistent with (2). That's the problem with Ilya's position, I think. Ilya starts with proposition (2); he then adopts an interpretation of "activity" that then proves proposition (2); and then uses (2) to show that the mandate is unconstitutional. But we need to start with proposition (1), not proposition (2), and they are very different.

If you start at (1), it's easy to square proposition (1) with the individual mandate. All you have to do is come up with a theory that allows the individual mandate but doesn't allow *everything*. One candidate for this theory is that the mandate is an effort to regulate commerce rather than something noncommercial. That theory permits the mandate but doesn't allow Congress to regulate noncommercial activity with no interstate nexus such as the possession of guns in *Lopez*.

Now I'm not saying that this candidate of a possible reading of (1) is necessarily correct. Maybe it's right, maybe it's wrong. There are versions of proposition (1) that permit the mandate and versions of (1) that do not. My point is only that starting with proposition (2) isn't helpful. Starting with proposition (2) rules out a lot of versions of (1) as an *assumption*: if you're not already inclined to interpret (1) as also implying (2), making that argument as an assumption is not going to be persuasive.

Notes

1. Thomas More Law Ctr. v. Obama, 720 F. Supp. 2d 882 (E.D. Mich. 2010).
2. *Id.* at 894.
3. *Thomas More Law Ctr.*, 720 F. Supp. 2d at 893. (emphasis added)
4. *Id.* at 894. (emphasis added)

5. *Id.* at 893.
6. *Id.* at 894.
7. Orin Kerr, "McDonald and the Mandate: A Response to Randy," *Volokh Conspiracy* (blog), October 17, 2010, http://www.volokh.com/2010/10/17/mcdonald-and-the-mandate-a-response-to-randy.
8. Randy E. Barnett, "Commandeering the People: Why the Individual Health Insurance Mandate Is Unconstitutional," *New York University Journal of Law and Liberty* 5, no. 581 (2011).
9. United States v. Comstock, 130 S. Ct. 1966–68 (2010) (Kennedy, J., concurring).
10. 505 U.S. 144 (1992).
11. 521 U.S. 898 (1997).
12. Liberty Univ. v. Geithner, 753 F. Supp. 2d 611 (W.D. Va. 2010).
13. Ilya Somin, "Michigan District Court Upholds Individual Mandate against Challenge by the Thomas More Law Center," *supra.*
14. Brief for the Washington Legal Foundation, *Sebelius*, 728 F. Supp. 2d 768, *supra.*
15. *Liberty Univ.*, 753 F. Supp. 2d at 620.
16. *Id.* at 633–34.
17. *Thomas More Law Ctr.*, 720 F. Supp. 2d at 894.
18. *Id.*
19. 514 U.S. at 566.
20. 130 S. Ct. at 1966 (Kennedy, J., concurring).
21. United States v. Lopez, 514 U.S. 580 (1995) (Kennedy, J., concurring).

4

More Decisions

On December 13, 2010, Judge Henry E. Hudson of the United States District Court for the Eastern District of Virginia struck down the individual mandate portion of the Affordable Care Act (ACA) as going beyond the scope of Congress's power under the Commerce and Necessary and Proper Clauses. He also severed the individual mandate from the rest of the act and left the balance of the law standing.

This issue, called "severability," would also reach the Supreme Court. Whenever a small part of a bigger statute is ruled unconstitutional, the question remains whether the entire law or just the smaller part must fall. When analyzing severability, courts look to whether the remaining parts of the statute are fully functional without the unconstitutional provision(s) and whether the downsized statute will still function in the way Congress intended.

Hudson's decision was much more significant than his previous denial of the government's motion to dismiss. Whereas denying a motion to dismiss merely allows the case to move forward to the "merits" of the legal arguments, Judge Hudson's decision was the first to say, "You not only have good enough arguments to proceed with the lawsuit, you have good enough arguments to win."

The game was afoot.

It was a bold move for a district court judge. Even many challengers believed it would be unlikely for any district court judge—the lowest level of conventional federal judges—to strike down the ACA. If the case were to be won, they believed, it would have to be won by appealing district court losses up to the circuit courts of appeals and, hopefully, the Supreme Court. Hudson's decision was a major and, for some, unexpected victory.

Later in this chapter, a second district court judge, Judge Roger Vinson of the United States District Court for the Northern District of Florida, would also strike down the individual mandate. Vinson, unlike Hudson, did not separate the individual mandate from the rest of the act. Instead, he ruled that the individual mandate was too fully integrated with the rest of the law to sever, thus the entire law had to fall.

***

Initial Thoughts on the Virginia Health Care Ruling

Jonathan H. Adler
December 13, 2010

The federal district court's decision declaring portions of federal health care reform unconstitutional reaffirms that the federal government has limited and enumerated powers.[1] The theories advanced by the federal government in support of the mandate were without bounds and could have justified virtually unlimited federal control of private activity. Reforming America's health care system is important, but just like everything else, from national security to environmental protection, it must be done in a way that's consistent with constitutional principles.

The district court properly recognized that the individual mandate represents the most far-reaching exercise of federal regulatory authority under the Interstate Commerce and Necessary and Proper Clauses in the nation's history. Certainly the argument can be made that the logic of prior decisions could support such an exercise of federal power (and Orin has made it), but it is also true that no prior case upheld a mandate of this sort.

As I've suggested before,[2] the question before the Court is in a similar posture to that in *United States v. Lopez*. The Court's expansive precedents have been given even more expansive interpretations by the majority of academic commentators, but the Court has also consistently maintained that federal regulatory authority has judicially enforceable limits and that upholding the individual mandate (much like upholding the Gun-Free School Zones Act) would make any such limits difficult, if not impossible, to discern.

The Court distinguished *Wickard* and *Raich* on the grounds that the individuals in those cases became subject to federal regulation due to affirmative actions each had taken. As the court noted, "In both cases, the activity under review was the product of a self-directed affirmative move . . . This self-initiated change of position voluntarily placed the subject within the stream of commerce. Absent that step, governmental regulation could have been avoided."[3] I think this is correct, and this is precisely the sort of distinction that courts must draw if there are to be judicially enforceable limits on the federal government's enumerated powers.

The federal government's strongest argument is that the individual mandate is necessary to facilitate other aspects of health care reform and thus must be valid as "necessary and proper" to the regulation of health insurance markets. But this argument proves too much. I've noted that the individual mandate does not, as written, truly solve the adverse selection problem created by other aspects of health care reform.[4] It only helps on the margin. If this is enough to satisfy the Necessary and Proper Clause then Congress could mandate that all individuals engage in *any* behavior that helps keep down health insurance costs by increasing the participation of healthy people in insurance pools or improving the health of those already in the pool. So for instance, Congress could mandate that all Americans join health clubs or purchase fruits and vegetables, for these too would help lower health care costs and facilitate achievement of the health care reform's goals.

Some may argue that Congress may have the power to mandate health care memberships or some such thing but that it would never do so because such an extreme step would be so politically unpopular (even more so than the individual mandate is). In this way, one could argue, individuals are protected from federal overreach. This is the argument Justice Harry Blackmun made for the Court in *Garcia v. SAMTA*.[5] Yet this rationale (if not *Garcia*'s precise holding) was soundly repudiated by the Supreme Court in its more recent federalism decisions. As the Court reaffirmed in *Lopez* and *Morrison*, federal power is proscribed by judicially enforceable limits, and it is the obligation of the Court to reject any theory of federal regulatory authority that is without limit.

The court also found the federal government's more recent claim that the mandate is really a tax unpersuasive. Based upon its review of the law, it concluded that the mandate is, "in form and substance, a penalty as opposed to a tax" and therefore could not be justified under the General Welfare Clause.[6]

Finally, I found interesting the court's discussion of how to handle this lawsuit as a "facial" challenge to the law. Virginia's lawsuit presents a facial challenge to the mandate, not a challenge to the constitutionality of its application in any given circumstance. The federal government argued this created an extremely high bar because Virginia would have to demonstrate that there is no instance in which the federal government could impose a mandate to purchase health insurance or regulate the health care choices made by the uninsured. The district court rejected this framing, and properly so. In a facial Commerce Clause challenge, the question is whether Congress had constitutional authority to enact the law that was enacted, not whether there is any conduct covered by the law in question that could, conceivably, be regulated. *United States v. Lopez* is instructive on this point: Alfonso Lopez was involved in a commercial gun sale; he was the mule. His specific conduct could have been subject to federal regulation as part of a broader regulatory scheme governing gun sales. Yet that is not what Congress enacted. Instead Congress enacted a prohibition of possession in or near schools, and that measure was unconstitutional *even though Lopez's specific conduct could have been reached under a different law.* So too here. That some private decisions concerning whether to purchase health care could be subject to federal regulation does not establish that the individual mandate is, as a facial matter, constitutional.

The Significant Error in Judge Hudson's Opinion

Orin S. Kerr
December 13, 2010

I've had a chance to read Judge Hudson's opinion, and it seems to me it has a fairly obvious and quite significant error. Judge Hudson assumes that the power granted to Congress by the Necessary and Proper Clause—"To make all Laws which shall be necessary and proper for carrying into Execution the foregoing Powers"—does not expand Congress's power beyond the Commerce Clause itself. The key line is on page 18:

If a person's decision not to purchase health insurance at a particular point in time does not constitute the type of economic activity subject to regulation under the Commerce Clause, then logically an attempt to enforce such provision under the Necessary and Proper Clause is equally offensive to the Constitution.[7]

Judge Hudson does not cite any authority for this conclusion—he seems to believe it is required by logic. But it is incorrect. The point of the Necessary and Proper Clause is that it grants Congress the power to use *means* outside the enumerated list of Article I powers to achieve the *ends* listed in Article I. If you say, as a matter of "logic" or otherwise, that the Necessary and Proper Clause only permits Congress to regulate using means that are themselves covered by the Commerce Clause, then the Necessary and Proper Clause is rendered a nullity. But that's not how the Supreme Court has interpreted the clause from Chief Justice John Marshall onwards. Indeed, as far as I know, not even the most vociferous critics of the mandate have suggested that the Necessary and Proper Clause can be read this way.

Given that existing Supreme Court case law gives the federal government a fairly straightforward argument in support of the mandate under the Necessary and Proper Clause, Judge Hudson's error leads him to assume away as a matter of "logic" what is the major question in the case. That is unfortunate, I think.

Further Thoughts on the Virginia Health Care Ruling and the Necessary and Proper Clause

Jonathan H. Adler
December 13, 2010

In his previous post, Orin criticizes Judge Hudson's opinion for implying that if Congress may not regulate inactivity under the Commerce Clause, it also may not reach such conduct under the Necessary and Proper Clause. This cannot be right because, as Orin notes, the whole point of the Necessary and Proper Clause is to give Congress the ability to execute its other enumerated powers. I accept this point, but I would caution against jumping to the opposite conclusion. Just because Congress has the power to enact measures that are necessary and proper to the execution of its power to regulate commerce—in this case, health care markets—that does not mean that Congress has the power to do anything and everything that, on the margin, facilitates or makes more efficient other federally enacted regulatory measures.

Identifying the line to distinguish between permissible and impermissible exercises of the federal government's power under the Necessary and Proper Clause is the task at hand, and existing precedent is only of limited use. The Court's decisions, from *McCulloch v. Maryland* to *Comstock*, only go so far in addressing this question. They clearly confirm that Congress can take some steps beyond the scopes of the other enumerated powers but also reaffirm that federal power is limited, and none of the relevant cases stand for the proposition that it is for

Congress, and Congress alone, to determine what may be enacted as necessary and proper to the execution of other constitutional measures.

This is why the individual mandate presents a difficult question. It is beyond dispute that, on the margin, requiring all Americans to purchase health care will reduce the costs of seeking to expand coverage by, for instance, prohibiting health insurers from denying coverage for preexisting conditions. But as I noted previously,[8] the same can be said for any measure that increases the participation of relatively healthy people in health insurance pools or that increases the average health of those that are insured. So unless one wants to adopt the view that *any* provision adopted as part of some broader legislative scheme is necessary and proper just because Congress says it is, so long as there is some plausible justification for its relation to the broader scheme, one needs to identify some alternative limit. This is something the individual mandate's defenders have yet to do.

One solution to the line-drawing problem is to argue that, at least for Commerce Clause purposes, there is a fundamental difference between regulating economic conduct—conduct that places an individual within or sufficiently proximate to the streams of commerce—and mandating conduct. This line is appealing because neither a prohibition nor conditional regulation curtails liberty as much as does an affirmative mandate. On this basis, one could argue that a direct mandate is not "proper," even if it might be useful or efficient. Drawing the line here is also appealing because there is no precedent for using the Necessary and Proper Clause in this fashion, at least not in the Commerce Clause context. Thus, a court can invalidate the individual mandate on this ground without challenging any of the relevant precedents and without undermining any other portions of the U.S. Code. Finally, if one accepts that a line must be drawn—and I recognize that some do not—this line is appealing because it is an administrable line, and its critics have yet to identify any viable alternative.

Thoughts on Today's Ruling Striking Down the Individual Health Insurance Mandate

Ilya Somin
December 13, 2010

Here are a few thoughts on today's federal district court ruling striking down the constitutionality of the Obamacare individual mandate. In my view, the strongest parts of Judge Henry Hudson's opinion are those where he rejects the federal government's arguments under the Commerce Clause and the Taxing and Spending Clause.

On the Commerce Clause, federal government lawyers argued that the mandate is justified because the state of not having health insurance qualifies as economic activity due to the fact that most people will eventually use health care in some form or other. As Judge Hudson points out, "the same reasoning could apply to transportation, housing, or nutritional decisions. This broad definition of the economic activity subject to congressional regulation lacks logical limitation and is unsupported by [the Supreme Court's] Commerce Clause jurisprudence."[9] The same logic would justify forcing people to purchase cars on the grounds that everyone eventually uses the market for transportation or forcing them to blog on the grounds that everyone uses the market for information in some way. I addressed this point more fully elsewhere.[10]

Judge Hudson also does a very good job of explaining why the government's claim that the mandate is a tax runs counter to existing Supreme Court precedent distinguishing taxes from regulatory penalties. The mandate is pretty clearly an example of the latter. Here, his reasoning is similar to that which I advocated in the amicus brief in the case that I wrote on behalf of the Washington Legal Foundation and a group of constitutional law scholars.[11] As the Supreme Court explained as recently as 1996 in *United States v. Reorganized CF&I Fabricators of Utah, Inc.*, "[a] tax is a pecuniary burden laid upon individuals or property for the purpose of supporting the Government."[12] By contrast, it went on to say, "if the concept of penalty means anything, it means punishment for an unlawful act or omission."[13] It's hard to think of a much clearer example of a fine used as "punishment for an unlawful act or omission" than the individual mandate. Various earlier Supreme Court decisions cited by Judge Hudson and in my brief take a similar view.

The weakest part of Judge Hudson's opinion is his analysis of the government's Necessary and Proper Clause argument, which merely claims that the Necessary and Proper Clause only authorizes legislation that is linked to an enumerated power but does not really explain why the mandate is not. In my view, a far better answer to the government's argument is that the mandate isn't "proper" even if it is "necessary" and that it runs afoul of the five-part test recently outlined by the Supreme Court in *United States v. Comstock*. I discussed both points in some detail in the amicus brief, and in a shorter form previously.[14] In fairness to the judge, his neglect of this point may have been due to the fact that the federal government gave it short shrift in their brief (allocating less than two pages to it buried in the middle of a fifty-page brief). While coblogger Orin Kerr and I believe that this is the government's strongest argument, few other commentators seem to agree. In today's *New York Times* Room for Debate[15] forum on Hudson's opinion, none of the contributors (including four prominent scholars who support the individual mandate) even mentioned this issue. Still, the opinion can and should have addressed this point much better.

Judge Hudson ruled that invalidating the mandate does not require invalidation of any other part of the health care bill. I'm not a real expert on the relevant law of "severability," so it's hard for me to say whether this part of the decision is correct. Still, it is relevant that the bill doesn't contain any severability clause of the sort normally used to ensure that the other parts of a law stay in place if one part is invalidated as unconstitutional. Moreover, a few other parts of the law are so closely connected to the mandate that it's hard to imagine that they are truly severable from it. The best example is the regulation forcing insurance companies to accept customers with preexisting conditions. Interestingly, the White House recently issued a statement claiming that these two provisions are not in fact severable (though federal government lawyers apparently argued otherwise in the litigation before Judge Hudson). My tentative view is that the White House is correct on this issue, and Judge Hudson is wrong.

Finally, it goes without saying that today's ruling is just one phase in a lengthy legal struggle. Ultimately, the issue will be decided by the federal courts of appeals, and very likely the Supreme Court. At the same time, it is significant that we now have a district court decision striking down the mandate, with a second one likely in the case filed by twenty state governments and the National Federation of Independent Business. The judge presiding over that case has already indicated considerable skepticism about the government's arguments and rejected the Taxing and Spending Clause claim outright. If the district courts had all uniformly upheld the mandate, appellate judges might have hesitated to challenge such a broad emerging judicial consensus. As things actually stand, the issue remains up for grabs. That in itself is a major change from just a few months ago, when conventional wisdom dismissed the antimandate lawsuits as frivolous grandstanding with virtually no chance of success.

A Brief Reply to Orin on the Necessary and Proper Clause

Jonathan H. Adler
December 14, 2010

Previously,[16] I wrote that "none of the relevant cases stand for the proposition that it is for Congress, and Congress alone, to determine what may be enacted as necessary and proper to the execution of other constitutional measures." Orin suggested that a passage from *United States v. Comstock* (quoting *Burroughs v. United States*) suggests otherwise, but I don't think so.

The passage at issue is:

> If it can be seen that the means adopted are really calculated to attain the end, the degree of their necessity, the extent to which they conduce to the end, the closeness of the relationship between the means adopted and the end to be attained, are matters for congressional determination alone.

This is true, as far as it goes. The "degree of necessity" and "closeness of the relationship" are left up to Congress, but these are not the only relevant questions under the Necessary and Proper Clause, as *Comstock* makes clear. Rather, the Court in *Comstock* explains, there are five factors for the Court to consider in evaluating the constitutionality of a congressional assertion of its Necessary and Proper Clause power. The passage Orin cites is from its discussion of the first. So even granting that the individual mandate passes this test does not establish that "it is for Congress, and Congress alone, to determine what may be enacted as necessary and proper to the execution of other constitutional measures."

The Doctrinal Limits of "Necessary" in the Necessary and Proper Clause

Randy E. Barnett
December 15, 2010

A couple days ago, Orin raised an interesting point about Judge Hudson's opinion in the challenge to the Affordable Care Act to which Jonathan has already responded. But I thought I would explain the source of the confusion, which lies not in Judge Hudson's opinion, but in Chief Justice William Rehnquist's opinion in *Lopez*.

The key is to understand three uncontestable propositions:

1. The "economic-noneconomic" distinction established in *Lopez* qualifies the substantial effects doctrine.
2. The substantial effects doctrine was first established and developed in *NLRB v. Jones & Laughlin Steel*, *United States v. Darby*, and *Wickard v. Filburn*.
3. In these New Deal cases, the power of Congress to reach intrastate activity that has a substantial effect on interstate commerce was justified by invoking *McCulloch v. Maryland* and the Necessary and Proper Clause. In *Wickard v. Filburn*, the Court wrote: "[E]ven if appellee's activity be local and *though it may not be regarded as commerce*, it may still, whatever its nature, be reached by Congress if it exerts a substantial economic effect on interstate commerce."[17] In other words, Congress could reach beyond its power of interstate commerce to reach intrastate activity that was not commerce because it was "necessary" to the execution of its Commerce Clause power.

This leads then to a conclusion that is not widely recognized:

4. **The "necessary" prong of the Necessary and Proper Clause is already being limited by a judicially administrable doctrine: the economic-noneconomic distinction.** To execute its commerce power under the existing Necessary and Proper Clause doctrine, Congress may only reach intrastate economic activity that substantially affects interstate commerce. According to this settled doctrine, however "necessary" it might otherwise be, it cannot reach intrastate noneconomic activity. Therefore, a claim that Congress can reach *inactivity* that substantially affects interstate commerce because it is "necessary" goes beyond the outer reaches of the Necessary and Proper Clause as established by *Lopez* and reaffirmed in *Morrison*.

The source of the confusion here is that, in *Lopez*, Chief Justice Rehnquist does not discuss the Necessary and Proper Clause underpinnings of the substantial effects doctrine, though he does expressly trace it back to the New Deal cases cited previously. But Justice Scalia makes this clear in his concurring opinion in *Raich*:

> Our cases show that the regulation of intrastate activities may be necessary to and proper for the regulation of interstate commerce in two general circumstances. Most directly, the commerce power permits Congress not only to devise rules for the

governance of commerce between States but also to facilitate interstate commerce by eliminating potential obstructions, and to restrict it by eliminating potential stimulants. See *NLRB v. Jones & Laughlin Steel Corp.* (1937). That is why the Court has repeatedly sustained congressional legislation on the ground that the regulated activities had a substantial effect on interstate commerce. *Lopez* and *Morrison* recognized the expansive scope of Congress' authority in this regard: "[T]**he pattern is clear**. Where economic activity substantially affects interstate commerce, legislation regulating that activity will be sustained."

This [Necessary and Proper Clause—RB] principle is not without limitation. In *Lopez* and *Morrison*, the Court—conscious of the potential of the "substantially affects" test to "'obliterate the distinction between what is national and what is local,'" rejected the argument that Congress may regulate noneconomic activity based solely on the effect that it may have on interstate commerce through a remote chain of inferences. "[I]f we were to accept [such] arguments," the Court reasoned in *Lopez*, "we are hard pressed to posit any activity by an individual that Congress is without power to regulate." Thus, although Congress' authority to regulate intrastate activity that substantially affects interstate commerce is broad, it does not permit the Court to "pile inference upon inference," in order to establish that noneconomic activity has a substantial effect on interstate commerce.[18]

To this Justice Scalia proposes a *second* Necessary and Proper Clause doctrine based on dictum from *Lopez*:

As we implicitly acknowledged in *Lopez*, however, Congress' authority to enact laws necessary and proper for the regulation of interstate commerce is not limited to laws directed against economic activities that have a substantial effect on interstate commerce. Though the conduct in *Lopez* was not economic, the Court nevertheless recognized that it could be regulated as "an essential part of a larger regulation of economic activity, in which the regulatory scheme could be undercut unless the intrastate activity were regulated." This statement referred to those cases permitting the regulation of intrastate **activities** "which in a substantial way interfere with or obstruct the exercise of the granted power."

The regulation of an intrastate **activity** may be essential to a comprehensive regulation of interstate commerce even though the intrastate **activity** does not itself "substantially affect" interstate commerce. Moreover, as the passage from *Lopez* quoted above suggests, Congress may regulate even noneconomic local **activity** if that regulation is a necessary part of a more general regulation of interstate commerce. The relevant question is simply whether the means chosen are "reasonably adapted" to the attainment of a legitimate end under the commerce power.[19]

Supporters of the constitutionality of the mandate mainly rely on this yet-to-be-established doctrine, which I predict *will* be accepted by the Court in an appropriate case involving intrastate noneconomic **activity**. But as Judge Hudson recognized, the mandate goes beyond intrastate activity to reach inactivity, so this is not that case.

Of course, the distinction between economic and noneconomic activity would not limit this new "Essential to a broader regulatory scheme doctrine" as it does the substantial effects doctrine. That is Justice Scalia's point. Because it has not yet been used to decide a case, however, the Court has not had occasion to identify a "limiting doctrine" so this new Necessary and Proper Clause doctrine does not destroy the scheme of enumerated powers.

When Chief Justice Rehnquist devised the economic-noneconomic distinction limiting the substantial effects doctrine of the Necessary and Proper Clause he did so by "looking back" and finding that, in all previous substantial effects doctrine cases, "the pattern is clear": they all involved the regulation of *intrastate economic activity*. And this is what Judge Hudson did in *Virginia v. Sebelius*. He looked back and saw a clear pattern: Every case in which the Necessary and Proper Clause was used to reach beyond interstate commerce involved "*activity*." Congress never before sought to reach beyond activity to reach inactivity. So that provides the requisite limiting doctrine to the yet-to-be-applied "Essential to a broader regulatory scheme doctrine" proposed by Justice Scalia.

Like the economic-noneconomic distinction, such a doctrine would provide a judicially administrable limit to the scope of "necessary" under the Necessary and Proper Clause without requiring a judicial examination of the more or less necessity of a measure, which the Court has refrained from doing (e.g., the passage quoted by Orin in *Comstock*). It provides a doctrinal line to prevent Congress from reaching matters that are remote from its power over interstate commerce—regardless of the degree of remoteness in any given case, which the courts will not assess.

How does the government attempt to limit the reach of its claimed power? It asserts that the health insurance market is special or unique and therefore different than other sorts of regulatory schemes that Congress might enact. But this attempt to limit the scope of its theory IS based on a judicial assessment of the more or less necessity of the insurance mandate, which is an approach that won't ultimately limit the power.

Does anyone want to bet serious money on whether Justice Scalia, the father of this newly minted Necessary and Proper Clause doctrine, won't see all this by the time the case reaches the Court, that he won't adopt Judge Hudson's distinction between activity and inactivity as a judicially administrable limit on his doctrinal creation, and that he won't distinguish *Raich* (and *Wickard*) from this case on this ground? I did not think so. Judge Hudson intuited all this in his ruling on Monday.

Orin's complaint about Judge Hudson's opinion only looks right if one fails to see that the substantial effects doctrine we are discussing *is already a Necessary and Proper Clause doctrine limiting "necessary."* The New Deal Court's decisions were much clearer and more careful about this than was Chief Justice Rehnquist's opinion in *Lopez*. After all, in their youths, the New Deal justices were trained to take enumerated powers seriously.

Thoughts on Justice Scalia's Wonderful Concurrence in *Gonzales v. Raich*

Orin S. Kerr
December 15, 2010

Many thanks to Randy Barnett for his thoughtful views on the relationship between the Necessary and Proper Clause and existing Commerce Clause doctrine. Randy's argument is more or less the one Justice Scalia makes in his concurring opinion in *Gonzales v. Raich*: That the "substantial effects" test in Commerce Clause doctrine should be read as actually being an interpretation of the Necessary and Proper Clause. If you take that view, then once you have analyzed the individual mandate under existing Commerce Clause doctrine, you're basically done: There is no more added power under the Necessary and Proper Clause, as the *Lopez* test has already factored in that power.

I have two responses to this argument. The first will be my emotional response, the response that reflects my values and my beliefs about the fundamental limits on federal government power. The second response will be my doctrinal response, the response that I think a lower-court judge should use when evaluating this argument.

1. **The Emotional Response**—I love it. This is a great way to reconceive the doctrine. It really does make conceptual sense that that the "substantial effects" doctrine is really about what is necessary and proper—they are both about the power to do things outside interstate commerce to try (in the aggregate) to regulate interstate commerce. And as someone who loves federalism, and who feels that it is extremely important that the federal government be a government of limited power, I find this theory tremendously appealing. It holds out the hope that there can be real limits on federal government power beyond the symbolic federalism of recent Supreme Court decisions.[20] As someone who was saddened by the expansive interpretation of federal government power in *Comstock*—recall my "shock"[21] at the breadth of [Solicitor General Elena] Kagan's oral argument—this gives me new hope. I hope the Supreme Court adopts this theory.
2. **The Doctrinal Response**—Justice Scalia's concurrence was the view of one justice, not a majority opinion of the Court. As best I can tell, existing doctrine has not adopted it. Indeed, Randy presents his argument as a chain of premises that reach "a conclusion that is not widely recognized"—a.k.a. a claim of where the Supreme Court should go in the future, not a claim as to where its precedents go at present.

I don't think Randy disagrees that current Supreme Court doctrine does not adopt this theory, as he presents his explanation as what he thinks the Supreme Court should do and what he thinks Justice Scalia will do—and suggests that Judge Hudson was essentially predicting Scalia's vote in his opinion.

I will leave to Randy the "legal realist" question of what Justice Scalia might do, as well as whether it actually matters to the outcome of any future Supreme Court case on the mandate (does anyone think Justice Scalia is the fifth vote on federalism issues?, etc.). Plus, I'm happy to let Judge Hudson "intuit" future votes of individual justices, if that's what he was actually doing in his opinion. But just as a matter of doctrine, it doesn't seem to me that Justice Scalia's views—as much as I personally find them appealing (see response 1)—are currently part of the existing law that lower court judges are duty bound to apply.

Of course, I'd be delighted if I'm wrong on this doctrinally. As I say in response 1, I find Scalia's view very appealing, so I mean that literally: I would be delighted if I'm wrong on this doctrinally. And if Scalia's view is adopted by the Supreme Court, I think it makes the constitutionality of the mandate a very close question. But whether I personally want the Supreme Court to adopt a view is unrelated to whether the Supreme Court has actually done so, and as best I can tell, it has not done so.

Constitutional Doctrine and the Constitutionality of Health Care Reform

David E. Bernstein
December 15, 2010

I've been following the debate both at the *Volokh Conspiracy* and elsewhere and find myself somewhat amused at the law professor conceit that the constitutionality of the individual mandate will be determined based on whether the "best" interpretation of Supreme Court precedent supports it or not.

Here's my take: What the opponents of the individual mandate had to do was provide plausible arguments that the individual mandate is distinguishable from precedents like *Wickard v. Filburn* and *Gonzales v. Raich*. Whether the *best* interpretation of those precedents supports the individual mandate is almost entirely irrelevant.

The modern Supreme Court is reluctant to directly overrule precedents, especially well-entrenched precedents, but is not at all reluctant to distinguish precedents, even when the distinctions in question are quite strained. I could present many examples, but just consider, for example, how *Boy Scouts of America v. Dale*[22] turned out not to be governed by *Roberts v. United States Jaycees*;[23] how the Court distinguished *Mathews v. Eldridge*[24] from *Goldberg v. Kelly*;[25] or how the Court has gone back and forth between relying on *Ex Parte Milligan*[26] and *Ex Parte Quirin*[27] in detainee cases without overruling either one of them or really explaining how they don't contradict each other.

So now that the opponents of the individual mandate have managed to make arguments that pass the laugh test, the Supreme Court's ultimate decision will involve such factors as the following: (1) How popular will the individual mandate, and health care reform more generally, be when the Court takes up the issue?; (2) How popular will President Obama be at that time? (3) The Republicans on the Court will undoubtedly be less likely to support a law passed with only Democratic support; (4) Will Justice Kennedy be more in the mood to be susceptible to the "Greenhouse Effect," or to cement his conservative credentials, which in part will depend on "how close to retirement he is"? (5) Does Justice Scalia think that invalidating the individual mandate will somehow hurt the cause of ultimately overruling *Roe v. Wade*, something that I think is always on Justice Scalia's mind? (6) Will the Republican House and the expanded Republican minority in the Senate show in any way that they take federalism and limited national government seriously, the way the *Contract with America* undoubtedly made *Lopez* more viable, and the Big Government conservatism of the Bush Administration helped lead to *Raich*? (7) Will the Court have other issues before it on which the conservative justices would rather spend their political capital? And so on.

For what it's worth, I remember law professors vigorously debating the law underlying the *Bush v. Gore* litigation. My eventual response was, "the conservative Republicans on the Court will undoubtedly see what's going on as the Democrat-dominated Florida Supreme Court trying to steal the election for Al Gore. And given that this case has unique facts that aren't clearly governed by contrary precedent, you can expect all of them to vote for Bush, and, contrariwise, the liberal Democratic justices to vote for Gore (though I was surprised that Justice Breyer went along with the majority's equal protection arguments, albeit not the remedy)."

UPDATE: I left out a crucial factor: If the liberals on the Court, like the dissenters in *Lopez*, are unable to articulate a limiting principle that would prevent their decision from giving the federal government an essentially plenary police power to regulate virtually all human activity and inactivity, the individual mandate is doomed. The conservative majority simply will not accept a doctrine that suggests that federal power is not one of limited and enumerated powers.

Broccoli, Slippery Slopes, and the Individual Mandate

Ilya Somin
January 25, 2011 3:26 pm

Opponents of the constitutionality of the individual mandate have emphasized that upholding the mandate would give Congress the power to mandate virtually anything, including forcing people to eat broccoli. Northwestern law professor Andrew Koppelman appears to agree, but argues that this slippery slope is nothing to worry about:

> One of the most rhetorically effective arguments that has been made against President Obama's health insurance mandate is that it places us on a slippery slope to totalitarian government. If the federal government can make us buy insurance, what can't it do?
>
> The Broccoli Objection, as I will call it, rests on a simple mistake: treating a slippery slope argument as a logical one, when in fact it is an empirical one.
>
> This basic point was made long ago in Frederick Schauer's classic article, "Slippery Slopes."[28] Schauer showed that any slippery slope argument depends on a prediction that the instant case will in fact increase the likelihood of the danger case. If there is in fact no danger, then the fact that there logically could be has no weight. For instance, the federal taxing power theoretically empowers the government to

tax incomes at 100%, thereby wrecking the economy. But there's no slippery slope, because there is no incentive to do this, so it won't happen.

Similarly with the Broccoli Objection. The fear rests on one real problem: there are lots of private producers, including many in agriculture, who want to use the coercive power of the federal government to transfer funds from your pockets into theirs. But the last thing they want to do is impose duties on individuals, because then the individuals will know that they've been burdened. There are too many other ways to get special favors in a less visible way.[29]

Koppelman makes an interesting point. But I think it ultimately fails for two reasons. First, even if Congress would never actually enact the broccoli mandate, the fact that it could do so under the same logic as the health insurance mandate highlights a logical flaw in the argument made by defenders of the latter. It strains credulity that a constitutional text that gives Congress the power to regulate interstate commerce gives it unlimited authority to force people to buy products they don't want, even within the borders of a single state.

Second, I think that Koppelman is right to point out that slippery slope scenarios must be evaluated based on their actual likelihood of occurring, as opposed to merely the logical possibility. But I think the likelihood of this is much greater than he admits. It's true that subsidies are easier to hide from the voters than purchase mandates. But the latter have their own advantages for politicians and interest groups. For example, in a time of tight budgets, a purchase mandate can transfer money to a favored industry without requiring additional government spending or tax increases. It's very hard for the federal government to directly transfer as much money to an industry as it would get from forcing millions of new customers to buy their products.

Moreover, there is a wide variety of ways that purchase mandates could be sold to the public. Congress needs not admit that they're intending to help powerful interest groups. The mandates could instead be defended as efforts to stimulate the economy by helping a vital industry (the same justification as was used to justify government bailouts of the banks and auto industry). Forcing people to purchase broccoli or other food could be defended as a public health measure. Indeed, paternalists of both the "libertarian" and traditional varieties have successfully advocated numerous coercive regulations on precisely those kinds of grounds. There is no reason why they couldn't use similar strategies to justify purchase mandates. An alliance between well-intentioned paternalists and industry interest groups is precisely the kind of "Baptist-bootlegger"[30] coalition that has often been successful in the past. Given widespread political ignorance,[31] voters will often be hard pressed to tell whether such proposals will really increase public health.

Finally, it's important to emphasize the sheer range of interests that come into play here. The logic of the pro–health care mandate argument can justify virtually any mandate to purchase or do anything. This opens the door to the machinations of an extraordinarily large number of interest groups. It seems very likely that at least a few of them will figure out a way to take advantage of the opportunity. Even if I can't figure out exactly how to do it, interest group leaders and other professional political strategists probably can.

Indeed, at least one industry interest group already *has* managed to do it. After all, the health insurance mandate was included in the health care bill in large part because insurance companies support it[32] and in spite of the fact that President Obama had strongly opposed the idea when Hillary Clinton proposed it during the 2008 presidential campaign.[33] Where the insurance industry leads, others might well follow.

Today's Florida District Court Ruling Striking Down the Obamacare Individual Mandate

Ilya Somin
January 31, 2011

Today's Florida district court ruling[34] that the individual mandate is unconstitutional is by far the best court opinion on this issue so far. Judge Roger Vinson provides a thorough and impressive analysis of the federal government's arguments claiming that the mandate is authorized by the Commerce Clause and the Necessary and Proper Clause and explains the flaws in each. He had already rejected the government's claim that the mandate is constitutional because it is a tax in a previous ruling. So far, all three federal courts that have considered the tax argument have rejected it, instead ruling (in my view, correctly) that the mandate is a penalty.

This is perhaps the most important of all the antimandate lawsuits because the plaintiffs include 26 state governments and the National Federation of Independent Business.

One of the best parts of today's opinion is Judge Vinson's critique of the federal government's argument that the mandate is constitutional under the Commerce Clause because the clause gives it the power to regulate "economic decisions":

> The problem with this legal rationale, however, is it would essentially have unlimited application. There is quite literally no decision that, in the natural course of events, does not have an economic impact of some sort. The decisions of whether and when (or not) to buy a house, a car, a television, a dinner, or even a morning cup of coffee also have a financial impact that—when aggregated with similar economic decisions—affect the price of that particular product or service and have a substantial effect on interstate commerce. To be sure, it is not difficult to identify an economic decision that has a cumulatively substantial effect on interstate commerce; rather, the difficult task is to find a decision that does not.
>
> The important distinction is that "economic decisions" are a much broader and far-reaching category than are "activities that substantially affect interstate commerce" [which Supreme Court precedent allows Congress to regulate]. While the latter necessarily encompasses the first, the reverse is not true. "Economic" cannot be equated to "commerce." And "decisions" cannot be equated to "activities." Every person throughout the course of his or her life makes hundreds or even thousands of life decisions that involve the same general sort of thought process that the defendants maintain is "economic activity." There will be no stopping point if that should be deemed the equivalent of activity for Commerce Clause purposes.[35]

Judge Vinson has a similarly compelling answer to the government's claim that choosing not to purchase health insurance is an "economic activity" because everyone participates in the health care market at some point:

> [T]here are lots of markets—especially if defined broadly enough—that people cannot "opt out" of. For example, everyone must participate in the food market. Instead of attempting to control wheat supply by regulating the acreage and amount of wheat a farmer could grow as in *Wickard*, under this logic, Congress could more directly raise too low wheat prices merely by increasing demand through mandating that every adult purchase and consume wheat bread daily, rationalized on the grounds that because everyone must participate in the market for food, non-consumers of wheat bread adversely affect prices in the wheat market. Or, as was discussed during oral argument, Congress could require that people buy and consume broccoli at regular intervals, not only because the required purchases will positively impact interstate commerce, but also because people who eat healthier tend to be healthier, and are thus more productive and put less of a strain on the health care system. Similarly, because virtually no one can be divorced from the transportation market, Congress could require that everyone above a certain income threshold buy a General Motors automobile—now partially government-owned—because those who do not buy GM cars (or those who buy foreign cars) are adversely impacting commerce and a taxpayer-subsidized business.[36]

As Vinson explains, both the "economic decisions" argument and the "health care is special" argument ultimately amount to giving Congress the power to mandate virtually anything and therefore conflict with the text of the Constitution and Supreme Court precedent. I previously addressed both arguments in more detail.[37] Judge Vinson also notes that the scenarios he raises are not merely a "parade of horribles," but have a realistic basis, a point that I also discussed previously.[38]

Turning to the Necessary and Proper Clause, Judge Vinson concedes that the individual mandate is "necessary" under existing Supreme Court precedent, but argues that it isn't "proper" because the government's logic amounts to giving Congress virtually unlimited power. I think this is exactly right; Vinson's analysis is actually very similar to my own[39] (which is not to even suggest that he got the idea there).

Vinson also notes that the mandate probably runs afoul of the five-part test recently outlined by the Supreme Court in *United States v. Comstock*, though he ultimately does not base his ruling on this point. I've advanced a similar interpretation of *Comstock* and its implications for the mandate case.[40] Overall, Judge Vinson's analysis of the Necessary and Proper Clause is a big improvement on Judge Henry Hudson's performance in the recent Virginia ruling striking down the mandate.

Unlike Judge Henry Hudson in the Virginia case, Judge Vinson ruled that the mandate is not "severable" from the rest of the health care bill and therefore invalidated it in its entirety. I think this may be somewhat too sweeping. However, Vinson is on strong ground in ruling that the mandate cannot be severed from the bill's provisions forcing insurance companies to cover people with preexisting conditions. As he emphasizes, the federal government itself has repeatedly stressed this point in the litigation.

Finally, Judge Vinson rejected the 26 states' argument that the funding provisions of the bill are unconstitutionally "coercive." I may have more to say on this issue in a later post.

As I have often noted in the past, this decision is just another step in an ongoing legal battle. Ultimately, the issue of the individual mandate will be resolved by the courts of appeals and probably by the Supreme Court. Still, Judge Vinson's ruling is a victory for opponents of the mandate. It's also extremely well written and thereby provides a potential road map for appellate judges who might be inclined to rule the same way.

UPDATE: In the following post, coblogger Orin Kerr takes Judge Vinson to task for holding that the mandate is not "proper" because it leads to unlimited federal power. Orin claims that this is inconsistent with the "words" of Supreme Court precedent, citing a dissent by Justice Clarence Thomas in *Gonzales v. Raich*. However, the words of actual Supreme Court precedent repeatedly emphasize that Congress's power is *not* unlimited. For example, in *United States v. Lopez*, the Court emphasized that "[t]he Constitution . . . withhold[s] from Congress a plenary police power that would authorize enactment of every type of legislation."[41] In its most recent Necessary and Proper Clause decision, *United States v. Comstock*, the Court similarly stated that there is no reason to "fear that our holding today confers on Congress a general 'police power, which the Founders denied the National Government and reposed in the States'" (quoting *United States v. Morrison*)[42]; the Court emphasized that the regulation it was upholding was "narrow" in scope. *Gonzales v. Raich* itself gives Congress virtually unlimited power to regulate "economic activity" but does not address the issue raised by the mandate case. Thus, if Judge Vinson is right that the federal government's argument for the mandate would give Congress unlimited power, then the mandate indeed conflicts with the words of Supreme Court precedent.

Orin is also wrong to suggest that Vinson "used a first principle to trump existing Supreme Court case law." Vinson in fact discussed those precedents, including *Raich*, in great detail and noted how the individual mandate case is distinguishable from them—for example, the discussion of *Raich* on pages 1283–85.

As I have argued elsewhere, both *Comstock*[43] and *Raich*[44] give Congress vastly greater authority than is actually authorized by the Constitution. But going way too far down this road is not the same as authorizing completely unlimited congressional power. At the very least, it certainly isn't what the words of the relevant Supreme Court precedents say they have done.

UPDATE 2: In an update to his post, Orin insists that Judge Vinson failed to consider existing precedent, which in Orin's view imposes only "symbolic" limits on congressional power. All I can say is that Vinson in fact discusses current precedent in great detail and explains why it doesn't cover the mandate case. Moreover, nowhere does that precedent state that the remaining limits to federal power are purely symbolic and would not strike down any significant congressional policies. Thus, if Vinson is correct in concluding that the argument for the individual mandate would give Congress unconstrained authority to mandate anything it wants, then the mandate really is contrary to existing precedent. At the very least, existing precedent certainly doesn't require upholding the mandate.

The Weak Link in Judge Vinson's Opinion Striking Down the Mandate

Orin S. Kerr
January 31, 2011

I agree with Ilya that "Judge Vinson's analysis of the Necessary and Proper Clause is a big improvement on Judge Henry Hudson's performance in the recent Virginia ruling striking down the mandate." Judge Hudson's opinion was pretty embarrassing on the Necessary and Proper Clause issue, while Judge Vinson gives the issue much more attention. At the same time, I think Judge Vinson's argument on the Necessary and Proper Clause is not persuasive, and in this post I want to explain why.

To understand Vinson's argument, you need to realize that conservatives and libertarians have been complaining for many decades that Commerce Clause doctrine has left Congress essentially unlimited power. Between *Wickard v. Filburn* and *Gonzales v. Raich*, conservatives and libertarians have complained that the federal government can justify pretty much anything. Remember how Justice Thomas began his dissent in *Raich* (emphasis added):

> Respondents Diane Monson and Angel Raich use marijuana that has never been bought or sold, that has never crossed state lines, and that has had no demonstrable effect on the national market for marijuana. **If Congress can regulate this under the Commerce Clause, then it can regulate virtually anything—and the Federal Government is no longer one of limited and enumerated powers.**[45]

Of course, the holding of *Raich* was that Congress *could* in fact regulate this under the Commerce Clause. Thus, in the view of Justice Thomas, existing Commerce Clause doctrine gave the federal government the power to "regulate virtually anything." According to Justice Thomas, existing Commerce Clause doctrine establishes a "Federal Government [that] is no longer one of limited and enumerated powers."

Now let's return to Judge Vinson's analysis of the Necessary and Proper Clause. The words of the relevant Supreme Court cases point to an extremely broad power, and Judge Vinson is supposed to be bound by those words. But Judge Vinson concludes that these words can't be taken at face value because "to uphold [the mandate] via application of the Necessary and Proper Clause would [be to] . . . effectively remove all limits on federal power."[46] He writes:

> [T]he Commerce Clause limitations on the federal government's power would definitely be compromised by this assertion of federal power via the Necessary and Proper Clause.

The defendants have asserted again and again that the individual mandate is absolutely "necessary" and "essential" for the Act to operate as it was intended by Congress. I accept that it is. Nevertheless, the individual mandate falls outside the boundary of Congress' Commerce Clause authority and cannot be reconciled with a limited government of enumerated powers. By definition, it cannot be "proper."[47]

This might work as a Supreme Court opinion that can disagree with precedent. But Judge Vinson is just a district court judge. And if you pair Justice Thomas's dissent in *Raich* with Judge Vinson's opinion today, you realize the problem: Judge Vinson is reasoning that existing law *must be* a particular way because he thinks it should be that way as a matter of first principles, not because the relevant Supreme Court doctrine actually points that way. Remember that in *Raich*, the fact that the majority opinion gave the federal government the power to "regulate virtually anything" was a reason for Justice Thomas to *dissent*. In Judge Vinson's opinion, however, the fact that the government's theory gave the federal government the power to "regulate virtually anything" was a reason it had to be inconsistent with precedent.

Obviously, I'm not arguing that Judge Vinson was bound by Justice Thomas's dissent. Rather, my point is that Judge Vinson should not have used a first principle to trump existing Supreme Court case law when that principle may not be consistent with existing case law. Either Justice Thomas is wrong or Judge Vinson is wrong, and Judge Vinson was not making a persuasive legal argument when he followed the first principle instead of the cases. Because Judge Vinson is bound by Supreme Court precedent, I would think he should have applied the cases.

Anyway, I realize this argument will only resonate with readers who care about binding precedent, which at times seems like a vanishingly small group of readers. But it does seem to be the weak link in Judge Vinson's opinion for the three of us who are interested in whether the decision is correct under existing law.

UPDATE: My coblogger Ilya Somin defends Judge Vinson by pointing out that the Supreme Court's majority opinions insist that the federal government does not have completely unlimited power. Ilya's argument is unpersuasive because the existence of nonzero limits in no way implies the existence of major limits. The current state of Commerce Clause doctrine is that there are certain largely symbolic limits on federal power but those limits are relatively minor—as Justice Thomas put it, Congress can regulate *virtually* anything. Judge Vinson says that this cannot be the law because it would make the federal government too powerful. But Judge Vinson does not consult existing doctrine before declaring the principle, and that's the problem: If you take existing doctrine seriously, it readily fits the mandate under the Necessary and Proper Clause.

Does Judge Vinson's Opinion Impose a "Major Limit" on Federal Power?

Jonathan H. Adler
February 1, 2011

In an addendum to his previous post, Orin writes "the existence of nonzero limits [on federal power] in no way implies the existence of major limits." Fine. But this does not mean that the limits on federal power that survive *Raich* are only "symbolic" nor does it mean that Judge Vinson is wrong. It is hard to see how a holding that would only prohibit a single federal enactment adopted in the nation's 200-plus-year history constitutes a "major limit" on federal power. The federal government is hardly limited, and yet invalidating the individual mandate would not threaten any other past or present exercise of federal power.

I also think Orin's argument that the individual mandate must be constitutional under existing precedent because dissenting justices argued that such precedents allow the federal government to regulate "virtually anything" is problematic. First, Orin is relying upon the opinions of *dissenting justices*, when the majority opinion in *Raich* maintained that limits on federal power remained. Second, the argument assumes what is at issue: whether the failure to purchase government-approved health insurance is an activity that can be regulated. In other words, one of the questions in the case is whether inactivity is anything at all or the absence of something that can be regulated. I agree with Orin that *Raich* is a problematic precedent, but I am not convinced it controls the outcome of this case.

A Comment on District Court Originalism

Orin S. Kerr
February 1, 2011

My earlier post on Judge Vinson's opinion seems to have caused a lot of confusion, so I thought I would try again to express my concerns with Judge Vinson's opinion a bit more clearly.

The core problem, I think, is that Supreme Court doctrine has strayed far from the original meaning of the scope of federal power granted by the Constitution. Today's constitutional doctrine permits a scope of federal power that is much broader than the original meaning of the Commerce Clause and the Necessary and Proper Clause would allow. When interpreting the scope of federal power, then, you need to decide what you will follow: The original meaning or case precedents. As I read Judge Vinson's opinion, he mixes the two. Judge Vinson jumps back and forth between purporting to apply Supreme Court precedents and purporting to interpret the Commerce Clause and the Necessary and Proper Clause in light of their original meanings. Judge Vinson spends about half of the legal analysis on original meaning and about half of the legal analysis on precedent, and he seems to treat both as important. In the critical passage on the Necessary and Proper Clause, Judge Vinson relies primarily on original meaning, specifically Federalist No. 33.[48]

Thus, for example, Judge Vinson rejects one of the arguments of amici on the ground that the result of the amici's argument "would, of course, expand the Necessary and Proper Clause far beyond its original meaning, and allow Congress to exceed the powers specifically enumerated in Article I. Surely this is not what the Founders anticipated, nor how that Clause should operate."[49] And critically, Judge Vinson writes that the mandate cannot be constitutional because "[i]f Congress is allowed to define the scope of its power merely by arguing that a provision is 'necessary' to avoid the negative consequences that will potentially flow from its own statutory enactments, the Necessary and Proper Clause runs the risk of ceasing to be the 'perfectly harmless' part of the Constitution that Hamilton assured us it was [in Federalist No. 33], and moves that much closer to becoming the 'hideous monster [with] devouring jaws' that he assured us it was not."[50]

If you are an originalist, as many VC readers seem to be, this is a very appealing argument. If you're a libertarian, as many VC readers seem to be, this is also a very appealing argument. But there's a technical problem here that I want to draw out: Judge Vinson is only a district court judge. Under the principle of vertical stare decisis, he is bound by Supreme Court precedent.[51] And when Supreme Court precedent conflicts with original meaning, Judge Vinson is bound to follow the former. Of course, that doesn't mean a district court judge can't discuss the original meaning of a constitutional provision in his opinion. But where the original meaning and case precedents conflict, the judge is stuck: Because he is bound by Supreme Court doctrine, the judge has to apply the doctrine established by the Supreme Court and has to ignore the original meaning.

If you're going to take that view, I think you have to confront the doctrinal test that the U.S. Supreme Court offered in a majority opinion just a few months ago in *United States v. Comstock*:

> [I]n determining whether the Necessary and Proper Clause grants Congress the legislative authority to enact a particular federal statute, we look to see whether the statute constitutes a means that is rationally related to the implementation of a constitutionally enumerated power.[52]

It seems to me that when the Supreme Court says that this is what "we look to see" when determining if a power falls within the Constitution, then that is a doctrinal test to which a trial judge is bound under the principle of stare decisis. That's especially true when a Justice Anthony Kennedy wrote a concurring opinion in *Comstock* treating it as a doctrinal test, and no one corrected him. At the very least, this is language worth mentioning to explain why it's *not* a test you think you're bound to as a trial judge. But Judge Vinson doesn't even mention this language. Instead, he focuses on Alexander Hamilton and Federalist No. 33. Given the gap between the original meaning of the scope of federal power and the case precedents, I don't think this approach is persuasive for a district court judge to take.

Was the Fifth Circuit Wrong in *Lopez*?

Jonathan H. Adler
February 6, 2011

In 1992, Alfonso Lopez Jr. brought a gun to Edison High School in San Antonio, Texas. He had been offered $40 to deliver the gun to a local gang member. Though originally charged under state law, the local charges were dropped when the Feds decided to prosecute him for violating the Gun-Free School Zones Act of 1990 (GFSZA). He was convicted and sentenced to six months in federal prison.

On appeal before the U.S. Court of Appeals for the Fifth Circuit, Lopez successfully argued that the GFSZA exceeded the scope of federal power. Specifically, Lopez argued, and the Fifth Circuit agreed, that this law could not be justified as a permissible exercise of Congress's power to "regulate commerce . . . among the several states." "The United States Constitution establishes a national government of limited and enumerated powers," the opinion began, followed by references to James Madison, *The Federalist Papers*, and the Tenth Amendment.

The Fifth Circuit's opinion was something of a surprise. The Supreme Court had not rejected a federal law for exceeding the scope of the Commerce Clause in over fifty years, and it was generally assumed (particularly among legal academics) that Congress could do anything it wanted in the name or regulating commerce, so long as it did not intrude upon the Bill of Rights. As Bruce Ackerman explained in volume 1 of *We the People*, after the New Deal revolution, "[a] commitment to federalism . . . was no longer thought to require a constitutional strategy that restrained the national government to a limited number of enumerated powers over economic and social life."[53] As a narrow majority of the Supreme Court had explained in *Garcia v. San Antonio Metropolitan Transit Authority*, the remaining safeguards on federal power were "political," not judicial. As a consequence, federal judicial opinions invalidating federal statutes for exceeding the scope of federal power were few and far between.

The Fifth Circuit recognized the tide of elite opinion supported the federal government's case, but it also noted that the constitutionality of the GFSZA was "a question of first impression in the federal courts." Although the Supreme Court had okayed ever-increasing assertions of federal power, Judge William Garwood's opinion repaired to the "fundamental postulate of our constitutional order" that federal power is limited. However broad the laws upheld in *Jones & Laughlin Steel*, *Darby*, *Wickard*, *Heart of Atlanta Motel v. United States*, *Hodel v. Virginia Surface Mining*, and *Perez v. United States* (to name but a few), federal power could not be infinite. And so the Fifth Circuit struck the GFSZA down.

The Fifth Circuit's opinion was subsequently vindicated by the Supreme Court in *United States v. Lopez*, but the appellate panel had no basis for predicting such an outcome at the time. As noted previously, it had been over half a century since the Court had felled a federal law on Commerce Clause grounds. Does this mean the Fifth Circuit was wrong when it decide *Lopez*? Or is it acceptable for lower courts to continue to observe the foundational principles of our constitutional order when considering cases of first impression, even when doing so requires swimming against the prevailing current of case law and academic opinion? Or does it all depend on how the Supreme Court ultimately rules?

Predicting How the Mandate Might Fare at the Supreme Court: Explaining Chief Justice Roberts's Vote—and Opinion Assignment—in *United States v. Comstock*

Orin S. Kerr
February 18, 2011

Legal debates over the constitutionality of the individual mandate generally focus on three different questions: (1) As a matter of constitutional theory, how should a court rule based on a normative theory of interpretation? (2) As a matter of existing doctrine, how does the mandate fit (or not fit) into existing law? (3) As a prediction, if the case reaches the Supreme Court, how might the justices rule? I have a question about (3) for those who think the Supreme Court will or very well might strike down the mandate: how do you explain Chief Justice John Roberts's vote and assignment in *Comstock*?

Let's recall a little recent history. At the same time that the individual mandate was being enacted in Congress, the Supreme Court heard a very significant case on the Necessary and Proper Clause, *United States v. Comstock*. The two overlapped: The Senate passed the individual mandate legislation on December 24, 2009, and oral argument in the *Comstock* case was a little more than two weeks later, on January 12, 2010. At oral argument, the United States made what I called at the time a "shockingly broad" argument in favor of nearly limitless federal power. The House passed the mandate legislation March 21, and President Obama signed it into law on March 23. Seven weeks later, on May 17, the Supreme Court handed down its opinion in *Comstock*. The set of opinions in *Comstock* began with a five-justice majority opinion by Justice Stephen Breyer—joined by Stevens, Ginsburg, Sotomayor, and Chief Justice Roberts—that largely reflected the tremendously broad rationale offered by the United States at oral argument. It then added concurring opinions by Justices Kennedy and Samuel Alito agreeing as to the result in that case but offering narrower rationales, followed by a dissent from Justice Thomas joined by Justice Scalia.

Now let's imagine what likely happened inside the Court during this time. The justices would have met shortly after argument in *Comstock* to take a tentative vote. Given the 7–2 outcome, with Roberts in the majority, it seems extremely likely that Roberts voted with the majority at conference and assigned the opinion to Justice Breyer. That would have been in mid-to-late January. It probably took Justice Breyer around two or more months to send around a draft majority opinion, so that would have been circulated shortly after Obamacare was enacted into law. The justices were surely aware of the health care law that Congress had just enacted. And yet, soon after, Chief Justice Roberts became the fifth vote for the majority opinion in *Comstock* that takes an extremely broad view of federal power. Notably, without Roberts's vote, the controlling opinion would have shifted to a narrower rationale like Kennedy's. But by joining the Breyer opinion, Roberts ensured that the opinion by Breyer—who dissented in *Lopez*, and who seems to believe in no limits on federal power at all—would become the law.

So here are my questions for those who think Roberts will vote to strike down the mandate: If Roberts will vote to strike down the mandate, why did he assign the *Comstock* opinion to Breyer (rather than Alito or Kennedy, as I predicted at the time)? And why did Roberts sign on to the extremely broad Breyer opinion to make that opinion the law shortly after Obamacare was passed?

Anyway, obviously this is a reading-the-tea-leaves, inside-baseball sort of post, but I suppose that's what happens when you're trying to predict how the Supreme Court might rule in a case.

Why the Obamacare Mandate Penalty Can't Be a Tax

David B. Kopel
Orange County Register, March 4, 2011

Within a year or two, the Supreme Court probably will decide whether the new federal mandate to purchase a particular type of health insurance is authorized by Congress's constitutional power to "regulate Commerce . . . among the several States." If the Obama administration cannot convince the court that the Commerce Clause allows Congress to force people to engage in commerce, the administration has a backup argument: The mandate is separately authorized by Congress's constitutional power to tax.

If this argument succeeds, the constitutional system of a federal government of limited, enumerated powers will, for all practical purposes, come to an end.

The Constitution grants Congress the "Power To lay and collect Taxes, Duties, Imposts and Excises." Pursuant to the Affordable Care Act, the penalty for not buying a congressionally designed health insurance policy will be collected by the Internal Revenue Service.

The Obama tax theory, in effect, would give Congress the power to make laws on any subject, impose a fine for noncompliance, have the IRS collect the fine, and then claim that the entire regulatory structure is part of the tax power. The result would nullify Article I of the Constitution, which carefully grants Congress 18 specific powers—and does not grant a general power to legislate on everything.

All three federal judges who have ruled on the Obamacare tax argument, even the one who upheld the Obama administration on the Commerce Clause issue, have rejected it.

The most obvious reason why these judges are correct is that the Affordable Care Act itself calls the penalty a "penalty" and not a "tax."

President Barack Obama, for his part, told CNN in September 2009 that the penalty is "absolutely not a tax."

It's true that the penalty is placed in the Internal Revenue Code, in a subtitle with the heading "Miscellaneous Excise Taxes." But the code itself declares that the headings have no legal significance, and no inferences can be drawn from them.

A leading Obamacare defender, Yale professor Jack Balkin, cites a 1937 case, *U.S. v. Sonzinsky*, where the Supreme Court upheld a $200 tax on the transfer of machine guns. Although the tax was meant to discourage machine guns rather than to raise revenue, the court said the judges should not engage in "[i]nquiry into the hidden motives" behind a tax.

Yet two judges agreed that *Sonzinsky* actually seals the case against the penalty: *Sonzinsky* also means that when Congress says that something is a "penalty" and is not a "tax," then courts should not speculate that Congress meant something else.

Could Congress rescue the law by amending it so that the word "penalty" was replaced with "tax"? Probably not, because the new "tax" would not be the type that Congress has the constitutional power to impose.

The Sixteenth Amendment grants Congress the power to "collect taxes on incomes, from whatever source derived." The Supreme Court has defined "derived" income to mean "undeniable accessions to wealth." Here, the mere refusal to purchase a product is not any kind of "income" or accession of wealth.

Likewise, the penalty cannot be an excise tax. An excise tax is imposed on an event or item, such as the acquisition of a machine gun. Again, there is no event to be taxed, and never in American history has a federal excise tax been imposed on an American's inactivity.

Thus, the tax is constitutionally a "direct tax"—similar to a head tax or a tax on real estate. The Constitution requires that such taxes be imposed "in Proportion to the Census." The mandate penalty is not so apportioned.

Congress does have nearly limitless authority to create income tax deductions and could have created one for the cost of buying approved insurance. Courts, however, will not be ruling on the constitutional bill that Congress might have enacted but, rather, on the unconstitutional one that Congress did enact.

Fourth Circuit Judges Baffled by the Proposed Activity-Inactivity Distinction

Orin S. Kerr
May 10, 2011

The challenge to the constitutionality of the individual mandate is based heavily on a proposed distinction—one that I believe was first articulated two years ago by our own Randy Barnett—that Congress can regulate "activity" but not "inactivity." I've expressed my own puzzlement as to what this distinction is supposed to mean. When Randy and I debated the constitutionality of the mandate in January, however, Randy poked fun at my puzzlement on the ground that "only a law professor" could fail to understand such a commonsense idea. Based on today's first appellate argument on the constitutionality of the mandate, it looks like appellate judges may have the same problem. Lyle Denniston reports,

> One thing about the fate of the new health care law emerged vividly in its first challenge Tuesday in a federal appeals court: the challengers cannot defeat the law in court unless they sharpen their argument that Congress has set out in a revolution-

ary new direction to control Americans' personal lives. They have built their challenge almost entirely on the premise that Congress can regulate "activity," but cannot regulate "inactivity." But that attempted distinction, so clear in the eye of the challengers, seemed fundamentally baffling—and thus probably unconvincing—to the three judges who heard just over two hours of argument in the Fourth Circuit Court in Richmond.

Circuit Judge Andre M. Davis wondered if "a mental process" is "activity," obviously implying that a person's specific choice not to buy insurance might be something Congress could regulate, even if "activity" were a necessary predicate. And, Davis asked, "You talked about 'inactivity.' Where in the cases do you find that?"[54]

Baffled That Anyone Is Baffled by the Activity-Inactivity Distinction

Jonathan H. Adler
May 11, 2011

The Fourth Circuit panel may have been baffled by the activity-inactivity distinction, as Orin reports, but it's really not a new idea. The distinction between activity and inactivity is not an alien concept to the law. We see this distinction where the law recognizes the difference between acts of commission and acts of omission, for instance, or where there are legal (or even constitutional) distinctions made between prohibitions or limitations on conduct, on the one hand, and mandated conduct, on the other. Furthermore, if one accepts a classical liberal conception of individual liberty, the former are a qualitatively lesser infringement upon liberty than the latter. This does not, by itself, establish that the activity-inactivity distinction should be recognized as a limitation on federal power under the Interstate Commerce and Necessary and Proper Clauses. Nor does it suggest that it is always easy to draw the line separating activity from inactivity, as there may be closes cases here (as elsewhere). It does, however, suggest that there should be a bit less bafflement about the underlying concept.

An obvious example where the law has long recognized a distinction between activity and inactivity is the duty to rescue. Under the common law, simple inactivity—a failure to rescue, by itself—can never be a source of liability. Rather, the duty to rescue only arises when one engages in certain activities—that is, when one takes certain affirmative steps, such as by creating an ultrahazardous situation entering a certain type of relationship with the individual in need of rescue becoming a common carrier, or taking initial steps toward rescue. And only after certain activities are engaged in can there be liability. Whether certain activities are, or should be, the source of a duty breach of which could result in liability has prompted significant debate, but the fact that the common law required activity of some sort before a duty could arise is clear. In other words, under the common law, activity could create the duty but inactivity could not.

We can also see analogous distinctions made in some areas of constitutional law. Under current First Amendment doctrine, for example, the government's ability to compel speech is greater once a speaker engages in a relevant activity than when a would-be speaker has done or said nothing. So for instance, the government can mandate that those engaged in dangerous activities post warnings or that potentially misleading speech be cured by disclaimers. But the government lacks any general ability to simply mandate speech across the board. Again, the law recognizes that engaging in certain sorts of activity may result in legal obligations where simple inactivity, doing nothing, does not.

One way to think about the activity-inactivity distinction is to recognize the difference between prohibiting conduct or imposing conditions on conduct, on the one hand, and mandating conduct on the other. We see this distinction in the Supreme Court's current federalism jurisprudence. The federal government may prohibit (preempt) states from engaging in certain activities under the Supremacy Clause. It may also subject states to generally applicable regulations if states engage in those activities that would make them subject to such rules, for example if states become market participants, employers, property managers, and so on. The federal government may not, however, simply commandeer states to engage in activities because that is what the federal government wants. That is, once states engage in certain activities, the federal government may be able to regulate how those activities are conducted, but it may not mandate that states engage in certain activities in the first place. Even under the Fourteenth Amendment, we see plenty of areas in which Congress may require states to administer state-run programs in a particular way, so as to ensure equal protection or prevent the infringement of fundamental liberties, but few if any in which "inactive" states are mandated to do something in the first place.

As noted previously, the idea that there is a fundamental difference between a prohibition or conditional regulation, on the one hand, and a mandate, on the other, follows from a classical liberal conception of individual liberty. From this perspective, a naked mandate—a requirement that one engage in an activity—is a greater imposition than a prohibition or a conditional regulation. Why? Think of it this way. At any given moment, a free individual can engage in a near-infinite set of activities (n). A government prohibition reduces this set by one (to $n - 1$). A conditional regulation has a similar effect, in that it imposes a burden on one activity, but it does not otherwise reduce the set of options. A mandate, on the other hand, requires that at a given moment the mandated individual engage in the required activity, to the exclusion of all else. If a person were mandated to wash his car, that time cannot be spent doing other things. The loss of opportunities is near infinite—indeed, it is $n - 1$—insofar as the mandate precludes the individual from doing other things simultaneously. Therefore, a simple prohibition or conditional regulation is a rather minor limitation on individual liberty, whereas a mandate is not.

The same logic applies to economic mandates. A free person can spend a dollar on a nearly infinite set of things. A prohibition on the purchase of a good or service reduces the set by one. You may not be able to buy X, but you still have a near-infinite set of options for how to use the dollar. A conditional regulation—if you buy X, you must also buy Y or may only buy X if it meets certain conditions—still does not impose a categorically greater imposition. You still have a near-infinite set of alternative uses for that dollar. When the government mandates that you purchase something, be it health care, a fitness club membership, broccoli, or whatever, you lose the ability to spend that dollar on anything else. Your set of options for that dollar has been completely extinguished, and the set of opportunities has been definitively reduced. This does not mean that mandates are necessarily unconstitutional, only that they are qualitatively different in a way that helps us understand the distinction between regulating activity and mandating activity (which is just another way of saying "regulating inactivity").[55]

To be clear, my argument in this post is not that an activity-inactivity distinction is self-evidently imposed by the Constitution (though I believe such a distinction is consistent with current precedent and ought to be adopted) or that the individual mandate should be held to be unconstitutional (though I believe that as well). My point here is simply that the activity-inactivity distinction is not some alien invention of libertarian academics and not qualitatively different from distinctions we see in the law and our legal tradition. Whether this means the distinction should be incorporated into (or made explicit within) existing enumerated powers doctrine is a separate question for another time.

Not So Baffled about the Activity-Inactivity Distinction

Randy E. Barnett
May 11, 2011

As one of the lawyers now representing the National Federation of Independent Business in the Eleventh Circuit, I was at yesterday's oral arguments in Richmond. I had a somewhat different take on the discussion of the activity-inactivity distinction. Lyle Dennison's account of the opening minutes is generally accurate, but there are two important qualifications. One that comes through a bit in his report is the panel's frustration that counsel for Liberty University was not directly answering its questions about the activity-inactivity distinction. So they kept reformulating their questions and prolonging the discussion, which led to the appearance, if not reality, of increasing "bafflement." Still, there is no question that, during this exchange, the panel conveyed a tone of skepticism about the utility of the distinction.

The initial argument in the *Liberty University* case ran almost double the allotted time. By the time Acting Solicitor General Neal Katyal got up to argue the Virginia case, Presiding Judge Dianna Motz invited him to focus on the standing issue. Near the end of his presentation, however, something very interesting occurred. I wish I had the transcript, but I have transcribed a portion of this exchange from the recording on the Fourth Circuit's website.

Judge Motz said she had a question to ask on the merits: Did not the term "regulate" in the Commerce Clause presuppose (or was predicated upon) some activity to be regulated? Here is what I have taken from the recording:

> My problem with that is, and I hear all that, but if you do not have activity, and for purposes now—instead of going back and telling me the sixteen reasons why you think this is an activity—just bear with me that this is not an activity, what do we do with the

word "regulation"? Because, you know, that—although it has not been pressed with any great concern here—in the research that we've done and apparently has now been done in other cases that you're going to face so you're going to have to deal with the question, that has always assumed that there's a *predicate* that's going to be regulated, an activity, if you will, and the regulation is right—the power that Congress has is "to regulate," and that's right *in* the Constitution. That is a constitutional provision. The "activity" isn't to be sure, but "regulation" would seem to think by John Marshall and others to imply a predicate to be regulated. If you don't have this activity predicate, what do you do?

To this Acting Solicitor General Katyal said he did not have an immediate response as it was not in the multiple briefs filed in this case, and that he "would want to have a lot more time to think about it." She then pressed him by saying "but it was in the Florida briefs"—to which I assume she was referring to the briefs in the Eleventh Circuit that had been filed about a week prior (interesting that she had read them)—and that "maybe you can think a little more about that regulation question" and address it in his rebuttal. Now this struck me at the time as an amazing moment. After receiving a polite "I don't know" answer from the Solicitor General, Judge Motz basically instructed him to sit down and think about it and come up with an answer.

In his rebuttal, Katyal said, even if you do think that Congress is regulating inactivity, with which he disagreed, *Raich* "went so far as to say that Congress can regulate even almost the textual opposite of what's in the text of the Constitution: commerce in a single state as opposed to among states, that is Congress is permitted to regulate intrastate activity so long as"—at which point, Judge Motz interrupted with "but it's the activity, see, that is still tied there. . . . and in our hypothetical situation, that I know you don't agree with what we are talking about here, is can you regulate something that is not an activity?"

Katyal's basic response to this was what matters is the effect on commerce, and the activity-inactivity distinction has never been the touchstone, and that under the Necessary and Proper Clause, Congress can fill in the gaps of a regulatory scheme to eliminate barriers. After some additional back and forth about child support orders that seem to require activity, Judge Motz said, "We know, as I understand it, we wouldn't have a Commerce Clause argument if Congress had straight-forwardly set up universal health care and required everybody to buy, right?" To which Katyal said "sure." Judge Motz then replied, "They didn't want to do that though. That wasn't, apparently—well in any event, for whatever reason, they didn't do that, so we don't have that situation. We have instead this, what we have." After Katyal replied that there may have been any number of policy reasons for this choice, which are beyond the purview of the courts, and that the Supreme Court says the test for this court is to evaluate whether Congress had a rational means, as long as Congress's means are rationally adapted to the ends, citing *McCullough* and *Comstock*. To this she replied: But "for the past fifty years they have attached to that, to the regulation [unintelligible] activity, and that is what we arguably don't have here . . . and which distinguishes this case from all those cases." In response, Katyal again voiced his disagreement that there was no activity here and asserted the Necessary and Proper Clause.

This whole exchange was very interesting and it was the point where Katyal clearly had the most difficulty. I thought it was highly significant that Judge Motz returned to this question at the end of several hours of argument that had moved far away from the merits, indicating that this was sincerely troubling her. Now I am NOT asserting that Judge Motz is going to vote to strike down the individual mandate as unconstitutional, though it is worth remembering that she was the judge who wrote the court of appeals opinion in *Comstock* holding that the sexual predator's law exceeded the power of Congress under the Necessary and Proper Clause, which was then reversed by the Supreme Court. Perhaps she was merely seeking help in writing an opinion to uphold the mandate. But she was quite clearly and genuinely *bothered*—not baffled—by the lack of activity.

Is the Proposed Activity-Inactivity Distinction Just the Common Law "Actus Reus" Requirement?

Orin S. Kerr
May 12, 2011

My coblogger Jonathan Adler is right, in a sense, that efforts to draw a doctrinal distinction based on the requirement of an "act" are not new in American law. But I think that's precisely the problem with the proposed activity-inactivity distinction in the mandate setting: American law has traditionally struggled with doctrines premised on act requirements, which generally end up being conceptually quite complicated. That doesn't mean that introducing such a distinction is wrong. But it does mean that proponents of the proposed distinction at least need to articulate what version of the distinction they want to draw if they expect appellate courts to adopt it.

First, some background. Law students first encounter act requirements when they study the "guilty act" requirement of common law criminal liability (in Latin, *actus reus*). For most law students, this subject arises near the beginning of their first semester. Students are told that there is an "act" requirement. But then they are forced to struggle with what the "act" means. Much to students' surprise, it turns out that the requirement of an "act" can be satisfied by a failure to act—an "omission"—at least in some circumstances. Specifically, the "omission" can lead to liability if there is a "duty," but when a duty exists is rather complicated. Plus some actions don't satisfy the requirement of an "act" because they must be "voluntary," with the catch that what counts as a "voluntary" act is actually rather unclear. Consider a person who commits a criminal act while sleepwalking. The person has "acted" in a common sense view, but have they committed an "act" for purposes of the "act" requirement? (Answer: No.) The discussion eventually veers into the philosophical, aided by the reality that no cases exist to answer how the distinction applies to a lot of the obvious hypotheticals. And for most students, that's just in the first few weeks of law school.

The important lesson for first-year law students is that distinctions such as "acts" and "omissions" that might seem clear at first blush can actually be very complicated. The proposed line can mean lots of different things, and students have to spend some time working through the possible meanings and grappling with the implications. Students that get the complications and ambiguities get an A. Students who continue to believe that there is a simple distinction—based, you know, on what seems to be an act—do not.

I think Jonathan's discussion of the common law act requirement highlights some of the difficulties.

The problem with Jonathan's "failure to rescue" example,[56] I believe, is that Jonathan is mixing up two different common law concepts: acts/omissions, on one hand, and legal duties, on the other. It's true that the law does not ordinarily impose liability for failure to rescue. But—at least from a criminal law perspective—that's because there is no duty to rescue, not because the law does not impose liability for inaction.

I think Jonathan recasts the common law doctrine of duties into a common law doctrine of acts and omissions by treating the creation of a duty as itself an act—he suggests that a person must "take certain affirmative steps" and enter into a relationship that creates a duty. But the common law doesn't require "certain affirmative steps" for the creation of a legal duty. A legal duty exists in seven different situations: (1) when a statute imposes a duty (such as a statute prohibiting leaving the scene of an accident), (2) when a special relationship exists (such as parents vis-à-vis their children), (3) when there is a contractual duty (such as a lifeguard who has agreed to watch the beach), (4) when a person voluntarily assumes care, (5) when the person has created the danger, (6) when the person has an affirmative duty to control others (such as an employer who has a duty to stop an employee from committing crimes), and (7) when a landowner invites people on to his property. Some of those ways generally will require the taking of affirmative steps (3, 4, 5, 7), while others generally will not (1, 2, 6). Either way, Jonathan's hypothetical is about when a legal duty exists, not about the distinction between acts and omissions.

Further, if the activity-inactivity distinction is simply about the common law voluntary act requirement, as Jonathan suggests, then I would think that the decision not to buy health insurance is an act that satisfies the common law standard. Under the common law standard, the decision not to deviate from a preset course of action over which a person has control can lead to liability. A common hypothetical in first-year criminal law classes is the driver who is driving down the highway with the cruise control on when he sees a little old lady slowly walking across the street. The driver realizes that if he does nothing, his car will hit and kill the little old lady. However, if he takes the car off cruise control and slows down, or if he comes to a stop, or if he turns the steering wheel a bit, his car will miss the little old lady and she will live. The driver decides he wants the old lady to die, so he does nothing and she is killed. The driver can't then avoid criminal liability on the ground that he never acted. In this setting, the law treats the failure to act as an "act" for purposes of the *actus reus* requirement. The decision not to act and stop the harmful event that the person has the capability to stop satisfies the act requirement.[57]

None of this means that there are no ways to draw a distinction between activity and inactivity. Obviously there are. The problem is that there are lots of *different* ways to draw the distinction. And it's genuinely hard to know what the distinction means unless its advocates tell us what line they are proposing.

From a purely strategic perspective, I suppose I can understand why proponents of the distinction have tried to avoid explaining it. If you have to explain it, you quickly expose the same conceptual problems that first-year law students encounter when they grapple with the common law "act" requirement. You either end up saying that the distinction is a formal requirement that is easily circumvented (e.g., the act requires physical motion) or else that it is some fairly minimal requirement (as with the common law act requirement in criminal law) or else that it is sort of substantive requirement that relies on some fairly complicated philosophical concepts that judges aren't likely to be very eager to adopt as constitutional law (e.g., the act must be such that it substantially interferes with the power of the state to impose an overly burdensome regulatory regime). None of these options are very appealing for proponents of the distinction. If you want to make the distinction seem intuitive—and thus something judges are more likely to adopt—it's preferable to rely on our vague sense that the line must be easy and to avoid acknowledging the difficult choices.

If the recent oral arguments are a sign, avoidance may work with some judges. That's especially true on the district court. But as the mandate moves up the ladder to the appellate courts, I think judges see the difficulty pretty easily. They naturally want some explanation of what version of the distinction proponents have in mind. Given that, I think it would be sensible for mandate proponents to be a lot more specific as to what version of the distinction they want the courts to adopt.

Hard Cases Make Bad Law: Activity-Inactivity Edition

Jonathan H. Adler
May 12, 2011

I appreciate Orin's thoughtful post responding to my post on the activity-inactivity distinction. I think it helps make my point that the basic distinction between activity and inactivity is readily understandable. What Orin points out, however, is that the precise contours of this distinction are a bit fuzzy and may be difficult to apply in some contexts. That is certainly true, but this is true of just about every important legal concept—a point, Orin notes, that we law professors dutifully seek to impress upon our students. But to say that a distinction is "complicated" or somewhat fuzzy is not to say that it is meaningless, unworkable, or inapplicable. It is merely to recognize that there are tough cases. I readily concede that point, but I also don't think it does much work in the context of this debate.

Throughout the law there are concepts that we understand and apply while recognizing the existence of residual ambiguity and definition problems. Under the First Amendment, for example, we know that some things are speech and others are not, but the precise line of demarcation is not always clear. Fortunately, most such distinctions, most of the time, are easy to apply—we know the difference between day and night even if twilight blurs the line of demarcation—and First Amendment law proceeds along quite well even though some residual ambiguity around the edges about what constitutes speech remains.

Returning to the examples of common law duties, all of the examples Orin gives in his posts, with the possible exception of the first (statutory impositions), are examples of positive duties that arise as a consequence of an individual's affirmative act. Indeed, this was the general nature of affirmative duties (as opposed to negative duties) at the common law. So, for instance, when one enters a relationship, duties attach as a consequence of that action that would not attach otherwise. Again, there are tough cases (e.g., some familial duties), but the basic concept is readily understandable. At common law, as a general rule, affirmative duties could only arise as a consequence of an affirmative act. Mere presence in the world was not enough. Again (and I repeat myself), there are tough cases and fuzzy lines, but the basic distinction is readily understandable if not perfectly definable.

Orin's suggestion that the mandate would satisfy an activity requirement of the sort we see in the common law rests on a clever sleight of hand. As Orin notes, "Under the common law standard, the decision not to deviate from a preset course of action over which a person has control can lead to liability." Exactly. The decision to engage in a particular course of conduct—the decision to act—leads to the creation of a duty not to cause harm as a consequence of said conduct. Any liability is a consequence of the duty that arises from the initial action. That is not the case with the mandate, as Congress is asserting the authority to require every person within the country to purchase a qualifying health care plan. This obligation is not contingent upon anyone having taken any action. It is an obligation that exists as a consequence of one's presence in the country. That Congress exercised some restraint by exempting some people is beside the point, just as it did not help that the Gun-Free School Zones Act only prohibited guns in or near schools.

This all leads to the question, which my prior post did not address, of how an activity-inactivity distinction would work in this context. My short answer is that an activity subject to federal regulation must be an affirmative act that, as a general matter, one may choose whether to undertake. In short, the federal government could impose an otherwise constitutionally permissible affirmative obligation contingent upon an individual taking an affirmative act. It would be a line much like that which we see in the case of affirmative duties under the common law and similar to that which we see in other federalism contexts.[58] Does this create a perfectly clear, bright line? Of course not. (What test in constitutional law does?) It does, however, create a distinction that fits well with similar distinctions we see elsewhere in the law.

Orin could no doubt respond with all sorts of examples in which this line could be difficult to apply. Tough cases there are and always will be, but the mandate, as written, would not be among them, nor would many (if any) other federal laws, save the child pornography example. Indeed, when the Supreme Court decided *United States v. Lopez*, the number of federal statutes called into question by the

Court's holding was far greater than the number potentially threatened by a decision striking down the mandate.

That Congress might be able to circumvent the line by replacing the mandate with some sort of broad conditional requirement does not defeat the argument for drawing the line in the first place. Again, when the Supreme Court decided *Lopez* there was some question whether Congress could reenact an equivalent ban on guns in or near schools by adding formal findings or a jurisdictional requirement, but that did not dissuade the Court from striking down the statute and embracing a previously unarticulated limitation on the scope of the commerce power. All that mandate opponents are really seeking is that the Court do the same thing here. Whether this argument will satisfy Justice Kennedy is something we'll just have to see.

The Activity-Inactivity Distinction Still Lives!

Randy E. Barnett
May 12, 2011

In light of Orin's post this morning I have four additional observations to add to my post of yesterday.

First, Acting Solicitor General Katyal did not question the meaningfulness of the activity-inactivity distinction. Instead, he argued that the statute regulated activity. That is a different claim than Orin has been making. In none of its briefs to date has the government adopted Orin's approach. Perhaps it should, and one day it will, but to date it has not engaged in the activity of making that particular argument. In my view, it would be a serious tactical mistake to do so; one which it has not made and I do not expect it to.

Second, by Orin's reckoning, Judge Motz must have not have been an "A" law student. Or more precisely, when she was (allegedly) "baffled" about the activity-inactivity distinction during the opening minutes of the oral argument, she was an "A" student, but later when she employed the activity-inactivity distinction repeatedly, she had digressed to being a "B" student or worse.

Third, cases involving "vicarious responsibility" are fascinating, which is why years ago I decided to teach the course on agency. But agency law requires a "principal" to enter into a specifically defined "consensual" relationship with an "agent" before holding the principal legally responsible for the acts of another. This reflects an exceedingly basic principle of private law—lest we could haul into court anyone with an ability to pay and sue them to compensate us for our losses. Any such defendant would be able to demur "why me?" and the complaint will be dismissed unless the plaintiff can make out a good "cause of action" for why this particular individual is vicariously responsible for the injuries for which compensation is being sought. But the act-omission distinction in criminal law and torts is challenging enough without moving our discussion into yet another doctrinal area.

Finally, given all Orin said about complexifying the act-omission distinction to first-year law students, it is a wonder that the law still accepts the distinction rather than repudiates it! Yet it does. Like much of the Socratic Method, the law professor's first year critique of the "act-omission" distinction exploits two conflicting intuitions held by ordinary people, which first-year law students still are when we get our hands on them. The first is the intuitive distinction between performing an action and not doing anything coupled with the further intuition that we should be held legally responsible for our voluntary acts and not for simply being alive. The second is the fact that a failure to act can sometimes result in the same consequences or effects as acting does. So if the law is aimed at avoiding these consequences or effects, then we should at least sometimes be held liable for our inaction. In short, the law professor confronts the moral intuitions of his or her students with a consequentialist critique. This conflict can then be heightened in class by pressing the fact that the law does—on relatively rare occasions—impose a "duty to act" on persons who are not acting and thereby hold them responsible for their inaction. But, and this is important, this consequentialist critique does not undermine *the meaningfulness of the act-omission distinction itself*, but instead it challenges the intuition that legal liability ought to turn on this distinction. Yet the legal distinction between acts and omissions lives on. As I once said when debating Orin, one would quite literally have to be deranged not to recognize the difference between acting and failing to act. While we may drive a very few law students mad, I believe that even most "A" students survive their exposure to first-year law professors with their basic intuitions largely intact. Some of them later go on to become judges.

The Need for Clarity of the Proposed Activity-Inactivity Distinction

Orin S. Kerr
May 12, 2011

In their posts, both Jonathan Adler and Randy Barnett suggest that it's OK for the proposed activity-inactivity distinction to be unclear because the *actus reus* distinction has been unclear for a long time and the world hasn't ended. I think this response fails to recognize an important difference between legal doctrines that rarely arise (and therefore can remain uncertain) and those that arise often (and therefore have more of a need to be clear). In this post, I wanted to explain the difference and why I think it matters.

Let's start with the *actus reus* requirement of criminal law. The exact contours of the act requirement are fuzzy because they almost never actually come up in real life. We know that the act requirement is minimal, and it's extremely rare for legislatures to enact a criminal law that doesn't obviously satisfy the act requirement. Plus courts construe criminal laws to impose an act requirement by statute even if it's not clear on the face of the statute. As a result, there are only a handful of cases that casebook authors can use, and they're mostly pretty terrible at describing the issue. To teach the material, law professors have to come up with all sorts of creative hypotheticals that just don't often come up in real criminal prosecutions: people who commit crimes while sleepwalking, under hypnosis, and the like. Such scenarios may make for good (or bad) movies, but they aren't the subject of real-world prosecutions and therefore aren't found in judicial decisions. Put bluntly, the ambiguities remain because the subject is more of theoretical than real-world significance. Most prosecutors, defense attorneys, and criminal trial judges go their entire careers without encountering a "voluntary act" problem.

In contrast, when the Supreme Court announces a limitation on the scope of federal power, it tends to come up again—and often quite quickly. The very sad reality is that Congress has little or no interest in federalism. The House and Senate love expanding the scope of federal law. And it's not just one party to blame, either. Neither party has a serious interest in federalism, as each side is quick to pass federal legislation that is really about state law concerns if the politics suit them.[59] As a result, if the Supreme Court adopts the activity-inactivity distinction, it seems likely that future Congresses will use whatever hook the Supreme Court says is required—and *not one iota more*—to make sure their laws pass judicial muster.

We saw this with Congress's reaction to *United States v. Lopez*, the 1995 decision striking down the Gun-Free School Zones Act. At the time, the law made it a crime "for any individual knowingly to possess a firearm at a place that the individual knows, or has reasonable cause to believe, is a school zone." After the Supreme Court struck down the statute, Congress simply reenacted it a few months later with a new interstate commerce hook. The current form of the statute makes it a crime "for any individual knowingly to possess a firearm *that has moved in or that otherwise affects interstate or foreign commerce* at a place that the individual knows, or has reasonable cause to believe, is a school zone" (new language in italics). Lower courts have upheld the amended statute, at least so far.

The lesson, I think, is that Congress will go right up to the line that the Supreme Court draws. If the Supreme Court strikes down the mandate because it regulates "inactivity," we can bet that some members of Congress will quickly submit a bill adding an "activity" requirement to the mandate. In light of that, I think it's important for proponents of the activity-inactivity distinction to be clear as to what kind of distinction they have in mind.

Notes

1. Commonwealth ex rel. Cuccinelli v. Sebelius, 728 F. Supp. 2d 768 (E.D. Va. 2010).
2. Jonathan H. Adler, "The Individual Mandate Debate as a Replay of United States v. Lopez," Volokh Conspiracy (blog), October 15, 2010, http://www.volokh.com/2010/10/15/the -individual-mandate-debate-as-a-replay-of-united-states-v-lopez/
3. *Sebelius*, 728 F. Supp. at 780.
4. Jonathan H. Adler, "Is the Individual Mandate 'Necessary?,'" *Volokh Conspiracy* (blog), October 14, 2010, http://www.volokh.com/2010/10/14/is-the-individual-mandate -necessary.
5. Garcia v. San Antonio Metro. Transit Auth., 469 U.S. 528 (1985).
6. *Sebelius*, 728 F. Supp. 2d at 788.
7. *Id.* at 779.
8. Jonathan H. Adler, "Initial Thoughts on the Virginia Health Care Ruling," *supra*.
9. *Sebelius*, 728 F. Supp. 2d at 781.

10. Ilya Somin, "Why Going without Health Insurance Isn't an 'Activity,'" *supra*.
11. Brief for the Washington Legal Foundation & Constitutional Scholars as Amici Curiae Supporting Respondents, NFIB v. Sebelius, 132 S. Ct. 2566 (2012) (No. 11-398).
12. United States v. Reorganized CF&I Fabricators of Utah, 518 U.S. 213, 224 (1996).
13. *Id.*
14. Ilya Somin, "Necessary and Proper Clause Doctrine and the Individual Mandate," *supra*.
15. "Room for Debate: A Fatal Blow to Obama's Health Law," *New York Times*, December 13, 2010, http://www.nytimes.com/roomfordebate/2010/12/13/a-fatal-blow-to -obamas-health-care-law.
16. Jonathan H. Adler, "Further Thoughts on the Virginia Health Care Ruling and the Necessary and Proper Clause," *supra*.
17. Wickard v. Filburn, 317 U.S. 111, 125 (1942).
18. Gonzales v. Raich, 545 U.S. 1, 35–36 (2005).
19. *Id.* at 36–37.
20. Orin Kerr, "The Rehnquist Court and Symbolic Federalism," *SCOTUSblog*, June 6, 2005, http://www.scotusblog.com/2005/06/the-rehnquist-court-and-symbolic-federalism.
21. Orin Kerr, "Oral Argument in *United States v. Comstock*," *Volokh Conspiracy* (blog), January 12, 2010, http://www.volokh.com/2010/01/12/oral-argument-in-united-states -v-comstock.
22. Boy Scouts of Am. v. Dale, 530 U.S. 640 (2000).
23. Roberts v. United States Jaycees, 468 U.S. 609 (1984).
24. Mathews v. Eldridge, 424 U.S. 319 (1976).
25. Goldberg v. Kelly, 397 U.S. 254 (1970).
26. Ex Parte Milligan, 71 U.S. (4 Wall.) 2 (1866).
27. Ex Parte Quirin, 317 U.S. 1 (1942).
28. Frederick Schauer, "Slippery Slopes," *Harvard Law Review* 99 (1985): 361.
29. Andrew Koppelman, "Health Care Reform: The Broccoli Question," *Balkinization* (blog), January 19, 2011, http://balkin.blogspot.com/2011/01/health-care-reform-broccoli -objection.html.
30. Bruce Yandle, "Bootleggers & Baptists in Retrospect," *Regulation* 22, no. 3 (1999): 5, http://www.cato.org/pubs/regulation/regv22n3/bootleggers.pdf.
31. Ilya Somin, "Knowledge about Ignorance: New Directions in the Study of Political Information," *Critical Review* 18, nos. 1–3 (2006): 255, http://papers.ssrn.com/sol3/ papers.cfm?abstract_id=916963.
32. Lisa Girion, "Private Insurance Companies Push for 'Individual Mandate,'" *Los Angeles Times*, June 7, 2009, http://articles.latimes.com/2009/jun/07/business/fi-healthcare7.
33. "Obama Flip Flops on Requiring People to Buy Health Care," PolitiFact, July 20, 2009, http://www.politifact.com/truth-o-meter/statements/2009/jul/20/barack-obama/ obama-flip-flops-requiring-people-buy-health-care.
34. Florida v. United States Dep't of Health & Human Servs., 780 F. Supp. 2d 1256 (N.D. Fla. 2011).
35. *Id.* at 1293, 1294.
36. *Id.* at 1289.
37. Ilya Somin, "Why Going without Health Insurance Isn't an 'Activity,'" *supra*.
38. Ilya Somin, "Broccoli, Slippery Slopes, and the Individual Mandate," *supra*.
39. Ilya Somin, "Necessary and Proper Clause Doctrine and the Individual Mandate," *supra*.
40. Ilya Somin, "Taking Stock of Comstock: The Necessary and Proper Clause and the Limits of Federal Power," *2009-2010 Cato Supreme Court Review* (2010): 236..

41. 514 U.S. at 566.
42. 130 S. Ct. at 1964.
43. Ilya Somin, "Taking Stock of Comstock."
44. Ilya Somin, "*Gonzalez v. Raich*: Federalism as a Casualty in the War on Drugs," *Cornell Journal of Law and Public Policy* 15, no. 3 (2006): 507.
45. Gonzales v. Raich, 545 U.S. 1, 57–58 (2005).
46. 780 F. Supp. 2d at 1298.
47. *Id.*
48. *Id.*
49. *Id.* at 1297.
50. *Id.* at 1298.
51. See, e.g., Winslow v. F.E.R.C., 587 F.3d 1133, 1135 (D.C. Cir. 2009): "Vertical stare decisis—both in letter and in spirit—is a critical aspect of our hierarchical Judiciary headed by 'one supreme Court.'" (citing U.S. Const. art. III, § 1).
52. 130 S. Ct. at 1956.
53. Bruce Ackerman, *We the People, Volume I: Foundations* (Cambridge, MA: Belknap Press, 1993).
54. Lyle Denniston, "Easy Outing for Health Care Law?," *SCOTUSblog*, May 10, 2011, http://www.scotusblog.com/2011/05/easy-outing-for-health-care-law.
55. A quick note on taxes: Taxes have the same effect as a mandate. This is why taxes are viewed with such hostility and suspicion, even if they are necessary. It is no accident that, in *McCulloch v. Maryland*, Chief Justice Marshall called the power to tax the "power to destroy" or that the founders felt the need to separately enumerate, and constrain, the taxing power.
56. Jonathan H. Adler, "Baffled That Anyone Is Baffled by the Activity/Inactivity Distinction," *supra*.
57. See, e.g., Moreland v. State, 139 S.E. 77 (Ga. 1927) ("owner of chauffeur-driven car is guilty of homicide when chauffeur drives negligently and gets into an accident that causes death, even though owner was not driving and was only passively sitting in the back of the car, as the driver failed to 'curb the operator of the car.'").
58. Jonathan H. Adler, "An Act/Omission Limitation on Federal Power Over States?," *supra*.
59. See Orin Kerr, "Are All Computer Crimes Now *Federal* Computer Crimes? A Review of Recent Legislative Changes," Volokh *Conspiracy* (blog), June 3, 2009, http://www.volokh.com/posts/1244004465.shtml.

5

Moving Up the Ladder

On June 29, 2011, the United States Court of Appeals for the Sixth Circuit upheld the individual mandate against a challenge brought by the Thomas More Law Center. Writing in concurrence with the panel was Judge Jeffrey Sutton, a noted conservative jurist and one-time clerk of Justice Antonin Scalia.

The decision was the first from a court of appeals, and the fact that Judge Sutton voted to uphold the individual mandate was seen by many as an evidence for how some of the conservative Supreme Court justices might rule.

Although it was looking increasingly likely that the Supreme Court would take the case, it was not yet a sure thing. If the challengers to the law could get just one circuit court to strike down all or part of the act, then a date with the Supreme Court was all but guaranteed. A circuit split—that is, a disagreement between two or more circuit courts about the constitutionality of a federal statute—is one of the best ways to get the Supreme Court to take a case.

That circuit split came in August when the Eleventh Circuit Court of Appeals, hearing the government's appeal from Judge Vinson's district court decision, upheld Judge Vinson and struck down the individual mandate as unconstitutional. The decision was coauthored by Judges Joel Dubina and Frank Hull. Hull, a President Bill Clinton appointee, was the first Democrat appointee to strike down the mandate.

Perhaps the most interesting part of the Eleventh Circuit's opinion is how parts of it resemble some conversations posted at the *Volokh Conspiracy* and collected in this volume. Take this passage, for example:

> It is striking by comparison how very different this economic mandate is from the draft. First, it does not represent the solution to a duty owed to the government as a condition of citizenship. Moreover, unlike the draft, it has no basis in the history of our nation, much less a long and storied one. Until Congress passed the Act, the power to regulate commerce had not included the authority to issue an economic mandate. Now Congress seeks not only the power to reach a new class of "activity"— financial decisions whose effects are felt some time in the future—but it wishes to do so through a heretofore untested power: an economic mandate.[1]

While there is no evidence that influence came directly from the *Volokh Conspiracy* blog, Randy Barnett, Ilya Somin, and David B. Kopel all contributed to briefs that were submitted to the Eleventh Circuit. Their writings for the court were of course influenced by the conversations on the blog.

The case had already gone further than many had imagined, and now a date with the Supreme Court was essentially inevitable.

***

Today's Sixth Circuit Decision Upholding the Individual Mandate

Ilya Somin
June 29, 2011

Today's 2–1 Sixth Circuit Court of Appeals decision[2] upholding the constitutionality of the individual mandate is undeniably a setback for mandate opponents. Up until now, judges' votes in the mandate cases had split along ideological and partisan lines. Every conservative Republican judge had voted to strike it down, while every liberal Democrat voted to uphold it. Even in the Sixth Circuit, two of the three judges fit the same pattern (Judge Boyce Martin and Judge James Graham in dissent). But Judge Jeffrey Sutton, a well-known conservative judge has now become the first exception to it. Like Martin, he voted to uphold the mandate as an exercise of Congress's powers under the Commerce Clause.

At the same time, Martin and Sutton's opinions highlight a central weakness of the pro-mandate position in even more blatant form than previous opinions upholding the mandate. Their reasoning has extremely radical implications. Unlike previous decisions upholding the mandate, which ruled that failing to purchase health insurance is "economic activity," Martin and Sutton conclude that Congress has the power to regulate inactivity as well, so long as the inactivity has some kind of "substantial" economic effect.

The Martin-Sutton approach thereby opens the floodgates to an unlimited congressional power to impose mandates of any kind. Any failure to purchase a product has some substantial economic effect, at least when aggregated with similar failures by other people. This is certainly true of failures to purchase broccoli, failures to purchase cars, failure to buy a movie ticket, and so on. Even failure to engage in noncommercial activity nearly always has such effects. For example, a mandate requiring people to eat healthy food and exercise every day can be justified on the grounds that it would increase economic productivity and also increase the demand for healthy food products and gym memberships. The district court rulings in favor of the mandate all embraced some version of the "health care is special" argument (or at least the argument that not purchasing health insurance is "economic activity") in order to avoid this slippery slope problem (albeit, unsuccessfully, in my view). By contrast, Martin and Sutton take us all the way to the bottom of the hill in one fell swoop.

Obviously, Congress will not enact every conceivable harmful mandate that the Martin-Sutton reasoning would authorize. But the risk of abuse is far from purely theoretical, since many interest groups can and will lobby for laws that compel people to purchase their products.[3]

The sweeping congressional power authorized by Martin and Sutton's opinions makes a hash of the text of the Constitution, which gives Congress the power to regulate interstate and foreign commerce, not a blanket power to mandate anything that has a "substantial" economic effect. It also makes most of the rest of Congress's Article I powers superfluous. For example, there would be no need for a separate power to tax. After all, failure to give the government some of your money voluntarily surely has substantial economic effects. Therefore, virtually any tax could be imposed through the Commerce Clause, without the need for a separate Taxing and Spending Clause. Similarly, failure to serve in the armed forces surely has substantial economic effects. The Commerce Clause therefore authorizes Congress to impose a draft and purchase military equipment, thereby making the power to raise armies superfluous.

The Sixth Circuit ruling would be defensible if it were compelled by Supreme Court precedent. However, both Martin and Sutton admit that the Supreme Court has never previously ruled on a case involving a mandate of this type and has also never previously addressed the issue of whether the Commerce Clause authorizes regulation of inactivity. Therefore, it's hard to defend their reasoning on the grounds that it was somehow compelled by precedent.

Martin and Sutton also both make the argument that a health insurance mandate is a special case because everyone will use health care at some point in their lives. This part of their reasoning adds little to previous statements of the same argument, which I criticized previously.[4] It also does not vitiate the radical implications of their rejection of the activity-inactivity distinction, since neither actually concludes that Congress's power to enact the mandate depends on health care's supposedly special nature.

Much of Judge Sutton's Commerce Clause argument relies heavily on the notion that the plaintiffs' case must fail as a "facial" challenge to the mandate because some possible applications of the law are constitutional even under his interpretation of the plaintiff's own theory of the case. He leaves the door open to "as-applied" challenges, suggesting that the mandate may still be unconstitutional as applied to people who have not previously purchased health insurance. I may take up this aspect of Sutton's argument in a follow-up post.

Finally, it's worth noting that Sutton and Judge Graham both reject the government's claim that the mandate is a valid exercise of Congress's power to tax, instead concluding that it is a penalty. Judge Martin avoids addressing this issue directly but does hold that the mandate is a penalty in the section of his opinion discussing standing. So far, the tax argument has been rejected by every judge who has ruled on it, including those who have upheld the law on other grounds.

Judge Sutton on the Individual Mandate

Orin S. Kerr
June 29, 2011

Of all the judges tasked with assessing the constitutionality of the individual mandate, the one to watch so far has been Judge Jeffrey Sutton of the Sixth Circuit. As some readers know, Judge Sutton is a Federalist Society favorite, one of Justice Scalia's favorite former clerks and a regular "feeder" judge to the Supreme Court. As a result, what Judge Sutton thinks about the constitutionality of the mandate actually matters a lot to the future debate over the mandate. In light of that, I think the important aspect of today's opinion from the Sixth Circuit is that Judge Sutton concluded that the mandate is constitutional.

I think Judge Sutton's separate opinion is excellent, but then it's easy for me to say, Judge Sutton's views closely match what I've been saying here and elsewhere for a long time, so maybe this just proves once again that "brilliant people agree with me."[5] In any event, in light of our many debates here on whether the proposed action-inaction distinction is clear and obvious (as Randy argues) or if it is actually quite complex and uncertain (as I have contended), I thought it would be worth posting Judge Sutton's discussion of why he finds it quite confusing:

> Level of generality is destiny in interpretive disputes, and it remains unclear at what level plaintiffs mean to pitch their action/inaction line of constitutional authority or indeed whether a workable level exists. Does this test apply to individuals who have purchased medical insurance before? Those individuals have not been inactive in any sense of the word when it comes to the medical-insurance market, yet plaintiffs say that Congress may not regulate them.
>
> What of individuals who voluntarily have insurance on the day the mandate goes into effect? One of the plaintiffs in this case, Jann DeMars, now has insurance, yet she claims Congress has no right to require her to maintain that coverage. It is not clear what the action/inaction line means in a setting in which an individual voluntarily (and actively) obtains coverage and is required only to maintain it thereafter. As to this group of individuals, why can't Congress regulate them, even under plaintiffs' theory of the case? We no longer are talking about a mandate imposed on the mere status of "existence" in the United States but on individuals who have voluntarily purchased medical insurance in an interstate market and who must maintain only what they chose to buy. At a minimum, this application of the law is constitutional.
>
> How would the action/inaction line have applied to Roscoe Filburn? Might he have responded to the Agricultural Adjustment Act of 1938 by claiming that the prohibition on planting more than 11.1 acres of wheat on his farm compelled him to action—to buy wheat in the interstate market so that he could feed all of his animals? And is it any more offensive to individual autonomy to prevent a farmer from being self-sufficient when it comes to supplying feed to his animals than an individual when it comes to paying for health care? It seems doubtful that the *Wickard* Court would have thought so. *See Wickard*, 317 U.S. at 129 (acknowledging that the law "forc[ed] some farmers into the market to buy wheat they could provide for themselves"). How would the action/inaction line apply if someone like Angel Raich sold her house, marijuana plants and all? The Controlled Substances Act would obligate

the new owner to act (by removing the plants), see 21 U.S.C. § 844, but it seems doubtful that he could sidestep this obligation on the ground that the law forced him to act rather than leaving him alone to enjoy the fruits of inaction.

There is another linguistic problem with the action/inaction line. The power to regulate includes the power to prescribe and proscribe. Legislative prescriptions set forth rules of conduct, some of which require action. See, e.g., 18 U.S.C. § 2250 (sex-offender registration); id. § 228 (child-support payments); see also *United States v. Faasse*, 265 F.3d 475, 486–87 (6th Cir. 2001) (en banc). The same is true for legislative proscriptions. Take the drug laws at issue in *Raich*, where Congress regulated by prohibiting individuals from possessing certain drugs. A drug-possession law amounts to forced inaction in some settings (those who do not have drugs must not get them), and forced action in other settings (those who have drugs must get rid of them).

An enforceable line is even more difficult to discern when it comes to health insurance and the point of buying it: financial risk. Risk is not having money when you need it. And the mandate is one way of ensuring that all Americans have money to pay for health care when they inevitably need it. In this context, the notion that self-insuring amounts to inaction and buying insurance amounts to action is not self-evident. If done responsibly, the former requires more action (affirmatively saving money on a regular basis and managing the assets over time) than the latter (writing a check once or twice a year or never writing one at all if the employer withholds the premiums). What is more, inaction is action, sometimes for better, sometimes for worse, when it comes to financial risk. When Warren Buffett tells shareholders that "[w]e continue to make more money when snoring than when active" or that "[i]nactivity strikes us as intelligent behavior," Chairman's Letter to Shareholders (Feb. 28, 1997), ¶¶ 72–73, available at http://www.berkshirehathaway.com/letters/1996.html, he is not urging the Board of Directors to place him in a Rip Van Winkle-like stupor for the next year. He is saying that, of the many buy and sell recommendations that came across his desk that year, the best thing he could have done is the informed, even masterful, inaction of saying no to all of them.

No one is inactive when deciding how to pay for health care, as self-insurance and private insurance are two forms of action for addressing the same risk. Each requires affirmative choices; one is no less active than the other; and both affect commerce. In affidavits filed in this case, the individual plaintiffs all mention the need to make current changes in their spending and saving practices to account for the need to pay for medical insurance in the future. Saving to buy insurance or to self-insure, as these affidavits attest, involves action. E.g., Ceci May 27, 2011 Decl., ¶ 7 ("Due to the added financial pressure [of the mandate], I have cut back on discretionary spending, such as costs associated with entertainment, like going to the movies, a restaurant, or sporting events."); Hyder May 28, 2011 Decl., ¶ 8 (same).[6]

Judge Sutton on Facial vs. As-Applied Challenges to the Individual Mandate

Ilya Somin
June 29, 2011

In his concurring opinion upholding the constitutionality of the Obamacare individual mandate, Sixth Circuit Judge Jeffrey Sutton argues that the plaintiffs' case must fail as a "facial" challenge to the law because there are some applications of the mandate that are clearly constitutional. On the other hand, he leaves the door open for future "as-applied" challenges, which contend merely that the law is unconstitutional in certain specific cases:

> For now, whatever else may be said about plaintiffs' activity/inactivity theory of commerce power, they have not shown that the individual mandate exceeds that power in all of its applications. Congress may apply the mandate in at least four settings: (1) to individuals who already have purchased insurance voluntarily and who want to maintain coverage, but who will be required to obtain more insurance in order to comply with the minimum-essential-coverage requirement; (2) to individuals who voluntarily obtained coverage but do not wish to be forced (at some indeterminate point in the future) to maintain it; (3) to individuals who live in States that already require them to obtain insurance and who may have to obtain more coverage to comply with the mandate or abide by other requirements of the Affordable Care Act; and (4) to individuals under 30, no matter where they live and no matter whether they have purchased health care before, who may satisfy the law by obtaining only catastrophic-care coverage. The valid application of the law to these groups of people suffices to uphold the law against this facial challenge.
>
> While future challenges to the law have hills to climb, nothing about this view of the case precludes individuals from bringing as-applied challenges to the mandate as the relevant agencies implement it . . . [7]

Sutton appears to be arguing that the plaintiffs' claim that the mandate is an unconstitutional regulation of inactivity does not apply to the first three of the previous situations because people who fall into these categories have already engaged in activity in the health insurance market. Therefore, the mandate could be imposed on them even under the plaintiffs' reasoning.

Sutton's analysis rests on a misinterpretation of the plaintiffs' argument. The key point is not that a given plaintiff hasn't engaged in economic activity but that the regulation imposed by Congress does not require any such activity as a prerequisite for covering them. The fact that some of the individuals covered by the mandate could be regulated by a more narrowly drawn law (e.g., one that covered only people who had already purchased health insurance) does not mean that the *present* mandate is constitutional as applied to them. Their having previously engaged in economic activity that Congress could regulate is purely coincidental. It is not the reason why the mandate applies to them under the terms of the law itself.

By Judge Sutton's reasoning, the Supreme Court should have rejected the facial challenges brought in *United States v. Lopez* and *United States v. Morrison*. In *Lopez*, the Court struck down a federal law banning possession of guns in a school zone as going beyond Congress's authority under the Commerce Clause. But surely some of the people whom that law could have been applied to were using guns that were purchased in interstate commerce or had brought the guns into a school zone in order to facilitate an interstate economic transaction (e.g., bringing in a gun in order to protect their sale of illegal drugs imported from abroad). In *Morrison*, the Court invalidated a federal law creating a civil penalty for gender-motivated crimes of violence. But some of the people covered by the law might have committed their crimes on interstate trains or buses or committed them for the purpose of interfering with women engaged in interstate economic transactions. By Judge

Sutton's reasoning, *Lopez* and *Morrison* struck down laws that did not "exceed" Congress's power "in all of [their] applications."

The Court ruled the way it did in *Morrison* and *Lopez* because the challenged laws, as actually written, did not require any kind of connection to interstate commerce as a legal prerequisite for their application. The fact that some potential defendants happened to have such a connection was legally irrelevant. The same reasoning applies to the individual mandate. Judge Sutton's approach, by contrast, would rule out virtually all facial challenges to any law, so long as there is even one conceivable situation where the law leads to a prosecution that could have been constitutional with a more narrowly drawn statute.

To illustrate my point a bit further, consider a hypothetical statute giving police the power to break into any house any time they want. In my view, that statute would be facially invalid. By contrast, Judge Sutton would have to uphold it against a facial challenge because some of the searches allowed by the statute would involve cases where the search was "reasonable" under the Fourth Amendment (e.g. because the authorities had probable cause to believe that a crime had recently been committed on the premises).

It is not entirely clear why Judge Sutton thinks that the plaintiffs' argument does not apply to his fourth category, people under the age of thirty who are only required to purchase "catastrophic" health insurance coverage under the law. Not having catastrophic coverage is no more "economic activity" than is not having a broader insurance policy. If the plaintiffs' theory applies to the latter case, it applies to the former as well. Judge Sutton seems to think that the two are different because congressional legislation requires some providers to provide emergency health care treatment for free. But it is not clear why this distinction should have any constitutional significance. If Congress required some supermarkets to provide free broccoli, would that justify a broccoli purchase mandate?

Re: Facial vs. As-Applied Challenges to the Individual Mandate

Jonathan H. Adler
June 30, 2011

Ilya's post addresses an important issue in Commerce Clause litigation: whether Commerce Clause challenges should be treated as facial or as-applied challenges and, if the former, how such challenges should be addressed. I largely agree with Ilya's post. Indeed, if anything, Ilya understates the point, particularly with regard to *United States v. Lopez*. Further, whatever the other merits of Judge Sutton's opinion—which is quite strong, even if I disagree with its conclusion—it mishandles this issue.

In his post, Ilya asks how Judge Sutton's reasoning would apply in *Lopez* if "some of the people whom that law could have been applied to were using guns that were purchased in interstate commerce or had brought the guns into a school zone in order to facilitate an interstate economic transaction."

This is not merely a hypothetical. It is, in fact, what happened in *Lopez*. Alfonso Lopez was not just some kid who happened to bring a gun to school. Rather, as the Fifth Circuit's opinion explains, he was a courier who had been paid to deliver the gun to a gang member. He was a delivery boy engaged in a commercial transaction. As a consequence, his possession was within the scope of the Commerce Clause power. Had Congress passed legislation prohibiting this sort of economic transaction, his Commerce Clause argument would have failed. The reason his Commerce Clause challenge prevailed was not because his conduct was beyond the scope of the commerce power. Rather, it prevailed because the statute at issue (the Gun-Free School Zones Act [GFSZA]) was not itself a proper exercise of that power. What the statute prohibited—possession, as such, in a school zone—was beyond the scope of the power, even though the statute reached conduct that could be reached constitutionally.

What the Court's handling of *Lopez* reveals is that the key question in a Commerce Clause challenge is the nature of the exercise of federal power, not whether, in a given case, the plaintiff's conduct could be regulated or prohibited constitutionally. This is why the GFSZA was invalidated when challenged by someone who was engaged in reachable conduct. It is also why the *Lopez* Court noted the lack of a jurisdictional element (e.g., a provision limiting the prohibition to gun possession "substantially related" to interstate commerce). The purpose of a jurisdictional element is to preserve a statute's constitutionality by confining its exercise to those activities within the scope of the Commerce Clause power.[8] Thus, a statute prohibiting the *commercial* possession of guns in or near a school is constitutional, but a statute imposing a blanket prohibition on gun possession in or near a school is not. In the former instance, Congress is engaged in a constitutional exercise of its power, in the latter it is not, even though the statutes overlap. Yet under Judge Sutton's approach, the GFSZA should have been upheld because it would be constitutional to prohibit participation in commercial gun transactions like the one in which Alfonso Lopez was engaged.

The traditional test for a facial challenge is whether there is any set of circumstances in which the statute's application would be constitutional. As *Lopez* shows, the proper way to apply this test is *not* to ask whether the statute reaches otherwise reachable conduct—commercial gun possession, the purchase of insurance, and so on. Rather, the question is whether the class of activities expressly subject to regulation—that is, the conduct that brings an individual within the scope of the statute at issue—is itself within the scope of the commerce power. As the Supreme Court has reiterated time and again (albeit mostly in cases upholding statutes against Commerce Clause challenge), what matters is what Congress did, not the specific conduct of the individual challenging the statute's constitutionality. This is why Lopez prevailed. Incidentally, it is also why Angel Raich lost. For in *Gonzales v. Raich* there was no question that Congress could regulate interstate commerce in drugs. Once the Court concluded that the class of activities subject to the statute—the sale, production, distribution, and possession of a controlled substance—was within the scope of the commerce power (supplemented by the Necessary and Proper Clause), Raich had to lose. Indeed, there is no Commerce Clause precedent in which the Supreme Court has upheld the broader statute but invalidated its application to a specific individual. If the relevant statutory provision is a permissible exercise of the commerce power, the challenge fails.

The preceding illustrates why the key issue is defining the class of activities subject to federal control. Listen to the oral arguments in the various circuit courts and notice how Acting Solicitor General Neil Katyal takes pains to define the class of activities subject to regulation in economic terms—as "financial decisions about how and when health care is paid for." Judge Martin's decision does much the same, characterizing the class of activities as "the practice of self-insuring for the cost of health care delivery."[9] The problem, in my view, is that these characterizations are not consistent with the statutory provision, as neither accurately characterizes the class as a whole Congress has sought to regulate.

It may be the case that most of those subject to the individual mandate are making "financial decisions" about how and when to pay for their health care or are engaged in self-insurance, but the statute does not limit its application to such people nor can all those subject to the mandate be characterized in such terms. Not only are there those who would otherwise never purchase health insurance. There are also those who, for whatever reason, religious or otherwise, will never purchase health care. (Indeed, under *Cruzan*, they have a fundamental right to refuse even potentially lifesaving care.) That Congress can reach most of those without insurance through other means is immaterial, just as it was immaterial that Congress could have prohibited what Alfonso Lopez actually did had it only passed a different statute. What matters is the statute that Congress actually passed and whether the class of activities over which Congress asserted its authority is, as a class, subject to federal jurisdiction.

So, contrary to Katyal's protestations at the various oral arguments and the opinions of Judges Martin and Sutton, the class of activities at issue is the mere presence in the country without qualifying health insurance, and the question really is whether Congress may mandate the purchase of a given good or service. In other words, the question is whether such a mandate itself is facially constitutional as an exercise of federal power, not whether we can identify a range of situations in which such a mandate could be constitutionally applied. (As-applied challenges should be reserved to claims that the mandate violates some other constitutional provision, such as the First or Fifth Amendment, in its application to specific individuals, e.g. someone with religious objections to medical care.)[10]

POSTSCRIPT: Just in case it was not clear, the previous argument is not sufficient to establish the unconstitutionality of the individual mandate. The point is rather to identify some of the problems with the way some have defended its constitutionality. Although I believe the mandate should be held unconstitutional, I have long conceded that this is a difficult case, particularly in light of *Gonzales v. Raich*, and one that implicates first principles about the nature of federal power and the Constitution.

SECOND POSTSCRIPT: I should also have noted that what this argument does is shift the focus from the Commerce Clause to the Necessary and Proper Clause. If a class of activities extends beyond the scope of the Commerce Clause itself (as I believe the class subject to the mandate does), the question becomes whether the broader class can be justified as necessary and proper to the overall scheme. Under *Gonzales v. Raich*, there is a strong argument in defense of the mandate on these grounds. Short of overturning *Raich* (which I would love to see the Court do), the strongest counterarguments are that mandating the purchase of a good or service is not "proper" to the execution of an enumerated power and that the argument for the mandate rests on an effectively unlimited conception of federal power that contravenes one of the motivating principles of *Lopez* and *Morrison*.

THIRD POSTSCRIPT: Some of the commenters in the following suggest my view requires a somewhat-radical "all-or-nothing" approach to Commerce Clause challenges. Yes and no. It is perhaps radical and "all or nothing" in that I believe that a given prohibition is either within the scope of enumerated powers or it is not. But what is "all or nothing" is a given statutory provision, not a statute in its entirety. This remains strong medicine but makes my position slightly less radical in its implications. What would this have meant for *Gonzales v. Raich*? This is a good question, and one I engaged elsewhere.[11] My first preference would have been for the Court to invalidate the prohibition on possession, thereby requiring Congress to add a jurisdictional element. Two alternatives that are less doctrinally satisfying but perhaps easier to swallow would have been either to hold that the Controlled Substances Act (CSA) did not reach noncommercial possession (effectively reading a jurisdictional requirement into the statute) or to have recognized a separate class of activities authorized by state law that could be analyzed independently. Either of these alternatives would have required a bit of work (particularly the latter), as there's little basis for either in the relevant case law.

The Individual Mandate and the Presumption of Constitutionality

Orin S. Kerr
June 29, 2011

One of the emerging criticisms of the Sixth Circuit opinion upholding the individual mandate—and especially Judge Sutton's separate opinion—is that the Sixth Circuit erred because the individual mandate should be presumed unconstitutional. Unless Supreme Court precedent is so clear that it compels a holding that the statute is constitutional, the argument runs, the mandate should be struck down. For example, Cato's Ilya Shapiro writes,

> Under a document establishing a government of enumerated and therefore limited powers, the burden is on that government to prove that it has the power to do something, not on the plaintiffs to disprove that power. Never has the Supreme Court ratified the federal power to force someone to buy a product in the marketplace under the guise of regulating commerce. Indeed, never, not even during the height of the New Deal, had Congress asserted such a power—until the health insurance mandate.

If I understand him correctly, our own Ilya Somin appears to be making a similar point with the following criticism:

> The Sixth Circuit ruling would be defensible if it were compelled by Supreme Court precedent. However, both Martin and Sutton admit that the Supreme Court has never previously ruled on a case involving a mandate of this type and has also never previously addressed the issue of whether the Commerce Clause authorizes regulation of inactivity. Therefore, it's hard to defend their reasoning on the grounds that it was somehow compelled by precedent.

More colorfully, commenter WolfWalker writes in response to me,

> There's simply no way that the mandate can be permitted under the spirit of the Constitution. This endless hairsplitting about "is it really most sincerely unconstitutional, or can we find a way to let it stand" is a corruption of the entire spirit of the Constitution, and the LIMITED FEDERAL GOVERNMENT that it was intended to create. The United States federal government is not a Windows system where anything that is not expressly forbidden is allowed. It's a Unix system, where any action that is not expressly permitted is forbidden.

I've heard others make similar arguments, both previously and in some of today's threads. The mandate is so exceptional, the argument goes, that those seeking to uphold its constitutionality must overcome a steep burden of proof.

It's worth noting, however, that the law is to the contrary. The United States Supreme Court has long imposed a presumption of constitutionality on judicial review of statutes, not a presumption of *un*constitutionality.[12] Further, the Court has described the presumption of constitutionality as "strong" when courts review an act of Congress.[13] As a result, the burden of proof here is on the plaintiffs, not the defendants.

I realize that the presumption of constitutionality is unpopular among many people who happen to think that the mandate is unconstitutional under existing precedents. Randy Barnett has argued[14] that the presumption of constitutionality is wrong, for example, and I believe Ilya Somin agrees. But lower court judges like those on the Sixth Circuit don't have the authority to ignore or overturn the long-standing Supreme Court case law that establishes the presumption of constitutionality. Obviously, this doesn't settle the constitutionality of the mandate; it only addresses who has the burden of proof. But I think it's a helpful point to keep in mind, as at least some of the criticism of the Sixth Circuit opinion appears to assume the contrary presumption.

The "Presumption of Constitutionality" and the Individual Mandate Cases

Ilya Somin
June 30, 2011

In a recent post, coblogger Orin Kerr argues that the "presumption of constitutionality" accorded to congressional legislation weighs in favor of the federal government in the individual mandate cases. In my view, courts should *not* grant either congressional or state legislation a presumption of constitutionality. Such deference is especially inappropriate in situations where the legislature is passing judgment on the scope of its own authority. When a person or political institution is acting as a judge in its own case, its conclusions should not be considered presumptively valid. The presumption is also particularly improper in an era where most members of Congress of both parties routinely fail to take their constitutional responsibilities seriously and usually just rely on the courts to sort out constitutional issues, as many did at the time the individual mandate itself was enacted.[29]

Nevertheless, Orin is right in pointing out that some Supreme Court decisions say that a presumption of constitutionality should be applied to congressional legislation. On the other hand, many Supreme Court decisions, including *Morrison* and *Lopez*, strike down federal legislation without any reference to the presumption. The presumption was also conspicuous by its absence when the Court struck down large parts of the Detainee Treatment Act in *Boumediene v. Bush*.

If such a presumption *had* been applied in those cases, the Court would probably have had to reach a different result. For example, in *Lopez*, there was a plausible argument that a statute banning the possession of guns in a school zone was constitutional under previous precedents that the *Lopez* majority did not wish to overturn because such possession has important economic effects. Justice Stephen Breyer did a good job of articulating this point in his dissenting opinion.

How can we reconcile those cases where the Court applies the presumption of constitutionality with those where it doesn't? The cynical answer is that the Court applies the presumption in cases where it wants to uphold the challenged statute and ignores it in cases where the majority wants to strike the law down. I suspect that this factor really does account for much of the variation between cases.

Less cynically, one might argue that the justices apply the presumption in cases where they think the statute is supported by well-established precedent but not where Congress has gone beyond the bounds of both previous decisions and the text of the Constitution itself. Applying this logic to the mandate case, I think it can be said that the presumption does not apply if you believe that the mandate is an unprecedented expansion of federal power that goes beyond previous precedent and is not supported by the text of the Constitution. Alternatively, if you think that the mandate is fairly similar to previous statutes that have been upheld by the Court or that it is authorized by the text of the Constitution, the presumption would apply.

The key question to ask is whether this case is more like *Lopez*, *Morrison*, and *Boumediene* or whether it is more similar to those cases where the Court has applied the presumption, such as *Watson v. United States*,[30] a case cited by Orin. For what it's worth, I think *Watson* is a clear example of a case where the majority thought that the challenged statute was constitutional on the merits, with or without a presumption of constitutionality. The Court emphasized that it was supported by common law principles and by many decades of precedent.

This, of course, suggests that the presumption applies only to those statutes that the courts are likely to uphold anyway. However, such an approach is consistent with the way the Court has applied the presumption over the last several decades. It's hard to point to any cases where the Court has used the presumption to uphold a congressional statute that it was otherwise inclined to strike down. As currently used by the Court, the presumption of constitutionality is mostly a way to seal the deal on a case the government was likely to win anyway. It turns a strong case into a slam dunk. But it can't be used to transform a probable loss for the federal government into a win.

Obviously, it is still possible to argue that the mandate should be upheld even without applying the presumption. The point of this post is simply that the presumption adds little or nothing to the federal government's case.[31]

More on the Presumption of Constitutionality

Orin S. Kerr
June 30, 2011

In his previous post, my coblogger Ilya Somin concludes that courts should not apply the presumption of constitutionality to the individual mandate

Ilya's analytical framework does not appear to me to be based on existing case law. First, some of the cases in which Ilya contends that the presumption was not mentioned actually recited it quite clearly. For example, *United States v. Morrison* says

> Due respect for the decisions of a coordinate branch of Government demands that we invalidate a congressional enactment only upon a plain showing that Congress has exceeded its constitutional bounds. See *United States v. Lopez*, 514 U.S., at 568, 577—578 (Kennedy, J., concurring); *United States v. Harris*, 106 U.S., at 635. With this presumption of constitutionality in mind, we turn to the question whether §13981 falls within Congress' power under Article I, §8, of the Constitution.[32]

It's true that not every decision recites the legal point that there is a presumption of constitutionality. But then not every decision recites the legal point that courts have the power of judicial review, and yet we don't consider the absence of that explicit point to be some sort of implicit overturning of *Marbury v. Madison*.

Ilya's effort to reconcile the cases into a view that the presumption applies depending on whether one thinks a statute is "unprecedented" and beyond the constitutional text strikes me as both inconsistent with the cases and based on a misunderstanding of the presumption. On the first point, consider one of Ilya's examples: the statute struck down in *Boumediene*. That statute was hardly unprecedented. It was actually just restoring the prior law before the Supreme Court creatively read its statues a few years earlier. Nor did it create some obvious textual problem. The Court struck it down, but I think not based on the theory Ilya suggests.

On the second point, some of the confusion may concern what it means to say there is a presumption of constitutionality. In my experience, discussions of presumptions and burdens of proof generally involve three possible issues:

1. *Who* has the burden of proof;
2. *How high* is the burden of proof; and
3. *What kind of evidence or argument* can be used to meet the burden of proof.

My sense is that the presumption of constitutionality is mostly just about question 1: *who* has the burden of proof. The cases sometimes talk about 2, but usually only in a vague sense (the presumption is "strong," etc.). In my view, it's pretty much impossible to dispute that there is a presumption of constitutionality in the question 1 sense: It has been repeated in hundreds of cases over two centuries. It's true that Supreme Court practice is not consistent on questions 2 and 3, but the law strikes me as extremely clear on question 1.

One final point: Ilya suggests in comments that if the presumption of constitutionality is only about question 1, then it isn't very important in a practical sense. I don't think that's right, though, in part because it rules out one of the approaches offered of the mandate opponents. In my experience, many of the arguments against the mandate include some sort of reference to the burden of proof being on the government. Some mention that the burden must be particularly steep. As a result of the presumption of constitutionality, however, I don't think those statements are correct.

The Presumption of Constitutionality Revisited

Ilya Somin
June 30, 2011

In his response to my post on the mandate cases and the presumption of constitutionality, Orin Kerr argues that the presumption applies to all cases where courts consider the constitutionality of congressional legislation.

Orin recognizes that the Supreme Court majority in fact fails to even mention the presumption in many controversial cases where it strikes down federal laws, such as *United States v. Lopez* and *Boumediene v. Bush*.[15] I would add to that list such other cases as *Reno v. ACLU*,[16] *New York v. United States*, and *Printz v. United States*—the latter two being major federalism cases. The Court did briefly mention the presumption at the start of its opinion in *United States v. Morrison* (I corrected my error on that point in an update to my previous post) but then completely ignores it in its actual analysis of the legal issues in the case. Thus, it seems clear that the Court routinely ignores the presumption in cases where it strikes down federal laws.

Orin suggests that the Court may be applying the presumption even in cases where it goes unmentioned. That is theoretically possible but highly unlikely in reality. If the Court were applying a presumption of constitutionality in closely contested cases such as *Lopez*, *Boumediene*, *Printz*, and *New York* (all 5–4 or 6–3 decisions that were highly controversial), one would expect the justices to at least mention that fact. Unlike judicial review, the presumption and its application are not uncontested background assumptions that nearly all jurists agree on. Rather, the degree of deference due to Congress is one of the main contested issues in federalism and separation of powers cases, including the ones listed previously.

In my previous post, I suggested that the Court chooses not to apply the presumption in situations where the majority believes the challenged statute has "gone beyond the bounds of both previous decisions and the text of the Constitution itself." Orin responds that that wasn't true in *Boumediene* because the statute struck down in that case "was actually just restoring the prior law before the Supreme Court creatively read its statues a few years earlier." Orin's interpretation of the statute may be correct. But it's not the view taken by the Supreme Court majority, which had interpreted the prior law as *not* allowing the kinds of military tribunals[17] that were explicitly permitted by the statute struck down in *Boumediene*. Even more importantly, the prior statute was itself a recent innovation arising from the war on terror. In the Supreme Court majority's view, it was not supported by previous judicial precedent or by long-standing practice. The majority opinion actually refers to what it calls "the lack of a precedent on point."[18]

Finally, Orin suggests that the presumption of constitutionality is merely about "who has the burden of proof" and wrongly interprets me as saying that a burden of proof makes no difference. What I actually said, in the comments to my previous post was this:

> If the presumption merely means that those challenging a law must present some proof of some kind that it's unconstitutional, then it makes little difference. Realistically, no court is likely to strike down a law without at least some showing of that type. However, those who argue for the presumption usually imply a significantly higher burden of proof, such as that the law must be upheld unless its unconstitutionality is unambiguously clear.

If Orin believes that the presumption requires only the sort of minimal burden of proof I described in my comment, then the difference between our views has little practical significance. I still think that the presumption doesn't apply at all (in some cases; as it didn't in *Lopez*, *Printz*, *Boumediene*, etc.). But there is little meaningful difference between not applying it at all and interpreting it to require some minimal proof of some kind. Realistically, no federal court is likely to strike down a law if the challengers have no argument at all against it. If, on the other hand, Orin would require a more substantial burden, things are different.[19]

Eight Things to Know about Yesterday's Sixth Circuit Decision

Randy E. Barnett
June 30, 2011

Volokh readers will remember when two widely respected conservative court of appeals judges, Judge Frank Easterbrook and Judge Richard Posner, were on a unanimous Seventh Circuit panel denying both the due process and privileges or immunities challenge to Chicago's handgun ban. One year later, the due process challenge was upheld 5–4 in *McDonald v. City of Chicago*. My friend and current adversary, Walter Dellinger said yesterday that the opinion by Judge Jeff Sutton to uphold the individual mandate "is a complete vindication of the constitutionality of the Affordable Care Act." Not so fast. Sutton's opinion was no surprise to anyone who was in the courtroom in Cincinnati. Nor would a contrary opinion have been surprising. Sutton was scrupulously critical of both sides that day. Indeed, his opinion shares the "on the one hand" and "on the other hand" character of his questioning. And it also bears some resemblance to Judge Easterbrook's opinion in *McDonald*.

Given that Dellinger's reaction is likely to be commonplace among the act's supporters, I thought it would be useful to offer a few observations about the Sixth Circuit decision generally and Judge Sutton's opinion in particular. Although each of these points merit further thought and more extensive treatment, it is also useful to present them more succinctly as a list.

1. **Yesterday's decision was 2–1.** The arguments in favor of the mandate that some find so persuasive were well presented by Judges Martin and Sutton. Yet they still failed to persuade Judge Graham. Unlike defenders of the Affordable Care Act (ACA), no challenger has ever claimed that this case is a slam dunk for unconstitutionality or that legal arguments supporting the ACA are frivolous. No challenger has ever predicted a unanimous Supreme Court decision. Just as the substance of Judge Martin's opinion could well end up being adopted by a majority of justices, so too could Judge Graham's analysis. (For the following reasons, I do not believe Judge Sutton's opinion, based as it is on a "Roach Motel" view of facial challenges, is as likely to form the basis of a Supreme Court majority opinion, but elements of it could.) This case remains a very difficult challenge for the courts and one that the Supreme Court will ultimately decide *de novo*. I do not believe that any of the justices on either side will be overly influenced by any of the lower court opinions, except as potential road maps to take them where they independently decide they want to go. In short, the Supreme Court justices' decisions will be made according to their own jurisprudential commitments, not those of inferior court judges who are subject to different constraints and norms. And this will also be true if one appeals court strikes down the mandate—just as the opinions of two district court judges who held the mandate unconstitutional did not dictate the outcome in the Sixth Circuit.

2. **Yesterday's decision affirmed 2–0 the unprecedented nature of this power.** Both Judge Sutton and Graham note that the power to impose economic mandates on the people is novel. (So far as I could tell, Judge Martin does not speak to the issue. He certainly cites no clear cut previous examples of such mandates.) Of course, it does not automatically follow from this that it is therefore unconstitutional, as evidenced by this 2–1 decision upholding the mandate. But it reaffirms that the Court will have to let Congress go where it has not gone before. That continues to create a challenge for the law's defenders, even under a "presumption of constitutionality." As Judge Sutton wrote (citing *Printz* among other cases), "Legislative novelty typically is not a constitutional virtue. More than once, and quite often in separation-of-powers cases, the Court has said that a '[l]ack of historical precedent can indicate a constitutional infirmity'" in a congressional act.[20]

3. **Yesterday's decision rejected the tax power argument 2–0–1.** A majority of the panel yesterday rejected the darling theory of law professors: that the "penalty" enforcing the "individual responsibility requirement" or mandate is an exercise of the tax power. And Judge Martin expressly declined to reach the issue. Once again, the tax power theory went nowhere. I won't rehearse all the reasons why the implications of this theory are too radical for any court to accept. But keep in mind that many of the same people who have been telling us that the Commerce Clause theory is a slam dunk *also* endorse the tax power theory.

4. **The Court rejected the objections to standing 3–0.** Some of the same folks who are so confidently opining on the scope of the commerce and tax powers—including the government—were also questioning the claimants' standing to challenge the ACA. The court unanimously rejected their view and reached the merits.

5. **Judge Martin accepted**[21] **the requirement the Congress must regulate activity.** Unlike the passage from Judge Sutton quoted by Orin, Judge Martin did not question the activity-inactivity distinction. "In applying this jurisprudence, our first duty is to determine the class of activities that the minimum coverage provision regulates."[22] And "[t]he minimum coverage provision regulates activity that is decidedly economic."[23] Later he writes, "far from regulating inactivity, the provision regulates active participation in the health care market."[24] For his Commerce Clause analysis, he accepted the government's characterization of the activity reached by the statute:

> By regulating the practice of self-insuring for the cost of health care delivery, the minimum coverage provision is facially constitutional under the Commerce Clause for two independent reasons. First, the provision regulates economic activity that Congress had a rational basis to believe has substantial effects on interstate commerce. In addition, Congress had a rational basis to believe that the provision was essential to its larger economic scheme reforming the interstate markets in health care and health insurance.

In short, the majority accepted the "class of activities" framework that I have advanced since December of 2009 and found the "practice of self-insurance" to be the relevant activity. Having been advanced by the government, this theory of the relevant "class of activities" was neither new nor surprising. The first step in any Commerce Clause analysis is to define the relevant "class of activities" and the litigants disagree about this definition.

6. **The use of "self-insurance" by the majority was problematic.** Neither Judge Martin nor Sutton spend much time explaining the concept of "self-insurance" upon which their opinions vitally depend. Wikipedia summarizes the conventional technical meaning of this activity: "Self-insurance is a risk management method in which a calculated amount of money is set aside to compensate for the potential future loss." In other words, companies "self-insure" when instead of entering a risk pool provided by an "insurance" company they create their own pool of funds from which to handle future losses. *This is a genuine activity.* Doing nothing and waiting to pay for something later—perhaps best called "self-financing"—is simply not the same thing. The key about "self-financing" is that it happens *when you receive services and are called upon to pay.* But this is not the class of activities *defined by the statute.* In this way, by misusing the term "self-insurance," both judges convert inactivity into a "class of activities." But that is merely semantic not substantive. It would only convince someone who really did not care whether Congress has the power to mandate activity. It would not convince anyone concerned about granting this new power to Congress. Judge Martin gives up considerable ground in a footnote, where he concedes: "We use the term self-insurance for ease of discussion. We note, however, that it is actually a misnomer because no insurance is involved, and might be better described as risk retention."[25] "Risk retention" is a somewhat more transparent way to describe doing nothing, but it is still seeking to use semantics to create a "class of activities" from nonactivity.

7. **The swing vote depended on a "Roach Motel" theory of facial challenges.** According to Judge Sutton's view of facial challenges, the mandate is constitutional as applied to anyone who already has insurance. Having once voluntarily chosen to get insurance, they can be mandated never to stop. Like the Roach Motel, once citizens check into the health insurance market, they can never check out. This implication of Judge Sutton's analysis is a sign of its weakness and why it won't be adopted the Supreme Court. Ilya and Jonathan have already ably explained some of the substantive difficulties with this approach. But the key is that his view of facial challenges was crucial to his decision because it allowed him to avoid the hardest issues posed by the mandate: compelling citizens into a market—here the insurance market—who are not currently in that market. (I realize that the government claims the "relevant market" is the health care market, but this rewriting of the statute has other problems.) If Judge Sutton is right about "facial challenges," and Judge Martin and others are right about the unavailability of "as-applied challenges" after *Raich* (as I think they are),

then there is really no justiciable way to adjudicate whether Congress has exceeded its Commerce Clause powers. Here is the basic logic:

"Facial" challenges will be denied so long as there are *any* constitutional applications of the law.

But, so long as Congress can reach a "class of activities," the courts will not carve out subclasses in an "as-applied" challenge to see if they may be beyond Congress's power.

This would be a radical conclusion I doubt the Supreme Court will adopt. By the time it reaches the Supreme Court, Judge Sutton's analysis of facial challenges will have been thoroughly vetted. In the end, the choices for the justices will be between something like Judge Martin's opinion or Judge Graham's. The "center" will not hold.

8. **Judge Sutton's challenge to the Supreme Court.** In *McDonald*, Judge Easterbrook protested that it was not for an "inferior" judge to extrapolate from recent Due Process Clause cases to strike down a handgun ban given nineteenth-century cases refusing to extend protection of the Second Amendment to the states. Judge Sutton does the reverse. His opinion concedes that this claim of power goes beyond anything the Constitution or Supreme Court has previously upheld. "The Court, for one, has never considered the validity of this type of mandate before, at least under the commerce power . . . Not only has the Court never crossed this line, neither has Congress . . ."[26] One might have imagined that, at this point, an inferior court judge might well have stopped and ruled for the challenger. Instead, Judge Sutton engages in extrapolation from "the language *and direction* of the Court's precedents . . ." In other words, he engages in just the form of extrapolation that Judge Easterbrook eschewed. His predictive approach to stare decisis closely resembles that which has been articulated here by Orin. To which Judge Graham offered his own prediction:

Notwithstanding *Raich*, I believe the Court remains committed to the path laid down by Chief Justice Rehnquist and Justices O'Connor, Scalia, Kennedy, and Thomas to establish a framework of meaningful limitations on congressional power under the Commerce Clause. The current case is an opportunity to prove it so.[27]

Indeed, Judge Sutton issues his own poignant challenge to the Supreme Court:

The Supreme Court can decide that the legend of *Wickard* has outstripped the facts of *Wickard*—that a farmer's production only of more than 200 bushels of wheat a year substantially affected interstate commerce. . . . A court of appeals cannot. The Supreme Court can decide that *Raich* was a case only about the fungibility of marijuana, . . . not a decision that makes broader and more extravagant assertions of legislative power more impervious to challenge. A court of appeals cannot.[28]

Whether or not an inferior court may, the Supreme Court not only can but must decide these questions. And so it will. About a year from now.

The "Unlimited Power" Argument and the Commerce Clause

Orin S. Kerr
August 17, 2011

There has to be some natural limit on how much commentary readers can bear on the individual mandate, but I wanted to respond to one argument that seems to be at the core of the arguments in the mandate debate. As the recent Eleventh Circuit decision and the recent *SCOTUSblog* symposium make clear, much of the constitutional argument against the individual mandate rests on the unlimited power argument: The mandate must be unconstitutional because upholding the mandate requires concluding that the federal government has unlimited power. If the mandate is within Congress's power, the thinking goes, then anything is within Congress's power—the federal government would have a general police power, which cannot be right.

I'm deeply sympathetic to the argument that current Commerce Clause doctrine gives the government too much power. At the same time, I think it's worth noting that arguments in support of the mandate do reflect a limitation on the scope of federal power: the line between regulating markets in goods and services and regulating outside of markets in goods and services. The basic idea is that Congress has Article I power to regulate markets in goods and services, as markets in goods and services are commerce. In contrast, Congress does not have a general Article I power to regulate on subjects *outside* of markets in goods and services, as that is not part of commerce.

Just to be clear, it's not the line I would propose if I could rethink Commerce Clause jurisprudence from first principles. But it does appear to be the line that current Supreme Court cases draw. Thus, in *Lopez*, the federal government couldn't ban possession of a gun in a school zone with no proven link to interstate commerce because it's extremely tenuous to argue that possessing a gun in a school zone is part of a market in goods and service. As the *Lopez* Court put it, "Section 922(q) is a criminal statute that by its terms has nothing to do with 'commerce' or any sort of economic enterprise, however broadly one might define those terms."[33] Thus, it couldn't be regulated. In contrast, in *Raich*, the federal government could regulate even intrastate possession of marijuana, as it is part of an effort to regulate a market in illegal goods and services for marijuana. The *Raich* court explained,

> Unlike those at issue in *Lopez* and *Morrison*, the activities regulated by the CSA are quintessentially economic. "Economics" refers to "the production, distribution, and consumption of commodities." Webster's Third New International Dictionary 720 (1966). The CSA is a statute that regulates the production, distribution, and consumption of commodities for which there is an established, and lucrative, interstate market. Prohibiting the intrastate possession or manufacture of an article of

commerce is a rational (and commonly utilized) means of regulating commerce in that product.[34]

Of course, I realize that there's a debate on how to apply that economic vs. noneconomic test (or perhaps more accurately, the market vs. nonmarket test). Mandate supporters generally look at the law from the perspective of Congress. They reason that Congress was trying to regulate a large chunk of the United States economy and that obviously relates to markets. In contrast, mandate opponents generally look at the law from the perspective of someone who does not participate in the market for health care. They reason that this application of the law doesn't regulate markets, as the person regulated was outside the market to begin with. But regardless of which application of the test is correct, the test itself does impose a limitation on the scope of federal power.

To be clear, I'm not saying that I personally like the current state of the law. I'm a federalism guy. I personally think the economic/noneconomic line isn't enough of a limitation on federal power. Lots of things relate to markets in some way, and when you can "aggregate" economic impact, that gives Congress an enormous amount of power. The Commerce Clause is not just about commerce, it's about *interstate* commerce. So I would be pleased if the Supreme Court ends up taking a more restrictive view of federal power than existing case law reflects. But while the economic/noneconomic line may not be enough of a limitation to me, I don't think it's accurate to say that it makes the federal government one of unlimited power.

Is the Individual Mandate "Unprecedented" Because It Is More Statist than Previous Laws or Because It Is More Market Oriented?

Orin S. Kerr
September 19, 2011

One of the common claims made by opponents of the individual mandate is that it is "unprecedented"—and therefore constitutionally suspect—for Congress to use the Commerce Clause power to mandate the purchase of a product. Never in United States history has Congress interfered so much with personal freedom so as to mandate the purchase of a product. If Congress can do this, the thinking runs, then individual freedom is lost because there are no limits on what other statist things the federal government can do. As a result, approving the mandate would enable unprecedented statism: if the federal government can cross this line, it can cross any line.

That's the narrative. At the risk of ticking off my fellow libertarians even more than I have already, however, I wonder if this narrative is somewhat backwards.

Here's my thinking. The basic goal of the Affordable Care Act is to make sure everyone has health care insurance. In the 1960s Great Society era, that goal would have been satisfied by establishing a government monopoly that forced government insurance on everyone. Consider the Medicare program, which was first established in 1965. Under Medicare, the federal government automatically provides health insurance to those 65 or older. The program is paid for with taxes paid by the country's employees, most of whom are under 65, who must pay a 2.9 percent payroll tax.

The 1960s Great Society way to establish health care for everyone would have been to extend Medicare so that it applies to everyone. The payroll tax would have been increased, and insurance would have been provided to everyone under a uniform plan run by the federal government. Throughout the debate over health care, first in the Clinton years and later with the Obama administration, the 1960s Great Society model was in play at times under the rubric of the "single-payer model." That's what those on the Left wanted in the current health care debate.

Pretty much everyone agrees that a single-payer government monopoly paid for out of payroll taxes would be constitutional. It's the old big-government way of doing things and is certainly not "unprecedented." It's old news. So if the Affordable Care Act had been based on that model, there would be no challenge to its constitutionality.

Now enter the individual mandate. In the health care debates, an individual mandate was considered a more market-oriented alternative to the single-payer model. As far back as 1992, the idea was pitched by the Heritage Foundation as the Heritage Consumer Choice Health Plan. It was then enacted in Massachusetts in 2006 under Republican Governor Mitt Romney. The basic idea is to reject a one-size-fits-all method of government control and to instead continue to allow private companies to offer health care plans, with the catch that everyone who can afford health care must buy it.

The end result is similar to that in a mandatory benefit program, in that everyone ends up with health care insurance. But under an individual mandate health care plan, private companies are allowed to compete among each other for customers. Instead of forcing the same benefit on everyone and using the tax system to force people to pay for it in payroll taxes, it maintains the basic dynamic of a purchased good and thereby retains some aspects of a market system based on competition among providers. Of course, it's not a free market by any stretch. Those who can afford it are *required* to purchase a good from one of the approved insurance companies, which libertarians will abhor. But on a scale from a total free market to total government control, the option is more market oriented than the Great Society approach—which would require the benefit to be provided and paid for without even the pretense of a market purchase.

Let's return to the title of the post, the question of why the mandate is "unprecedented." If I understand the way in which mandate challengers use that term, the mandate isn't unprecedented because the government has never been this statist. To the contrary, it is "unprecedented" because it is the first time that a major federal government benefit program rejected the 1960s Great Society model and instead tried to adopt a more market-oriented approach to benefits. That is, the mandate is unprecedented because it tries to create a federal government benefit program while maintaining the basic market dynamic of goods being bought and sold instead of a government monopoly dynamic of paying for benefits through taxes. As far as I know, it's the first time a federal government program has tried to use that kind of hybrid government-market model.

Why does this matter? I think it matters in part because it suggests that the arguments of the mandate challengers are libertarian only in the short run. In the short run, we know that between a 1960s Great Society model and an individual mandate model the individual mandate model was more politically popular—and that even it barely squeaked through Congress. As a result, if you can get the individual mandate struck down, then the effect is likely to keep away either kind of health care system as long as the current political picture stays roughly steady. That's why the argument looks libertarian today and presumably why so many libertarians embrace it: for the foreseeable future, it would have the libertarian result of leading to neither a government monopoly nor an individual mandate model of health care. The former would be ruled out by public opinion and the latter by the courts.

In the long term, however, the argument of the mandate opponents doesn't strike me as a particularly libertarian. If the courts conclude that the mandate approach is unconstitutional, then the more market-oriented approach to benefits would be ruled out. Congress would have a choice: don't mandate benefits or else mandate using a 1960s Great Society government monopoly model. Depending on what kinds of policies are popular in the future, the result may be to push future Congresses to embrace the government monopoly model *more*. If Congress had the determination to pass a benefits program but the more market-oriented approach were ruled out, then it would presumably proceed with a government monopoly program instead. Perhaps the Constitution requires that. But it doesn't strike me as a libertarian result.

Is the Mandate More "Market Oriented" than Available Alternatives (and Does It Matter)?: A Response to Orin

Jonathan H. Adler
September 21, 2011

Orin Kerr's post suggesting that the individual mandate is less of a threat to liberty than some of the available alternatives has drawn quite a response. See, for instance, the posts by Timothy Sandefur at PLF[35] and Trevor Burrus at Cato@Liberty.[36] They make some important points, but I wanted to add a few of my own.

First, I think there's too much attention paid to whether the individual mandate is or is not "unprecedented" and what conclusions we should draw from that observation. As a simple factual matter, it is true that the federal government has never sought to use the commerce power to mandate the purchase of a good or service from private firms. But this fact, by itself, does not establish that the mandate is unconstitutional. At most, it requires greater analysis as there is no clear analog from prior cases or government actions to which one can turn and may justify some resort to constitutional first principles (as in *Lopez*) to answer the question. (As a related matter, whether one program or another is more or less of a threat to individual liberty may or may not be relevant to the constitutional question.)

Second, many of the prior, government-run programs adopted in the past are actually far more market oriented than the individual mandate, let alone the entire health care reform law. Traditional welfare programs, for instance, involve the direct provision of cash or vouchers that the recipients decide how to spend. Even though there are sometimes restrictions placed on how such assistance may be used, this approach remains far more market oriented—and "libertarian"—than a mandate. Indeed, individual providers of eligible goods and services compete against each other more in this context than insurance companies will under the individual mandate and the health care reforms other measures. Even Medicare, despite all of its problems, is more market oriented in many ways than the current reforms, in that recipients still get to choose among providers, and does less to distort health care markets than regulatory mandates. Further, as the example of Medicare shows, direct government provision of a benefit does not necessarily become "monopoly" provision. Medicare is a "mandatory" program, but recipients are free to decide whether they will partake in the program and may supplement it as they choose. Of course, that one program is more "market oriented" than another is a different question from whether one is more or less constitutionally suspect.

Third, it is generally accepted that the primary constraints on the federal government's exercise of its taxing and spending are political, not judicial. That is, we let the political process discipline the federal government's excesses when it taxes or spends too much or on the wrong things. Judicial intervention is generally reserved for ensuring that the government does not subvert political accountability or use these powers to achieve otherwise unconstitutional ends (as with the unconstitutional conditions doctrine). The "political safeguards" approach to federalism advocated by Herbert Wechsler and Justice Harry Blackmun has been decisively rejected because it is too easy for the federal government to subvert political accountability when it is using other powers.

Fourth, there are many areas in which it is recognized that allowing the federal government to compel activity by others is a greater threat to liberty and does more to undermine political accountability than to allow the government to act directly. I'll give just two quick examples.

1. Commandeering: Under cases like *New York v. United States* and *Printz v. United States*, the federal government may not compel state governments or state officials to implement a federal program. Part of the rationale is that it is better to force the federal government to implement such measures itself and that the risk of the federal government overreaching as a result is less than the threat to political accountability of letting the federal government be the states' puppet master.
2. Compelled vs. government speech: Current doctrine concerning compelled commercial speech (marketing orders and the like) subject government mandates that private parties speak to a greater level of scrutiny than the government's use of taxes or special assessments to fund the same message. In other words, current doctrine is more suspicious of efforts by the

government to force, say, fruit growers to espouse the government's message than it is of efforts by the government to tax the very same fruit growers so that the federal government can itself promulgate the same message. As with commandeering, part of the concern here is political accountability. It is easier to hold the government accountable when it must openly raise revenues and act itself than when it can dictate that others devote their resources in a manner the government prefers.

Finally, Orin's post suggests a false dichotomy insofar as it implies that the only relevant options for health care reform are something like the individual mandate and government monopoly provision. In reality, there are many ways to expand health care coverage or otherwise reform health care. Not only are there less intrusive ways of subsidizing health care for those in need, there are less intrusive (and more effective) ways of enhancing competition within health care markets. So invalidating the mandate does not necessarily mean that we'd eventually get something worse—but even if it did, that would not resolve the constitutional question.

Should Libertarians Prefer the Single-Payer Model to the Individual Mandate? A Response to Adler and Burrus

Orin S. Kerr
September 21, 2011

I appreciate the responses of Jonathan Adler and Trevor Burrus to my post questioning whether the mandate challenge would further libertarian ends. To recap, in my post I agreed that in the short run, given prevailing political winds, the mandate challenge would further libertarian preferences. But I questioned whether that would be true in the long run: it seemed to me that given shifting political views, the argument against the mandate might have the ironic effect of ruling out a less bad option (mandates) and thereby resulting in Congress embracing more bad options in the future (traditional 1960s Great Society government benefit programs). Adler and Burrus have both disagreed, and I want to respond here.

1. In his response, Jonathan Adler argues that I have presented a false choice between two lousy options, and that better options are available:

Orin's post suggests a false dichotomy insofar as it implies that the only relevant options for health care reform are something like the individual mandate and government monopoly provision. In reality, there are many ways to expand health care coverage or otherwise reform health care. Not only are there less intrusive ways of subsidizing health care for those in need, there are less intrusive (and more effective) ways of enhancing competition within health care markets. So invalidating the mandate does not necessarily mean that we'd eventually get something worse . . .

Just to be clear, I agree that it doesn't *necessarily* mean that. I'm only asking about the chances that it would.

I realize that, for us smaller-government types, my framing of the issue is a little like the game "would you rather," in which someone poses two terrible options and asks which you would prefer. If someone asks if you would you rather be eaten alive by hungry mountain lions or torn limb from limb by a grizzly bear, it's natural to say that neither sounds good and you would prefer option C. But it seems to me that although Adler, Burrus, and I have preferences that are significantly more market oriented than either of the options on the table—and significantly more market oriented than most voters—our being out of sync with majority preferences means that having views on the relatively desirability of bad options is an important concern. (It's not something you hear much in politics, as everyone fears that acknowledging a result is less bad will be misconstrued as saying it is good. But, fortunately, none of us are running for office.)

2. Jonathan Adler argues that a single-payer model would actually be preferable to an individual mandate from a libertarian perspective. I think there are two different questions here: first, what a person has to do to get a benefit, and second, what a person can then do with the benefit following receipt. Jonathan focuses on the latter and notes that in the model of a government-provided benefit program, the recipients may be able to do as they please with the benefit. But I would think the comparison here is the former question, not the latter. Whether the government provides health insurance or a person buys it, once a person has that insurance, they use it in the same way. The relevant distinction is in how a person obtains the benefit, not what they do with it. In the 1960s model, the government just provides it. In the mandate model, individuals buy it with their own money from one of the approved sellers.

Both are bad options from a libertarian perspective, but I would think that the former is somewhat worse. I'm certainly not an expert in this, so if I am missing the boat I'd be happy to change views. But here's my perhaps amateurish thinking. First, in general, permitting private companies to compete means choice and competition, which generally lead to more freedom and incentives to improve. That's the thinking behind school vouchers, for example, and I would think it applies to health insurance, too.

Second, my sense is that a mandate approach is easier to limit and control. In a 1960s benefit system, benefits seem to magically appear, and recipients become deeply invested in seeing those benefits preserved and expanded. People don't feel like they're buying something, and thus should expect value for their money: Instead they feel like they're getting free stuff and they pretty much always want and welcome more. The taxes that are imposed to pay for the program become largely hidden,[37] as they are deducted from employee paychecks before employees ever see the money. That's why entitlement programs are so hard to keep in check once created.

In contrast, I would think that a mandate approach leads to more account-ability. When the law forces people to buy something, it forces people to confront what the law is doing. The coercion and the trade-offs are more in the open, as people are forced to repeatedly buy a product and to give up their money for it. They are forced to see what the products are, and to see how much they cost, and they are much more sensitive to those costs and the effect of government regulation on them when they choose which plan to buy. My sense is that that would be preferable to us smaller-government types: the urge to limit government is much sharper when people are regularly confronted with the fact that the government is forcing them to pay for something they may or may not want.

3. I read Trevor Burrus as arguing that a single-payer model would be preferable to the mandate because it is politically tougher to enact. The individual mandate is *really* a tax-and-benefit program, the argument runs, but styling it as something other than a tax lets the administration pass it more easily—and thus get all the big government Obama wants without having to admit he wants higher taxes. As a result, we may be better off if a mandate approach is off the table and the government has to pitch taxes as taxes.

I can appreciate that argument in the short term, but I'm not sure it works in the long term. While raising taxes is a political nonstarter in today's GOP,[38] that hasn't been nearly as much the case in the past. That's how taxes got to where they are today; why they used to be higher (think of the marginal tax rates of 70 percent on high income earners in the 1970s[39]); and why even antitax President Reagan raised taxes a number of times. Taxes have never been popular, obviously. But I don't think we can assume that today's attitudes toward taxes are fixed.

Single-Payer, the Individual Mandate, Liberty, and Accountability: A Surreply to Orin

Jonathan H. Adler
September 21, 2011

Would defeating the individual mandate today lead to something worse tomorrow? I don't know. I don't have a crystal ball but neither does Orin. We can't answer this question, but we can identify reasons why mandate-style approaches to health care reform can increase the threat to individual liberty and undermine democratic accountability. My previous point was not that a single-payer plan is necessarily preferable to the individual mandate on libertarian grounds, as it would depend on how such a system was designed and implemented. But I would argue that upholding the mandate risks greater threats to liberty insofar as (a) mandate-style measures help hide the real costs of health care reforms, thereby undermining democratic accountability, and (b) it would set the precedent that the federal government's regulatory power could be used to mandate the purchase of a good or service from private firms. Direct government provision or subsidization of health care services does not suffer from the first problem as the costs are readily identifiable through the budget process (which is precisely why we got the mandate in the first place). And direct government provision or subsidization of health care services does not suffer from the second problem as the relevant precedent has already been set.

Orin seems to equate the financial cost of government programs with the extent to which they impair individual liberty. The cost of a government program may be a rough proxy for the extent to which liberty is impaired, but it is just that. Freedom is about more than the size of one's tax bill. Zeroing out government expenditures altogether might reduce the tax burden, but insofar as some governmental functions may enhance liberty (such as national defense, police, judicial systems, etc.), it would not maximize individual liberty.

In any event, the individual mandate and other measures constraining health care markets may not increase the tax burden, but that does not mean they are "free." Health insurance must be paid for either way; the mandate just keeps more of it off the federal government's ledger. Indeed, the individual mandate was expressly designed to facilitate redistributive policies that could not be adopted directly—and this is so precisely because the mandate and associated insurance reforms are less transparent than taxes and direct expenditures. If the American people want a given degree of economic distribution, so be it, but neither liberty nor accountability is furthered by allowing such redistribution to occur off budget through the imposition of regulatory dictates.

I will admit I am a bit perplexed by Orin's reference to school vouchers, as vouchers have far more in common with traditional government programs than does the mandate. The "thinking behind school vouchers" is that a given good—education, health care, whatever—should be funded out of tax revenues but that control over how the benefit is used remains with the recipient. This sounds more like a traditional benefit program than the recent reforms. Indeed, there are quite a few mandate opponents who support reforms that would "voucherize" existing and proposed benefit programs. The reason entitlement programs are so hard to control is not tax withholding but that the budgets for such programs are on auto-pilot and not limited by appropriations and so are more difficult to restrain than discretionary expenditures.

Insofar as Orin's concern is that opposition to the individual mandate cannot produce a relatively stable political outcome unless and until its opponents find some other way to satisfy the demand for health care "reform," I would agree with him. However much I dislike much of the recent health care reforms, it was responding to some real (and some perceived) needs and deficiencies of the current system. It is also true that many conservatives and libertarians (and even more Republicans) devote far more time and effort to tearing down proposed reforms than proposing positive solutions of their own. (I've made similar complaints about the Right's approach to environmental policy for years.) So I share the concern that defeating the mandate could be a Pyrrhic policy victory if there are not serious efforts made to improve the health care system and (in particular) expand access to care. But I don't see why such concerns counsel against opposing the mandate, let alone why such concerns should be relevant to the constitutional debate.

Oral Argument in the D.C. Circuit Mandate Case

Randy E. Barnett
September 27, 2011

Last Friday, I attended the oral argument in the *Seven-Sky v. Holder* case in the Court of Appeals for the D.C. Circuit. There has been very little press attention paid to this hearing, most likely because the press was anticipating important developments in the Eleventh Circuit case involving the 26 state attorneys general and the National Federation of Independent Business (in which I am involved). But the hearing was very interesting if for no other reason than the intellectual fire power of the panel: Judges Harry Edwards, Laurence Silberman (who previously wrote opinions holding that the independent counsel law and the D.C. gun ban were unconstitutional), and Brett Kavanaugh. The lawyers for each side had their ups and downs. The low point for the government was when Judges Kavanaugh and Silberman pressed counsel for about ten minutes for a single example of any economic mandate that would be unconstitutional under the government's theory of constitutionality. To their evident frustration, she refused to provide any such example. The low point for the challengers was attempting to wrestle with Judge Kavanaugh's reading of the text of the Anti-Injunction Act (AIA) and with Judge Silberman's capacious interpretation of *Wickard v. Filburn*.

Near the end of the government's time, however, Judge Kavanaugh laid out an explicit four-point analysis that summarized several lines of questions and that might well provide the structure for a majority opinion in the case. So far as I know, this has gone unreported. (Note: I have not seen a transcript of the argument so this is reconstructed from my notes and, except where I use quotation marks, does not purport to be a verbatim account. Comments in brackets were not necessarily stated by him but are my reactions and interpretations.)

1. First, although judges should approach all acts of Congress with a presumption of constitutionality, given that in 220 years the Congress has never claimed the attractive power to mandate that private citizens send their money directly to private companies, judges should at least be "hesitant" before endorsing such a power. [Elsewhere in the argument Judge Kavanaugh noted that this principle was identified in *Printz* when Justice Scalia was evaluating the constitutionality of the power to commandeer state governments as a necessary and proper means of executing the commerce power: "[I]f, as petitioners contend, earlier Congresses avoided use of this highly attractive power," wrote Justice Scalia, "we would have reason to believe that the power was thought not to exist." Ultimately, Justice Scalia characterized a state commandeering power as "improper."]
2. Second, this claim of power is "uncabined." [As evidenced by the governments adamant refusal in oral argument to identify any economic mandate that would be outside the power of Congress to enact. A fact-based evaluation that "health care is different" does not provide a judicially administrable

limit. This was a major concern expressed by Judges Dubina and Hull in their jointly authored Eleventh Circuit opinion.]

3. Third, Congress could have accomplished all or most of what it wanted to accomplish simply by exercising its tax power but it chose not to. [Although earlier in the argument Judge Kavanaugh pressed counsel for Seven-Sky on the tax power theory, this comment seemed to signal that he was not persuaded by the government's tax power theory, which remains the darling of the law professoriate. I could be wrong about this signal, but Judge Kavanaugh did seem to say that Congress chose not to use its tax power.]

4. Therefore, why then open a new chapter of congressional power by extending the commerce power in so dangerous a way? Here Judge Kavanaugh made what was, for me at least, a new argument against sustaining this power: unlike the tax power that is limited to monetary exactions (except for penalties imposed for failure to make payments), sustaining economic mandates under the commerce power would empower Congress to impose any penalty up to and including prison terms for violating its economic mandates. Judge Kavanaugh seem sincerely troubled by the dangerous nature of this new (i.e. unprecedented) expansion of federal power from what has previously existed until now. [True, the ACA contains only tepid penalties, but if the Commerce Clause rationale is successful, the sky is the limit.]

While some press accounts have focused on Judge Kavanaugh's forceful questioning about the AIA—and it was indeed forceful—I thought the government's counsel was effective in countering his textual analysis to the point where he volunteered that it was a "close" issue. In the end, I feel confident that the AIA issue will not prevail, especially given that both the government and the challengers agree it does not apply for good reasons, and all but two federal judges so far have concurred in this assessment.

Of greater concern is Judge Silberman's interpretation of *Wickard*, but that issue merits a separate post.

UPDATE: When I expressed the opinion that, "*In the end*, I feel confident that the AIA issue will not prevail," I was speaking of the legal challenges to the ACA as a whole, not to the outcome of the D.C. case in particular. Judge Kavanaugh's concerns were serious and genuine, and I am hopeful but not "confident" that the government's textual arguments, and a nice metaphor offered by the counsel for Seven-Sky, were enough to satisfy him.

What about *Wickard*?

Randy E. Barnett
October 14, 2011

A few weeks ago, I blogged about oral argument in the D.C. Circuit Court of Appeals in the *Seven-Sky v. Holder* case. In my post, I expressed some concern about a colloquy between Judge Silberman and Ed White, counsel for the American Center for Law and Justice, about the scope of congressional power upheld in *Wickard v. Filburn*. In particular, Judge Silberman asked counsel for both sides to comment on what he presented as the "logic" of *Wickard*. Here is the exchange with passages of particular interest highlighted in bold and italics I have added:

MR. WHITE: Because I think as the Middle District of Pennsylvania noted just last week, the judge was bound by Stare Decisis, is it's not just the outer reaches where you're looking at *Wickard* and *Raich*, which are basically the same case even though it's a different substance, but you look at *Lopez* and *Morrison*–

JUDGE SILBERMAN: **That's not true. They're not really the same case.** I think *Wickard* goes, forgive me for stopping you, but **I think *Wickard* goes further.** *Wickard*, if you read it carefully, applied in the following situation. **You have a small farmer who wishes to grow wheat for the purpose of baking bread for his own family *and only for his own family* and nevertheless, he can be barred from doing so. Now, in a sense, that is a greater exercise of Governmental power than this case because as Justice Jackson pointed out, the purpose of the statute was to force that farmer to buy wheat in the interstate market. He couldn't grow it himself, even to feed his own family.**

MR. WHITE: I will address that after I address this first point, okay? Where when you look at *Lopez*, when I say they're basically the same case, I think the Supreme Court in *Raich* said they're very similar, similar circumstances, okay, and I understand there are nuances to everything, is that when you look at *Lopez* and *Morrison*, the Court said, you know, the line is drawn between economic and non-economic activity. Here, we have really the absence of commerce activity. And said you also have to consider the limits of federalism because that's very hard because we, we are a country with a free market economy. We're not, you know the Soviet Union with a centralized, controlled command economy where the Federal Government tells us everything, what to do. And especially when we go back to when you talk about Massachusetts, the states, and that's where people (indiscernible) liberty to, the states are supposed to be laboratories of experimentation and if the situation in Massachusetts really seems to work over the course of time, other states can adopt that and can move on. Now, going to *Wickard*, *Wickard* is more of a limitation. When we talked about Congress says, you were talking earlier about Congress can regulate and prohibit as they did, *Wickard* is a limitation in the sense that Filburn was still able to grow a percentage of his acreage of wheat.

JUDGE SILBERMAN: That's only because there was an exemption for small farmers. But the *logic of Jackson's opinion*, it seems to me, made it quite clear he could have been barred from growing any wheat whatsoever.

MR. WHITE: Well, if–

JUDGE SILBERMAN: And even to feed his own family.

MR. WHITE: Well–

JUDGE SILBERMAN: Force him to buy in the interstate, in the open market.

MR. WHITE: Well, I do not think–

JUDGE SILBERMAN: **Which is sort of a mandate, isn't it?**

MR. WHITE: Well, not really. If anything, it's a limitation or a prohibition. If Congress said we're, in effect, going to outlaw wheat growing–

JUDGE SILBERMAN: Sort of reminds me of let them eat cake.

MR. WHITE: And unfortunately, that might be where we're going if this, you know, if Congress has this unlimited power. They are letting eat cake.

In my experience, the seminal New Deal opinions, broad as they were, were not nearly as broad as constitutional law professors later made them out to be. Because of the gloss on these decisions that has been applied over the decades, one needs to examine what they actually said. To evaluate the interpretation of *Wickard* articulated by Judge Silberman, it is useful to read the relevant portion of Justice Robert Jackson's opinion[40] in its entirety to preserve context, once again with the most relevant passages indicated in bold, and with some comments in brackets:

> The effect of **consumption of home-grown wheat** on interstate commerce is due to the fact that **it** [i.e. the consumption of home-grown wheat] constitutes *the most variable factor* in the disappearance of the wheat crop. **Consumption on the farm where grown** appears to vary in an amount greater than 20 percent of average production. The total amount of **wheat *consumed as food varies but relatively little***, and use as seed is relatively constant. [ME: When Justice Jackson is discussing "home-grown wheat" and "consumption on the farm where grown," which he characterizes as "the most variable factor," he distinguished this from "wheat consumed as food," which he said "varies but relatively little." So Justice Jackson's references to "home-grown wheat" and "consumption on the farm where grown" do not include either "wheat consumed as food" or wheat "use[d] as seed." So contrary to the way it is often taught, *Wickard* does not equate "home consumed wheat" or wheat "consumption on the farm where grown" with wheat consumed "as food" on the farm. This is simply a misreading of the terminology of Jackson's opinion.]
>
> The maintenance by government regulation of a price for wheat undoubtedly can be accomplished as effectively by sustaining or increasing the demand as by limiting the supply. The effect of the statute before us is to restrict the amount which may be produced for market and the extent, as well, to which one may forestall resort to the market by producing to meet **his own needs**. [ME: Given the previous paragraph, these "needs" are a reference to using wheat on the farm to feed livestock rather than buying wheat from other farmers. It is not a reference to wheat consumed as food.] That appellee's own contribution to the demand for wheat may be trivial by itself is not enough to remove him from the scope of federal regulation where, as here, his contribution, taken together with that of many others similarly situated, is far from trivial. *Labor Board v. Fairblatt*, 306 U.S. 601, 306 U. S. 606 et seq.; *United States v. Darby* supra at 312 U.S. 123.
>
> It is well established by decisions of this Court that the power to regulate commerce includes the power to regulate the prices at which commodities in that commerce are dealt in and practices affecting such prices. One of the primary purposes of the Act in question was to increase the market price of wheat, and, to that end, to limit the volume thereof that could affect the market. It can hardly be denied that **a factor of such volume and variability** as home-consumed wheat [ME: i.e., not "wheat consumed as food," the volume of which "varies but relatively little" (see previous)] would have a substantial influence on price and market conditions. This may arise because being in marketable condition such wheat overhangs the market, and, if induced by rising prices, tends to flow into the market and check price increases. But if we assume that it is never marketed, it supplies a need of the man who grew it which would otherwise be reflected by purchases in the open market.

[ME: Again, purchases in the market for livestock feed, not bread for the family table.] Home-grown wheat [ME: i.e., wheat grown on the farm to feed to livestock] in this sense competes with wheat in commerce. **The stimulation of commerce is a use of the regulatory function quite as definitely as prohibitions or restrictions thereon.** [ME: "Stimulation" does not here refer to a mandate but to the incentive created from the prohibition.] This record leaves us in no doubt that Congress may properly have considered that **wheat consumed on the farm** [ME: this is economic activity] where grown, if wholly outside the scheme of regulation, would have a substantial effect in defeating and obstructing **its purpose to stimulate trade** therein at increased prices.

It is said, however, that this Act, *forcing* **some farmers into the market to buy what they could provide for themselves,** is an unfair promotion of the markets and prices of specializing wheat growers. It is of the essence of regulation that it lays a restraining hand on the self-interest of the regulated, and that advantages from the regulation commonly fall to others. The conflicts of economic interest between the regulated and those who advantage by it are wisely left under our system to resolution by the Congress under its more flexible and responsible legislative process. Such conflicts rarely lend themselves to judicial determination. And with the wisdom, workability, or fairness, of the plan of regulation, we have nothing to do.

The first thing to note is that it is entirely proper to construe the **holding** of *Wickard* in light of the relevant facts of the case, in particular the nature of the statute that was under consideration. The facts are these: (1) The Court never addressed the power of Congress to regulate the activity of growing wheat to feed one's family; what it might or might not have said about this claim of power is a matter of speculation—remember that the Court was so bothered by restricting this intrastate activity of farmers that they held the case over another term for reargument. (2) The Agricultural Adjustment Act (AAA) did not apply even to all commercial farms, much less all individuals in the United States; it applied to farms over a certain acreage. (3) Perhaps most importantly, the AAA did not involve a federal mandate that those farmers to which it did apply, much less all individuals in the United States, purchase wheat or wheat products from the interstate market; instead, it prohibited the covered farmers from growing more than a set quota of wheat. (4) Under the AAA upheld by the Court, farmers were only *indirectly* "forced" to enter the market for interstate wheat by the exercise of Congress to prohibit them from growing more than a certain amount of wheat, not from *directly* mandating they do so; and remember, when Justice Jackson uses the word "forcing," he is paraphrasing an objection to the scheme.

So the proposition that *Wickard* extends beyond these facts depends entirely on how one defines its "logic." But I do not believe that the logic of Justice Jackson's opinion is accurately reflected in Judge Silberman's summary.

The logic of *Wickard* is that people's economic activity—such as the activity of wheat farmers—may be "**restrict[ed]**" even if such a restriction has the effect of "forcing" them into the interstate market over which Congress has control. The Court in *Wickard* scarcely could imagine, much less endorse, a direct command by Congress to farmers that they must buy interstate wheat. The power to "stimulate" commerce by resorting to regulations, prohibitions, as well as taxation and subsidies that are within the power of Congress to impose is simply not the same as the power to mandate commerce.

In short, there are many things that Congress can try to accomplish indirectly *with its enumerated powers* even though it has no enumerated power to do them directly. So rather than mandate that all home owners in flood plains buy flood insurance, Congress can deny home owner's federally guaranteed mortgages unless they obtain flood insurance. Instead of mandating people buy American cars, it can pay "cash for clunkers." Conversely, just because Congress can "force" farmers into the interstate wheat market by using its power to cap their production of wheat, it does not entail that Congress also has the power to command or mandate that farmers buy interstate wheat and imprison any farmer who disobeys.

Remember, as Judge Kavanaugh observed in oral argument, unlike tax subsidies or other incentives, once the power to mandate economic activity is recognized under the Commerce Clause, there is absolutely nothing preventing Congress from criminalizing failures to engage in the mandated activity. The price of forgoing a subsidy, or even giving up a regulated activity altogether to avoid a regulatory scheme—for example, by selling one's farm or quitting the practice of medicine—is entirely different than the consequences of refusing to obey a government mandate to engage in activity, which can be punishable by fine or imprisonment. The fact that the sanction for violating *this* mandate is limited to a fine is beside the point, since the "logic" of finding it to be a Commerce Clause regulation will allow Congress to impose any of its usual regulatory punishments for failing to comply with Commerce Clause regulations or prohibitions.

Furthermore, unlike the power to prohibit, the power to mandate commerce is not *incidental* to the power to *regulate* commerce but is an awesome, dangerous, and independent power in its own right that the Constitution did not delegate to the Congress. If such a power to mandate economic activity exists, it would need to be authorized by the Constitution, as it may well be authorized by a state constitution to the extent that it, unlike the U.S. Constitution, grants a broader police power to its legislature. Of course, the police power of states is subject to other federal constitutional constraints (e.g. the Fourteenth Amendment). In addition, state police powers are subject to an important structural constraint: companies and individuals can flee a state for another with less objectionable laws. By contrast, the federal government is subject both to Bill of Rights constraints and the textual constraint imposed by the list of limited enumerated powers. But that textual constraint only operates if federal judges hold the line on these textually defined powers.

There is probably more to say—pro and con—on *Wickard* than I have said here, but this post has already grown far longer than I intended. So let me conclude with the following observation. If the logic of *Wickard* is read as broadly as the questions posed by Judge Silberman, then the command of another canonical Supreme Court decision would have to be discarded:

> The powers of the Legislature are defined and limited; and that those limits may not be mistaken or forgotten, the Constitution is written. To what purpose are powers limited, and to what purpose is that limitation committed to writing, if these

limits may at any time be passed by those intended to be restrained? The distinction between a government with limited and unlimited powers is abolished if those limits do not confine the persons on whom they are imposed, and if acts prohibited and acts allowed are of equal obligation.[41]

Wickard need not, and ought not, be interpreted as transgressing against *Marbury v. Madison*.

UPDATE: I had an additional thought: It is quite clear after *Raich* that Congress now *does* have the power to prevent a person from growing wheat to feed his own family. Whereas we claimed that growing something in your own backyard was noneconomic activity, the majority in *Raich* reached its result by characterizing the manufacture or consumption of a commodity as an "economic activity." This is the sense in which *Raich* is conventionally and correctly interpreted as a step beyond *Wickard*. If Angel Raich obeys that prohibition, she could then be "forced" into the illicit marketplace for her marijuana. But this does not entail that Angel Raich or Dianne Monson can be compelled to grow marijuana or that Roscoe Filburn can be compelled to grow wheat. Nor does it entail that any of them can be directly compelled to buy marijuana or wheat in the marketplace. I did not want to leave the impression that because *Wickard* may be limited to the restriction of commercial farming, which in the aggregate has a substantial effect on interstate commerce, that this limit was not expanded by *Raich*, now allowing Congress to reach just this activity.

Moreover, even if the "logic" of *Wickard* or *Raich*, extending beyond their facts, might be used to justify a mandate of economic activity, there are other cases with their own logic that cut the other way. For example, *Lopez* and *Morrison*'s logic is that Congress lacks a general police power, that its powers are limited and enumerated, and that these limits justify some judicial enforcement. The logic of *Printz* is that even a necessary mandate on state governments is an improper means of regulating commerce, in that case because it commandeers the legislatures of the states in violation of the principles underlying the Tenth Amendment. The Tenth Amendment, after all, protects the reserved powers of the people equally with the powers of the states. Or the *Bond v. United States*[42] case from last term that affirms that the scheme of federalism based on enumerated powers was intended to protect individual liberty (and for this reason can be asserted by individuals objecting to a federal statute). The logic of all these cases bears on the ACA case, not just *Wickard*, even if *Wickard*'s logic is broader than its holding.

Farmer Filburn's Wheat

Jonathan H. Adler
October 16, 2011

As an addendum to Randy's post on *Wickard v. Filburn*, I wanted to point out some additional facts about the case and farmer Roscoe Filburn's activity in particular. It is commonly asserted that Farmer Filburn was barred from growing extra wheat for consumption by his family. This is simply false.

The Agricultural Adjustment Act expressly applied to the growing of wheat for the purpose of feeding livestock, and this is what farmer Filburn was doing. Filburn grew the extra wheat for the primary purpose of feeding his dairy cows. For Filburn, the excess wheat was an input of production in a broader commercial enterprise, and that is why he went over his allotment.

Filburn grew 11.9 acres of excess wheat—more than double his quota. The extra acreage generated 239 bushels. How much is that? As Jim Chen points out in his informative essay on the case: "To consume 239 excess bushels, the Filburn family would have had to consume nearly forty-four one-pound loaves of bread each day for a year."[43] Filburn's livestock may have been able to consume this much wheat, but his family sure couldn't.

Whether or not *Wickard* can or should be read as authority for the proposition that Congress could prohibit a farmer from growing wheat for (in Judge Silberman's words) "the purpose of baking bread for his own family and only for his own family," this is not an accurate characterization of what Farmer Filburn had done to violate the AAA.

On November 8, 2011, the United States Court of Appeals for the District of Columbia Circuit upheld the Affordable Care Act. (Ed.)

Kavanaugh on the Case for Not Deciding the Constitutionality of the Mandate

Orin S. Kerr
November 8, 2011

Judge Kavanaugh wrote a separate opinion[44] in the D.C. Circuit's mandate case that many readers will overlook: it's based on the tax code, and the opinion itself acknowledges that its analysis is dense and difficult. ("The Tax Code is never a walk in the park. . . . I caution the reader that some of the following is not for the faint of heart.") At the same time, Kavanaugh's opinion closes with a very interesting prudential case for not deciding the merits of the mandate and instead deciding the case on Anti-Injunctive Act grounds. Among them, Kavanaugh argues that if the Court doesn't decide the issue now, it may never have to decide the issue because the statute could be easily amended to make the mandate easily constitutional under the taxing power. It's an interesting read, and one that I suspect may get some attention when the case reaches the Supreme Court.

As an aside, it's interesting that the circuit court decisions on the mandate have included three opinions by leading lights of the Federalist Society—Judges Silberman, Sutton, and Kavanaugh—and that *none of them* voted to strike down the mandate. These three judges are hugely influential in the conservative legal community, and the conservative justices and clerks on the Court watch their work closely. Although a split is a split, and the Court is extremely likely to take a mandate case, the absence of a vote to strike down the mandate among the opinions from Judges Silberman, Sutton, and Kavanaugh can't be welcome by mandate opponents.

Notes

1. Florida v. U.S. Dep't of Health & Human Servs., 648 F. 3d 1235, 1291 (2011); Cf. Randy Barnett, "No Commandeering." *infra*.
2. Thomas More Law Ctr. v. Obama, 651 F. 3d 529 (6th Cir. 2011).
3. See Ilya Somin, "Broccoli, Slippery Slopes, and the Individual Mandate," *supra*.
4. Ilya Somin, "Why Going without Health Insurance Isn't an 'Activity,'" *supra*.
5. Orin Kerr, "Brilliant People Agree with Me," *Volokh Conspiracy* (blog), August 4, 2010, http://www.volokh.com/2010/08/04/brilliant-people-agree-with-me.
6. *Thomas More Law Ctr.*, 651 F. 3d at 560–61 (opinion of Sutton, J.).
7. *Id.* at 565–66 (opinion of Sutton, J.).
8. See, e.g., United States v. Jones, 529 U.S. 848 (2000).
9. *Thomas More Law Ctr.*, 651 F. 3d at 544 (opinion of Martin, J.).
10. For those interested in more about this question, I recommend the work of a former student: Nathaniel Stewart, "Turning the Commerce Clause Challenge 'On Its Face': Why Federal Commerce Clause Statutes Demand Facial Challenges," *Case Western Reserve Law Review* 55 (2004): 161.
11. Jonathan H. Adler, "Is Morrison Dead? Assessing a Supreme Drug (Law) Overdose," *Lewis and Clark Law Review* 9 (2005): 751, 770–76.
12. See, e.g., O'Gorman & Young, Inc. v. Hartford Fire Ins. Co., 282 U.S. 251, 257–58 (1931) (citing cases).
13. See, e.g., United States v. Watson, 423 U.S. 411, 416 (1976).
14. Randy E. Barnett, *Restoring the Lost Constitution: The Presumption of Liberty* (Princeton, NJ: Princeton University Press, 2004).
15. Boumedience v. Bush, 553 U.S. 723 (2008).
16. Reno v. Am. Civil Liberties Union, 521 U.S. 844 (1997).
17. Hamdan v. Rumsfeld, 548 U.S. 557 (2006).
18. Boumediene v. Bush, 553 U.S. 752 (2008).
19. I should emphasize that the point is not just that the Court failed to explicitly mention the presumption of constitutionality in the cases I listed. Even more importantly, it also failed to *apply* the doctrine with or without mentioning it, even though it would clearly have been relevant if it did apply. Nowhere in these opinions is there any indication that the majority was deferring to Congress or presuming that Congress's statute was constitutional.
20. *Thomas More Law Ctr.*, 651 F. 3d at 559 (opinion of Sutton, J.).
21. UPDATE/CORRECTION: In editing Judge Martin's opinion for the supplement to my casebook, I came across the following caveat, which detracts from my characterization of his opinion as "accepting" the requirement that Congress must regulate activity:

> As long as Congress does not exceed the established limits of its Commerce Power, there is no constitutional impediment to enacting legislation that could be characterized as regulating inactivity. The Supreme Court has never directly addressed whether Congress may use its Commerce Clause power to regulate inactivity, and it has not defined activity or inactivity in this context. However, it has eschewed defining the scope of the Commerce Power by reference to flexible labels, and it consistently stresses that Congress's authority to legislate under this grant of power is informed by "broad principles of economic practicality." *Lopez* (Kennedy, J., concurring); see *Wickard* (explaining that Congress's power cannot be determined "by reference to any formula which would give controlling force to nomenclature such as 'production' and 'indirect' and foreclose consideration of the actual effects of the activity in

question upon interstate commerce." . . . Thus, the provision is constitutional notwithstanding the fact that it could be labeled as regulating inactivity.). 651 F. 3d at 547–48.

Before and after this passage, Judge Martin adopts and employs the "class of activities" analysis without questioning it, and he then finds the existence of activity. In his very next sentence he writes the sentence I quoted previously: "Furthermore, far from regulating inactivity, the minimum coverage provision regulates individuals who are, in the aggregate, active in the health care market." But, despite the ambiguity created by his clear acceptance of the "class of activities" mode of analysis, I no longer think it accurate to claim that he "accepted" that Congress "must regulate activity." It would be more accurate to say that "Judge Martin declined to uphold the law on the ground that Congress may regulate inactivity, preferring instead to find that Congress had indeed regulated activity in this case." I regret the error.

22. *Thomas More Law Ctr.*, 651 F. 3d at 542.
23. *Id.* at 544.
24. *Id.* at 547.
25. *Id.* at 543n3.
26. *Id.* at 558.
27. *Id.* at 573 (Graham, J., dissenting).
28. *Id.* at 559–60 (opinion of Sutton, J.).
29. Matt Cover, "When Asked Where the Constitution Authorizes Congress to Order Americans to Buy Health Insurance, Pelosi Says: 'Are You Serious?,'" CNSNews.com, last modified October 22, 2009, http://cnsnews.com/node/55971.
30. Watson v. United States, 552 U.S. 74 (2007).
31. UPDATE: It turns out that the Supreme Court did briefly mention the presumption at the start of its opinion in *United States v. Morrison*. I apologize for the error. At the same time, the presumption seems to play little if any role in the Court's analysis of the decision. It is not mentioned at all after this one line near the beginning: "Due respect for the decisions of a coordinate branch of Government demands that we invalidate a congressional enactment only upon a plain showing that Congress has exceeded its constitutional bounds . . . With this presumption of constitutionality in mind, we turn to the question whether §13981 falls within Congress's power under Article I, §8, of the Constitution." *Morrison*, 529 U.S. at 607.
32. *Id.*
33. United States v. Lopez, 514 U.S. at 561 (1995).
34. *Raich*, 545 U.S. at 25–26.
35. Timothy Sandefur, "Privatization, Regulation, and Freedom of Choice—or, Orin Kerr Doesn't Get It. Again," *PLF Liberty Blog*, September 20, 2011, http://plf.typepad.com/plf/2011/09/privatization-regulation-and-freedom-of-choiceor-orin-kerr-doesnt-get-it-again.html.
36. Trevor Burrus, "The Difference Between Governments Where There Is Responsibility, and Where There Is None," *Cato At Liberty* (blog), September 20, 2011, http://www.cato.org/blog/difference-between-governments-where-there-responsibility-where-there-none.
37. See Dean Stansel, "The Hidden Burden of Taxation: How the Government Reduces Take-Home Pay," *Cato Policy Analysis* no. 302 (1998), http://www.cato.org/pubs/pas/pa-302.html.
38. "What Is the Taxpayer Protection Pledge?," Americans for Tax Reform, http://www.atr.org/taxpayer-protection-pledge.

39. "U.S. Federal Individual Income Tax Rates History, 1913–2011," Tax Foundation, http://taxfoundation.org/article/us-federal-individual-income-tax-rates-history-1913–2011-nominal-and-inflation-adjusted-brackets.

40. 317 U.S. 111, 127–29 (1942).

41. Marbury v. Madison, 5 U.S. 137, 176–77 (1803).

42. Bond v. United States, 131 S. Ct. 2355 (2011).

43. James Ming Chen, "The Story of Wickard v. Filburn: Agriculture, Aggregation, and Commerce," in *Constitutional Law Stories*, ed. Michael C. Dorf (New York: Foundation Press, 2008).

44. Seven-Sky v. Holder, 661 F. 3d 1 (2011).

6

The Big Show

On November 14, 2011, the Supreme Court agreed to hear the cases of *National Federation of Independent Business v. Sebelius* and *Florida et al. v. Department of Health and Human Services.*

There were two cases because both the government and the plaintiffs—the National Federation of Independent Business (NFIB), Florida, and 25 other states—appealed to the Supreme Court. The government had little choice but to appeal Judges Joel Dubina and Frank Hull's decision if they were to save President Barack Obama's signature legislative achievement. The NFIB and Florida appealed the Eleventh Circuit's decision to not sever the individual mandate and its decision to uphold the Medicaid expansion.

The Supreme Court would hear four questions: (1) whether the individual mandate is constitutional; (2) whether the Medicaid expansion is constitutional; (3) whether the mandate, if declared unconstitutional, could be severed from the rest of the act; and (4) whether the Anti-Injunction Act (AIA), a nineteenth-century law that prohibits legally challenging a tax before that tax is collected, foreclosed the plaintiffs' challenge to the individual mandate. The last question was closely tied to whether the mandate's penalty could be upheld as a tax. The individual mandate comes into force in 2014, and thus no one had yet been fined for not complying. If the Anti-Injunction Act prevented the preemptive challenge to the mandate's penalty, then the entire case would be kicked out of court without a decision on Obamacare's constitutionality.

The Court's decision to hear the Medicaid expansion question and the Anti-Injunction Act question surprised everyone. No lower court had yet struck down the Medicaid expansion, which was challenged under the theory that Congress cannot go too far in offering states money as an inducement to change their laws. Prior decisions had said that federal funding could be used as an enticement but not as extortion. The line between the two, however, had long been unclear.

The Court also granted five-and-a-half hours of oral argument, a surprisingly long time. Arguments would be held on March 26 through March 28, 2012. Everyone knew that, barring exceptional circumstances, the fate of the law would be known by late June 2012.

***

How Should the Supreme Court Rule on the Individual Mandate?

Orin S. Kerr
January 20, 2012

Now that the mandate case has reached the Supreme Court, the case triggers conflicting instincts for me. On one hand, as I've said before, I'm a federalism guy. I think limits on federal power play a critical role in our federal system, and I think Supreme Court doctrine has erroneously permitted the federal government to become too big and plays too intrusive a role in American society. The Commerce Clause was never intended to give the federal government a general police power. It was meant to just allow the federal government to regulate interstate commerce. That part of me would cheer if the Supreme Court struck down the mandate.

On the other hand, I'm also a Burkean conservative, stare decisis guy, and I'm acutely aware of the Supreme Court's long struggle to identify principled and workable limits on the scope of the Commerce Clause. History has shown that it's surprisingly hard to do and that unprincipled or unstable lines don't last and just destabilize the law for a short window before being rejected. My comfort with the Court striking down the mandate therefore varies considerably based on *how* the Court could do it. Let's imagine, hypothetically, that the Supreme Court strikes down the mandate but does not identify any genuinely principled or workable doctrine to justify it. The Court's decision merely reopens the hornet's nest of line-drawing problems that the Court has long struggled with in the Commerce Clause setting, with the significant likelihood that in twenty years the Court will abandon its reasoning. In that case, the Burkean conservative part of me would be dismayed by the Court's decision. Sure, the federalism guy side of me would be happy, but it would be outweighed by my Burkean objections. But if we imagine a hypothetical opinion invalidating the mandate that *did* identify such a principle, and the principle proves a lasting one, then my Burkean concerns could be addressed and my reaction would be different.

That explains why I have posted a lot of "law professor hypotheticals" about the implications of the mandate challenge. The more I see the theory driving the challenge as workable and principled, the more I favor it. I can't gauge how much the challenge triggers my Burkean objections without understanding exactly what it is and how it might work.

Now add another consideration. I also value the Supreme Court deciding cases independently of politics as much and often as possible. This is a sort of Wechslerian neutral principles idea that the justices shouldn't be political actors in robes. It's horribly out of fashion in the faculty lounge, to be sure, but the neutral principles part of me is pretty dubious about the mandate challenge because the challenge seems so transparently political. The Affordable Care Act is President Obama's signature legislative achievement. Everyone who opposes the constitutionality of the mandate just so happens to also oppose the mandate politically. And the most commonly asserted constitutional argument against the mandate wasn't even thought up until around just before the mandate was passed, only to be readily embraced by the same folks that tried to stop the legislation in Congress but failed.

The obvious political valence of the mandate challenge gives me a lot of pause, and it adds a significant complication in my view of what the Court should do. On one hand, it's obvious that any decision striking down the president's signature legislation would have enormous political ripple effects. Given that the theory behind the challenge was largely made up to stop the mandate, and it's hard to imagine more than five votes to strike down the mandate, that would make the Supreme Court a political player in ways that dwarf recent examples. The narrative of the decision as deeply political would resonate with a lot of people. But my concerns go beyond that. Because I don't like it when the Court's decisions have an obvious political valence, I start to care about the vote count and the political resonance of the opinions. All other things being equal, I'd greatly prefer a vote lineup that didn't break along the obvious 5–4 political lines and that is written in ways that echo partisan concerns. I would prefer a lineup with cross-party voting and with opinions that have more lasting and long-term legal gravitas; something that tells us that there is more than just politics afoot here.

Where do these and other sometimes-competing concerns lead? In my case, they lead me to conclude that I can't know what I would prefer the Supreme Court to do unless I know what the options are. I'm less concerned with whether the Court strikes down or upholds the mandate than how it does so. If I can dream about a perfect world, I would like to see a 9–0 decision that identifies a widely shared neutral principle deeply rooted in precedent that also limits the scope of the federal government in a significant way, but that's a pipe dream. To borrow from Donald Rumsfeld, you go into Court with the justices and the precedents you have, not the justices and the precedents you might want.

The realistic options therefore are much more confined. When I imagine the realistic options, I can imagine both a hypothetical majority opinion striking down the mandate, which I would prefer to a hypothetical dissent upholding it, and a hypothetical majority opinion upholding it, which I would prefer to a hypothetical dissent striking it down. It depends on how the opinions are written, what they would say, and whether they would identify clear lasting principles outside of the short-term political environment of the present. For example, is a hypothetical decision upholding the mandate a 5–4 Breyer opinion that dismisses federalism, or is it an 8–1 John Roberts opinion that recognizes the great value of federalism but concludes reluctantly in a Sutton-esque way that the lack of a principle and the weight of stare decisis dooms the challenge? Is a hypothetical decision striking down the mandate one that is easily circumvented by a future Congress and is easily construed as a one-time-only way to stop legislation most Republicans oppose, or is a deeper principle adopted?

No Commandeering

Randy E. Barnett
January 20, 2012

In his thoughtful post, Orin says he would support striking down the individual insurance mandate on federalism grounds if the Supreme Court provided a "genuinely principled or workable doctrine to justify" its decision. "[I]f we imagine a hypothetical opinion invalidating the mandate that did identify such a principle, and the principle proves a lasting one, then my Burkean concerns could be addressed. . . ." Of course, he admits that his crosscutting considerations are "competing" and therefore difficult to satisfy. Indeed, he characterizing satisfying them all as a "pipe dream."

But I think there is an existing constitutional doctrine already limiting the commerce power of Congress that does satisfy most of Orin's competing considerations: the doctrine established by the Court in *New York v. United States* in an opinion by Justice Sandra Day O'Connor that bars Congress from commandeering state legislatures by mandating that they enact laws. *New York* has been widely accepted and applied without raising the sort of insuperable line-drawing problems that concern Orin and the underlying noncommandeering principle has been extended to bar commandeering of state executive branch officials[1] and the state judiciary.[2] This line of cases is now twenty years old and considered well settled. Congress has been able to legislate quite extensively without running afoul of the prohibition on state mandates (though the Medicaid requirements of the Affordable Care Act are now testing the boundaries of this structural constraint). So the noncommandeering principle as applied to states seems to satisfy Orin's Burkean concerns.

Notice that, in each of these cases, the Congress was purporting to exercise its power to regulate interstate commerce under the Commerce Clause, and the Court did not question that this was indeed the legitimate *end* or purpose of the challenged legislation. What was at issue was the *means* that Congress used to effectuate this end. In *Printz v. United States*, the government justified its choice of means under the Necessary and Proper Clause. Writing for the Court, Justice Antonin Scalia did not question the measure's necessity but concluded that the means employed was "improper." In this respect, Justice Scalia's decision in *Printz* is quite different than his concurring opinion in *Gonzalez v. Raich* that solely concerned the necessity of the prohibition of homegrown marijuana in states that authorized its possession and use. In *Raich*, no one questioned the propriety of the means that Congress had used to effectuate its commerce power. Furthermore, in none of these noncommandeering cases was this restriction on the propriety of the means chosen to effectuate the commerce power based on the protection of "liberty" in the Due Process Clause of the Fifth Amendment. Instead, it was based on the "structural" principle of limited state sovereignty that the Court concluded was presupposed by the Tenth and Eleventh Amendments. While states may be regulated in how they conduct their affairs by, for example, barring them from engaging in racial or sex discrimination, and they may be barred from certain activities altogether, they may not be "mandated" to enact legislation or enforce federal law.

Of course, the obvious objection to applying the noncommandeering doctrine in the ACA challenge is not Burkean but legal: it is *individuals* and not the states who are being commandeered by the Affordable Care Act, so the existing noncommandeering doctrine does not apply. Yet the principal textual basis for the decisions in *New York* and *Printz* was the Tenth Amendment that reads, "The powers not delegated to the United States by the Constitution, nor prohibited by it to the states, are reserved to the states respectively, *or to the people.*" The Tenth Amendment, therefore, protects *popular* as well as state sovereignty. Indeed, it protects them equally. (The Virginia legislature initially refused to ratify the Tenth Amendment precisely for this reason.) Requiring citizens to "consent" to contracts is very much the same as requiring states to enact legislation. As the famed contracts scholar Lon Fuller wrote, the "power of the individual to effect changes in his legal relations with others [by entering contracts] is comparable to the power of a legislature. It is, in fact, only a kind of political prejudice which causes us to use the word 'law' in one case and not in the other . . ."[3]

The principle that the people may not be commandeered is reflected in several other constitutional provisions. The Third Amendment bars the commandeering of the people's houses to quarter the military during peacetime ("No soldier shall, in time of peace be quartered in any house, without the consent of the owner, nor in time of war, but in a manner to be prescribed by law."). The Fifth Amendment bars the commandeering of private property ("[N]or shall private property be taken for public use, without just compensation."). The Fifth Amendment also stipulates that no person "shall be compelled in any criminal case to be a witness against himself." And the Thirteenth Amendment bars the commandeering of a person's labor by private parties or by the government itself ("Neither slavery nor involuntary servitude . . . shall exist within the United States").

Of course, like every legal principle, there are exceptions to the noncommandeering principle. Soldiers may be quartered in private homes in wartime if authorized by law. Private property may be taken "for public use" provided "just compensation" is made. Involuntary servitude may be imposed "as a punishment for crime whereof the party shall have been duly convicted." In addition, the people may be "commandeered" by the federal government to serve in the military, to file federal tax returns, to serve on juries in federal court, and to serve on a *posse comitatus*. The first of these exceptions, however, was expressly grounded on what the Supreme Court characterized as "the exaction by government from the citizen of the performance of his *supreme and noble duty* of contributing to the defense of the rights and honor of the nation . . ."[4] Likewise, the other duties can be considered duties of citizens owed to the government itself. Moreover, none of these duties of citizenship have ever been associated with the commerce power.

While the existence of exceptions does make line drawing more difficult, this is pervasive in all of law. And the historical exceptions to the principle against commandeering the people are all specifically or narrowly defined and deeply rooted in the nation's traditions, which is exactly the "conservative" criterion by which the Supreme Court defines exceptions to legislative powers on behalf of individual liberty under the Due Process Clause. So the relevant question is whether a duty of citizenship to buy private insurance is deeply rooted in the nation's tradition? Or more broadly, is there "a supreme and noble duty" of American citizenship to do anything that Congress in its discretion deems it necessary to its regulation of interstate commerce? Analyzing a claimed "duty" of citizenship the way the Supreme Court now analyzes claims of liberty would yield a ready answer.

Of course, although the noncommandeering principle is based on both the text of the Constitution (as just described), its application in this case would be "novel." But this is due entirely to the novelty of the individual insurance mandate. Simply because the mandate is literally unprecedented so too would be any doctrine directly addressing it, however fundamental the principle being effectuated. *Printz* too considered a "novel" claim of power to control state executives, thus requiring the identification of a new rule of law. Yet, as Justice Scalia wrote, "[I]f . . . earlier Congresses avoided use of this highly attractive power, we would have reason to believe that the power was thought not to exist."[5]

Barring the government from commandeering the people by imposing economic mandates upon them would not affect any other law ever enacted by Congress because such mandates are unknown in our history. Such a ruling would not bar Congress from using its tax powers when it has the political will to do so (subject, of course, to whatever doctrines now limit that power). Such a ruling would not bar states from exercising such a power if it was authorized by a state's constitution (subject, of course, to other constitutional limitations on state powers). Such a ruling would only require the conclusion that just as the Constitution did not delegate to Congress the power to commandeer state legislatures as a means of exercising its commerce power neither did it delegate the power to commandeer the people as a whole to enter into contractual relations with private companies. In short, if a majority of justices have the will to invalidate the individual insurance mandate, they surely have the way.

A Response to Randy on "No Commandeering"

Orin S. Kerr
January 20, 2012

Thanks very much to Randy for his post arguing that his "no commandeering of the people" theory could be the argument that addresses my different concerns and create a sound way to strike down the mandate. Like all of Randy's work, it is engaging, interesting, and important. But of the different arguments Randy offers to invalidate the mandate, I find the "no commandeering of the people" argument the least persuasive. Here's a rundown of why.

First, the "commandeering of the people" claim reads like an emanations-and-penumbras argument, in which we look to various bits and pieces of the Constitution to try to assemble them into a brand-new principle to get to where we want to go. Maybe I'm too sensitive to constitutional claims that rely on implicit principles of the Third Amendment. But that kind of legal reasoning gives my

Burkean instincts the heebie-jeebies. In my experience, the point of emanations-and-penumbras arguments is to present something new as if it were something old (but just not quite previously recognized). I get the move, but here it seems pretty clear that the argument is new. As Randy concedes, the existing doctrine is about commandeering the states, not about commandeering the people.

Even if this is to be recognized as a new constitutional principle, it's not clear how it works. First, it's not clear to me how saying you have to pay an extra fee if you don't buy health insurance "commandeers" anything. True, it's an incentive to do something. But it's a relatively modest one and strikes me as far short of the coercive take-over implied by the concept of commandeering. And if we say that this sort of modest incentive amounts to commandeering, then isn't most of what the government does commandeering? For example, does the home mortgage deduction commandeer you to buy a house? And more obviously, doesn't the draft commandeer you to join the military?

Randy introduces several limitations on the theory that lead him to conclude that the mandate is the first case of the relevant kind of commandeering and therefore is the only legislation that needs to be invalidated. But his limitations strike me as rather arbitrary. First, Randy limits his proposal to "economic" commandeering. That presumably would deal with the draft cases. But if the Constitution is to be read to prohibit commandeering, isn't economic commandeering the least offensive kind? A draft forcibly making someone go off to fight a war (and risk death in combat) seems exponentially more offensive than making someone pay a few hundred bucks through a lower tax refund if their income is above a certain amount. And isn't the limitation to "economic" commandeering an odd fit with the tax power? Under Randy's theory, as I understand it, it seems that Congress is actually perfectly free to engage in economic commandeering as long as it does so through something formally called a tax. If economic commandeering is to be recognized as a core constitutional prohibition, it seems surprising that it could be so easily done under the tax power.

Finally, there's my Wechslerian neutral principles reaction. One of Randy's selling points for the no-commandeering argument is that it could be adopted in a way that only strikes down the mandate. He writes, "In short, if a majority of justices have the will to invalidate the individual insurance mandate, they surely have the way." Although potentially appealing to the Burkean instinct, from a Wechslerian perspective, that's a bug rather than feature. A novel argument that manages to only strike down the one law we don't like is not based on an appeal to lasting principle. Instead, it appeals to expedience; it gets us where we want to go. From a Wechslerian neutral principles perspective, I'd be much more drawn to a principle that has all sorts of results that we don't like. The more we don't like the results, the more we have an indication that we are adopting the principle because of its constitutional truth and not because we don't like the Affordable Care Act.

"This Far and No Further": Baselines and the Individual Insurance Mandate

Randy E. Barnett
January 22, 2012

Much of the difference of opinion over the constitutionality of the individual insurance mandate turns on a difference of opinion about the appropriate baseline for evaluating congressional power. For sixty years, law professors taught that Congress had unlimited discretion with respect to using its commerce power to regulate the national economy. They held this view notwithstanding that the Supreme Court had never enunciated such a position and that we now know that some justices on the New Deal Court considered doing so in *Wickard v. Filburn* but declined to pull that trigger. Virtually all "progressive" academics—and many, if not most, "conservatives" whose constitutional views were formed before 1995—accepted and continue to accept this proposition as the baseline against which congressional legislation was to be assessed.

Regardless of whether this was ever the baseline accepted by the Supreme Court, in 1995, the Supreme Court *arguably* (more on this in a moment) rejected it in favor of another: Congress has discretion with respect to all the powers that have been upheld up to that point, but any claim of implied congressional power beyond that point was constitutionally suspect. Because Congress had never before attempted to regulate wholly intrastate noneconomic activity, a majority of the Court in *United States v. Lopez,* and again in *United States v. Morrison* (over the impassioned dissent of those justices who hewed to the other baseline), said it would not recognize this new extension of power. *Raich* can be understood as an effort to restrain Congress from exercising a power it had long used: the power to regulate the intrastate cultivation, possession, and distribution of an intoxicating substance. It can also be understood as an effort to sustain an "as-applied" challenge to a facially constitutional exercise of the commerce power, and no such challenge had ever before succeeded.

Since *Lopez* and *Morrison* have now become fixed poles of constitutional decision, there are two competing readings of these cases depending on which baseline one holds. Those who continue to hold the baseline of unlimited Congressional discretion—whose politics can be progressive *or* conservative—construe *Lopez* and *Morrison* as identifying a relatively narrow exception to this power. Since the individual insurance mandate does not clearly fall within this exception, it is therefore deemed by them to be clearly constitutional. This is why, I believe, so many constitutional law professors thought this case was so easy.

In contrast, those who interpret Chief Justice Rehnquist's opinions in *Lopez* and *Morrison* as rejecting that baseline in favor of the position that Congress may go as far as it has gone in the past but no further view the mandate quite differently. Because the power to require all citizens to enter into contracts with private companies is a new or "unprecedented" claim of power, it is at minimum constitutionally suspect and at maximum unconstitutional. Given the baseline, the burden is on the government to justify this expansion of federal power as both necessary *and* proper. As important, there must be some identifiable and judicially administrable limit on its exercise.

Ultimately, it will be up to the individual justices to decide what baseline they wish to employ. Do *Lopez* and *Morrison* represent merely symbolic "sport" cases as so many academics now believe? Or did these cases (along with cases such as *New York*, *Printz*, and *Alden v. Maine*) establish a post–New Deal baseline ("this far and no further") beyond which Congress may not go without meeting a serious burden of justification? Because this case will tell us what baseline the Roberts Court wishes to affirm for the future, it is both a very big deal and not all that easy to predict simply on the basis of prior cases and doctrines. If the Roberts Court adopts the first baseline, however, it will not only be repudiating what I believe to be the best reading of the Rehnquist Court's landmark decisions establishing the so-called New Federalism, it will finally be doing what even the New Deal Court could not bring itself to do. Regardless of how they eventually rule, one can well understand why the Court would feel the need for three days of oral argument to consider this decision.

Understanding Justice Scalia's Concurring Opinion in *Raich*

Randy E. Barnett
March 9, 2012

There has been a lot of chatter lately about how Justice Scalia's concurring opinion in *Raich* somehow binds him to rule for the government in the challenge to the ACA. As the lawyer for Angel Raich, I admit to being disappointed by the outcome of the case, by Justice Scalia's vote, and by his opinion. But during the course of that litigation, I became very familiar with the issues raised by that case and since then have come to appreciate the problem with which Justice Scalia was wrestling. There are two very important implications of his opinion in *Raich*, and neither benefits the government's case.

First, as I explained in my 2010 New York University Law and Liberty article,[6] Justice Scalia clearly locates the "substantial affects" doctrine of *United States v. Darby Lumber Co.* and *Wickard*, as well as the "essential to a broader regulation of interstate commerce" dicta in *Lopez*, in the Necessary and Proper Clause, not in the Commerce Clause—and in particular in the word "necessary" in that clause. Why is this so important? Because if the substantial affects doctrine is viewed as resting on the Commerce Clause, then there is a temptation to *add* the Necessary and Proper Clause to it as an additional theory of power and failing to realize that *Lopez* and *Morrison* were actually limiting the scope of the Necessary and Proper Clause, not the Commerce Clause. In short, there are judicially enforceable doctrinal limits to the scope of the Necessary and Proper Clause.

Moreover, if the substantial effects and essential to a broader regulatory scheme doctrines are both grounded in the word "necessary," then there is still the issue of whether a particular means deemed "necessary" is also *proper*. In *Printz*, for example, Justice Scalia concluded that imposing a mandate on—or "commandeering" of—state legislatures to enact legislation, *however essential it might have been to the regulatory scheme in that case*, was still an improper means of effectuating

Congress's commerce power. True, *Printz* was based on the protection of states afforded by the Tenth Amendment, but the Tenth Amendment applies equally "to the people" as it does to the states. And, in *Comstock*, Justice Scalia joined Justice Thomas's dissenting opinion that reaffirmed Justice Scalia's characterization of the Necessary and Proper Clause as "the last best hope of those who defend *ultra vires* congressional action."[7]

In *Raich*, we never denied the proposition that the "essential to a broader regulatory scheme" doctrine was grounded in the Necessary and Proper Clause but argued instead throughout the litigation that whether a law was "essential," and therefore "necessary," had to survive greater scrutiny than mere rational basis review. When Justice Scalia adopted a rational basis approach to ascertaining "necessity," however, we lost his vote. (Significantly, Justice Anthony Kennedy, in his concurring opinion in *Comstock*, recently advocated a heightened rational basis scrutiny in Commerce Clause cases.)

In our challenge to the Affordable Care Act, we are not asking for any heightened scrutiny of the "necessity" of the mandate for the broader regulatory scheme of the ACA, and neither are we challenging this crucial aspect of Justice Scalia's opinion in *Raich*. Indeed, our severability analysis hinges on Congress's finding that the mandate was "essential" to its scheme of regulating insurance companies. Rather, we are making two claims not addressed in *Raich* by either the majority or by Justice Scalia.

- First, that the mandate is not necessary "*to carry into execution*" Congress's power over interstate commerce. Unlike in *Raich*, those who fail to purchase health insurance in no way obstruct the ability of Congress to enforce its regulations on insurance companies. Instead, Congress wants to ameliorate the negative *consequences* of *successfully* executing its insurance company regulations by forcing these citizens to compensate the insurance companies for the cost of the regulation by transferring their wealth to these companies. These consumers are being forced to buy expensive policies priced *far above their actuarial risk* for the purpose of providing what amounts to a subsidy or transfer payment to the insurance companies. In other words, the need for the mandate assumes that insurance companies *will comply* with Congress's commerce power regulation but suffer economically as a result. Neither the Court in *Raich* nor Justice Scalia were addressing this claim of power by the government in any way.
- Second, unlike in *Raich*, we are claiming that, however "necessary" they may be, mandates of this sort are an improper means of executing the commerce power of Congress. I won't elaborate on this claim here, except to note that it is precisely Justice Scalia's opinions in *Raich* and *Printz* that make so very clear why this claim is a serious one that must be addressed.

But there is a second important lesson to be drawn from Justice Scalia's opinion in *Raich*. Put simply, *Raich* was an "as-applied" Commerce Clause challenge. In *Raich*, we conceded that Congress had the power to prohibit the interstate commerce in marijuana but claimed that a subset of the national market in marijuana—namely, wholly intrastate cultivation and possession that was authorized by the laws of some states—was outside of the power of Congress to reach. Yet no such challenge has ever succeeded. (Think *Wickard*, *Heart of Atlanta Motel v. United States*, *Perez v. United States*, etc.) Recently, my colleague, Nick Rosenkranz has argued that, on textualist grounds, no such challenge *should* ever succeed.[8] When we litigated *Raich* the significance of this aspect of the case was not well understood, but I think it accounts for why Justice Scalia was moved to offer the Necessary and Proper Clause analysis he did.

In *Raich*, we were asking the court to carve out a subset of the class of activities Congress sought to regulate and find that *this subset* was beyond its power under the Commerce Clause. In his concurring opinion, Justice Scalia was wrestling with the following practical issue: given the fungible nature of the commodity, what if "to carry into execution" its power to prohibit interstate marijuana, Congress decided it was "necessary" to regulate the subset of activities involving the identical commodity inside a state, regardless of whether it was being bought and sold and was therefore "noneconomic?" He concluded that Congress could draw the circle—that is, define the class—as widely as it had a rational basis for believing it needed to be drawn to enable it to *effectively enforce* its regulation of interstate commerce that is within its powers. If so, as Justice Stevens suggested during his questioning of Paul Clement in oral argument, there was simply no way to win an "as-applied" Commerce Clause challenge by identifying a subset of the class of activities that Congress sought to regulate.

But the challenge to the individual mandate is a *facial* challenge like that in *Lopez* and *Morrison*. Unlike "as-applied" challenges, facial challenges *have* succeeded (even where a subset of the class, like guns that had moved in interstate commerce, might well have been within the power of Congress to reach). Indeed, in his dissenting opinion in *Raich*, Justice Clarence Thomas noted in a footnote that the majority's decision had no effect on future facial challenges, such as those brought in *Lopez* and *Morrison*. Unlike *Raich*, we are facially challenging the claim that Congress has the power to impose mandates to engage in economic activity by entering into contracts both because (a) such mandates are not necessary *to carry into execution* the regulation of the insurance companies *and* because (b) the unprecedented claim of power to impose a mandate to enter into contracts with private companies is highly *improper*. The "subset" enforcement problem Justice Scalia was grappling with in the "as-applied" challenge in *Raich* simply does not exist here.

Just because the individual insurance mandate is unprecedented does not automatically render it unconstitutional—though, in *Printz*, Justice Scalia affirmed that the fact that so attractive a power has never before been claimed by Congress is evidence the power does not exist. But the unprecedented nature of the mandate *does* make this a case of first impression, which means it is not directly covered by either the majority's or Justice Scalia's opinion in *Raich*. To distinguish his opinion in *Raich* from this case, Justice Scalia would not even have to break a sweat.

Public Opinion, the Individual Mandate, and the Supreme Court

Ilya Somin
March 19, 2012

A recent *Washington Post* / ABC poll shows that 68 percent of the public wants the Supreme Court to strike down the individual health insurance mandate.[9] That includes 42 percent who want the Court to invalidate the entire Affordable Care Act and 26 percent who want it to strike down the mandate alone. If forced to choose, 52 percent of those who want the Court to strike down only the mandate would prefer for the Court to get rid of the entire law, if that is the only way to rule the mandate unconstitutional. That means that some 55 percent would rather have the Court invalidate the entire law than leave the mandate in place. By a 52–41 margin, respondents in the *Washington Post* / ABC poll also say that they disapprove of the health care law overall.

Support for invalidating the mandate cuts across ideological lines, with even a slight 48–44 plurality of Democrats saying they want the court to strike it down. These results are similar to those reached in other recent polls on the constitutionality of the mandate.

These poll results do not prove either that the law is unconstitutional or that the justices are necessarily going to rule the way the public wants. The public's knowledge of constitutional law is weak, and the justices don't always rule in accordance with public opinion.

However, the overwhelming public support for striking down the mandate does suggest that if a majority of the Court wants to invalidate this law, they probably won't be prevented from doing so by fear of a political backlash. Usually, the Court hesitates to strike down major legislation strongly supported by the president and his party because doing so could result in a political confrontation that the Court is likely to lose, as happened during the New Deal period. In this case, however, strong public opposition to the mandate—along with extensive opposition in Congress—insulate the Court from any such backlash. The situation is in sharp contrast to what happened in the 1930s, when many of the laws struck down by the Court had broad bipartisan support.[10]

The situation is also different from what happened after the *Citizens United v. Federal Election Commission* decision in 2010,[11] the most recent Supreme Court ruling that generated extensive public opposition. In that case, the Court endorsed a result contrary to majority opinion, though I believe it was a correct one.

In fact, the Court could well generate greater public anger if it upholds the mandate than if it strikes it down. Many more people want the law struck down than want the Court to uphold it. As the case of *Kelo v. New London* dramatically demonstrates,[12] public outrage can be stimulated by a decision upholding an unpopular law just as readily as by striking down a popular one.

A Bug or a Feature?

David E. Bernstein
March 20, 2012

Jonathan Cohn notes that the question of whether the ACA's (Obamacare's) Medicaid mandate is unduly coercive to the states is the "sleeper issue of the case": "The Affordable Care Act expands Medicaid eligibility guidelines significantly, so that, starting in 2014, anybody with income below 133 percent of the poverty line can receive it. The result will be approximately 15 million more people with Medicaid coverage."[13]

Given that the U.S. Supreme Court has never defined precisely how far the federal government may go in "bribing" states before the bribes become an offer the states can't refuse and thus unconstitutionally coercive, some of the justices might find that this is a mechanism for overturning the ACA without having to revisit the Court's Commerce Clause precedents.

Cohn reprints an email from University of Michigan law professor Sam Bagenstos, in which he details the potential consequences of such a ruling:

> If the Court holds that the ACA's Medicaid expansion is unconstitutional, such a holding could put any number of cooperative state-federal programs at constitutional risk. The most obviously vulnerable would be Medicaid itself—even as it existed before the ACA's amendments to it. If the petitioners are right that the large amount of federal money at stake coerces states into accepting new Medicaid conditions by leaving them with no realistic choice but to accept them, then it is hard to explain why the same large amount of federal money does not coerce states into continuing to accept the conditions that have long applied to Medicaid funding. The many federal statutes that impose conditions on federal aid to education would also be at severe constitutional risk, because those conditions are attached to large amounts of federal funding that states may feel they cannot realistically turn down. These statutes include Title I of the Elementary and Secondary Education Act—the most recent reauthorization of which was the No Child Left Behind Act—and Title IX of the Education Amendments of 1972.

Cohn (and Bagenstos) obviously think they are recounted a parade of horribles, but these sorts of programs are among the worst the federal government has to offer, not necessarily because of their substance but because they undermine political accountability. The states get money from the federal government, with strings attached. Congress is happy because it gets to spend more money, and state and local officials are happy because they can claim credit for spending the money without being accountable for raising it. But local citizens who are unhappy with the relevant "strings" have no recourse to their local government because the locals are just following orders from the Feds. It's the worst of all worlds and a great example of a very dysfunctional version of federalism—congressional overspending; centralized rules from agencies in Washington, D.C.; and no accountability at the level where the money is spent and the rules implemented. If the ACA challenge leads to a constitutional rethinking of (mostly) funded federal mandates, that strikes me as a feature, not a bug. (Note that there is nothing stopping any or all the states from enacting their own, self-funded versions of Medicaid, NCLB, Title IX, etc. and that at least some federal mandates, even if coercive, are constitutionally valid under Congress's "Section 5" power to enforce the Fourteenth Amendment.)

The Congress-Can-Do-Whatever-It-Wants Power

David E. Bernstein
March 23, 2012

As I've argued several times before, the Supreme Court's conservative majority will not uphold the individual mandate if the mandate's defenders are unable to come up with a limiting principle that will prevent a decision upholding the law from eviscerating any remaining limits on Congress's power to regulate interstate commerce (which is not to say that the majority will necessarily uphold the law if such a limiting principle is articulated).

I leave it to those who have studied the briefs in detail to discuss whether the government and its amici have come up with such a principle. But with friends like *New York Times* columnist Linda Greenhouse, they don't need enemies. Greenhouse wrote,

> If the commerce power extends to backyard marijuana growing (as it did to backyard wheat growing in the famous New Deal case of *Wickard v. Filburn*), the notion that Congress somehow lacks the power to regulate, restructure *or basically do whatever it wants in the health care sector*, which accounts for 17 percent of the gross domestic product, is far-fetched on its face.[14]

Greenhouse's reasoning is sloppy. First, *Wickard v. Filburn* didn't apply to "backyard" wheat growing, the farm in question was a large commercial operation, and the wheat in question was fed to the farm's cattle, which were sold on the interstate market. But more important, *Wickard* and *Raich* were both *as-applied* challenges, while the challenge to the individual mandate is a *facial* challenge.

So what Greenhouse is arguing is that because the Supreme Court has in the past refused to countenance as-applied challenges that sought to exempt local activity from a concededly broader scheme of the regulation of interstate commerce, facial challenges to laws on the grounds they don't regulate interstate commerce to begin with are also out of bounds. In other words, Congress can do whatever it wants, at least so long as it identifies an important economic "sector" to which its regulation pertains.

In the health care area, can Congress in fact require everyone to eat broccoli? Exercise twice a day in government-run health care facilities with a government-mandated exercise program? Prohibit people from picking wild blueberries for their own consumption? According to Greenhouse, Congress can do any of those things, even though there is no commerce, much less interstate commerce, involved, so long as it can argue that by doing so it's really trying to regulate the "health care sector."

Maybe it's a good idea to give Congress the power to regulate whatever and however it wants, though I really doubt it. More to the point, I'm quite sure that the conservative majority is not willing to endorse the proposition that the commerce power is really the Congress-can-do-whatever-it-wants power.

Bonus foolishness from Greenhouse: She touts Nancy Pelosi's infamous "are you serious?" response to questions about the ACA's constitutional basis as evidence that the ACA is in fact constitutional, as opposed to what is really is, evidence that Pelosi and her allies treated the idea that the health care law needed to be within Congress's enumerated powers with thinly veiled contempt. This is a very good reason for the Court not to defer to Congress's view of the scope of its commerce power, though of course, lack of deference doesn't dictate the outcome one way or the other.

The Individual Mandate Case Is Not Easy

Ilya Somin
March 23, 2012

Linda Greenhouse[15] and Dahlia Lithwick[16] have attempted to resuscitate the claim that the individual mandate is so obviously constitutional that only ignorance or political bias can lead anyone to believe otherwise.

Such claims were perhaps understandable back when this litigation began. But even then, there was no expert consensus on the constitutionality of the mandate.[17] They are even more dubious now, after several lower court decisions have ruled against the mandate. Even the decisions upholding it all acknowledge that the case raises novel issues. And all of them spend many pages explaining their reasoning, which is not what you would normally see in an easy open-and-shut case.

It's also worth noting that many leading constitutional federalism scholars believe that the law is unconstitutional, including Gary Lawson (one of the top experts on the Necessary and Proper Clause), Steve Calabresi (who is one of the legal scholars who signed on to the amicus brief I wrote for the Washington Legal Foundation), Richard Epstein, and, of course, coblogger Randy Barnett. If the case were an easy one, we would not have such a deep division among legal experts and jurists.

You can say that the experts who think the mandate is unconstitutional are just politically biased. But of course the same charge can be levied at Greenhouse, Lithwick, and the overwhelming majority of commentators on the other side. Greenhouse makes much of the fact that two conservative judges have voted to uphold the mandate. But a Democrat-appointed judge—Frank Hull of the Eleventh Circuit—voted to strike it down. These exceptions do not change the fact that the overwhelming majority of conservative and libertarian experts believe that the law is unconstitutional, while the overwhelming majority of liberal ones believe the opposite. Such ideological polarization among experts is actually yet another sign that the issue is not an easy one. If it were, we would be more likely to see an expert consensus developing.

Greenhouse and Lithwick's argument is not helped by the various factual and analytical errors they make in their pieces. Perhaps the most important is Greenhouse's fallacious assertion (seemingly endorsed by Lithwick) that the plaintiffs' argument is "[b]asically just one word . . . : 'unprecedented.'" In reality, the plaintiffs have never argued that the unprecedented nature of the mandate by itself proves that it is unconstitutional. Rather, their brief repeatedly emphasizes that the main reason to strike down the mandate is that there is no logical way to uphold it without giving Congress virtually unlimited authority to impose other mandates. So far, the federal government has failed to come up with any limiting principle that proves otherwise, as I've explained in some detail elsewhere.[18] If the federal government loses this case, it will be because of that failure, not because only ignorant or politically biased people can believe that law is unconstitutional. As David Bernstein puts it, the Court majority is not going to buy the notion of a "Congress-can-do-whatever-it-wants power."

Greenhouse also claims that *Gonzales v. Raich* and *United States v. Comstock* clearly dictate the outcome of the mandate case. She does not even consider ways in which these cases differ from the mandate issue. As I explained in the WLF amicus brief, some elements of *Comstock* actually help the antimandate plaintiffs. Ironically, Greenhouse previously cited my article explaining why *Comstock* does not dictate the outcome of the mandate case as evidence that even "critics of the newly enacted health care law" believe that *Comstock* requires the mandate to be upheld.

I do not mean to suggest that there isn't a substantial case in favor of the constitutionality of the mandate. Some of the law's defenders have made serious and insightful arguments on its behalf (e.g. Brian Galle, Neil Siegel, and my former colleague Max Stearns). The Supreme Court's precedent on the relevant issues is complex and unclear enough that both sides can make a good case for their position. In my view, the antimandate side does have an overwhelming advantage under the text and original meaning of the Constitution. But textualism and originalism are not, and probably cannot be, the only interpretive methodologies used by the courts.

Be that as it may, public debate over this important issue is not improved by claims that the case for the mandate is so obviously right that no informed person can reasonably disagree with it.

Can the Federal Government Pass a Compulsory Education Law?

David E. Bernstein
March 24, 2012

I was trying to think of a good example to illustrate the federal government's lack of a general police power as opposed to the states' inherent police power, an example that doesn't implicate serious "substantive due process" concerns. So here goes:

all states have compulsory schooling laws, some to age 18, others to age 16. No one seriously questions the constitutionality of these laws.

But let's say the federal government decided to pass legislation, modeled on longstanding state laws, requiring all residents of the United States to attend school until age 18 or face some penalty—a fine, or being drafted into "national service," or whatever. A resident of a state where schooling is only mandatory until age 16 sues, claiming that this is beyond Congress's enumerated powers.

The government claims that it has the authority under its commerce power to require school attendance. After all, not only is education a huge percentage of the American economy, the federal government already regulates the education market to a substantial degree and spends tens of billions of dollars annually for education, money that will to some extent be wasted if children don't continue their education at least through high school. Thus, it's both necessary and proper that the government impose an education mandate to ensure that its education policies will be successful.

To the argument that a 16-year-old dropout isn't engaged in economic activity, the government argues that staying out of school is itself an economic activity because, among other things, it reduces the amount of federal and state aid to one's school, makes one less marketable in the employment market, reallocates resources that would otherwise be spend on the dropout's education, and makes it more likely that one will need to spend money on education in the future. Moreover, no one is really "out" of the education market because everyone is learning things all the time, whether from TV, one's friends, Facebook, or formal schooling. Finally, by dropping out of school, a 16 year old is raising the expected costs to the government and society of future crime, welfare payments, and the like.

Anyone think the government should win?

False Arguments in Favor of the Mandate

Jonathan H. Adler
March 25, 2012

There are serious arguments in support of the constitutionality of the individual mandate (just as there are serious arguments against it). There are also quite a few bad arguments and quite a few that rest on patently false premises. A common example of the latter is that the mandate does not require anyone to engage in commercial activity because all Americans will, in one way or another, eventually engage in health care markets. This is not true.

Here's an example: Walter Dellinger, in today's *Washington Post*,[19] asserts, "The mandate does not force people into commerce who would otherwise remain outside it." This is false, as Dellinger's essay effectively acknowledges when it goes on to note that health care is "an activity in which virtually everyone will engage." This latter statement may be true. "Virtually everyone" may acquire health care—but "virtually everyone" is not "everyone." Most people may purchase health care at some point in their lives, but some will not. Some people will refuse to purchase health care for religious reasons. Some will not purchase health care because they are lucky enough not to need such care before a sudden death. Still others may decide not to purchase health care because they have chosen to remove themselves from commerce—consider a survivalist or other person who decides to live in a shack, growing their own food, and not engaging in commerce with others. All but the former *are* forced to enter into commerce but "would otherwise remain outside it." Indeed, under *Cruzan v. Director, Missouri Department of Health*, there is a fundamental right to refuse even lifesaving health care. Therefore, the government cannot assume that each and every person will, at some point, use (let alone purchase) health care, as every American has the right to decide otherwise. These facts clarify the nature of the legal case for the mandate. Specifically, in order to sustain the mandate, the Court must conclude that Congress has the power to force *all* Americans to engage in commerce simply because *most* Americans already do.

Dellinger goes on to say that "people who go without insurance often shift the costs of their health care to other patients and taxpayers. That situation is different from what happens with any other type of purchase." This latter claim isn't true either. Those who fail to acquire adequate levels of disaster insurance "often shift the costs" of disaster assistance on to others, as the federal and state governments regularly provide assistance to disaster victims above and beyond what their insurance provides. And yet the federal government does not mandate the purchase of flood or other disaster insurance.

That there is some number of people, however small, who would otherwise not engage in health care markets and that there are other contexts in which the underinsured shift costs on to others does not establish that the mandate is unconstitutional. But the persistence of arguments that rest on false premises is further evidence that the individual mandate case is not as easy as some like to suggest. After all, if this were such an easy case, advocates would not need to stretch the facts or make false claims to make their case.

Shortcomings of the "Everyone Uses Health Care" Rationale for the Individual Mandate

Ilya Somin
March 25, 2012

The biggest weakness in the case for the constitutionality of the individual health insurance mandate is that it collapses into a rationale for virtually unlimited federal power.[20] To deal with this problem, defenders of the mandate have put forward a variety of arguments claiming that health care is a special case.

The most popular one, recently restated by Walter Dellinger and Linda Greenhouse, is that health care is a special case because everyone or almost everyone uses it at some point in their lives. However, there is a serious flaw in this argument that mandate defenders have yet to find a way around. I have pointed it out several times over the last two years:

The fact that most people eventually use health care does not differentiate health insurance from almost any other market of any significance. If you define the relevant "market" broadly enough, you can characterize any decision not to purchase a good or service exactly the same way. Notice that the government does not argue that everyone will inevitably use health *insurance*. Instead, they define the market as "health *care*." The same bait and switch tactic works for virtually any other mandate Congress might care to impose.[21]

Interestingly, Greenhouse unintentionally illustrates this point herself. As she puts it,

> The uninsured don't exist apart from commerce. To the contrary, their medical care results in some $43 billion of uncovered health care costs annually and, through cost-shifting, adds $1,000 a year to the average cost of a family insurance policy. People who don't want to buy broccoli or a new car can eat Brussels sprouts or take the bus, but those without health insurance are in commerce whether they like it or not.[22]

Brussels sprouts and buses are indeed alternatives to broccoli and cars. But Brussels sprouts are still part of the food market and buses part of the market for transportation, in the same way as health insurance and other forms of health care provision are both part of the health care market. Thus, people "who don't want to buy broccoli or a new car" are still "in commerce" just like people who don't want to buy health insurance.

You can use similar reasoning to justify virtually any other mandate. Every good that we might be required to purchase or use is part of some broader market that all or most of us will not avoid. How about a mandate requiring people to read and study *Volokh Conspiracy* blog posts? After all, everyone at least to some degree uses the market for "information." And if you don't get information from the VC, you are still likely to get it from other (surely inferior) sources.

As Jonathan Adler points out,[23] it is not in fact true that everyone uses the health care market. A few people do manage to avoid it. By contrast, the market for food really *is* literally impossible to avoid for anyone who wants to remain alive for more than a short time. Even if you grow all your own food without using any tools purchased from others, you would still be engaging "economic activity" as the Supreme Court defines that term. Far from distinguishing this case from the broccoli mandate, the "everyone uses health care" argument actually provides stronger support for food purchase mandates than for the health insurance mandate.

Mandate defenders have also advanced several other rationales for why this is a special case.[24] These rationales all suffer from much the same weaknesses as the "everyone uses health care" argument: their reasoning can justify virtually any other mandate, including the broccoli mandate, the car purchase mandate, and others.

So far, all the king's horses and all the president's men have yet to figure out a way to make this mandate special again. Indeed, it's noteworthy that the seriously flawed "everyone uses health care" argument remains the most popular of the different rationales for why the mandate is a special case. If the many outstanding lawyers and legal scholars on the pro-mandate side have not come up with anything better after two years of effort, that may indicate that no better argument is possible.

None of this will matter if the Court is willing to follow the lead of the D.C. Circuit, which upheld the mandate despite acknowledging that there are no limits to the federal government's logic. But, like David Bernstein,[25] I highly doubt that a majority of the justices are going to endorse the notion that congressional power is essentially unlimited.

Guns, Broccoli, and the Individual Mandate: Thoughts on the Eve of Argument

Jonathan H. Adler
March 26, 2012

Prevailing elite opinion is dismissive of the arguments against the mandate, just as it was dismissive of the challenge [in *Lopez*] to the Gun-Free School Zones Act (GFSZA). Yet then, as now, defenders of the federal law have a difficult time reconciling their arguments with meaningful limits on federal power. Asked to identify something beyond the scope of the federal commerce power in *Lopez*, the solicitor general (SG) came up empty. Asked to identify how the Supreme Court could uphold federal power to compel participation in commerce as a regulation in commerce, without green-lighting a near infinite power to command private activity, the SG's office has also had a difficult time identifying the class of activities subject to regulation. This is one reason the SG's office has shifted its emphasis from "commerce" to what is "necessary and proper" and remains concerned about the "broccoli question."

Whereas some academics and commentators protest the mandate presents an easy case, those who actually have to argue the case in court recognize the need to reaffirm limits on federal power, even as they approve of the individual mandate. The difficulty in maintaining this position is one reason I have become more skeptical of the mandate's constitutionality over time. Harvard's Charles Fried may be comfortable proclaiming that Congress has the power to command all Americans to purchase broccoli or any other good or service, but he also felt Congress had the power to regulate the possession of guns in or near schools. Indeed, as the University of Pennsylvania's Ted Ruger recently recounted, Fried did not even teach the Commerce Clause prior to *Lopez*, as he did not believe the clause was relevant anymore. Many of those defending the mandate today felt much the same way and have sought to minimize the importance of *Lopez* (and *Morrison*) ever since. Yet the Fifth Circuit then, and the Eleventh Circuit now, took the admonition that ours is a government of limited and enumerated powers more seriously and invalidated an unprecedented assertion of federal power as a step too far. Then, a majority of the Supreme Court followed suit. Will they now?

As I noted two years ago,[26] the statutory provisions at issue in *HHS v. Florida* are far more consequential provision than was at issue in *Lopez*. Few Americans had heard of the GFSZA, and even fewer had an opinion as to its constitutionality. Does this mean the challenges will fail? It is much easier for a court to invalidate a small piece of symbolic legislation than a major social reform. And yet the Court has, at times, been willing to cut wide swaths through the federal code or confront the political branches. Dozens of statutory provisions were invalidated by *INS v. Chadha*, and the Court's aggressive review of the political branches' wartime policy decisions in *Boumediene v. Bush* were unprecedented, so it's not as if the Court has not flexed its muscles in the recent past.

The GFSZA may have been obscure, but that also meant it was not unpopular. If, as many believe, the Court is somewhat responsive to political pressures and popular sentiment, this could influence how the Court evaluates arguments that Congress has gone too far. Polls continue to show widespread opposition to the mandate and widespread skepticism about its constitutionality. Indeed, it's not very often that a majority of states unite against a federal statute, particularly when preemption, sovereign immunity, or other state prerogatives are not at stake. Thus, a decision to strike down the mandate may offend academics and other legal elites, but it would not swim against the prevailing political tide or pick a fight with the political branches, as the Court did in *Boumediene*.

If pressed to make a prediction, it's always safer to assume the federal government will prevail before the High Court. It remains relatively rare for the Supreme Court to strike down a federal law. Yet the Court has confounded such expectations before—and there's a nontrivial chance it could do so again. Here's hoping.

Notes

1. Printz v. United States, 521 U.S. 898 (1997) (majority opinion by Scalia, J.).
2. Alden v. Maine, 527 U.S. 706 (1999) (majority opinion by Kennedy, J.).
3. Lon Fuller, "Consideration & Form," *Columbia Law Review* 41 (1941): 799, 806–7.
4. *Selective Draft Law Cases*, 245 U.S. 366, 390 (1918).
5. *Printz*, 521 U.S. at 905.
6. Randy E. Barnett, "Commandeering the People: Why the Individual Health Insurance Mandate Is Unconstitutional," *New York University Journal of Law and Liberty* 5 (2010): 581–637.
7. *Printz*, 521 U.S. at 923.
8. Nicholas Quinn Rosenkranz, "The Subjects of the Constitution," *Stanford Law Review* 62 (2010): 1209.
9. Scott Clement, "Toss Individual Health Insurance Mandate, Poll Says," *Washington Post* (blog), March 19, 2012, http://www.washingtonpost.com/blogs/behind-the-numbers/post/toss-individual-health-insurance-mandate-poll-says/2012/03/18/gIQAaZtpLS_blog.html.
10. Randy Barnett, "Barry Cushman on Bipartisan Support for the New Deal," *Volokh Conspiracy* (blog), March 15, 2012, http://www.volokh.com/2012/03/15/barry-cushman-on-bipartisan-support-for-the-new-deal.
11. Citizens United v. FEC, 558 U.S. 310 (2010).

12. Ilya Somin, "The Limits of Backlash: Assessing the Political Response to Kelo," *Minnesota Law Review* 93 (2009): 2100.

13. Jonathan Cohn, "Obamacare on Trial: Case of the Century," *New Republic* (blog), March 18, 2012, http://www.newrepublic.com/blog/jonathan-cohn/101826/health-reform -supreme-court-challenge-commerce-necessary-proper-medicaid?.

14. Linda Greenhouse, "Never Before," *Opinionator* (blog), March 21, 2012, http:// opinionator.blogs.nytimes.com/2012/03/21/never-before/?scp=6&sq=health%20 care&st=cse.

15. *Id.*

16. Dahlia Lithwick, "It's Not about the Law, Stupid," Slate.com, last modified March 22, 2012, http://www.slate.com/articles/news_and_politics/jurisprudence/2012/03/ the_supreme_court_is_more_concerned_with_the_politics_of_the_health_care _debate_than_the_law_.single.html.

17. Ilya Somin, "The Myth of an Expert Consensus on the Constitutionality of an Individual Health Insurance Mandate," *supra.*

18. Ilya Somin, "A Mandate for Mandates."

19. Walter Dellinger, "5 Myths about the Health-Care Law," *Washington Post*, March 23, 2012, http://www.washingtonpost.com/opinions/5-myths-about-the-health-care-law/ 2012/03/19/gIQAHJ6JWS_story.html.

20. Ilya Somin, "Will the Supreme Court Give Congress an Unlimited Mandate for Mandates?," *SCOTUSblog*, August 10, 2011, http://www.scotusblog.com/2011/08/ will-the-supreme-court-give-congress-an-unlimited-mandate-for-mandates.

21. Ilya Somin, "Why the Individual Heath Care Mandate Is Unconstitutional," JURIST, last modified May 4, 2011, http://jurist.org/forum/2011/05/ilya-somin-mandate-is -unconstitutional.php.

22. Greenhouse, "Never Before."

23. Jonathan H. Adler, "False Arguments in Favor of the Mandate," *supra.*

24. I give a detailed critique of them in Somin, "A Mandate for Mandates," and in the amicus brief I wrote on behalf of the Washington Legal Foundation and a group of constitutional law scholars, *supra.*

25. David Bernstein, "The Congress-Can-Do-Whatever-It-Wants Power," *supra.*

26. Jonathan H. Adler, "What Will the Courts Do with the Individual Mandate?," *supra.*

7

Argument

On Monday, March 26, oral arguments began in *NFIB v. Sebelius*. The allotted time had been extended from an already unprecedented five-and-a-half hours to six. First up was the Anti-Injunction Act (AIA), for which the Court appointed a lawyer, Robert A. Long, to argue that the AIA barred all challenges to the mandate (the Court occasionally appoints lawyers to give arguments that neither party is willing to give).

March 27 was the big day: oral arguments over the individual mandate. Former Bush Administration Solicitor General Paul D. Clement argued for Florida and the 25 other states, Michael D. Carvin of the Washington, D.C., law firm Jones Day argued for the NFIB, and Solicitor General Donald B. Verrilli Jr. argued for the government.

On March 28, the Court heard arguments on the issue of severability and the Medicaid expansion. On severability, Clement argued that if the mandate is unconstitutional then the entire law must fall. Deputy Solicitor General Edwin Kneedler argued that the entire law shouldn't fall but only those parts closely tied to the mandate, such as the guaranteed issue and community ratings provisions. Finally, another Court-appointed lawyer, H. Bartow Farr III, argued that the entire law could keep going without the mandate. On the Medicaid expansion question, Clement and Solicitor General Verrilli crossed swords again

***

Is the Individual Mandate Really a Mandate?

Orin S. Kerr
March 26, 2012

In today's argument, Chief Justice John Roberts had an interesting series of questions on a matter that we debated a bit here at the blog: If the penalties for violating the individual mandate are really weak, is the regulation really a "mandate"? The exchange arose when Greg Katsas (a lawyer challenging the mandate) argued that the Anti-Injunction Act does not apply because the real purpose of the lawsuit is to challenge the individual mandate, not the collection of taxes, and that the mandate and the penalty for violating the mandate should be construed as two very different things. That led to this exchange:

> *CHIEF JUSTICE ROBERTS*: The whole point—the whole point of the suit is to prevent the collection of penalties.
> *MR. KATSAS*: Of taxes, Mr. Chief Justice.
> *CHIEF JUSTICE ROBERTS*: Well prevent the collection of taxes. But the idea that the mandate is something separate from whether you want to call it a penalty or tax just doesn't seem to make much sense.
> *MR. KATSAS*: It's entirely separate, and let me explain to you why.
> *CHIEF JUSTICE ROBERTS*: It's a command. A mandate is a command. If there is nothing behind the command. It's sort of well what happens if you don't file the mandate? And the answer is nothing. It seems very artificial to separate the punishment from the crime.
> *MR. KATSAS*: I'm not sure the answer is nothing, but even assuming it were nothing, it seems to me there is a difference between what the law requires and what enforcement consequences happen to you. This statute was very deliberately written to separate mandate from penalty in several different ways.
>
>   They are put in separate sections. The mandate is described as a "legal requirement" no fewer than 20 times, three times in the operative text and 17 times in the findings. It's imposed through use of a mandatory verb "shall." The requirement is very well defined in the statute, so it can't be sloughed off as a general exhortation, and it's backed up by a penalty. . . .
> *CHIEF JUSTICE ROBERTS*: Why would you have a requirement that is completely toothless? You know, buy insurance or else. Or else what? Or else nothing.
> *MR. KATSAS*: Because Congress reasonably could think that at least some people will follow the law precisely because it is the law.[1]

It's hard to make any firm conclusions from the exchange, of course. But the challenge to the minimum coverage provision is premised on the idea that the mandate is really a genuine mandate, not just some sort of generalized incentive, and that argument rests in significant part on seeing the mandate as separate from the penalty. We'll have to wait and see tomorrow how many justices accept that framing of the statute.

Thoughts on the Individual Mandate Oral Argument

Ilya Somin
March 27, 2012

Today's oral argument was a good day for the antimandate plaintiffs and a troubling one for the law's defenders. I have long argued that the weakest point in the federal government's case is the failure to provide a coherent explanation of why the rationale for the health insurance mandate doesn't also justify virtually any other mandate Congress might impose. All the conservative justices raised this exact issue during the course of today's oral argument, with the exception of the usually silent Clarence Thomas, whom few doubt will vote to strike down. And none of them seemed satisfied with Solicitor General Donald Verrilli's answers. This does not bode well for the mandate.

I was also very happy to see this exchange between Verrilli and Justice Antonin Scalia regarding the Necessary and Proper Clause:

> *JUSTICE SCALIA*: Wait. That's—it's both "Necessary and Proper." What you just said addresses what's necessary. Yes, has to be reasonably adapted. Necessary does not mean essential, just reasonably adapted. But in addition to being necessary, it has to be proper. And we've held in two cases that something that was reasonably adapted was not proper, because it violated the sovereignty of the States, which was implicit in the constitutional structure.
>
> The argument here is that this also is—may be necessary, but it's not proper, because it violates an equally evident principle in the Constitution, which is that the Federal Government is not supposed to be a government that has all powers; that it's supposed to be a government of limited powers. And that's what all this questioning has been about. What—what is left? If the government can do this, what—what else can it not do?
>
> *GENERAL VERRILLI*: This does not violate the norm of proper as this Court articulated it in *Printz* or in *New York* because it does not interfere with the States as sovereigns. This is a regulation that—this is a regulation—
>
> *JUSTICE SCALIA*: No, that wasn't my point. That is not the only constitutional principle that exists.
>
> *GENERAL VERRILLI*: But it—
>
> *JUSTICE SCALIA*: An equally evident constitutional principle is the principle that the Federal Government is a government of enumerated powers and that the vast majority of powers remain in the States and do not belong to the Federal Government.[2]

Scalia makes the key points that (1) a federal law must be both "necessary" *and* "proper" to be authorized by the Necessary and Proper Clause, and (2) a statute cannot be proper if the legal rationale for it would justify nearly unlimited federal power. These are exactly the arguments that we advanced in the amicus brief on this very issue that I wrote on behalf of the Washington Legal Foundation and a group of constitutional law scholars.[3]

I'm not saying that Scalia necessarily got the argument from us, or even that he read the brief. But whatever led him to take up this point, I'm very happy that he raised it. It is the key weakness in the federal government's Necessary and Proper Clause argument, which is otherwise fairly strong—a weakness that the federal government almost completely ignored in their petitioner's brief for the Supreme Court. The federal government has tried to turn the Necessary and Proper Clause into a mere "necessary clause." But, if Scalia's views are any indication, the Supreme Court majority doesn't seem to be buying it.

As I explain in the amicus brief, this point also enables Scalia to distinguish his concurring opinion in *Gonzales v. Raich*, which many defenders of the mandate have been relying on. *Raich* did not address the issue of propriety. And in his concurring opinion in that case, Scalia emphasized (as he had in previous opinions) that "proper" is an independent limit on congressional power under the clause, separate from necessity.

Before the oral argument, I thought that the plaintiffs had about a 30 to 40 percent chance of winning. I believed it was likely that the federal government would manage to persuade at least one conservative justice to buy one of their many "health care is special" rationales for the mandate. Now, I think the chances of the mandate being invalidated are at least 50 percent. The conservative justices just don't seem to be biting on the "health care is special" hook.

On the other hand, it is still too early for mandate opponents to celebrate. The federal government has a whole raft of different "health care is special" arguments. If the feds can persuade just one of the conservative justices to accept just one of these theories, they can still win. We certainly cannot rule out such a scenario. It could still easily happen. But unlike in high school debate, quantity of arguments in a major Supreme Court case is rarely a good substitute for quality. And the quality of the government's "health care is special" arguments is at the very least highly suspect.

Has the Pro-ACA Side Come Up with a "Limiting Principle"?

David E. Bernstein
March 27, 2012

Sorry to keep reiterating this point, but I've contended since December 2010 that if the pro–Affordable Care Act (ACA) side is unable to articulate a limiting principle that would prevent their decision from giving the federal government an essentially plenary police power to regulate virtually all human activity and inactivity, the individual mandate is doomed. The conservative majority simply will not accept a doctrine that suggests that federal power is not one of limited and enumerated powers.

Unfortunately for the law's defenders, the solicitor general (SG) today lapsed into incoherence when Justices Samuel Alito, Anthony Kennedy, and Antonin Scalia asked him to identify a limiting principle (check out various liberal blogs for apoplectic reactions to SG Verrilli's performance). Justice Stephen Breyer later tried to step in and articulate three such principles:

> First, the Solicitor General came up with a couple joined, very narrow ones. You've seen in *Lopez* this Court say that we cannot, Congress cannot get into purely local affairs, particularly where they are noncommercial. And, of course, the greatest limiting principle of all, which not too many accept, so I'm not going to emphasize that, is the limiting principle derived from the fact that members of Congress are elected from States and that 95 percent of the law of the United States is State law.[4]

So (1) even Breyer was unable to articulate exactly (or even approximately) what limiting principle the SG had come up with; (2) everyone knows that defeating *Lopez*'s limitations on the commerce power has largely become a statutory drafting game to find a federal jurisdictional hook, however remote, and an unsuccessful ACA challenge would make it that much more difficult to find any examples regarding which such a hook couldn't be found. Moreover, reliance on *Lopez* is a bit rich coming from Breyer, who dissented in *Lopez* and would undoubtedly vote to overturn it tomorrow if he could; and (3) this is not a limit, it's judicial abdication, though it's what Breyer really believes. Even though he knew—and said!—that his colleagues aren't going to be persuaded by this, he apparently couldn't resist throwing it in anyway, as the "greatest limiting principle." Ego over effectiveness, I suspect.

So far, we seem to be left with the "health care is special" argument, which is not a limiting *principle* but could persuade a conservative justice or two to join a limited *holding*. Yet Justice Kennedy suggested today that if the ACA is upheld, the government will soon be back arguing that some other sector of the economy is "special." Not a good day for limiting principles.

Four Thoughts on the Individual Mandate Argument

Orin S. Kerr
March 28, 2012

I've now made it through the full transcript of this morning's argument. Here are four thoughts:

1. This was a huge day for the challengers to the mandate. The challengers have an uphill battle because they need to sweep all four of the Republican nominees who are potentially in play—Roberts, Alito, Scalia, and Kennedy. Based on today's argument, it looks like *all four* of those Justices accepted the basic framing of the case offered by the challengers to the mandate. In particular, they all seem to accept that a legal requirement of action is quite different from a legal requirement regulating action, and that therefore the expansive Commerce Clause precedents like *Raich* did not apply to this case. That was the key move Randy Barnett introduced, and the four key justices the challengers needed seemed to accept it. Just as a matter of precedent, that doesn't seem to me consistent with *Wickard v. Filburn*, which stated that "[t]he stimulation of commerce is a use of the regulatory function quite as definitely as prohibitions or restrictions thereon."[5] But putting aside precedent, the four key justices all appeared to accept Randy's basic framing. That was an enormous accomplishment for the challengers.

2. Based on today's argument, I think it's a toss-up as to which side will win. My sense is that Scalia is very clearly against the mandate, and Alito seemed to lean that way. Roberts also seemed more on the antimandate side than the pro-mandate side. It's a cliché, but the key vote seems to be Justice Kennedy. As my friend and fellow former Kennedy clerk Steve Engel told the *Wall Street Journal* today, "It's entirely possible he doesn't know yet which way he's going to go."[6] And yet assuming the justices feel bound to the usual practice of finishing up the term's opinions by late June, there isn't much time. These opinions are hugely important and yet will have to be written very quickly, which doesn't bode well for their likely quality.

3. If the Court does end up striking down the mandate, this will be the second consecutive presidency in which the Supreme Court imposed significant limits on the primary agenda of the sitting president in ways that were unexpected based on precedents at the time the president acted. Last time around, it was President George W. Bush and the war on terror. The president relied on precedents like *Johnson v. Eisentrager*[7] in setting up Gitmo. But when the Court was called on to review this key aspect of the president's strategy for the war on terror, the Court maneuvered around *Eisentrager* and imposed new limits on the executive branch in cases like *Rasul v. Bush*[8] and *Boumediene v. Bush*. The president's opponents heralded the Court's new decisions as the restoration of the rule of law and the application of profound constitutional principle. Meanwhile, the president's allies condemned the decisions as the products of unbridled judicial activism from a political court. If the mandate gets struck down, we'll get a replay with the politics reversed. Just substitute Obama for Bush, health care reform for the war on terror, the individual mandate for Gitmo, and *Wickard* for *Eisentrager*.

4. Purely from the perspective of a legal nerd, what fun it is to live in such interesting times. Those of us who follow the Supreme Court and teach or write in areas of public law are always dependent on what the Court does. If the Court does boring and expected things, then following the Court can be a bit routine. But this term the Court has been pretty darn exciting to watch. Whatever you think of the umpire, the game sure is entertaining.

Crediting/Blaming the VC for the Possible Defeat of the Individual Mandate

Ilya Somin
March 28, 2012

Adam Teicholz of the *Atlantic* claims that the *Volokh Conspiracy* deserves much of the credit or blame for the possible upcoming defeat of the individual mandate in the Supreme Court:

> Blogs—particularly a blog of big legal ideas called *Volokh Conspiracy*—have been central to shifting the conversation about the mandate challenges. At *Volokh*, Barnett and other libertarian academics have been debating and refining their arguments against the mandate since before the ACA was signed. At the beginning, law professor Jonathan Adler fleshed out the approach that came to typify the elite conservative response for the first months of the public debate: the Founders never intended for the Constitution to permit such broad federal power, but given New Deal-era precedent, the mandate, if it became law, would pass muster. Things changed on *Volokh* around the time that it became clear that an insurance mandate would be part of whichever health care reform package passed into law.
>
> One congressional floor speech seemed to mark a tonal turning point for *Volokh*, the moment its writers realized their power to shape debate. On December 22, 2009, Democratic Senator Max Baucus quoted the post by Jonathan Adler mentioned above. Adler clearly resented that Baucus had taken his lawyerly evaluation of the case, stripped out the interesting part (that a pure reading of the Constitution weighs

against the mandate, even if precedent weighs in its favor), and used it in a political context—and he responded on *Volokh* directly to the senator.[9] If the world was going to use *Volokh* as a political tool, then he could, too. There followed months of posts by various *Volokh* bloggers, alongside increasingly sophisticated legal arguments, about just how reasonable, how comfortably within bounds the legal arguments against the mandate were. By the following year, a district court judge had cited Barnett in his opinion striking down health care reform, and Barnett himself had left behind his March 2010 conclusion that the Supreme Court would need to risk its credibility in a politically charged case, *Bush v. Gore*-style, to overturn the mandate.[10]

I am flattered by this estimate of our influence. But there are a number of flaws in Teicholz' account. First and foremost, it is simply not true that we all thought that the individual mandate would pass muster under current precedent until the exchange between Jonathan Adler and Senator Max Baucus led us to "realize [our] power to shape debate."

We knew we had that "power" long before the Adler-Baucus debate. Several of us had influenced public debate through blogging previously. Eugene Volokh has had a lot of influence on public debate over free speech, gun rights, and other issues. Todd Zywicki's excellent blogging about bankruptcy issues has been extremely influential for years. My own blogging about post-*Kelo* eminent domain reform and property rights has impacted debate over those issues and led to invitations to testify before the U.S. Senate Judiciary Committee and other government bodies.

Randy Barnett believed that the individual mandate could not be justified under current precedent all along, which I think was also true of David Kopel. As for me, I always believed that the mandate was unconstitutional but initially thought that it could be justified under the Supreme Court's decision in *Gonzales v. Raich*[11] (which I have long argued was wrongly decided). What changed my mind was a close rereading of *Raich* with the individual mandate case specifically in mind. I obviously can't speak for Jonathan Adler, but I suspect that the evolution of his views was similar.

Randy and I also initially believed that striking down the mandate would be more politically difficult for the Supreme Court than is likely actually to be the case. That's because we (or at least I) failed to foresee that the mandate and the health care bill as a whole would remain so unpopular for so long. I'd like to think that some of that unpopularity was the result of our efforts. But the lion's share was surely caused by other factors. If we really had the power to swing public opinion massively, I would long since have persuaded the public to oppose the war on drugs and support legalization of organ sales.

Where we did have some influence is in debunking the myth that the constitutionality of the mandate was a no-brainer backed by an overwhelming consensus of expert opinion.[12] But we could not have done that were we not (1) recognized academic experts on these issues ourselves and (2) able to point to other well-known experts who also believed the mandate to be unconstitutional, many of them not VC-ers. The latter include such prominent constitutional law scholars as Richard Epstein, Steve Calabresi, Steve Presser, and Gary Lawson.

Randy, of course, played an especially vital role by developing crucial legal arguments that had a huge influence. But those arguments would have been of little avail if they could not persuade judges and other experts, as well as lay public opinion. The world is full of laws that are widely disliked but have no chance of getting invalidated by a court because the arguments against them have no credibility with legal professionals.

Teicholz also errs in thinking that our arguments against the mandate fell by the wayside when the case reached the Supreme Court and the antimandate lawyers started using "better-trodden" arguments—implying that our points were mainly for the purpose of influencing the lay public. In reality, Tuesday's oral argument overwhelmingly focused on the point that I and others here have been pushing for a long time: that the government's rationales for the mandate lacks any logical limitations and could therefore justify virtually any mandate of any kind. Several of the justices also suggested that the mandate is constitutionally dubious because it does not regulate any preexisting economic activity—the main argument that Randy has been emphasizing since 2009.[13] Some of Justice Scalia's questions on the Necessary and Proper Clause almost exactly mirrored the central point of an amicus brief I wrote on behalf of the Washington Legal Foundation and a group of constitutional law scholars[14] (though I reiterate that I have no way of knowing whether he got the idea from my brief).

Finally, Teicholz writes as if it is somehow unusual for lawyers to be "waging this battle not only in the courtroom but in the court of public opinion," suggesting that Randy's dual role as lawyer and public advocate is particularly "unusual for an appellate lawyer." In reality, two-track strategies in important constitutional cases are far from new. The abolitionist movement arguably pioneered this kind of approach in the 1840s and 1850s when they challenged the Fugitive Slave Act and other proslavery laws. The NAACP pursued a similar strategy since the early 1900s, as have feminists, environmentalists, gay rights advocates, gun rights advocates, property rights supporters, and many others. Randy's role is also far from "unusual" among lawyers involved in high-profile constitutional cases of this kind. As far back as the 1940s, Thurgood Marshall was both the lead appellate litigator for the cause of black civil rights and a major public spokesman for that cause. These historical precedents (many of them by left-wing movements) are what led me to suggest back in March 2010 that a similar strategy could work in this case.[15]

What happened here is just one of many examples of conservatives and libertarians adapting strategies that were mostly pioneered by the political left. Such borrowing from the Left is at the heart of much of what conservative and libertarian activists for legal change have achieved over the last thirty years.[16] Ironically, some on the Left don't recognize the influence of their own tactics when they are adopted by adversaries. Perhaps they should recall that imitation is the sincerest form of flattery.

SG Verrilli Relies on the Constitution's Preamble

David E. Bernstein
March 28, 2012

In his closing remarks at today's oral argument over the Medicaid expansion, SG Verrilli urged the Court, notwithstanding concerns about limiting the federal government, to uphold not just the Medicaid provision but the entire ACA. His rationale was in part that the people's democratically elected representatives, after much thought, decided that the ACA was the best way to deal with America's health care problems. But he also referred, twice, to the fact that the Medicaid provision and the ACA more generally are important to "secure the blessings of liberty" for those individuals who would otherwise face health care crises.

I find this an odd strategic choice for Verrilli to have made in his very last remarks to the Court. It's not uncommon for liberals to refer to the Constitution's preamble—"We the People, in order to form a more perfect Union, establish Justice, ensure domestic tranquility, provide for the common defense, **promote the General Welfare and secure the Blessings of Liberty**"—as a counterweight to the notion that the federal government's powers are significantly limited by their enumeration. But I've never heard of a *conservative* buying into the idea that the goals set forth in the preamble have any particular weight in constitutional interpretation, at least not when set in opposition to specific constitutional provisions. Indeed, if anything, I think a typical reaction of Federalist Society types is that reliance on the preamble as the last refuge of those who don't have a serious constitutional argument to make; "you mean you're not an originalist or a textualist and you want us to engage in 'living constitutionalism' with regard to all sorts of very specific and substantive constitutional provisions, but then you want us to take the *preamble* seriously?"

This strikes me as part of a pattern I detect throughout this litigation and especially in the SG's oral argument: the government's lawyers seem to have no idea how conservative jurists typically think about the Constitution. Instead, they make arguments that would get almost unanimous nods of approval in the Harvard (or Columbia, the SG's alma mater) Law School faculty lounge but are not remotely persuasive to the other side.

Verrilli, after all, had months to come up with a succinct, plausible, limiting principle in defense of the individual mandate. He should have been able to repeat this backwards, forwards, upside down, and in his sleep. Yet he could barely explain himself yesterday, when given the opportunity by three different justices. Given his reputation as one of the country's top appellate lawyers, a tempting explanation is that he couldn't believe that anyone except perhaps Thomas was really concerned about that issue.

Democratic Congressmen on Constitutional Authority for the ACA

David E. Bernstein
March 28, 2012

Most of us know that when then-Speaker Nancy Pelosi was asked where the Constitution gives Congress the power to enact an "individual mandate," she replied with a mocking "Are you serious? Are you serious?"

Here are a few more pearls of constitutional wisdom from our elected representatives:

- Representative John Conyers cited the "Good and Welfare Clause" as the source of Congress's authority (there is no such clause).[17]
- Representative Fortney "Pete" Stark responded, "[T]he federal government can do most anything in this country."[18]
- Representative James Clyburn replied, "There's nothing in the Constitution that says the federal government has anything to do with most of the stuff we do. How about [you] show me where in the Constitution it prohibits the federal government from doing this?"[19]
- Representative Phil Hare said, "I don't worry about the Constitution on this, to be honest [. . .] It doesn't matter to me." When asked, "Where in the Constitution does it give you the authority . . . ?" He replied, "I don't know."[20]
- Senator Daniel Akaka said he is "not aware" of which Constitutional provision authorizes the health care bill.[21]
- Senator Patrick Leahy added, "We have plenty of authority. Are you saying there's no authority?"[22]
- Senator Mary Landrieu told a questioner, "I'll leave that up to the constitutional lawyers on our staff."[23]

Something to keep in mind when someone argues that the Supreme Court should defer to the constitutional wisdom of its coequal branches.

UPDATE: The point is not that leading Democrat politicians are especially ignorant or dismissive of the constitutional bases for what they do. I doubt Republicans would do better. The point is, as suggested previously, that this ignorance/dismissiveness undermines the argument that the Supreme Court should defer to Congress as a coequal branch making independent constitutional determinations. For such deference to make sense, members of Congress have to actually be making such determinations.

Nearing the End of the Search for the Nonexistent Limiting Principles

David B. Kopel
March 29, 2012

With the Supreme Court probably voting on the constitutionality of Obamacare (a term the president proudly embraces) on Friday, the health control law's academic friends are diligently attempting to do what the entire United States Department of Justice could not do after two years of litigation: articulate plausible limiting principles for the individual mandate. Over at *Balkinization*, Neil Siegel offers "Five Limiting Principles."[24] They are:

1. The Necessary and Proper Clause. "Unlike other purchase mandates, including every hypothetical at oral argument on Tuesday, the minimum coverage provision prevents the unraveling of a market that Congress has clear authority to regulate." This is no limitation at all. Under modern doctrine, Congress has the authority to regulate almost every market. If Congress enacts regulations that are extremely harmful to that market, such as imposing price controls (a.k.a., "community rating") or requiring sellers to sell products at far below cost to some customers (e.g., "guaranteed issue") then the market will probably "unravel" (i.e., the companies will lose so much money that they will go out of business). So to prevent the companies from being destroyed, Congress forces other consumers to buy products from those companies at vastly excessive prices (e.g., $5,000 for an individual policy for a healthy 35-year-old whose actuarial expenditures for health care of all sorts during a year is $845).

    So Siegel's argument is really an antilimiting principle: if Congress imposes ruinous price controls on a market to help favored consumers, then Congress can try to save the market's producers by mandating that disfavored consumers buy overpriced products from those producers.

2. The Commerce Clause. "The minimum coverage provision addresses economic problems, not merely social problems that do not involve markets." This is true and is, as Siegel points out, a distinction from *Lopez* (carrying guns) and *Morrison* (gender-related violence). However, it's pretty clear under long-established doctrine that the commerce power can be used to address "social problems that do not involve markets."[25] Personally, I thought that Chief Justice Melville Fuller's dissent in *Champion v. Ames*[26] had the better argument, but *Champion* and its progeny are well-established precedents, so proposed limiting principle (2) does not work, unless we overrule a century of precedent.

    Besides that, (2) does not work for the same reason that (1) does not work. If Congress forced food producers to sell products to some consumers at far below cost, then Congress could (for economic, not social/moral motives) force other consumers to buy overpriced food, so that the producers do not go bankrupt. Imagine that instead of the Food Stamp program (general tax revenue given to one-sixth of the U.S. population to help them buy food), Congress forced grocery stores to sell food to poor people at far below cost. And instead of raising taxes in order to give money to the grocery stores to make up for their losses on the coerced sales, Congress instead forced other consumers to spend thousands of dollars on food from those same stores, which would be sold to those consumers at far above its free-market price.

If there's a limiting principle, the only one seems to be that in order to mandate the purchase of a product Congress must also inflict some other harm on the producers of the product, which the coerced purchases will ameliorate.

3. "Collective action failures and interstate externalities impede the ability of the states to guarantee access to health insurance, prevent adverse selection, and prevent cost shifting by acting on their own. Insurers operate in multiple states and have fled from states that guarantee access to states that do not." This is really a policy argument for Obamacare. Hypothesizing that it's a good policy argument, it's not a limiting principle. That the advocates of Obamacare think that the policy arguments for their mandate are better than the policy arguments for other mandates does not provide courts with a limiting principle of *law*.

Moreover, the policy argument is wrong. It's true that some insurance companies stop operating in states where the law forces them to sell insurance to legislatively favored purchasers at far below the actuarial cost of the insurance, with the legislature failing to compensate the companies for the enormous resulting losses. If you make it difficult for companies to operate profitably in your state, then they will eventually stop operating in your state. It's not a collective action problem, it's just a problem of several states enacting laws that prevent companies from covering their costs. Any state with guaranteed issue and other price controls can solve the problem immediately by simply using tax revenues to pay compensation for the subsidy which the state law forces the insurance companies to provide to certain consumers.

Obamacare is a particularly weak case in which to argue that the federal government is riding the rescue of the states to solve a collective action problem. For the first time in American history, a *majority* of the states are suing to ask that a federal law be declared unconstitutional. These states are taking collective action to stop the federal government from *imposing* a problem on them.

4. The tax power. "[T]he minimum coverage provision respects the limits on the tax power. The difference between a tax and a penalty is the difference between the minimum coverage provision and a required payment of say, $10,000 that has a scienter requirement and increases with each month that an individual remains uninsured. Unlike the minimum coverage provision, such an exaction would be so coercive that it would raise little or no revenue. It would thus be beyond the scope of the tax power."

Let's put aside the fact that however ingenious the progressive professoriate's tax arguments have been, the chances that the individual mandate is going to be upheld under the tax power appear to be at most 1 percent greater than the chance that Buddy Roemer will be the next president of the United States.

Presuming that Siegel's tax justification for the individual mandate is valid, it is an antilimiting principle. Congress can indeed mandate eating hamburgers, smoking, not smoking, not eating hamburgers, or anything else Congress wants to mandate, as long as Congress sets the "tax" at a level that will raise a moderate amount of revenue, does not include a scienter requirement, and does not make the "tax" increase each month that the individual refuses to do what Congress mandates.

5. Liberty. "The minimum coverage provision does not violate any individual rights, including bodily integrity and substantive due process more generally. These rights would be violated by a mandate to eat broccoli or exercise a certain amount." Pointing to the existence of the Bill of Rights is *not* an example of a limiting principle for an enumerated federal power. The Constitution does not say that Congress may do whatever it wishes as long as the Bill of Rights protections of liberty are not violated. Ordering New York State to take title to low-level radioactive waste generated within the state (*New York v. United States*) did not violate any person's substantive due process rights, but the order was nonetheless unconstitutional because it exceeded Congress's powers. The federal Gun-Free School Zones Act did not, as applied, violate the Second Amendment rights of Alfonso Lopez, who was carrying the gun to deliver it to a criminal gang. Yet the act still exceeded Congress's commerce power. A limiting principle must limit the exercise of the power itself, not merely point out that the Bill of Rights protects some islands of liberty, which the infinitely vast sea of federal power might not cover.

Finally, I certainly agree with Professor Siegel that the Fifth Amendment's liberty guarantee (and its Fourteenth Amendment analogue for the states) *should* be interpreted to say that no American government can order people to consume a certain amount of healthy food or to exercise. But there is no major case that is on point for this. The argument for a new unenumerated right "not to eat the minimum quantity of nutritious food which government scientists have determined is essential for good health" is something that would have to be built almost entirely by extrapolation from cases that have nothing to do with food. I hope that courts would accept the argument, but if the political culture ever moved far enough so that a nutrition mandate could pass a legislature, I'm not as certain as Professor Siegel that courts would overturn the mandate. The odds of winning a case against a nutrition mandate will be better if the judges who decide that case have not grown up in a nation where a federal health control mandate is the law of the land.

Justice Kennedy, "Actuarial Risk," and the Individual Mandate's Unconstitutionality

Randy E. Barnett
March 29, 2012

As most experts and commentators have observed, Justice Kennedy and the other more conservative justices all strongly suggested during oral argument that the mandate was unprecedented and unbounded (and thus likely unconstitutional). Orin and some others, however, have highlighted a few questions by Justice Kennedy concerning "actuarial risk" that seem favorable to the government. (Indeed, it is quite striking that these may be the *only* moments of six hours of oral argument that are.) In particular, they have emphasized the following questions:

> "Is the government's argument this—and maybe I won't state it accurately. It is true that the noninsured young adult is, in fact, an actuarial reality insofar as our allocation of health services, insofar as the way health insurance companies figure risks. That person who is sitting at home in his or her living room doing nothing is an actuarial reality that can and must be measured for health service purposes; is that their argument?"[27]

> "But [the uninsured] are in the market in the sense that they are creating a risk that the market must account for?"[28]

> "And the government tells us that's because the insurance market is unique. And in the next case, it'll say the next market is unique. But I think it is true that if most questions in life are matters of degree, in the insurance and health care world, both markets—stipulate two markets—the young person who is uninsured is uniquely proximately very close to affecting the rates of insurance and the costs of providing medical care in a way that is not true in other industries."[29]

I do not pretend to know how Justice Kennedy is going to vote in this case. But the oral argument itself reveals why he may well have been just putting the government's argument in the best possible light rather than adopting it himself. Specifically, elsewhere, he and others strongly suggested that the "actuarial risk" concern is (1) a legally inadequate limiting principle, (2) a factually inapposite justification, and (3) redressable through alternative constitutional means.

I. Legally Inadequate Limiting Principle

Justice Kennedy's "actuarial risk" questions are being read to suggest that the uninsured "affect" commerce in the sense that they externalize the risk of unaffordable illness on the public. But, as Justice Kennedy and Chief Justice Roberts principally emphasized, there is no principled reason why that is the *only* economic effect flowing from the nonpurchase of a product that Congress can seek to undo by compelling the product's purchase.[30] Nothing in the Commerce

Clause or the Necessary and Proper Clause conceivably limit Congress to regulating nonpurchase of a product *if and only if* that nonpurchase externalizes risk rather than having a different type of unwanted economic effect. For example, Detroit's economic woes are no less "proximately" caused by the fact that Americans don't want to buy domestic cars. Indeed, to the contrary, they are *more* "proximately" caused: when an individual choose not to buy a domestic car, the "effect" on GM and others is direct and immediate (and as Paul Clement argued, unemployed workers shift costs to the employed); whereas when an individual chooses not to buy insurance, the "effect" on health insurers and health care providers *if* that individual *later* incurs an unaffordable illness is contingent and remote.

II. Factually Inapposite Justification

Moreover, the "internalize-actuarial-risk" defense of the mandate cannot be squared with the fact that the mandate forces individuals to purchase insurance that is neither actuarially priced (due to the community-rating requirement that bars consideration of actual health status) nor limited to unaffordable illness (due to minimum-essential-benefits requirements that drastically exceed catastrophic coverage). Chief Justice Roberts and Justice Alito principally emphasized this mismatch in the government's theory,[31] and Mike Carvin returned to the point in direct response to Justice Kennedy's final question about the issue.[32] The mismatch demonstrates that the predominant purpose and effect of the mandate is instead to stimulate demand for its own sake—that is, to force young, healthy individuals who will *not* incur unaffordable illnesses to subsidize the costs of old, sick individuals who will. But that is precisely the rationale that even the solicitor general disavowed.[33]

III. Alternative Constitutional Means

Finally, as Justice Kennedy himself observed, Congress has myriad legitimate alternatives to address those who externalize risk. Namely, it can incentivize them to internalize risk (by rewarding those who do so or by sanctioning those who fail to pay for costs they incur) or it can force them to internalize risk (through proper use of the tax power). For that reason, as Justice Kennedy suggested, there is no reason to stretch the commerce power[34] and thereby "[change] the relationship of the Federal Government to the individual in a very fundamental way."[35]

Again, you never know what any justice will do, but sitting in the courtroom, I sensed that Justice Kennedy had an impassioned concern for how upholding the mandate would fundamentally change the relationship of the individual to the federal government. These other questions were raised later and with much less intensity. But I could be wrong about this.

Some Tentative Thoughts on the Medicaid Case

Ilya Somin
March 29, 2012

In all the hoopla over the individual mandate, most people (myself emphatically included) have not devoted enough attention to the other big Obamacare case before the Court: the 26 states' challenge to the part of the act requiring the states to massively expand Medicaid coverage (covering every nonelderly with an income up to 138 percent of the poverty line) or face the loss of all their federal Medicaid funds. Medicaid is a huge program that represents some 40 percent of all federal grants to state governments, according to the states' brief. In cases such as *South Dakota v. Dole*,[36] the Supreme Court has ruled that Congress has very broad discretion in imposing conditions on spending grants offered to states but also warned that such conditions are unconstitutional if they are so onerous as to be "coercive." What qualifies as "coercion" in this context? The Court has never favored us with an explanation, and the whole concept is murky at best.

In this case, the states' strongest argument is that, if anything is "coercive," it's the threat of withdrawing such a massive proportion of all their federal funds, especially after the states have become dependent on Medicaid grants over a period of many years. If this isn't coercion through funding conditions, it's hard to see what is. On the other hand, as the federal government points out, it's hard to draw a clear line here. And, if the states wanted to avoid dependency, they could simply have refused to participate in Medicaid in the first place.

My interpretation of yesterday's Medicaid oral argument is that there probably aren't five votes to overturn this part of the law. The liberal justices strongly support the federal government's position, while several of the conservatives are at the very least on the fence. I conjecture that the real purpose of the Court's surprising decision to hear this case was to try to develop a clearer definition of what counts as "coercion" rather than a desire to invalidate this part of Obamacare. However, Lyle Denniston of *SCOTUSblog*—who is much more sympathetic to the federal government's position than I am—thinks there is a good chance that the law will be struck down.[37]

What should the Court do? I honestly don't have a very clear answer. My own view is that the coercion test is both unclear and doesn't have much basis in the text and original meaning of the Constitution. On that, I tend to agree with the Court's liberal justices. On the other hand, the Taxing and Spending Clause only gives Congress the power to spend money for the purposes of providing for the common defense, paying the federal debt, and advancing the "general Welfare." I think that the Court is wrong to interpret "general welfare" to include essentially anything that Congress thinks might potentially be beneficial. If that were correct, the power to spend for the common defense and the debts of the United States would be essentially superfluous. I developed this argument in more detail in one of my first academic articles back in 2002.[38] The original meaning of "general welfare" is much narrower, as is well explained in by John Eastman.[39]

However, fully endorsing my approach or Eastman's theory would require the Court to reverse important precedents and undercut major existing government programs on which both state governments and large numbers of people have become heavily dependent. It's both unrealistic and undesirable for the Court to try to do something like that in one fell swoop.

I would therefore prefer for the Court to move incrementally in the direction of tightening up its definition of "general welfare" without massively disrupting long-established major existing programs. How best to do that is a very difficult question to which I don't have any particularly good answer. Eastman, however, presents some interesting arguments about how the coercion theory can be used to bring us closer to the original meaning of "general welfare" in his amicus brief in the Medicaid case.[40] I tentatively think his approach is probably superior to the available alternatives. But I readily admit that I'm not really sure about how best to deal with this difficult conundrum.

Regardless, it will be interesting to see whether a majority of the justices can agree on a clearer definition of "coercion" and if so what it is.

Why Did Legal Elites Underestimate the Case against the Mandate?

Jonathan H. Adler
March 30, 2012

Greg Sargent is one of many commentators wondering, "How did legal observers and Obamacare backers get it so wrong?"[41] I think he's asking the wrong question. A better question to ask is why did so many expect legal elites to have any particular insight into the current court? After all, many of the legal experts who were so dismissive of the arguments against the mandate were equally dismissive of the federalism arguments that prevailed in cases like *United States v. Lopez, New York v. United States,* and *City of Boerne v. Flores.* Many of the legal academics who ridiculed Randy Barnett's work on the mandate, and who were relied upon by legal journalists and commentators, thought their schools were advancing viable legal claims in *Rumsfeld v. FAIR.*[42] Oops. Premier appellate litigators may have a good sense of how the Court is likely to assess complex constitutional law claims, but elite legal academics, not so much.

What explains this state of affairs? I believe there are several factors at work, but one in particular is the increasing separation of the legal academy from the practice of law—a separation that is greatest in fields, such as constitutional law, that touch on broad questions of public policy. At many schools, academics are more interested in developing a comprehensive theory of justice than in divining the nuances buried in the Court's cases. Junior academics are routinely discouraged from doctrinal scholarship and pushed to develop broad, overarching, and original theories for what the law should be. Constitutional scholarship in particular is increasingly focused on theory and less on the law. In some corners, it's more important to reconcile one's claims with the writings of John Rawls than the opinions of John Roberts.

This divide explains why so many legal academics were dismissive of some of the concerns raised in this week's oral arguments, such as the need for a limiting principle. The solicitor general's office has taken this concern seriously from day one, as have a few liberal legal academics (e.g. Neil Seigel, Michael Dorf), whereas others, such as Andrew Koppelman, have been sneeringly dismissive of this argument from the get-go. Even if Koppelman were right as a matter of first principles, he's clearly wrong as a matter of current doctrine as understood by the current Supreme Court, though you wouldn't know it from what he's written.

Another factor that contributes to this problem is the relative lack of ideological diversity within legal academia. The current Supreme Court has a right-leaning majority, but legal academia leans decidedly to the left. On many faculties there are few, if any, professors with any particular appreciation or understanding (let alone sympathy) for the jurisprudential views of a majority of the current justices. This means that when ideas are floated in the faculty lounge, they may get a far more sympathetic hearing than they would ever receive in court. So, for instance, it's easy for Jack Balkin to dismiss an argument premised on *Bailey v. Drexel Furniture* because it's a *Lochner v. New York*–era decision, even though *Bailey* remains good law.[43] A practicing lawyer would have been less likely to make this mistake. Indeed, the SG actually cited *Bailey* approvingly this week in his argument before the Court.

In teaching our students to be effective lawyers, it is important that we teach them how to understand opposing legal arguments on their own terms. Effective appellate attorneys are conscious of this problem and devote substantial energy trying to get inside the minds of their opponents. As I've heard Paul Clement (among others) explain, you can't effectively advocate your own position until you truly understand the other side. This can be difficult to do, particularly when we have strong feelings about a subject. Someone who believes the Patient Protection and Affordable Care Act is a long-overdue step toward remedying the profound injustices of the American health care system is not predisposed to embrace arguments that the PPACA is unconstitutional. And if those same academics both lack colleagues with opposing points of view and have no particular professional interest in making sure they fairly consider the other side, it is easy for them to overlook the strength of opposing arguments and reduce them to caricatures. Ridiculing the need for a limiting principle or other antimandate arguments may get approving nods in the faculty lounge, but, as we saw this week, it won't receive an equally warm welcome in court.

Legal Elites and Predictions of the Court: A Slightly Different View

Orin S. Kerr
April 2, 2012

Several of my cobloggers have suggested recently that liberal academics were surprised by the oral argument in the health care cases because they are out of touch with conservative thought. I don't think that's accurate, though, because the premise strikes me as wrong: I don't think there has been a major gap between liberal academics and Supreme Court lawyers and conservative academics and Supreme Court lawyers on the odds of what the Supreme Court might do. My sense is that folks on both sides were surprised by how the argument went. One side quite pleasantly, the other side quite unpleasantly. But my sense is that both sides were surprised.

I think it's worth stepping back and recognizing that at the beginning of the debate over the mandate, everyone saw the mandate challenge as a serious long shot. Randy Barnett has acknowledged that when the mandate debate began, he thought it "a long shot" just to make it to the Supreme Court (much less to win). In a 2010 essay in the *Washington Post*,[44] Randy acknowledged that "the smart money" was against the mandate challenge and recognized that the prospect that the Court might strike down the mandate might seem "farfetched," but suggested that it just might happen if the stars aligned as they did in *Bush v. Gore*. More recently, when the Court granted cert and scheduled six hours of oral argument time, folks on both sides of the aisle began to realize that there was a serious chance that the Court would strike down the mandate: While there was a modest difference between conservative and liberal opinion among Supreme Court clerks and Supreme Court lawyers on the chances the law would be upheld going into the argument, it was actually relatively narrow, with both sides still thinking that odds favored upholding the mandate. Given this history, I have a hard time seeing a major gap between conservative and liberal "elites" on the purely predictive question of what the Court might do.

Of course, some liberal academics were quite harsh in dismissing arguments against the mandate. Some may have used dismissive language for tactical reasons: defining the challenge as outside the realm of serious academic debate might (at the margins) make it less likely to be taken seriously by the courts. And these efforts were then countered by efforts of mandate opponents who argued in response that the issue should be considered mainstream and not frivolous and thus (at the margins) make the challenge more likely to be taken seriously by the courts. But viewing these sorts of squabbles in light of last week's oral arguments doesn't suggest that liberal academics fail to understand conservative thought. Rather, it just suggests that both sides were trying to define the mainstream with the hope that it might (somehow) influence how the justices approached the case and that five justices seemed to accept the definition of one side and four justices accepted the definition of the other side.

President Obama versus the Constitution

David B. Kopel
April 2, 2012

President Obama today fired his opening salvo in an unprecedented attack on the Constitution of the United States. Regarding the impending Supreme Court ruling on the health control law, the president said, "Ultimately, I'm confident that the Supreme Court will not take what would be an unprecedented, extraordinary step of overturning a law that was passed by a strong majority of a democratically elected Congress."

His factual claims are false. His principle is a direct assault on the Constitution's creation of an independent judicial branch as a check on constitutional violations by the other two branches.

It is certainly not "unprecedented" for the Court to overturn a law passed by "a democratically elected Congress." The Court has done so 165 times, as of 2010.[45]

President Obama can call legislation enacted by a vote of 219 to 212 a "strong" majority if he wishes. But there is nothing in the Constitution suggesting that a bill that garners the votes of 50.3 percent of the House of Representatives has such a "strong" majority that it therefore becomes exempt from judicial review. To the contrary, almost all the 165 federal statutes that the Court has ruled unconstitutional had much larger majorities, most of them attracted votes from both Democrats and Republicans, and some of them were enacted nearly unanimously.

That the Supreme Court would declare as unconstitutional congressional "laws" that illegally violated the Constitution was one of the benefits of the Constitution, which the Constitution's advocates used to help convince the people to ratify the Constitution. In Federalist No. 78, Alexander Hamilton explained why unconstitutional actions of Congress are not real laws, and why the judiciary has a duty to say so:

> There is no position which depends on clearer principles, than that every act of a delegated authority, contrary to the tenor of the commission under which it is exercised, is void. No legislative act, therefore, contrary to the Constitution, can be valid. To deny this, would be to affirm, that the deputy is greater than his principal; that the servant is above his master; that the representatives of the people are superior to the people themselves; that men acting by virtue of powers, may do not only what their powers do not authorize, but what they forbid. . . .
>
> Nor does this conclusion by any means suppose a superiority of the judicial to the legislative power. It only supposes that the power of the people is superior to both; and that where the will of the legislature, declared in its statutes, stands in opposition to that of the people, declared in the Constitution, the judges ought to be governed by the latter rather than the former. They ought to regulate their decisions by the fundamental laws, rather than by those which are not fundamental.[46]

Because Hamilton was the foremost "big government" advocate of his time, it is especially notable that he was a leading advocate for judicial review of whether any part of the federal government had exceeded its delegated powers.

Well before *Marbury v. Madison*, the Supreme Court recognized that the people had given the Court the inescapable duty of reviewing the constitutionality of statutes that came before the Court. The Court fulfilled this duty in cases such as *Hylton v. United States*[47] (1796) (is a congressional tax on carriages a direct tax, and therefore illegal because it is not apportioned according to state population?), and *Calder v. Bull*[48] (1798) (is Connecticut's change in inheritance laws an *ex post facto* law?). The Court found that the particular statutes in question did not violate the

Constitution. (The *Ex Post Facto* Clause applies only to criminal laws; the carriage tax was an indirect tax, not a direct tax.) However, the Court's authority to judge the statutes' constitutionality was not disputed.

It would not be unfair to charge President Obama with hypocrisy given his strong complaints[49] when the Court did *not* strike down the federal ban on partial birth abortions and given his approval[50] of the Supreme Court decision (*Boumediene v. Bush*) striking down a congressional statute restricting habeas corpus rights of Guantanamo detainees. (For the record, I think that the federal abortion ban should have been declared void because it was not within Congress's interstate commerce power and that *Boumediene* was probably decided correctly, although I have not studied the issue sufficiently to have a solid opinion.) The federal ban on abortion and the federal restriction on habeas corpus were each passed with more than a "strong" 50.3 percent majority of a democratically elected Congress.

As a politician complaining that a Supreme Court that should strike down laws he doesn't like while simultaneously asserting that a judicial decision against a law he does like is improperly "activist," President Obama is no more hypocritical than many other presidents. But in asserting that the actions of a "strong" majority of Congress are unreviewable, President Obama's words are truly unprecedented. Certainly no president in the last 150 years has asserted that a "strong" majority of Congress can exempt a statute from judicial review. President Abraham Lincoln's first inaugural address criticized the *Dred Scott v. Sandford* majority for using a case between two private litigants for its over-reaching into a major national question, but Lincoln affirmed that the Court can, and should, provide a binding resolution to disputes between the parties before the Court. And in 2012, the government of the United States *is* one of the parties before the Court. The government is before the Court in part because the government filed a petition for writ of certiorari to ask the Court to use its discretion to decide the case.

Alone among the presidents, Thomas Jefferson appears as a strong opponent of judicial review *per se*. Notably, he did not propose that Congress be the final judge of its own powers, especially when Congress intruded on matters that the Constitution had reserved to the states. Rather, Jefferson argued that in such a dispute the matter should be resolved by a convention of the states, and the states would be make the final decision. Given that 28 states have already appeared as parties in court arguing that the individual mandate is unconstitutional, we can make a good guess about what a convention would decide about the constitutionality of the health control law.

President Obama, however, wants Obamacare to be reviewable by no one: not by the Supreme Court, not by the states. You can find professors and partisans who have argued for such lawlessness, but for a president to do so is unprecedented.

The people gave Congress the enumerated power "[t]o regulate Commerce . . . among the several States." According to the Obama administration, this delegation of power also includes the power to compel commerce. Opponents contend that the power to regulate commerce does not include the far greater power to compel commerce and that the individual mandate is therefore an *ultra vires* act by a deputy (Congress) in violation of the grant of power from the principal (the people). Seventy-two percent of the public, including a majority of Democrats, agrees that the mandate is unconstitutional. Few acts of Congress have ever had such sustained opposition of a supermajority of the American public.

President Obama today has considerably raised the stakes in *Sebelius v. Florida*. At issue now is not just the issue of whether Congress can commandeer the people and compel them to purchase the products of a particular oligopoly. At issue is whether the Court will bow to a president who denies the very legitimacy of judicial review of congressional statutes—or at least those statutes that garnered the "strong" majority of 219 out of 435 representatives.

The *Washington Post* on *Lochner* and the ACA

David E. Bernstein
April 9, 2012

Supreme Court reporter Robert Barnes has a piece today about the role of *Lochner v. New York* in the ACA litigation.[51] The solicitor general told the Court at oral argument that invalidating the ACA would bring back *Lochner*, and last week President Obama said, "A law that was passed by Congress on an economic issue, like health care, that I think most people would clearly consider commerce—a law like that has not been overturned at least since *Lochner*."

Of course, this is lots of fun for me, as my formerly obscure (to my relatives and friends) interest in *Lochner* now has some popular currency. (It shouldn't hurt book sales, either[52]).

But I wonder if raising *Lochner* is really helpful to the ACA's proponents. First, liberals and conservatives mean two different things when they criticize *Lochner*. Barnes quotes me as follows:

> "Liberals see the court as unduly interfering with progressive legislation meant to help people who needed it," Bernstein said. "Conservatives draw a different lesson: They see it as a symbol of judicial activism," creating a right beyond those enumerated in the Constitution.

The SG and president used *Lochner* in the former sense, but that doesn't seem likely to sway the Court's conservatives. Indeed, Chief Justice Roberts jumped all over the SG when he suggested that the ACA challenge resembled *Lochner*: "It seems to me it's an entirely different question when you ask yourself whether or not there are going to be limits on the federal power, as opposed to limits on the states, which was the issue in *Lochner*." In other words, this is an enumerated powers case, not an unenumerated rights case, and therefore *Lochner* is irrelevant.

Moreover, to the extent that Justice Kennedy is likely to be the swing vote, he seems perhaps the least likely justice to be swayed by accusations of "Lochnering." Kennedy is, I think, the only justice who has had dissenters from both left and right accuse him of repeating *Lochner*'s mistakes. Just last term, in *Sorrell v. IMS Health Care, Inc.*,[53] Justice Breyer twice raised *Lochner* in his dissent to Justice Kennedy's majority opinion. Back in 2003, Justice Scalia, dissenting from Kennedy's opinion in *Lawrence v. Texas*,[54] suggested that the Fourteenth Amendment no more protects the right to engage in homosexual sodomy than it does the right to "[work] more than 60 hours per week in a bakery" (alluding to the facts of *Lochner*).

Kennedy is also the least shy "conservative" justice about relying on the Fourteenth Amendment to protect economic rights, the underlying "sin" of *Lochner* for both Left and Right. Unlike Thomas and Scalia, he happily joins opinions invalidating state punitive awards as violating the Due Process Clause. And then there's his lone opinion in *Eastern Enterprises v. Apfel*, in which he wrote, "Although we have been hesitant to subject economic legislation to due process scrutiny as a general matter, the Court has given careful consideration to due process challenges to legislation with retroactive effects."[55] He then proceeded to argue that the legislation in question fails a due process analysis.

So I'm not sure what the strategy of raising *Lochner* is supposed to accomplish, but it doesn't seem well designed to get the government five votes in the ACA litigation.

The Different Meanings of Judicial Activism—and Why They Matter for the Individual Mandate Case

Orin S. Kerr
April 9, 2012

If the Supreme Court strikes down the individual mandate, would that be an example of judicial activism? It depends what you mean by judicial activism, I think. In my experience, there are several different things people might mean when they label a judicial decision as "activist." Two of the meanings aren't very helpful, but I think three of them are, and I think it's worth keeping in mind the different meanings of the term when discussing whether a decision striking down the mandate might (or might not) be activist.

Here are the different things a person might mean when they accuse a Supreme Court decision of being activist. The meanings can overlap, to be clear, but it is helpful to keep them analytically separate:

1. **The decision was motivated by the justices' personal policy preferences or was result oriented.** In some instances, a decision is labeled "activist" when we think that the decision was based on the justices' own personal policy preferences or preferred outcomes. Of course, it's hard for us to know what subjectively motivated the justices. But we have an idea that judges should follow law, not just strike down laws and practices that they don't personally like. So when we think that a judge struck down a law in large part because he didn't like the law as a matter of policy or because he wanted one side to win and the other side to lose for reasons not concerning the legal merits of the case, we might call the decision "activist." This version of judicial activism stands in opposition to the rule of law; it expresses the fear that judges are just doing what they personally like. (A sample statement from

the Right: "*Roe v. Wade* is an activist decision because the justices in the majority just tried to enact their prochoice views." A sample statement from the Left: "The activist justices in the *Bush v. Gore* majority voted as they did because they wanted Bush to be president.")

2. **The decision expands the power of courts to determine the rules of our society.** A second reason to label a decision activist is if it expands the power of the courts to define rules. If an area of law used to be a matter of legislative or executive discretion, but then the courts step in and define the rules themselves, we might call the decisions doing so "activist" in the sense that the judges actively took over an area relative to some prior standard of judicial deference. This kind of activism can be good or bad depending on whether you think the judges properly stepped in, so this version of activism isn't necessarily a bad thing. But it is a second way of describing whether a decision is activist. (A sample statement from the Right: "The Warren Court's activist criminal procedure decisions largely eliminated the role of Congress in defining criminal procedure rules." A sample statement from the Left: "In *Citizens United v. Federal Elections Commission*, the activist Supreme Court narrowed the legislative options Congress has in enacting campaign finance reform.")

3. **The decision was not consistent with precedents.** In other instances, a decision can be labeled "activist" when it is not consistent with precedent or overrules precedent. If everyone had one understanding of the law, and then the Supreme Court comes along and announces a new understanding, then the decision might be seen as activist in the sense that the Court is setting a new direction for the law. Once again, this can be a good thing or a bad thing, depending on what one thinks of stare decisis or whether one agrees with the prior precedents. But this is a third way of describing whether a decision is activist that is often seen in the public debates over the Courts. (A sample statement from the Right: "In *Roper v. Simmons*, the judicial activists on the Left were not bothered by the contrary precedent in *Stanford v. Kentucky*; faced with an adverse precedent, they just overruled it." A sample statement from the Left: "Conservative activists on the Court want to overturn *Grutter v. Bollinger* and end affirmative action.")

4. **The decision struck down a law or practice.** This fourth interpretation of judicial activism simply looks at whether the court upheld the law or practice as constitutional or struck it down as unconstitutional. By this account, a decision is activist if it strikes down a law or practice (for whatever reason) and not activist if it upholds the law or practice. (Example from the Right: "During the Bush administration, an activist majority of the Court repeatedly invalidated the administration's policies in the war on terror; they should have showed some restraint instead." An example from the Left: "During the Rehnquist Court, the conservative justices were the true judicial activists because they voted to strike down federal legislation more often than liberal justices.")

5. **The decision was wrong.** A final interpretation of judicial activism is that the phrase just indicates agreement or disagreement with the court's

decision. An activist decision is a decision the speaker thinks is wrong, by whatever standard the speaker adopts; a decision is not activist if the speaker thinks the decision is correct. From this perspective, activism is just a statement of agreement or disagreement with the Court's reasoning. (An example from the Right: "*Kelo v. New London* is an activist decision; how can the justices interpret the Takings Clause that way?" An example from the Left: "The Supreme Court's recent strip-search case is written by activist justices who just don't get the Fourth Amendment.")

These different understandings can overlap, of course, and I think the overlapping meanings explain a lot about debates over judicial activism. First and most obviously, people tend to use the phrase "judicial activism" most easily when most or all the different meanings apply. But on the other hand, because there is no one meaning of the term, debates over judicial activism tend to run in circles because people just use different meanings of judicial activism in response to critiques. For example, imagine a liberal analyst looks at *Citizens United* and proclaims it activist based on meanings (2) through (4) and perhaps (1) as well; a conservative wishing to defend *Citizens United* would likely counter with meaning (5). But as the politics of the case shift so do allegiances to the different meanings. For example, if the same conservative and liberal switch from discussing *Citizens United* to *Boumediene v. Bush*, the arguments switch too: now the conservative will raise meanings (1) through (4) and the liberal will counter with meaning (5).

One response to these changing usages is just to give up and say that the term "judicial activism" is useless. But I don't think that's justified. We need language to evaluate what the Supreme Court does, and some of these meanings capture genuinely important dynamics about the role of the courts. In my view, meanings (1) through (3) are useful ways of labeling conduct as activist or not—especially if we specifically explain which meaning we have in mind, the terms allow us to have a useful debate about the proper role of the courts. On the other hand, I personally find meanings (4) and (5) pretty unhelpful. In my view, (4) isn't helpful because everyone agrees with the basic notion of judicial review (yes, even President Obama). Meaning (5) isn't helpful because no two people seem to agree on when a decision is "right" or "wrong."

So would a hypothetical decision striking down the mandate be activist under meanings (1) through (3)? Evaluating (1) is always tricky because it's a subjective question. We can't know with any certainty what the justices subjectively wanted. But if the case ends up 5–4, with the justices appointed from the party that supported the law on one side and the justices appointed from the party that opposed the law on the other, a lot of folks will assume that the decision is activist in the sense of meaning (1). That argument will be a lot weaker if the vote isn't 5–4 (compare debates over *Bush v. Gore*, where a common response of those who defend the case from accusations of activism is that parts of the case were 7–2). But if the votes line up in the predictable political way, then claims of activism based on argument (1) will be common.

As for meaning (2), I think accusations that a decision striking down the mandate would be activist in the (2) sense would be pretty weak, at least assuming the decision tracked the arguments made by the challengers. The main reason is that the argument made by the challengers would be very easily circumvented in a future case. The challengers agree that a future Congress could reenact the same law simply by clearly labeling it a tax or by structuring the law as an entitlement. As a result, the challenge to the mandate isn't making it impossible to enact health care reform, it's merely trying to invalidate the one way that Congress happened to have enacted health care reform, without blocking others. Further, a decision striking down the mandate wouldn't in any way limit state governments. As a result, I don't think a decision striking down the mandate would be particularly activist in the (2) sense.

On the other hand, I think a decision striking down the mandate would be justifiably criticized as activist in the (3) precedential sense. As I have explained many times before, I think existing Commerce Clause precedents combined with the presumption of constitutionality point pretty clearly in the direction of upholding the mandate. There's a reason why it never occurred to any one that a mandate might be constitutionally problematic until this very controversial legislation was written, went through the legislative process, and was about to pass. It wasn't until that late stage that many critics of the legislation came to the conclusion that the precedents actually pointed the other way (a judgment timed in such a way to suggest motivated reasoning is at work). So given that I read the precedents that way, I think a decision pushing the law in the opposite direction (however justified or unjustified) would be fairly labeled activist in the (3) sense.

So what's the bottom line? In my view, it's this: depending on how the decision might be written, a decision striking down the mandate could fairly be called activist in some ways but not in other ways. It depends on which meanings of "activism" you find useful, and different people will disagree on which meanings of activism are useful.

The Myth That the Individual Mandate Addresses Cost Shifting by the Uninsured, Part Two: "Bronze Plans" Are Not the Same as Catastrophic Coverage

Randy E. Barnett
April 12, 2012

One of the myths of the Affordable Care Act is that it designed to address the costs imposed on the health care system by uninsured healthy younger people who may incur unexpectedly high medical costs from, say, being hit by a bus and who then shift these costs to those who have insurance. As I have discussed previously,[56] several commentators have suggested that Justice Kennedy could uphold the mandate on the limited theory that the mandate uniquely requires individuals to pay to cover their own "actuarial risk"—that is, the chance that they will suffer an unexpected, catastrophic health care cost that they could not pay for out of pocket.

Among the flaws that I identified with this purportedly narrow defense of the mandate is that it is factually inaccurate: Obamacare does not simply make people buy catastrophic coverage that would cover their own unaffordable risks at a price that reflects their actuarial risk. Instead, as several of the justices recognized, it makes them buy comprehensive policies for a wide range of services they don't need in order to subsidize the law's other costly requirements, at a price in excess of the actuarial risk that they pose to the system. Rather than being a scheme to insure against the risk posed by younger persons, the Affordable Care Act creates a system of a government-mandated, privately administered redistribution of wealth from the young and healthy to older baby boomers.

An Associated Press (AP) reporter, however, recently suggested otherwise, cobbling together several comments from "insurance experts" under the provocative headline "Supreme Court Misunderstanding on Health Overhaul?"[57] According to the story, whereas the justices "seemed to be under the impression that the law does not allow most consumers to buy low-cost, stripped-down insurance to satisfy its controversial coverage requirement[, i]n fact, the law provides for a cheaper 'bronze' plan that is broadly similar to today's so-called catastrophic coverage policies for individuals."

This story might be used by those desperately seeking a limiting principle for the mandate, but the story's key factual contention is flatly false. As Chief Justice Roberts and Mike Carvin both correctly pointed out during oral argument, even a "bronze" plan must cover a wide array of costly "essential health benefits"— including contraceptives, maternity and newborn care, counseling, physical therapy, preventive services, and pediatric oral and vision care—that drastically exceed the types of unpredictable and unaffordable costs covered by normal catastrophic plans (and which might potentially result in cost shifting). As the article admits,

> The health care law does impose a minimum set of "essential health benefits" for most insurance plans. Those benefits have yet to be specified, but are expected to reflect what a typical small-business plan now offers, with added preventive, mental health and other services.

That is precisely why premiums for bronze plans would cost between $4,500 and $5,000 per year under the act (as estimated by the Congressional Budget Office [CBO]), whereas true catastrophic plans are currently available for around $420 per year (as quoted online for a policy that covers a thirty-year-old nonsmoker, doesn't cover preventative and other nonessential services, and carries a $10,000 deductible).

Thus, while the AP story emphasizes that "bronze" plans, compared to the other Obamacare plans, will have relatively high cost sharing by the insured through deductibles and so on, that is utterly irrelevant. *Compared to the catastrophic plans banned by the ACA,* "bronze" plans will still cost roughly ten times more than what is needed for healthy young people to internalize their own "actuarial risk." And the reason that the act imposed all these costly and gratuitous "benefits" on young people who don't need or want them—rather than allowing them to purchase insurance that would avoid "cost shifting"—was for the avowed purpose of having healthy people significantly lower others' insurance premiums by overpaying for their own insurance.

In this way, the proposed rationale for upholding the individual mandate does not match the actual statutory scheme. Yet again, as with other theories, such as the tax power theory, defenders of the Affordable Care Act have to rewrite the bill in order to justify it.

Nonlegal Arguments for Upholding the Individual Mandate

Ilya Somin
May 21, 2012

Both sides in the individual mandate litigation have developed a wide range of legal arguments to support their position. Some defenders of the mandate have also emphasized several nonlegal reasons why they believe the Court should uphold the law. These arguments have gotten more emphasis since the Supreme Court oral argument seemed to go badly for the pro-mandate side. The most common are claims that a decision striking down the mandate would damage the Court's "legitimacy," that a 5–4 decision striking down the mandate would be impermissibly "partisan," and that it would be inconsistent with judicial "conservatism."

Even if correct, none of these arguments actually prove that the Court should uphold the mandate as a legal matter. A decision that is perceived as "illegitimate," partisan, and unconservative can still be legally correct. Conversely, one that is widely accepted, enjoys bipartisan support, and is consistent with conservatism can still be wrong. *Plessy v. Ferguson*[58] and *Korematsu v. United States*[59] are well-known examples of terrible rulings that fit all three criteria at the time they were decided.

In addition, all three arguments are flawed even on their own terms.

I. A Decision Striking Down the Mandate Is Likely to Enhance the Court's Legitimacy More than It Undermines It

Claims that a decision striking down the mandate will undermine the Court's "legitimacy"[60] founder on the simple reality that an overwhelming majority of the public wants the law to be invalidated.[61] Even a slight 48–44 plurality of Democrats agree, according to a *Washington Post* / ABC poll.[62] Decisions that damage the Court's legitimacy tend to be ones that run contrary to majority opinion, such as some of the cases striking down New Deal laws in the 1930s. By contrast, a decision failing to strike down a law that large majorities believe to be unconstitutional can actually damage the Court's reputation and create a political backlash, as the case of *Kelo v. City of New London*[63] dramatically demonstrated.

Striking down the mandate will damage the Court's reputation in the eyes of many liberals and some legal elites. But a decision upholding it will equally anger many conservatives and libertarians, including plenty of constitutional law experts. There is not and never has been an expert consensus on the constitutionality of the mandate. Any decision the Court reaches is likely to anger some people, both experts and members of the general public. But more are likely to be disappointed by a decision upholding the law.

Ultimately, the Court should not base its decision in this case on "legitimacy" considerations. If the justices believe that the mandate is constitutional, they should vote to uphold it despite the possible damage to their reputations. But it would be a terrible signal if key swing justices refused to strike down a law merely because their reputations would be damaged in the eyes of a small minority of the public and a vocal faction of the legal elite. It would certainly call into question their willingness to make unpopular decisions that are compelled by their duty to uphold the Constitution, including in cases where they must strike down unconstitutional laws that really do enjoy broad public support.

II. An Impermissibly "Partisan" Decision?

Any decision striking down the mandate is likely to pit the five conservative Republican justices against the four liberal Democrats. Some commentators, such as Larry Lessig[64] and Jonathan Cohn,[65] claim that such a result would be impermissibly "partisan," creating a perception that the Court is only willing to strike down "liberal" laws.

This sort of argument urges judges to engage in genuinely political decision making in order to avoid the mere appearance of it. If a Republican-appointed justice votes to uphold a law he believes to be unconstitutional in order to avoid the appearance of "partisanship," he would be allowing political considerations to trump his oath to uphold the Constitution.

Even if there *is* a judicial duty to avoid the appearance of a partisan split, why doesn't it fall on the liberal justices just as much as the conservatives? If one or more of the liberal justices were to join the five conservatives in striking down the mandate that would diminish the appearance of partisanship just as much as a conservative "defection" to the liberal side would.

Finally, this line of criticism overlooks an important reason why decisions enforcing limits on congressional power often have an ideological division: the Court's liberals have consistently voted against nearly *all* structural limits on congressional power under the Commerce Clause, the Necessary and Proper Clause, and the Tenth Amendment. Thus, the Court enforces such limits only in those cases where the five conservative justices can agree among themselves. The only way for the conservatives to avoid the appearance of partisanship in this area would be complete abdication of judicial enforcement of structural limits on congressional power.

III. Consistency with Judicial "Conservatism"

Jeffrey Rosen[66] and others have argued that a decision against the mandate would be inconsistent with "conservative" attacks on "judicial activism" and deference to legislative judgment. Judicial conservatism is not a single, unitary entity. All sorts of decisions can potentially be justified on "conservative" grounds.

However, one major strand of conservative legal thought over the last thirty years has been the need to enforce constitutional limits on federal government power. This idea would be completely undercut by a decision upholding the mandate, since all the government's arguments in favor of the mandate amount to a blank check for unconstrained congressional power. As I explain in detail in an amicus brief for the Washington Legal Foundation and a group of constitutional law scholars, the government's various "health care is special" arguments collapse under close inspection.[67]

Conservative support for judicially enforced limits on federal power is in some tension with loose conservative rhetoric about "judicial activism," which is one reason why I have long been critical of such rhetoric. However, for most on the Right, "judicial activism" is not coextensive with any judicial overruling of statutes but rather with departures from the text and original meaning of the Constitution. And the originalist case against the mandate is very strong.

Conservatives and others can disagree among themselves as to how much deference should be given to Congress in any given case. In considering this issue, they should weigh two points that Rosen advanced in his important 2006 book *The Most Democratic Branch: How the Courts Serve America*.[68]

Although generally advocating judicial deference to Congress, Rosen notes two important exceptions to this principle. The first is that "[w]hen Congress's own prerogatives are under constitutional assault (in cases involving legislative apportionment or free speech, for example), it may be less appropriate for judges to defer to Congress's self-interested interpretations of the scope of its own power." Obviously, there are few more "self-interested" interpretations of "the scope of its own power" than one that would give Congress virtually unlimited power to impose any mandate it wants.

Second, Rosen suggests that "[f]or the Court to defer to the constitutional views of Congress, Congress must debate issues in constitutional (rather than political) terms."[69] In order to deserve deference, Congress needs to take the relevant constitutional issues seriously. In the individual mandate case, congressional Democrats notoriously demonstrated utter contempt for the constitutional issues and plenty of ignorance to boot.[70]

In fairness, their performance was no worse than that of the GOP when they controlled Congress during the Bush years. Far from generating serious constitutional deliberation in the legislative branch, the judiciary's tendency to defer to Congress on federalism issues has had the opposite effect. Both parties give short shrift to constitutional limits on federal power because judicial deference has created a political culture in which almost anything goes. More careful judicial scrutiny of Congress's handiwork might lead Congress to start taking the Constitution seriously again. That result should be welcomed by conservatives, libertarians, and liberals alike.

A nondeferential posture by the Court wouldn't necessarily lead to the invalidation of the mandate. It merely means that the justices should give little weight to Congress's "self-interested" interpretations of its own power and instead come to their own independent judgment on the constitutional issues at stake.

Ultimately, the Court should not decide the individual mandate case based on these sorts of nonlegal considerations. It is more important that its decision be right than that it be perceived as legitimate, nonpartisan, or conservative. But even on its own terms, the nonlegal case for upholding the mandate is not as impressive as its advocates claim.

No, the Supreme Court Is Not Poised to Adopt a Radical Libertarian Agenda, and Certain Commentators Should Be Embarrassed for Suggesting Otherwise

David E. Bernstein
May 23, 2012

Consider each of the following arguments in its historical context:

1. It's the 1930s. The Scottsboro Boys are represented by a known Communist Party (CP) front, beholden to the agenda Josef Stalin and his minions have dictated to the CP, including the creation of a separate country for American blacks in the "Black Belt." The Supreme Court should rule against the Scottsboro Boys because otherwise the Court will be well on its way to adopting the Communist agenda.
2. It's the 1980s. The Equal Employment Opportunity Commission (EEOC) is before the Supreme Court arguing that Title VII protects women from sexual harassment. The intellectual energy behind this claim comes from radical feminist Catherine MacKinnon, who also supports such things as "comparable worth" and a ban on indecent sexual speech. The Supreme Court should rule against the EEOC, lest it be well on its way to adopting the radical feminist agenda.
3. It's the 2000s. Various war on terror detainees are challenging their detention. While the detainees have some mainstream support, much of the energy behind their challenges comes from elements of the radical left who, for example, want the U.S. Constitution to be subordinated to "international law" as elaborated by left-wing nongovernmental organizations (NGOs) and who in some cases adhered to an ideology most would describe as "anti-American." The Supreme Court should rule against the detainees, lest it be well on its way to adopting the radical Left's agenda.

Obviously, these arguments are all flawed; the strength and validity of legal arguments before the Court does not depend on who is representing the parties nor on whether the relevant legal arguments were invented or influenced by "radicals" who have a political agenda that extends well beyond the precise issues before the Court. Nor does adopting one argument supported by "radicals" in any way obligate the Court to adopt the "radicals'" agenda in any future litigation. Not surprisingly, the Court rejected arguments to the contrary in all the previous examples, which were made especially vociferously in examples one and three.

This has not prevented a meme from developing, led by some prominent Supreme Court commentators who should know better, that if the Court invalidates the ACA it will somehow be well on its way to adopting a broader libertarian agenda supported by some of those, including some of my cobloggers, who helped craft the arguments against the ACA currently before the Court.

In fact, if the Court rules against the ACA, the other 90-plus percent of the U.S. government loathed by libertarians will still be going strong.

Those Supreme Court watchers who are pushing the "libertarians are coming" meme are well aware that the Supreme Court has historically never strayed much from mainstream public and elite opinion, both of which remain decidedly not libertarian. Nor is there any particular reason to believe that John Roberts, Samuel Alito, and others are in thrall to libertarian ideology. So all we have left is the disreputable rhetorical technique of trying to associate in the public mind sound legal arguments with unpopular "radicals" and to eke out a victory on the basis of the libertarian equivalent of Red-baiting rather than on the merits. To say the least, such arguments do no credit to those advancing them.

The Search for a Limiting Principle for Federal Power: Collective Action Problems

Jonathan H. Adler
May 29, 2012

Many of those who urge the Supreme Court to uphold the constitutionality of the individual mandate recognize that the Court is unlikely to take this step without identifying a "limiting principle" that cabins the scope of federal power in some meaningful way. While some deride the search for a limiting principle as unnecessary, others recognize that the Supreme Court has repeatedly reiterated the need for a limiting principle in its enumerated powers jurisprudence. In *Gibbons v. Ogden*, for example, Chief Justice John Marshall noted that "the enumeration presupposes something not enumerated,"[71] making clear that enumerated powers are necessarily limited powers. More recently, in *United State v. Lopez*, the Court rejected the government's proffered justification for the Gun-Free School Zones Act because it contained no such limiting principle. As Chief Justice William Rehnquist explained, "if we were to accept the Government's arguments, we are hard pressed to posit any activity by an individual that Congress is without power to regulate."[72]

One of the more popular limiting principles proposed by progressive academics in support of the individual mandate is that the federal government is authorized to act where action is (or could be) necessary to solve a collective action problem among the states. As Jeffrey Rosen put it in his exchange with Randy, the Court could uphold the mandate and Congress would still be unable to regulate noneconomic activity "where there are no collective action problems that make it impossible for the states to act on their own."[73] The case for a "collective-action federalism" of this sort has been made at greater length by Neil Siegel and Robert Cooter in the *Stanford Law Review*.[74]

The theory of collective-action federalism, particularly as articulated by Cooter and Siegel, is elegant and compelling. It outlines an internally coherent constitutional architecture that has much to recommend it. Yet it has one fundamental problem: *the theory of collective-action federalism cannot provide a plausible account of the Court's current federalism jurisprudence.* Were the Supreme Court to uphold the individual mandate on these grounds, it would repudiate the rationales of several recent Supreme Court opinions, including some written by Justices Scalia and Kennedy.

The collective-action theory of the federal government's enumerated powers seems plausible if one only looks at the Court's recent Commerce Clause cases. On the one hand, neither *Lopez* nor *Morrison* dealt with the sort of problem beyond the capacity of state governments. *Wickard* and *Raich*, on the other hand, dealt with national markets in commodities that states could not effectively regulate (or so our federal representatives could have rationally concluded). So far so good, but this hardly exhausts the universe of enumerated powers cases.

Although the collective action theory of federalism may be able to account for *Lopez* and *Morrison*, it is utterly unable to account for *New York v. United States* or *Printz v. United States*. Both cases involved clear collective-action problems related to economic activities, and in both cases, the laws were struck down on federalism grounds. The law in *New York* was an effort to induce states to provide for the disposal of low-level radioactive waste, which no state wanted to do on its own. It was based on an agreement among several states expressly predicated on the idea that collective action was necessary to solve the problem. No matter, for it sought to commandeer the states. The law in *Printz* could likewise be seen as an effort to solve a collective-action problem as no state would be able to prevent the purchase of guns without a background check if individuals could easily cross state lines to purchase a gun elsewhere.

In neither case was the existence of a collective-action problem enough to save the law. In each case, the Court concluded that the federal law at issue was not "necessary and proper" to carry into execution an exercise of the federal government's power to regulate commerce among the states despite the existence of a collective action problem. Cooter and Siegel did not even try to account for these cases in their *Stanford Law Review* piece. Indeed, neither case is cited (nor are the sovereign immunity cases, which likewise press against their theory).

The collective-action theory also has problems explaining the outcomes of recent decisions in which the Court construed the scope of federal statutes narrowly so as to avoid potential constitutional problems. In *SWANCC v. Army Corps of Engineers*[75] and *Rapanos v. United States*,[76] a majority of the Court adopted a narrowing interpretation of the scope of regulatory jurisdiction over "waters of the United States" under the Clean Water Act to avoid an interpretation of the act that could exceed the scope of the federal government's Commerce Clause power. The theory of federal power necessary to uphold such a broad assertion of regulatory authority could likewise justify federal regulation of local land use. Yet under the collective action theory of federalism, the Court's concerns were unwarranted, as federal legislators could reasonably believe that states would not adopt sufficiently stringent regulations governing water pollution, wetlands development, or even land use generally, due to fears of interstate competition. As previously stated, the collective-action theory of federalism would readily embrace assertions of federal power the Supreme Court has recently rejected.

In sum, the collective-action theory of the federal government's enumerated power may be a coherent theory, but it cannot be reconciled with the whole of the Supreme Court's federalism jurisprudence of the past twenty years. If a majority of the Court is to find a limiting principle for the scope of federal power that will both uphold the individual mandate and be consistent with existing precedent, they will have to look elsewhere.

Origins of Commerce Clause Objections to the Individual Mandate

David E. Bernstein
June 11, 2012

As noted previously on this blog, Democrats in Congress essentially ignored plausible constitutional objections to the ACA's individual mandate, and therefore have only themselves to blame if the law is declared unconstitutional.

A countermeme has spread on the liberal Left that constitutional objections to the ACA's individual mandate were somehow invented circa late 2009, whereas previously all mainstream constitutional commentators, including conservatives, would have conceded that such mandates were constitutional. Here's Andy Koppelman:

> The constitutional limits that the bill supposedly disregarded could not have been anticipated because they did not exist while the bill was being written. They were invented only in the fall of 2009, quite late in the legislative process. The first exploration of Congress's authority to enact a mandate was a paper by Mark Hall, which he posted on SSRN in February, 2009. . . .[77]

Of course, there was little reason for anyone to have written about a mandate before such a mandate was being actively considered by Congress, given that President Obama had promised NOT to enact a mandate in his 2008 campaign.

But more to the point, constitutional objections based on the Commerce Clause to federal health care mandates are hardly novel. Here's attorney David Rivkin writing in the *Wall Street Journal*—hardly an obscure venue—in **1993**:

> In the new health-care system, individuals will not be forced to belong because of their occupation, employment, or business activities—as in the case of Social Security. **They will be dragooned into the system for no other reason than that they are people who are here**. If the courts uphold Congress's authority to impose this system, they must once and for all draw the curtain on the Constitution of 1787 and admit that there is nothing that Congress cannot do under the Commerce Clause. The polite fiction that we live under a government of limited powers must be discarded—Leviathan must be embraced.
>
> The implications of this final extension of the commerce power are frightening. If Congress can regulate you because you are, then it can do anything to you not forbidden by the handful of restraints contained in the Bill of Rights. For example, if Congress thinks Americans are too fat—many are—and this somehow will affect interstate commerce—who's to say it doesn't?—can it not decree that Americans

shall lose weight? [Bernstein: Or "eat broccoli"] Indeed, under the new system, any activity that might increase the costs of health care might be regulatable.[78]

The Clinton administration was sufficiently concerned about constitutional objections to its health care proposals that according to the November 15, 1993, *Washington Times*, the administration asked that Congress

[r]equire lawyers to file within one year after the massive plan becomes law any challenges to its basic constitutionality; Give exclusive jurisdiction to an unusual panel of three judges from the U.S. District Court for D.C.; Forbid those federal judges from issuing temporary restraining orders or injunctions to stop the plan while the case is being litigated; Send appeals only directly to the Supreme Court; and consolidate separate cases.[79]

The constitutional hubbub over Hillarycare was especially remarkable given that this was pre–*Lopez* and *Morrison*—that is, before the only two modern cases to declare that there are limits to federal authority under the Commerce Clause. The objections weren't developed further at the time because Hillarycare never came close to enactment.

In short, the meme that conservatives expressed no constitutional objections to federal health care mandates until they became associated with Barack Obama is, in a word, false.

UPDATE: Just to preempt further comments along similar lines, the issue is not whether you can find any conservative politicians or intellectuals who supported federal mandates as an alternative to a fully nationalized health care system. Rather, the point Koppelman and others seem to be making is that the constitutional arguments against mandates were so unprecedented, so out of the blue, that you couldn't expect Democrats in Congress to be aware of them. I think that's false.

FURTHER UPDATE: A decent historical analogy (but in reverse) would be the National Labor Relations Act, passed in 1935. "Mainstream" opinion at the time was that the act was unconstitutional, and the Supreme Court would so hold. But reasonable observers were also aware that (a) the Court could choose to distinguish past precedents, even if tenuously, and uphold the act; and (b) there was growing sentiment that the scope of the Commerce Clause should be broadened, and this might rescue the act. So Congress passed it anyway, and the Supreme Court, following an election in which the pro–"Big Government" side won handily, decided that the Commerce Clause could be expanded without (yet) completely abandoning its prior jurisprudence.

How Much Will the Ruling in the Health Care Case Matter?

Orin S. Kerr
June 19, 2012

The Supreme Court will hand down its decision in the Affordable Care Act case in a few days, and there's lots of apocalyptic rhetoric from both sides about what a decision affirming or reversing might mean for the law and for the Supreme Court. I agree that the decision is likely to be hugely important. But I also think there are some reasons why the mandate decision may end up being less significant than many people think.

First, the challenge to the mandate has had an enormous impact even if the mandate is upheld. The political, rhetorical, and legal attacks on the mandate have caused a significant shift in how the legal culture on both sides of the aisle construes federalism issues. By the end of the Rehnquist Court in 2005, the Rehnquist federalism revolution was mostly dead. When Rehnquist and Sandra Day O'Connor departed and were replaced with justices seemingly less committed to federalism than they, the prospect for any federalism revival at the Court seemed dim. I remember attending the oral argument in *United States v. Comstock* in January 2010 and being aghast at how uninterested in federalism the conservative justices were. In just two years, opposing the mandate on constitutional grounds rooted in federalism principles has become the standard Republican position. This change has dramatically revived the Right's interest in limited federal power and has signaled to the Left that federalism concerns must be taken seriously. That reemergence of interest in federalism will continue whether the Court strikes down the ACA or upholds it.

Second, if the oral argument in the mandate case is a good guide, the Court may end up with a test that strongly discourages mandates whether or not this particular mandate is upheld. At oral argument, Justice Kennedy suggested that perhaps mandates should require some sort of special justification or heightened scrutiny to be allowed, with the big question then being whether the health care market regulated in this case satisfied that heightened scrutiny. If the Court ends up adopting a test like that, the Court will effectively blunt the possible future use of mandates even if the Court concludes that the health care market is unique and satisfies the heightened scrutiny. Given that the mandate has polled terribly, it's not likely that Congress would be rushing to enact one in the future anyway. I suspect the polling numbers alone would persuade future Congresses that designing programs to use a mandate instead of the 1960s-style entitlement is a political loser. But even if the politics alone doesn't end mandates, I suspect a higher degree of scrutiny for mandates would achieve that goal.

Third, we may end up in the same place over time in terms of health care laws no matter how the Court rules. If the Supreme Court upholds the Affordable Care Act, it seems reasonably likely that Congress will repeal parts of it over the next ten years (including the very unpopular mandate). If the Supreme Court strikes down only the mandate, the Court will bring us to a similar position. If the Court strikes down the entire law, it seems reasonably likely that some version of the Affordable

Care Act (minus the unpopular mandate) will be enacted in the next ten years. And if we're left with a law without mandates, it's not clear if it will last over time or will prove ineffectual and be replaced by something else. It's important to remember that the objection to the ACA is procedural in nature. The challenge is about how Congress can achieve its goal, not whether a national health care law can be enacted if people want one. So while striking down the entire mandate would restart the process on a health care law, there's a sense in which all the roads may be leading to the same place over the long run.

Fourth, although there have been a lot of claims about how a decision in the mandate case might impact public perceptions of the Supreme Court, I tend to discount such claims. Public opinion about the Supreme Court seems to be relatively insensitive to individual decisions: Gallup's poll suggests that the Court's approval rating ranges from about 40 percent to 60 percent over the years.[80] Changes in the ratings seem to coincide more with confirmation hearings (which in recent years have often correlated with a bump in approval ratings) than with particular decisions. That would make some sense, I suppose—Supreme Court confirmation hearings are major stories every day for at least ten weeks or so, while even major Supreme Court decisions are major stories only for a few days tops. Maybe the mandate case is so big that it would be different, but I'm not confident of that. So on balance I don't think a ruling on the mandate is likely to make much difference one way or the other.

The mandate case is still hugely important, of course. The size and scale of the ACA is so vast that any case on its constitutionality will have major effects. The legislative process can be heavily path dependent, so which path the Court takes may make a big difference even over time. The Medicaid expansion issue from day three is potentially a big sleeper issue that may have major impact, too. And importantly, part of my argument is premised on a particular view of how the justices might craft the opinion (especially my second point); if I end up being wrong on that, which is certainly possible, then it's hard to predict how much impact the decision might have. But for the previous reasons, I think there's a decent possibility that the decision in the health care cases may have less impact than many are expecting.

Correcting Misconceptions about the Roberts Court

Jonathan H. Adler
June 25, 2012

The Supreme Court has not yet ruled against the individual mandate, and who knows whether it will. Yet this has not stopped commentators from making sweeping charges about the Court. Many commentators, for instance, are charging that the Roberts Court is "activist." For some, "activist" is just a label for judges that make decisions they don't like; one man's "activist" is another's constitutional paladin. For others, however, the label "activist" is used to describe a court that is particularly "active" in overturning precedent and invalidating laws and thereby altering the course of the law. So, for instance, James Fallows claims[81] the Court, and Chief Justice Roberts and Justice Alito in particular, "actively second-guess and re-do existing law" and Jeffrey Toobin charged "the current Court has matched contempt for Congress with a disdain for many of the Court's own precedents."[82]

The problem with these characterizations of the court is that if by "judicial activism" one means a willingness to overturn precedents and invalidate federal laws, the Roberts Court is the *least activist* court of the postwar period. As a recent *New York Times* analysis showed, thus far the Roberts Court has overturned prior precedents and invalidates federal laws at a significantly lower rate than its predecessors.[83] Further, many of the Court's most "activist" decisions, so defined, have moved the law in a more liberal direction (see, e.g., *Boumediene* and *Kennedy v. Louisiana*[84]) or were broadly supported First Amendment decisions (e.g. *United States v. Stevens*[85]). This does not mean the Roberts Court's decisions are correct and there are exceptions to every rule. Nor does the Court's past conduct necessarily predict the future. It does, however, mean that when one looks at the Court's overall behavior (and not at a single case) it is inaccurate to say that this Court is particularly "activist" in moving the law in a conservative direction by overturning precedents and invalidating federal laws.

UPDATE: Here is the relevant quote from the *Times* article: "The Roberts court is finding laws unconstitutional and reversing precedent—two measures of activism—no more often than earlier courts." The data accompanying the article shows this is an understatement. Specifically, the data show the following:

- The Warren, Burger, and Rehnquist Courts overturned precedents at an average rate of 2.7, 2.8, and 2.4 per term, respectively. The Roberts Court, on the other hand, has only overturned an average of 1.6 precedents per term.
- The Warren, Burger, and Rehnquist Courts struck down an average of 7.9, 12.5, and 8.2 laws per term, whereas the Roberts Court has only invalidated an average of 3 laws per term.

The data are through 2010, but adding the past two terms would not change much.

Notes

1. Transcript of Oral Argument at 65-67, U.S. Dep't of Health & Human Servs. v. Florida, 132 S. Ct. 2566 (2012) (March 26, 2012) (No. 11-398) http://www.supremecourt.gov/oral_arguments/argument_transcripts/11-398-Monday.pdf (Monday argument).
2. Transcript of Oral Argument at 27-29, U.S. Dep't of Health & Human Servs. v. Florida, 132 S. Ct. 2566 (2012) (March 27, 2012) (No. 11-398), http://www.supremecourt.gov/oral_arguments/argument_transcripts/11-398-Tuesday.pdf (Tuesday argument).
3. Brief for the Washington Legal Foundation & Constitutional Scholars as Amici Curiae Supporting Respondents, NFIB v. Sebelius, 132 S. Ct. 2566 (2012) (No. 11-398).
4. Transcript of Oral Argument (Tuesday argument) at 77.

5. *Wickard*, 317 U.S. at 128.
6. Brent Kendall, "Kennedy Leaves Both Sides Hopeful," *Wall Street Journal*, March 27, 2012, http://online.wsj.com/article/SB1000142405270230417710457730805247799189 4.html.
7. Johnson v. Eisentrager, 339 U.S. 763 (1950).
8. Rasul v. Bush, 542 U.S. 466 (2004).
9. Jonathan H. Adler, "The Constitutionality of an Individual Mandate—A Reply to Senator Max Baucus," *supra*.
10. Adam Teicholz, "Did Bloggers Kill the Health Care Mandate?," *Atlantic*, last modified March 28, 2012, http://www.theatlantic.com/national/archive/2012/03/did-bloggers -kill-the-health-care-mandate/255182/#bio.
11. Ilya Somin, "Gonzalez v. Raich and the Individual Mandate," *supra*.
12. Ilya Somin, "The Myth of an Expert Consensus on the Constitutionality of an Individual Health Insurance Mandate," *supra*.
13. Randy Barnett, Nathaniel Stewart, and Todd F. Gaziano, "Legal Memorandum 49: Why the Personal Mandate to Buy Health Insurance Is Unprecedented and Unconstitutional," Heritage Foundation, last modified December 9, 2009, http://www.heritage .org/research/reports/2009/12/why-the-personal-mandate-to-buy-health-insurance -is-unprecedented-and-unconstitutional.
14. See Brief for the Washington Legal Foundation et al., U.S. Dep't of Health & Human Servs. v. Florida, 132 S. Ct. 2566 (2012) (No. 11-398).
15. Ilya Somin, "Legal Action and Political Action as a Two-Track Strategy for Opposing Obamacare," *supra*.
16. Ilya Somin, "Lessons from the Rise of Legal Conservatism," *Harvard Journal of Law and Public Policy* 32 (2009): 415.
17. Kerry Picket, "Conyers Fabricates Constitutional Law Citing 'Good and Welfare' Clause," *Washington Times*, last modified March 23, 2010, http://www.washington times.com/weblogs/watercooler/2010/mar/23/conyers-makes-constitutional -law-citing-good-and-w.
18. "PETE STARK:—The Federal Government Can Do Most Anything in This Country," YouTube video, 3:37, posted by "Steve Kemp," August 1, 2010, http://www.youtube .com/watch?v=W1-eBz8hyoE.
19. "Judge Napolitano v James Clyburn Debating Constitutionality of Federal Health Care," YouTube video, 2:41, posted by "TruthSeeker120," September 8, 2009, http:// www.youtube.com/watch?v=00Xcqp46A64.
20. Damon W. Root, "I Don't Worry about the Constitution on This, to Be Honest," *Reason Hit & Run* (blog), last modified April 2, 2010, http://reason.com/ blog/2010/04/02/i-dont-worry-about-the-constit.
21. Nicholas Ballasy, "Sen. Akaka Says 'I'm Not Aware' of Constitution Giving Congress Authority to Make Individuals Buy Health Insurance," CNSNews.com, last modified November 11, 2011, http://cnsnews.com/news/article/sen-akaka-says-i-m-not-aware -constitution-giving-congress-authority-make-individuals.
22. Matt Cover, "FLASHBACK: Senate Judiciary Chairman Leahy on Obamacare Mandate: 'Nobody' Questions Our Authority," CNSNews.com, last modified December 13, 2010, http://cnsnews.com/news/article/flashback-senate-judiciary-chairman-leahy-obama care-mandate-nobody-questions-our.
23. Nicholas Ballasy, "Sen. Landrieu Declines to Say Where Constitution Authorizes Congress to Force Americans to Buy Health Insurance, Saying She'll Let 'Constitutional Lawyers on Our Staff' Handle That," CNSNews.com, last modified December 9, 2010,

http://www.cnsnews.com/news/article/sen-landrieu-declines-say-where-constitution
-authorizes-congress-force-americans-buy.

24. Neil Siegel, "Five Limiting Principles," *Balkinization* (blog), March 28, 2012, http://
balkin.blogspot.com/2012/03/five-limiting-principles.html.

25. See, e.g., Caminetti v. United States, 242 U.S. 470 (1917) (holding that Congress can
use the interstate commerce power to criminalize interstate travel by people intending to engage in noncommercial extramarital sex); Champion v. Ames, 188 U.S. 321
(1903) ("What clause can be cited which, in any degree, countenances the suggestion
that one may, of right, carry or cause to be carried from one state to another that which
will harm the public morals?").

26. Champion v. Ames, 188 U.S. 321 (1903).

27. Transcript of Oral Argument at 57-58, U.S. Dep't of Health & Human Servs. v. Florida,
132 S. Ct. 2566 (2012) (No. 11-398), http://www.supremecourt.gov/oral_arguments/
argument_transcripts/11-398-Tuesday.pdf (Tuesday argument).

28. *Id.* at 71.

29. *Id.* at 106.

30. See, e.g., Tr. 16:18–17:7, 39:6–43:8.

31. See, e.g., Tr. 31:24–34:22.

32. *Id.* at 104:24–106:8.

33. *Id.* at 16:22–25.

34. *Id.* at 25:3–10.

35. *Id.* at 31:11–16.

36. South Dakota v. Dole, 483 U.S. 203 (1987).

37. Lyle Denniston, "Argument Recap: Will Medicaid Be Sacrificed?," *SCOTUSblog*,
March 28, 2012, http://www.scotusblog.com/2012/03/argument-recap-will-medicaid
-be-sacrificed.

38. Ilya Somin, "Closing the Pandora's Box of Federalism: The Case for Judicial Restriction of Federal Subsidies to State Governments," *Georgetown Law Journal* 90 (2002):
461.

39. John Eastman, "Restoring the General to the General Welfare Clause," *Chapman Law
Review* 4 (2001): 63.

40. Brief for the Center for Constitutional Jurisprudence et al. as Amici Curiae Supporting Petitioners, Florida et al. v. U.S. Dep't of Health & Human Servs., 132 S. Ct. 2566
(2012) (No. 11-400).

41. Gary Sargent, "How Did Legal Observers and Obamacare Backers Get It So Wrong?"
Washington Post (blog), March 29, 2012, http://www.washingtonpost.com/blogs/
plum-line/post/how-did-obamacares-backers-get-it-so-wrong/2012/03/29/gIQAr
H5wiS_blog.html.

42. Rumsfeld v. Forum for Academic & Institutional Rights, 547 U.S. 47 (2006) (holding
unanimously that the government can withhold funding from universities that refuse
to give military recruiters access to school resources).

43. Jack Balkin, "The Inevitable Conservative Argument That Health Care Reform Is
Unconstitutional," *Balkinization* (blog), August 22, 2009, http://balkin.blogspot
.com/2009/08/inevitable-conservative-argument-that.html; see also, Jonathan H.
Adler, "Is Obamacare Constitutional?," *supra.*

44. Randy E. Barnett, "Is Health Care Reform Constitutional?" *Washington Post*, March 21,
2010, http://www.washingtonpost.com/wp-dyn/content/article/2010/03/19/AR20100
31901470.html.

45. Cong. Research Service, *The Constitution of the United States: Analysis & Interpretation,*
Doc. No. *111–39* (Washington, D.C.: Government Printing Office, 2010), 201.

46. Alexander Hamilton, *Federalist No. 78*, ed. Clinton Rossiter (1961).

47. Hylton v. United States, 3 U.S. 171 (1796).

48. Calder v. Bull, 3 U.S. 386 (1798).

49. Wanda Franz, "*Gonzalez v. Carhart*: A Litmus Test for Presidential Candidates," *National Right to Life News* 34 (2007): 3, http://www.nrlc.org/news/2007/NRL08/PresidentColumnPage3.html. Quoting then-Senator Barack Obama, "I strongly disagree with today's Supreme Court ruling, which dramatically departs from previous precedents safeguarding the health of pregnant women. As Justice Ginsburg emphasized in her dissenting opinion, this ruling signals an alarming willingness on the part of the conservative majority to disregard its prior rulings respecting a woman's medical concerns and the very personal decisions between a doctor and patient. I am extremely concerned that this ruling will embolden state legislatures to enact further measures to restrict a woman's right to choose, and that the conservative Supreme Court justices will look for other opportunities to erode *Roe v. Wade*, which is established federal law and a matter of equal rights for women."

50. Dotcomabc, "Kaffee v. Jessup II: Obama and McCain Square Off on Habeas Corpus Rights for Accused Terrorists," *Political Punch* (blog), June 14, 2008, http://abcnews.go.com/blogs/politics/2008/06/kaffee-vs-jessu.

51. Robert Barnes, "Health Care Arguments Recall a Supreme Court That Is an Equal-Opportunity Offender," *Washington Post*, April 8, 2012, http://www.washingtonpost.com/politics/health-care-arguments-recall-supreme-court-case-that-is-an-equal-opportunity-offender/2012/04/08/gIQAmhrO4S_story.html.

52. David E. Bernstein, *Rehabilitating Lochner: Defending Individual Rights against Progressive Reform* (Chicago: University of Chicago Press, 2011).

53. Sorrell v. IMS Health, Inc., 131 S. Ct. 2653 (2011).

54. Lawrence v. Texas, 539 U.S. 538 (2003).

55. 524 U.S. 498, 547 (1994) (Thomas, J., concurring).

56. Randy Barnett, "Justice Kennedy, 'Actuarial Risk,' and the Individual Mandate's Unconstitutionality," *supra*.

57. Ricardo Alonso-Zalvidar, "Supreme Court Misunderstanding on Health Overhaul?" Associated Press, April 11, 2012, http://news.yahoo.com/supreme-court-misunderstanding-health-overhaul-164816921.html.

58. Plessy v. Ferguson, 163 U.S. 537 (1896) (upholding the constitutionality of "separate but equal").

59. Korematsu v. United States, 323 U.S. 214 (1944) (permitting the internment of Japanese-Americans during World War II).

60. Jonathan Cohn, "Obamacare Is on Trial. So Is the Supreme Court," *New Republic* (blog), March 29, 2012, http://www.tnr.com/blog/jonathan-cohn/102204/supreme-court-roberts-kennedy-health-mandate-legitimacy#.

61. Ilya Somin, "Public Opinion, the Individual Mandate, and the Supreme Court," *supra*.

62. Scott Clement, "Toss Individual Health Insurance Mandate, Poll Says," *Washington Post* (blog), March 19, 2012, http://www.washingtonpost.com/blogs/behind-the-numbers/post/toss-individual-health-insurance-mandate-poll-says/2012/03/18/gIQAaZtpLS_blog.html.

63. Kelo v. City of New London, 545 U.S. 469 (2005) (promoting "economic development" can be a valid "public use" under the Fifth Amendment's Takings Clause).

64. Lawrence Lessig, "Why Scalia Could Uphold Obamacare," *Atlantic*, April 13, 2012, http://www.theatlantic.com/national/archive/12/04/why-scalia-might-uphold-obamacare/255791.

65. Cohn, "Obamacare Is on Trial."

66. Jeffrey Rosen, "Second Opinions: Obamacare Isn't the Only Target of Conservative Judges," *New Republic*, May 4, 2012, http://www.tnr.com/article/politics/103090/magazine/conservative-judges-justices-supreme-court-obama.

67. Brief for the Washington Legal Foundation et al., *Sebelius*, 132 S. Ct. 2566, *supra*.

68. Jeffrey Rosen, *The Most Democratic Branch: How the Courts Serve America* (New York: Oxford University Press, 2006).

69. *Id.* at 10.

70. David E. Bernstein, "Democratic Congressmen on Constitutional Authority for the ACA," *supra*.

71. Gibbons v. Ogden, 22 U.S. 1, 195 (1824).

72. United States v. Lopez, 514 U.S. 549, 564 (1995).

73. Jeffrey Rosen, "Are Liberals Trying to Intimidate John Roberts?," *New Republic*, May 28, 2012, http://www.newrepublic.com/article/politics/103656/obamacare-affordable-care-act-critics-response.

74. Neil Seigel and Robert Cooter, "Collective Action Federalism: A General Theory of Article I, Section 8," *Stanford Law Review* 63 (2010): 115.

75. Solid Waste Agency of N. Cook Cnty. v. Army Corps of Engineers, 531 U.S. 159 (2001).

76. Rapanos v. United States, 547 U.S. 715 (2006).

77. Andrew Koppelman, "Origins of a Health Care Lie," Salon.com, last modified May, 31, 2012, http://www.salon.com/2012/05/31/origins_of_a_healthcare_lie/singleton.

78. David B. Rivkin Jr., "Health Care Reform vs. the Founders," *Wall Street Journal*, September 29, 1993.

79. Frank J. Murray, "Shelter Sought for Health Care Plan; Congress Asked to Curb Lawsuits," *Washington Times*, November 15, 1993, A10.

80. "Supreme Court Approval Results," Gallup, http://www.gallup.com/poll/4732/supreme-court.aspx#1.

81. James Fallows, "5 Signs of Radical Change in U.S. Politics," *Atlantic*, June 24, 2012, http://www.theatlantic.com/politics/archive/2012/06/5-signs-of-a-radical-change-in-us-politics/258904.

82. Jeffrey Toobin, "Money Unlimited: How John Roberts Orchestrated the *Citizens United* Decision," *New Yorker*, May 21, 2012, http://www.newyorker.com/reporting/2012/05/21/120521fa_fact_toobin.

83. Adam Liptak, "Court under Roberts Is Most Conservative in Decade," *New York Times*, July 24, 2010, http://www.nytimes.com/2010/07/25/us/25roberts.html?_r=0.

84. Kennedy v. Louisiana, 554 U.S. 407 (2008) (holding that the Eighth Amendment does not permit the state to punish the crime of rape of a child with the death penalty).

85. United States v. Stevens, 130 S. Ct. 1577 (2010) (striking down a federal law prohibiting depictions of animal cruelty as a violation of the First Amendment).

8

Decision Time and Aftermath

The last week of June, which is the last week of a Supreme Court term, is always a busy time for Court watchers. The Court often waits until then to issue the biggest and most controversial decisions, which are also usually the longest ones.

On June 26 and 27, the Court issued decisions at the usual 10 a.m. eastern time. Each day held the possibility that the Obamacare decision would come down, and disappointment when it didn't. When June 28 arrived, the last day of the Court's October 2011 term, a decision was essentially certain.

The decision, which weighed in at nearly two hundred pages, shocked nearly everyone, especially the *Volokh Conspiracy* bloggers.

***

Lose the Battle, Win the War?

Jonathan H. Adler
SCOTUSblog, June 28, 2012

For those who opposed the individual mandate and hoped to see the entire Patient Protection and Affordable Care Act (PPACA) struck down, today's Supreme Court decision is a disappointment. Yet for those who hoped the Court would reaffirm that the Constitution creates a federal government of limited and enumerated powers and that it is the responsibility of the Court to enforce such limits, there is much to like in today's decision. While the Court upheld the PPACA, it reaffirmed the foundational principles of the nation's constitutional structure and confirmed that the federalism decisions of the Rehnquist Court were not aberrations. In a very real sense, proponents of federalism may have lost the battle, but won the war.

The opening of Chief Justice John Roberts's opinion for the Court is a clear and forceful restatement of the notion that the enumeration of powers in Article I is meant to limit the federal government. This limitation, Roberts notes for the Court, is no less important for the preservation of individual liberty than the Bill of Rights. This opening section effectively repudiates the notion, briefly embraced by the Court in *Garcia v. San Antonio Metropolitan Transit Authority*, that the primary safeguards against federal overreach are political. It has been quite some time since these principles attracted such broad agreement on the Court. Though the chief justice upholds the individual mandate as an exercise of the taxing power, this provides insulation against the exercise of such powers in the future. Never again will Congress be able to pretend that a penalty of this sort is anything but a tax. As a consequence, such measures will only be adopted when they are truly supported by the people.

It would be tempting to read the chief justice's discussions of the Commerce and Necessary and Proper Clauses as mere dicta. It would also be wrong, as these analyses form an essential predicate to his ultimate conclusion that the mandate could be upheld as a tax. As the entire Court accepts, the most natural reading of the minimum coverage provision is as an economic mandate adopted pursuant to the Commerce Clause. It is only after rejecting the possibility that the mandate could be justified in this manner that the chief returns to the text to see if it is susceptible to an alternative construction. Thus, the only reason the chief justice even considers whether the mandate could be considered a tax, the statutory text notwithstanding, is because of his prior conclusion on the Commerce and Necessary and Proper Clauses. Thus this decision provides five firm votes for meaningful limits on the most expansive of Congress's powers.

The chief justice's opinion also confirms that he is a judicial minimalist—and more so than any other member of the Court. His decision to adopt a narrowed, if strained, interpretation of the minimum-coverage provision so as to preserve the statute's constitutionality is of a piece with what he has done before, in cases like *NAMUDNO v. Holder*[1] and *FEC v. Wisconsin Right to Life*[2] (and, according to Jeffrey Toobin's reporting, was prepared to do in *Citizens United v. Federal Election Commission*). When possible, the chief justice prefers to decide less, leave precedents undisturbed and, as in this case, avoid overturning a federal statute—even if it means stretching statutory text or adopting stingy interpretations of prior opinions. Whether or not one likes this approach to judicial decision making, it is what we have come to expect. It is thus no surprise that, as a 2010 *New York Times* analysis found, the Roberts Court overturns precedents and invalidates federal statutes far less often than did the Rehnquist, Burger, and Warren Courts.[3]

While commentators largely focused on the Commerce and Necessary and Proper Clauses, the Court's treatment of the spending power is likely to have the greatest practical effect. For years, the Court has insisted that Congress's power to impose conditions on the receipt of federal funds is limited without ever finding a limit it would enforce. The criteria outlined in *South Dakota v. Dole* made for a nice test, but it was a test that nearly every statute passed. Today, however, seven justices concluded that Congress could not condition the receipt of existing Medicaid funds on state acceptance of a Medicaid expansion, putting teeth into *Dole's* admonition that Congress could not use the promise of federal funds to "coerce" state obedience.

The Court's decision on the Medicaid expansion dramatically reduces the pressure for states to accept this part of the PPACA. It will also limit the federal government's ability to direct state implementation in other areas by threatening the withdrawal of federal funds. Given the frequency with which Congress uses the power of the purse to induce state cooperation, new rounds of litigation on the spending clause are sure to follow. *Dole* upheld a threat to withhold 5 percent of federal highway funds if states refused to adopt a 21-years-old drinking age. But will courts uphold a threat from the Environmental Protection Agency to shut off the lion's share of highway funds should states not adopt sufficiently stringent pollution controls on local businesses? Perhaps not.[4]

NFIB v. Sebelius does not end the legal wrangling over the PPACA. Rather, this case is only the beginning. Barring action by Congress, the Court will see this statute again. Several additional PPACA lawsuits are already pending in federal court. These suits challenge everything from the structure of the Independent Payment Advisory Board to the mandate that employers provide contraception coverage as part of employees' health insurance plans, and more are on the way.[5]

The Court decided this case, but it did not resolve the legal or political debate over health care reform. It did, however, decide this case in a way that reaffirmed foundational federalist principles, thus ensuring that federalist arguments will continue to receive a fair hearing from the judiciary. If mandate opponents had to lose this case, this was the way to lose it.

A Taxing but Potentially Hopeful Decision

Ilya Somin
SCOTUSblog, June 28, 2012

Today's 5–4 Supreme Court decision upholding the individual health insurance mandate is an extremely frustrating result for those of us who argued that the mandate is unconstitutional. One might even call it taxing. The plaintiffs came about as close as one can to winning a major constitutional case without actually winning it. It is the legal equivalent of losing the World Series after leading in the bottom of the ninth inning in the seventh game. It is not a happy day for supporters of limited government.

Yet the Court also offers us a measure of hope and vindication. A majority of the justices rejected claims that the mandate is authorized by the Commerce Clause and Necessary and Proper Clause. That has little immediate impact but bodes well for the future. The numerous pundits who claimed that this case was a slam dunk for the federal government turned out to be spectacularly wrong. The struggle over the constitutional limits on federal power is far from over.

I. A Partial Victory for Federalism

Although he cast the deciding vote in favor of the mandate, Chief Justice John Roberts's opinion actually rejected the federal government's main argument for the law: the assertion that the mandate is authorized by the Commerce Clause, which gives Congress the power to regulate "[c]ommerce . . . among the several states." As Roberts puts it "the power to regulate commerce presupposes the existence of commercial activity to be regulated."[6] But, he continues, the mandate "does not regulate existing commercial activity. It instead compels individuals to become active in commerce by purchasing a product, on the ground that their failure to do so affects interstate commerce."[7] If Congress can "regulate individuals precisely because they are doing nothing,"[8] it could impose pretty much any mandate of any kind. It could force people to purchase broccoli, cars, movie tickets, or any other product. By endorsing this distinction between regulation of activity and inactivity, Roberts validated the main argument advanced by the mandate's opponents.

Roberts's opinion also has a compelling answer to the many who argued that the mandate is justified by precedents such as *Wickard v. Filburn*, which ruled that the Commerce Clause allows Congress to limit the amount of wheat farmers can grow on their land: "The farmer in *Wickard* was at least actively engaged in the production of wheat, and the Government could regulate that activity because of its effect on commerce."[9] By contrast, "[t]he Government's theory here would effectively override that limitation, by establishing that individuals may be regulated under the Commerce Clause whenever enough of them are not doing something the Government would have them do."[10]

Roberts also rejected the federal government's various arguments to the effect that this mandate is constitutional because health insurance is a special case. The government's central "health care is special" argument was that this market is unique because it involves a product everyone uses at some point. But this analysis relies on shifting the focus from health insurance (the product actually covered by the mandate) to health care, claiming that the former is just one way to obtain the latter. But pretty much any product government might force you to buy is part of some larger market that is difficult to avoid. Not everyone purchases broccoli. But everyone does participate in the market for food. As Roberts puts it, "Everyone will likely participate in the markets for food, clothing, transportation, shelter, or energy; that does not authorize Congress to direct them to purchase particular products in those or other markets today. The Commerce Clause is not a general license to regulate an individual from cradle to grave, simply because he will predictably engage in particular transactions."[11]

For similar reasons, Roberts rejected the government's argument that the mandate is authorized by the Necessary and Proper Clause, which gives Congress the power to "make all Laws which shall be necessary and proper for carrying into Execution" other powers granted to Congress under the Constitution. Roberts recognizes that the Supreme Court has defined the term "necessary" very broadly. But even a "necessary" law may be unconstitutional if it is not also "proper." As Roberts puts it, "Even if the individual mandate is 'necessary' to the Act's insurance reforms, such an expansion of federal power is not a 'proper' means for making those reforms effective."[12] In this case, Roberts contends that the law is improper because, under the government's logic, Congress would "[n]o longer . . . be limited to regulating under the Commerce Clause those who by some preexisting activity bring themselves within the sphere of federal regulation."[13] The individual mandate, he explains, "vests Congress with the extraordinary ability to create the necessary predicate to the exercise of an enumerated power."[14]

Overall, the chief justice endorsed the central arguments of the plaintiffs, as has a majority of the Court. The four dissenting justices—Samuel Alito, Anthony Kennedy, Antonin Scalia, and Clarence Thomas—also concluded that the mandate exceeds Congress's Commerce and Necessary and Proper powers. This has potentially significant implications for future legislation imposing mandates under the Commerce Clause.

II. The Taxing and Spending Clause

After agreeing with the plaintiffs on so much, Roberts still voted to uphold the mandate because it is a "tax" authorized by Congress's power under the Taxing and Spending Clause. He endorsed an argument that had been rejected by every lower court ruling that addressed it. Even the lawyers for the federal government seemed to have little confidence in it, as indicated by the fact that they relegated it to a brief section near the very end of their brief.

The ruling also runs counter to repeated statements by President Obama and numerous congressional Democrats, who assured us that the mandate was not a tax. As the president put it in 2009, "for us to say that you've got to take a responsibility to get health insurance is absolutely not a tax increase." It is perhaps not surprising that Roberts voted to uphold the mandate. But it is a huge shock that he did so on the basis of the government's weakest argument, one that even most liberal lower court judges had rejected.

Roberts argues that the mandate is a tax because it imposes only a monetary penalty on those who fail to comply, the mandate does not apply to people too poor to pay income taxes, and the fine is collected by the IRS. He admits that this not the "most natural interpretation" of the law.

The text of the statute refers to the fine as a "penalty," not a tax. And the Supreme Court has repeatedly distinguished between taxes and penalties, defining the latter as "an exaction imposed by statute as punishment for an unlawful act" or omission. The health insurance mandate fits the definition of penalty almost perfectly: it imposes a fine as punishment for the unlawful refusal to purchase government-mandated health insurance.

Chief Justice Roberts claims that this is not a real penalty because "the mandate is not a legal command to buy insurance"[15] but merely a requirement that violators pay a fine to the IRS. Failure to purchase health insurance, is therefore, not really "unlawful." The logic here is underwhelming. Is speeding or jaywalking not really unlawful if the penalty for it is a fine payable to the Treasury and the very poor are exempt from it?

Moreover, pretty much any other mandate can be magically converted into a tax so long as it is structured in the same way as this mandate is. Congress can therefore use similar fines to force people to purchase broccoli, cars, or just about anything else. The danger here is not just theoretical. Numerous interest groups could potentially lobby Congress to enact a law requiring people to buy their products, just as the health insurance industry did in this case.

In his discussion of the Commerce Clause, Roberts ruled that the Constitution denies Congress the power to "bring countless decisions an individual could potentially make within the scope of federal regulation and . . . empower Congress to make those decisions for him." Yet having closed the front door of the

Commerce Clause, the chief justice has now "empowered" Congress to make those same decisions for us through the tax power.

III. Prospects for the Future

Today's decision is unlikely to be the last word on the constitutional limits of federal power. As the close 5–4 division in the Court shows, the justices remain deeply divided on federalism issues. Both Chief Justice Roberts's opinion and the powerful four-justice dissent reaffirm the need to enforce limits on congressional authority. And both accept all or most of the main constitutional arguments against the mandate. The latter will constrain future mandates imposed under the Commerce and Necessary and Proper Clause. No one can any longer say that the case against the mandate was a sure loser that could only be endorsed by fringe extremists or people ignorant of constitutional law.

Defenders of extremely broad federal power won an important battle today. But the war will continue.

Major Limits on the Congress's Powers, in an Opinion Worthy of John Marshall

David B. Kopel
SCOTUSblog, June 28, 2012

"The States are separate and independent sovereigns."[16] So affirms the Court today by a 7–2 vote, in the most important decision ever defining the limits of Congress's power under the Taxing and Spending Clause.

While the constitutional implications are tremendous, the practical effect on state budgets may be even greater. Today (and from now on!), states do not need to provide Medicaid to able-bodied childless adults. Likewise, states today have discretion about whether to provide Medicaid to middle-class parents. Undoubtedly, some states will choose to participate in the Affordable Care Act's (ACA's) massive expansion of medical welfare, but fiscally responsible states now have the choice not to.

It's true that the ACA contained a promise that the federal government would pay for most of the ACA expansion in the next several years. But history has shown that planning one's budget based on fiscal promises from Congress is reckless. While much of the legal commentariat treated the Medicaid mandate as a throwaway issue, the precedents against it were stronger, more numerous, and more recent than those involving the individual mandate. Since the late 1980s, the Court has repeatedly affirmed the central importance of state sovereignty in our constitutional structure. The Court's sovereignty decisions have involved not only the Commerce Clause, but many other enumerated congressional powers, ranging from the Patent Clause to Section 5 of the Fourteenth Amendment. Today, the Court affirms that the Taxing and Spending Clause is just like the rest of Congress's powers: it too must conform to the principles of state sovereignty, which pervade the Constitution and which are affirmed by the Tenth Amendment and given additional protection by the Eleventh Amendment.

During the late 1930s and early 1940s, a supine Court abdicated its constitutional duty of enforcing constitutional limits on congressional power. It was then that Chief Justice Harlan Stone called the Tenth Amendment a "truism."[17] Today, *Darby*'s characterization of the Tenth Amendment must be understood according to the literal meaning of "truism": a self-evident or obvious truth. It is self-evident that when the people of the United States ratified the Constitution, they gave Congress and the national government only some of the sovereignty that had previously inhered in the states.

In *South Dakota v. Dole*,[18] a divided Court had upheld a conditional grant under the Taxing and Spending Clause: if states did not raise their drinking age to 21, then states would lose 5 percent of their federal highway grants. Chief Justice William Rehnquist's majority opinion characterized the cutoff as "a relatively mild encouragement to the States."[19] He also cautioned that a cutoff might be so severe as to be unconstitutionally coercive, infringing the states' rights to self-government. Since then, academics have struggled to figure out a test for when a cutoff might violate *South Dakota v. Dole*. Lower federal courts have never enforced *Dole*'s anticoercion rule.

Today, for the first time, a federal court finds that a spending cutoff violates *Dole*. In *Dole*, the revenue at issue amounted to less than one-half of one percent of the state's budget. The Medicaid cutoff, however, constitutes at least 10 percent of a typical state's budget. So "[i]n this case, the financial 'inducement' Congress has chosen is much more than 'relatively mild encouragement'—it is a gun to the head."[20]

The chief justice seems to be saying that one-half of 1 percent is OK, and 10 percent is obviously far too much. So quantity does have a constitutional quality. Although lower courts that wish to follow the Supreme Court's guidance will probably conclude, in future cases, that 7 percent is too much and 2 percent is not, the issue is not solely quantitative.

As Chief Justice Roberts explains, the Medicaid mandate significantly changed the program:

> The original program was designed to cover medical services for four particular categories of the needy: the disabled, the blind, the elderly, and needy families with dependent children. See 42 U.S.C. §1396a(a)(10). Previous amendments to Medicaid eligibility merely altered and expanded the boundaries of these categories. Under the Affordable Care Act, Medicaid is transformed into a program to meet the health care needs of the entire nonelderly population with income below 133 percent of the poverty level.[21]

Accordingly, transformation is a clear indicia of unconstitutionality. If a federal grant program involves A and is later expanded to also include B, and Congress threatens to withhold the A funds from states that do not participate in B, the cutoff is unconstitutional.

Under Chief Justice Roberts's opinion, unconstitutionality does not necessarily require transformation and 10 percent. He quoted *Steward Machine Company v. Davis*,[22] the first case to articulate the coercion principle. *Steward* "did not attempt to 'fix the outermost line' where persuasion gives way to coercion."[23] In today's case, "we have no need to fix a line either. It is enough for today that wherever that line may be, this statute is surely beyond it."[24] Since the Medicaid mandate is "surely" over the line, we can infer that cutoffs less extreme than the Medicaid mandate may still be over the line.

The analysis I have discussed previously is from part IV-A of Chief Justice Roberts's opinion, which was joined by Justices Elena Kagan and Stephen Breyer. Justice Breyer has previously been unwilling to accept any structural limits on federal power, while Justice Kagan's views on the subject had been uncertain.

In a dissenting opinion, Justice Scalia wrote—on behalf of Justices Kennedy, Alito, and Thomas—that "Seven Members of the Court agree that the Medicaid Expansion, as enacted by Congress, is unconstitutional." It is rare to see seven justices, across ideological divides, declaring unconstitutional a major portion of one of the most important laws enacted by Congress in decades.

Chief Justice Roberts aims to emulate Chief Justice John Marshall, and *NFIB v. Sebelius* takes several big steps in that direction.

First, on the Necessary and Proper Clause, *NFIB* brings interpretation of the clause back to Marshall's originalist opinion in *McCulloch v. Maryland*[25]: The clause grants Congress no additional powers. Rather, per Marshall and Roberts, the clause simply restates the background principle that Congress can exercise powers that are merely "incidental" to Congress's enumerated powers. For example, since the Constitution expressly gives Congress the power to establish the rules of bankruptcy, Congress can enact laws against bankruptcy fraud.

While the Marshall Court had provided authoritative constructions of the Necessary and Proper Clause (*McCulloch*) and the Commerce Clause,[26] the Taxing and Spending Clause has lacked one—until today.

The Roberts opinion also brings to mind Chief Justice Marshall's opinion in *Marbury v. Madison*.[27] Under intense political pressure from a president and his allies who demand that the judiciary submit to their unchecked will, the chief justice gives them the result they want in a particular case. Yet wrapped within that victory is a dramatic strengthening of the power of the federal courts to check the current president and Congress and every future one.

In *Marbury*, the strengthening was the affirmation of judicial review itself. In *NFIB*, it is the first decision striking a Taxing and Spending Clause enactment because of coercion; the Necessary and Proper Clause restored to its pristine 1819 status; and a vibrant, broad construction of the Commerce Clause limits from *United States v. Lopez*.[28]

None of this comes for free. Marbury was unjustly denied his commission as justice of the peace for the District of Columbia. Chief Justice Roberts's ruling that the individual mandate is justified under the tax power is intellectually indefensible. He expressly says that the mandate is not a direct tax (e.g., a tax just for being alive). Accordingly, if the tax is constitutional, then it must be some form of "indirect tax"—such as an excise tax or a duty. He writes that the individual mandate merely "makes going without insurance just another thing the Government taxes, like buying gasoline or earning income."[29] Taxes on buying gasoline or on the salary from your job are straightforward excise taxes.

But the problem for Roberts is that excise taxes have always and only been applied for doing something (e.g., buying gas) or for owning something (e.g., a carriage).[30] There is literally no constitutional or tax law precedent for the notion that an individual can be subject to an excise tax merely for choosing not to buy a product. (The only thing that is even close to an exception to this rule is that a trust can be taxed for not distributing its assets pursuant to the terms of the trust. But a trust, unlike an ordinary American citizen, is an artificial legal person that was created for the sole purpose of performing an activity that the trust then refused to perform.)

Some modern scholars say that Chief Justice Marshall, too, had to cheat to get the result he wanted: that *Marbury* was incorrect to claim that Article III of the Constitution barred Congress from giving the Supreme Court original jurisdiction to issue writs of mandamus. Perhaps so.

But the bottom line is this: whatever political benefit President Obama gains from the continuing legal enforceability of his unpopular health control law and its widely disliked individual mandate, plaintiffs who wish to challenge congressional and presidential overreaching have much stronger Supreme Court precedent than they did yesterday.

Is This 1936?

David E. Bernstein
SCOTUSblog, June 29, 2012

Before the ACA decision was announced, many liberal pundits warned that the Supreme Court was on the verge of repeating its mistake in 1936, when the Court revealed that it retained a 5–4 majority hostile to broad regulation of economic activity. These pundits suggested that if the modern Court invalidated the ACA, it would be repeating the mistake of its conservative New Deal–era predecessor. The Court would then face a backlash of the sort that led to Franklin D. Roosevelt's Court-packing plan and ultimately to the famous "switch in time that saved nine."

Now that the Court has voted 5–4 to uphold the ACA, I want to suggest a different historical analogy, also focusing on 1936. What if the Court's ACA decision, like the Court's controversial 1936 ruling invalidating a state minimum wage law, turns out to be the last gasp of a dying constitutional regime?

In the early part of the twentieth century, traditional views of legislative authority gave way to more statist progressive assumptions. While progressives thought of themselves as under siege, in retrospect we can say that the pre–New Deal era was one of progressive dominance. The problem legal progressives faced, however, was they were never able to achieve a strong majority on the Supreme Court. Disappointing appointees (James McReynolds by Woodrow Wilson), bad luck in the timing of vacancies (Harding's four nominees), and an unwillingness by most of the justices with a long pre-Court progressive record to reconsider constitutional verities stymied progressive reform on the Supreme Court. The Court, nevertheless, did gradually and grudgingly uphold most of the novel regulations that came before it but failed to relinquish the underlying ideological underpinnings of traditional constitutional doctrine.

The old Warren Court regime is not as thoroughly discredited as the Gilded Age Court was by the 1930s, and the modern era is perhaps not as thoroughly conservative as the early twentieth century was progressive. But conservative jurists have made remarkable strides in persuading legal elites that originalism and textualism are first rather than last resorts. Conservatives have controlled the executive branch for the majority of time since Reagan was elected, but a combination of disappointing appointments (David Souter); inopportune timing on the loss of the Senate (Robert Bork); and a reluctance by various of the conservative justices, save Thomas, to question the underpinnings of the preexisting constitutional regime has stymied radical change.

But what if Mitt Romney gets elected in 2012, and what if the current 5–4 conservative majority ultimately becomes a 7–2 majority, as Breyer and Ruth Bader Ginsburg leave the Court? The Harriet Miers debacle suggests that conservative constituencies will no longer tolerate a Republican nominee who is not a "sure thing."

As important, the ACA litigation shows that ideas once deemed beyond the pale in "respectable" legal circles have now become mainstream among elite conservative lawyers. Indeed, though the individual mandate was upheld, the five conservative justices expressed a willingness to put real, substantive limits on the scope of the commerce power (*Lopez* and *Morrison* were easily evaded). The five conservatives, plus two liberal justices, also endorsed substantive limits on the spending power, the first time such limits were applied to Congress since the 1930s.

Like the other Justice (Owen) Roberts in 1936, the current Justice Roberts unexpectedly voted with a 5–4 majority to continue the old regime. But while the justices continued to dance in 1936, the music had died. Not only did the first Justice Roberts soon become a consistent vote to uphold New Deal legislation, but a series of FDR appointments unleashed a wave of liberal jurisprudence that ultimately went far beyond the progressives' original goal of keeping the courts out of economic matters.

The conservatives on the Court have already rewritten the constitutional law of campaign finance, sovereign immunity, and more but only tenuously with five vote majorities. A 7–2 or better majority would expand those rulings but, more important, expand conservative jurisprudence into areas not currently considered in play. What would happen to the Contracts Clause with a 7–2 conservative majority? Could vouchers for religious grade schools become mandatory, not just permitted? What powers now denied to the states would be allowed, and what powers now allowed to the federal government would be denied? Or maybe disputes between more "activist" and less "activist" justices and between libertarian-leaning and more authoritarian conservatives would mimic the infamous Douglas-Black-Frankfurter debates of the early Warren Court. The old regime would be overthrown, but progress toward affirmative conservative goals for an indefinite period of time.

No one can accurately predict these things, of course, just as no one could have predicted that FDR's war on an activist judiciary would ultimate result in *Brown v. Board of Education*,[31] *Roe v. Wade*,[32] and the like.

The obvious caveat is that Mitt Romney may not get elected and if he does he may not get to appoint any justices. Moreover, the Warren Court revolution was given crucial support by Eisenhower appointees, and it's hard to imagine that future Democratic nominees will play a similar role on a future conservative Court.

But then history never repeats itself precisely. So my point is simply that despite the Obama administration's victory today, we *may* be on the cusp of new and unpredictable era in conservative jurisprudence. Liberal pundits were sure that the Commerce Clause challenge to the individual mandate would lose 8–1, and that the Taxing and Spending Clause challenge to Medicaid expansion was even more frivolous. These pundits may be in for even greater surprises in the relatively near future.

The Conservative John Roberts

Orin S. Kerr
June 28, 2012

I suspect a lot of conservative readers are pretty upset with Chief Justice Roberts right now. The position that the mandate is unconstitutional had become the standard Republican position, echoed by nearly every prominent conservative whether or not they know anything about constitutional law. So there will be a lot of folks on the right who see Roberts as some kind of traitor, or at least not a real conservative. Roberts took a liberal position, the argument will run, so he must be a liberal.

I don't think that's right. Reading over the Roberts opinion, the opinion strikes me as quite conservative. The opinion starts from the premise that the federal government is a government of limited powers. The opinion goes on to reject the federal government's power to regulate inactivity under the Commerce Clause. It then goes on to reject a broad reading of the Necessary and Proper Clause. The opinion also imposes new limits on the federal government's ability to force the states to adopt federal programs, striking down the condition that Congress can withdraw all Medicaid funding if a state refuses to go along with the Medicaid expansion.

These sections of the opinion are all about the need to narrow Congress's power, and they impose new limits on federal power that have not been seen before. They nicely match what a lot of conservatives have been saying about the Affordable Care Act. Roberts even comes very close to using the broccoli hypothetical—he ends up using a generic example of "vegetables" instead of broccoli, but he's singing the conservative tune on these parts of the opinion.

Of course, Roberts ultimately concludes that the mandate is constitutional on the ground that the mandate can be read to work like a tax—and that so read, the law is constitutional. But methodologically, I don't think there is anything "liberal" about that approach. The ultimate question on the taxing power was whether to read a particular law formally or functionally: do you look at whether the law *says* that it is tax or do you look at whether it *acts* like a tax? There are pros and cons to each approach. But there's nothing jurisprudentially liberal about taking the functional approach; it's just the alternative way to assess the scope of the tax power.

Some will argue that the tax power argument comes off as a technicality, and the fact that the case hinges on a technicality suggests that Roberts was really just looking for a way to uphold the mandate. But it's important to remember that the entire challenge to the Affordable Care Act was premised on a technicality. Everyone challenging the Affordable Care Act agreed that Congress could enact a single-payer system. Everyone challenging the Affordable Care Act agreed that Congress could enact the same law as it did if it only chose the formal label of a tax. So the nature of the challenge to the mandate was a bit of a "gotcha" argument: The major legislative achievement of the Obama administration should be struck down because of the technical way it was done, even though Congress could have passed the same legislation with a few changes if only the Court had announced those changes beforehand rather than after. In part, that was the strategy behind the challenge: make the challenge so narrow that the challenge really just applied to this one law. The thinking was that this would make it more likely that the Court would strike down the act. But that also meant that the Court had an easy way to uphold the law, as they could just read the technicalities accordingly.

The result is an opinion that happens to please today's liberals and annoy today's conservatives because the liberal law that was passed and that conservatives hate remains on the books. But the key opinion that leads to that result is not a liberal opinion; rather, it strikes me as a largely conservative opinion that just happens to get to a liberal result.

The Perils of Shortsightedness

David E. Bernstein
June 28, 2012

As readers now know, the Court has upheld the ACA, 5–4, with Roberts in the majority.

As I noted several times on this blog, the Bush administration had one primary criterion for its judicial nominees: whether a nominee was likely to vote in favor of the government in war on terror cases.

I know, for example, of at least two law professors who were interviewed for circuit court judgeships but were never nominated almost certainly because they were considered not consistently trustworthy on war on terror issues.

Here is what I wrote in the wake of the Harriet Miers's nomination:

What do Miers and Roberts have in common? They both have significant executive branch experience, and both seem more likely than other potential candidates to uphold the Administration on issues related to the War on Terror (e.g., *Padilla* and whether a citizen arrested in the U.S. can be tried in military court). Conservative political activists want someone who will interpret the Constitution in line with conservative judicial principles. But just as FDR's primary goal in appointing justices was to appoint justices that would uphold the centerpiece of his presidency, the New Deal, which coincidentally resulted in his appointing individuals who were liberal on other things, perhaps Bush sees his legacy primarily in terms of the War on Terror, and appointing justices who will acquiesce in exercises of executive authority is his priority, even if it isn't the priority of either his base or the nation as a whole. Such justices may be coincidentally conservative on other issues, just as FDR's nominees moved the USSC generally to the Left.

Now we have some data. Alito voted with the conservatives in favor of federalism and Roberts, continuing his pattern in past cases, did not.

It was utter foolishness for the Bush justice department to be so myopically focused on one particular issue when appointing justices who are expected to serve for decades. That said, the relevant lawyers at justice were almost certainly following the wishes of their boss, who seemed to have no fixed ideology beyond his desire to avenge 9/11 and prevent its recurrence. Nevertheless, my strong sense is that the lawyers in question did not just acquiesce but were willingly complicit, letting themselves get wrapped up in the issue of the moment.

Was the Dissent Originally a Majority Opinion?

David E. Bernstein
June 28, 2012

The four-justice dissent, at least on first quick perusal, reads like it was originally written as a majority opinion, for example, it refers to Justice Ginsburg's opinion as "the dissent." (Update: Ginsburg did in fact technically dissent on the Commerce Clause issue, but I think it's unusual to refer to an opinion written by the winning side as "the dissent." Other reasons that the dissent reads like a majority are described as follows.)

Back in May, there were rumors floating around relevant legal circles that a key vote was taking place and that Roberts was feeling tremendous pressure from unidentified circles to vote to uphold the mandate. Did Roberts originally vote to invalidate the mandate on Commerce Clause grounds and to invalidate the Medicaid expansion and then decide later to accept the tax argument and essentially rewrite the Medicaid expansion (which, as I noted,[33] citing Jonathan Cohn, was the sleeper issue in this case) to preserve it? If so, was he responding to the heat from President Obama and others, preemptively threatening to delegitimize the Court if it invalidated the ACA? The dissent, along with the surprising way that Roberts chose to uphold both the mandate and the Medicaid expansion, will inevitably feed the rumor mill.

More Hints That Roberts Switched His Vote

David E. Bernstein
June 28, 2012

Reader Stuart Buck provides more detail as to why the dissent reads like a majority opinion:

1. The dissent has a whole section on severability that is completely beside the point except on the assumption that the mandate had been struck down, and now "We" have to decide whether and what to preserve of the rest of the act now that the mandate is gone.

2. Notice also that the response to Roberts is tacked on at the end, rather than worked into the body. For example, one would have expected the joint dissent to directly take on Roberts's application of the Anti-Injunction Act, but the brief section on that act only mentions what "the Government" argues.[34]

3. On top of that, the joint dissent's sections on the Commerce Clause and the Medicaid Expansion are just as long or longer than what Roberts writes (16 pages on the Commerce Clause and 21 pages on the Medicaid Expansion, compared to Roberts's 16 pages and 14 pages respectively). Yet the dissenters never write in the vein of saying, "we agree with the Chief Justice's opinion, but write to add a crucial discussion of some complexity." The analysis agrees with Roberts, and makes essentially the same points in "We" language. There's no reason for the dissenters to do this at such length, unless their opinion is what came first.

UPDATE: Ed Whelan notes a related theory:[35] Roberts assigned the opinion to himself and wrote most of what became the four-justice dissent. He then switched on the tax issue, and the four dissenters adopted most of his original majority opinion as a dissent. This would explain why the dissent is unsigned. Other blogs are noting that Justice Ginsburg directs much of her ire at the chief, which is the sort of things justices do when they think they've lost someone's vote, not when they are trying to keep a tenuous vote to uphold the law in question on board.

I should note that I think the Supreme Court is a political body (which is not to say that its decisions are primarily motivated by partisanship or political ideology) and that one can expect that the Court's rulings are affected by outside events. As I noted long ago, the challenge to the individual mandate would have stood no chance if the president and the ACA were riding very high in the polls, as the Court would not have had the political wherewithal to write what would be seen as a radical opinion invalidating a popular law from a popular president. Similarly, the level of heat defenders of the ACA were giving the Court could have persuaded Roberts that discretion was the better part of valor. (By contrast, for example, historians seem to think that FDR was relieved that the Supremes removed the National Industrial Recovery Act albatross from his neck.) Perhaps, as Rick Hasen suggests, he'd rather save his political capital for the affirmative action and voting rights cases that are coming up, especially since he found a way to give the "Right" a partial victory in his Commerce Clause reasoning and to limit the spending power.[36]

I don't find it at all illegitimate for political actors to put pressure on the Court, so long as they stay within proper legal bounds and keep their rhetoric within the broad boundaries of decency. But it is ironic that while liberal critics were quick to accuse the Court of playing politics by taking seriously the Obamacare challenges, it may turn out that it was only politics that saved the ACA.

We Lost on Health Care, but the Constitution Won

Randy E. Barnett
Washington Post, June 29, 2012

The legal challenge to the Affordable Care Act, which I advocated as a law professor before representing the National Federation of Independent Business as a lawyer, was about two huge things: saving the country from Obamacare and saving the Constitution for the country.

On Thursday, to my great disappointment, we lost the first point in the Supreme Court's 5–4 ruling to uphold the health care law. But to my enormous relief, we won the second. Before the decision, I figured it was all or nothing. But if I had been made to choose one over the other, I would have picked the Constitution.

In November, voters can still fight Obamacare. Yet no single election could have saved the Constitution from the court.

This battle for the Constitution was forced upon defenders of limited government by Congress in 2010, when it insisted in the health care bill that it was constitutional to require all Americans to purchase insurance or pay a fine. Lawmakers argued that this mandate was justified by the Constitution's Commerce and "Necessary and Proper" Clauses. Had we not contested this power grab, Congress's regulatory powers would have been rendered limitless.

They are not. On that point, we prevailed completely. Indeed, the case has put us ahead of where we were before Obamacare. The Supreme Court has definitively ruled that the Commerce and Necessary and Proper Clauses and the spending power have limits; that the mandate to purchase private health insurance, as well as the threat to withhold Medicaid funding unless states agree to expand their coverage, exceeded these limits; and that the court will enforce these limits.

On the Commerce Clause, Chief Justice John G. Roberts Jr. and four dissenting justices accepted all of our side's arguments about why the insurance mandate exceeded Congress's power. "The individual mandate cannot be upheld as an exercise of Congress's power under the Commerce Clause," Roberts wrote. "That Clause authorizes Congress to regulate interstate commerce, not to order individuals to engage in it."

Roberts adopted this view for the precise reason we advanced: granting Congress this power would gravely limit the liberties of the people. As he put it: "Allowing Congress to justify federal regulation by pointing to the effect of inaction on commerce would bring countless decisions an individual could *potentially* make within the scope of federal regulation, and—under the Government's theory—empower Congress to make those decisions for him."

Regarding the Necessary and Proper Clause, supporters of the health care overhaul had invoked the power of Congress "to make all laws which shall be necessary and proper for carrying into execution the foregoing powers," seeing it as a constitutional carte blanche to adopt any means to facilitate the regulation of insurance companies. Roberts squarely rejected this argument: "Even if the individual mandate is 'necessary' to the Act's insurance reforms, such an expansion of federal power is not a 'proper' means for making those reforms effective."

For these reasons, the court held that economic mandates are unconstitutional.

As for the spending power, while the court has previously invalidated statutes that exceeded the Commerce Clause, not since the New Deal had it rejected a law for exceeding the spending power of Congress—until Thursday. The court invalidated the part of the Affordable Care Act that empowered the Department of Health and Human Services to coerce the states by withholding Medicaid funding for existing programs unless the states accepted new coverage requirements.

All of this represents a fundamental departure from how most law professors viewed constitutional law before Thursday.

So if we prevailed on all our arguments about economic mandates, how could the Affordable Care Act be upheld? Roberts accomplished this by rewriting the law's "individual responsibility requirement" so that it was no longer a mandate but merely an option: get insurance or pay a mild "tax" penalty. Contrary to the statute, he ruled that anyone who did not have to pay the penalty would have no legal duty to get insurance. So, because there is no mandate, the tax penalty is constitutional.

In perhaps the most important passage of his opinion, Roberts insisted that "without deciding the Commerce Clause question, I would find no basis to adopt such a saving construction" of the penalty. This makes his analysis of the Commerce Clause a binding holding for future courts to follow.

True, Congress can now essentially tax people for not buying broccoli. But this power is not nearly as dangerous as the commerce power that was rejected. Congress can punish violations of its commerce power regulations with imprisonment. But under the tax power, the worst that can happen is a fine. And if lawmakers try similar legislation in the future, everyone will know that Congress is raising taxes and can fight back politically.

For more than two years, our lawsuit held Obamacare's legitimacy in limbo—long enough for the American people to organize politically, take the House from the Democrats, and thrust the issue into the center of the presidential campaign.

On Thursday, President Obama said: "The highest court in the land has now spoken." However, there is an even higher authority that must issue its verdict on the matter: the American people. Now that the Constitution is safe, voters can achieve what we didn't in court. Mitt Romney has made repealing and replacing the law his top priority.

"What the court did not do on its last day in session, I will do on my first day if elected president of the United States," he reaffirmed Thursday. "And that is I will act to repeal Obamacare."

He can also waive the collection of this tax by executive order, and the next Congress can repeal the tax using reconciliation, without the possibility of a Senate filibuster.

But voters can do something more. They can demand that the next president nominate justices who agree with the current majority of the court that Congress has only limited and enumerated powers—nominees who will enforce the original meaning of our whole Constitution, not just their favorite parts, and who, when pressured, won't wilt from the task. If they succeed, then this decision will mark a historic turning point in constitutional law.

During the New Deal-era, Americans acquiesced to an enormous expansion of federal power that they were promised would end the Great Depression. And the Supreme Court eventually expanded its interpretation of federal power accordingly. In contrast, during the Great Recession, millions of Americans were appalled by government bailouts, the horrific increases in spending and debt, and the intrusion into their lives that is coming with Obamacare. They responded by demanding a return to the Constitution's constraints on federal power. This fall, they can demand that the next president nominate justices with the fortitude to return Congress to the original meaning of the powers provided to it by the Constitution.

For now, the president still has his signature law to campaign on, and the country still has its Constitution. Those who value our republican system of limited federal powers should put their disappointment with the decision aside and breathe a sigh of relief about the bullet we dodged and the good legal precedent we set. Then they can get to work to achieve politically the complete victory that the chief justice denied us.

Do the Court's Commerce Clause and Necessary and Proper Clause Rulings in the Individual Mandate Case Matter?

Ilya Somin
June 29, 2012

As I pointed out yesterday at *SCOTUSblog*,[37] five justices, including Chief Justice Roberts, accepted all the plaintiffs' major arguments against the individual mandate with respect to the Commerce and Necessary and Proper Clauses. But how much does that conclusion actually matter? My tentative view is that it will have little immediate effect but may well be significant in the future.

One possible reason to dismiss the importance of the Court's treatment of these issues is that it might have been mere dictum.[38] After all, the Court upheld the mandate based on the Tax and Spending Clause, so the other two issues were not essential to the outcome. However, as coblogger Jonathan Adler points out,[39] Chief Justice Roberts's controlling opinion explicitly holds that this analysis was essential to the outcome.

One can still argue that the Commerce and Necessary and Proper analysis was dictum on the grounds that it was not seen as essential by the other four justices who voted to uphold the mandate. But to the extent that the chief justice's opinion is controlling, as that of the majority justice who concurred on "the narrowest ground,"[40] it is his position that matters. Moreover, as a practical matter, lower courts are unlikely to simply ignore a position that was forcefully endorsed by five Supreme Court justices in a major case.

Even if the chief justice's Commerce and Necessary and Proper analysis does bind lower courts, it's possible it will not have much effect in practice. As Roberts emphasizes, the mandate exceeded the scope of those powers because it sought to regulate inactivity. No other current federal law does the same thing on the basis of those two clauses. But, as I explained in this article,[41] the power to impose purchase mandates is one that Congress would have strong incentives to abuse in the future. So even if this case's Commerce Clause and Necessary and Proper Clause rulings will not endanger any present laws, they could cut off future mandates.

Obviously, Congress can circumvent the limits on Commerce Clause mandates by trying to structure future mandates on inactivity as taxes, utilizing Roberts's reasoning on why the health insurance mandate is a tax as a guide. However, the jury-rigged nature of Roberts's analysis and the possibility that it was developed primarily to avoid having to strike down this particular statute makes it possible that the Court will back off at least some of it in future cases. Even if it does not, having to use the tax power at least prevents Congress from punishing mandate violators with prison time instead of fines.

Moreover, the doctrinal impact of this decision potentially goes beyond mandates in one important sense. Chief Justice Roberts and (less clearly) the four dissenting justices all reaffirmed the proposition that laws authorized by the Necessary and Proper Clause must be "proper" as well as "necessary." As Roberts put it, "Even if the individual mandate is 'necessary' to the Act's insurance reforms, such an expansion of federal power is not a 'proper' means for making those reforms effective." This was the central theme of the amicus brief I wrote for the Washington Legal Foundation.[42] Roberts did not give anything approaching a comprehensive definition of "proper." But his emphasis on the idea that it imposes independent limitations on congressional power could well lead to future litigation on the subject.

The greatest potential significance of the Court's Commerce and Necessary and Proper ruling, however, lies less in the doctrinal details and more in the fact that five justices were willing to endorse a strong substantive limit on these powers. That is both symbolically significant and a potential signal for future cases.

Obviously, whether Roberts's analysis will really have an effect on future cases depends in large part on future Supreme Court appointments and the political situation. If, for example, Barack Obama gets reelected in November and replaces one or more conservative Supreme Court justices with liberals, yesterday's Commerce and Necessary and Proper ruling will likely be ignored or overruled. But for reasons David Bernstein emphasizes, it's also possible that things will move in the opposite direction.[43] Some liberal observers fear such a result.[44] It is still too early to say whether this part of the individual mandate decision will turn out to be an outlier or a sign of things to come.

A Simple Solution to the Holding vs. Dictum Mess

Ilya Somin
July 2, 2012

Much literal and blogospheric ink has already been spilled over the question of whether the Court's conclusion that the Commerce Clause does not authorize the individual mandate is part of the holding or mere dictum. I think, however, that there is a fairly simple solution to the problem: Just look at what the Court itself said the holding was. In part III-C of Chief Justice Roberts's opinion, which is a part of the opinion of the Court joined by the four liberal justices, Roberts writes: "The Court today holds that our Constitution protects us from federal regulation under the Commerce Clause so long as we abstain from the regulated activity."[45] The fact that the four liberals joined this part of the opinion suggests that they recognize that the chief justice's reasoning about the Commerce Clause is part of the holding, even though they don't agree with it. Perhaps they joined this part because they realize that this conclusion did in fact enjoy the support of five justices (Roberts and the four conservative dissenters). In any event, it seems to me that the official opinion of the Court is the best possible authority on what is and is not part of the holding.

It is not completely clear whether this statement is meant to cover the Commerce Clause as augmented by the Necessary and Proper Clause, as well as the former alone. But given the reasoning of the rest of Roberts's opinion (which covers both), I think the former interpretation is more likely.

I should add that I owe this point to coblogger Jonathan Adler, who could not post it himself right now, and therefore authorized me to do it.

There are also other reasons[46] for concluding that the Commerce Clause reasoning is part of the holding as well.

UPDATE: Coblogger David Post responds to this post as follows:

> That cannot be the right answer. A court's holding defines the scope of its power; holdings must be obeyed, by citizens and by other (lower) courts. Dicta is the stuff that doesn't have to be obeyed. Saying "just look at how the Court itself defined its holding" is like saying: "Just let Congress decide on the scope of its powers." Courts cannot be allowed to define the scope of their own power because if they are, they'll do what all institutions do when allowed to define the scope of its own power: expand it unmercifully. Of course Roberts and the four justices who are with him on this question would like it to be called a "holding"! They think they're right, and they'd like to have their view on the matter obeyed by others. But the holding/dictum distinction prevents them from doing that, over and over and over again. Courts don't have to be obeyed when they propound on something they didn't have to propound upon for the purpose of deciding the case the way they decided it. To decide that the mandate is within Congress's taxing power, they didn't have to decide that it is not within its Commerce Clause power.[47]

I remain unpersuaded. The distinction between holding and dictum is an issue of technical legal doctrine. The Supreme Court is the ultimate arbiter of such issues in the U.S. federal courts. If it were not, lower courts could disobey Supreme

Court decisions they disagree with simply by declaring that they are dicta rather than holding. Moreover, the Supreme Court has issued many decisions expounding on what qualifies as dictum or holding. It would make little sense for them to do so if they did not have the power to define the difference.

It is also worth noting that the section of Roberts's opinion I refer to was joined not by "the four justices who are with him on this question" but by the four who do not. The latter, too, recognize that the Commerce Clause is part of the holding.

David claims that his position is supported by the Federalist Papers, which stresses the need for constraints on institutional power. Of course the Federalist Papers never says that courts lack the power to define the distinction between dictum and holding. Federalist 78 specifically indicates that "[t]he interpretation of the laws is the proper and peculiar province of the courts."[48] The holding-dictum distinction is just one facet of "the interpretation of the laws." Part of the task of interpreting the Constitution and statutes challenged as unconstitutional is determining what reasoning is needed to explain why they are upheld or struck down.

Allowing the Court to determine the scope of its own holding hardly makes its power unlimited, certainly not more so than the power to declare laws unconstitutional in the first place. There are, in fact, many other constraints on judicial authority, such as the nomination process and the courts' dependence on other branches of government to enforce their decisions. Federalist 78 implicitly prerefutes David's argument as follows:

> Whoever attentively considers the different departments of power must perceive, that, in a government in which they are separated from each other, the judiciary, from the nature of its functions, will always be the least dangerous to the political rights of the Constitution; because it will be least in a capacity to annoy or injure them. The Executive not only dispenses the honors, but holds the sword of the community. The legislature not only commands the purse, but prescribes the rules by which the duties and rights of every citizen are to be regulated. The judiciary, on the contrary, has no influence over either the sword or the purse; no direction either of the strength or of the wealth of the society; and can take no active resolution whatever. It may truly be said to have neither FORCE nor WILL, but merely judgment; and must ultimately depend upon the aid of the executive arm even for the efficacy of its judgments. . . .
>
> It can be of no weight to say that the courts, on the pretense of a repugnancy, may substitute their own pleasure to the constitutional intentions of the legislature. This might as well happen in the case of two contradictory statutes; or it might as well happen in every adjudication upon any single statute. The courts must declare the sense of the law; and if they should be disposed to exercise WILL instead of JUDGMENT, the consequence would equally be the substitution of their pleasure to that of the legislative body. The observation, if it proved any thing, would prove that there ought to be no judges distinct from that body.[49]

Similarly, "[i]t can be of no weight to say that the courts," on the pretense of a holding, may substitute their own pleasure for the reasoning actually needed to resolve a case. One can argue that the Court's definition of its own holding is wrong, just as one can argue that the holding itself is wrong. But, in a hierarchical judicial system, lower courts cannot ignore the former any more than they can ignore the latter.

The Unprecedented Uniqueness of Chief Justice Roberts's Opinion

Randy E. Barnett
July 5, 2012

I have been out of town and not keeping up with all the chatter about the news that Chief Justice Roberts changed his vote after conference from invalidating the ACA, at least in part, to a vote to uphold it. The obvious question arises: was this switch motivated by legal considerations or by the sort of political considerations that had been urged upon him, after the case was submitted, by supporters of the ACA? Of course, deciding what motivated any particular decision must necessarily be judged by circumstantial evidence. Unless he expressed his motivations to others, only the chief justice has personal knowledge of exactly why he changed his vote (assuming that the reporting of this vote change is accurate). The same was true of why five of the nine Supreme Court justices ruled the way they did on the remedy issue in *Bush v. Gore* (after seven justices found an equal protection violation in the way Florida was counting its ballots). Yet, at least in academic circles, this speculation has taken on the status of ontological truth: the five "Republican" justices handed the election to "their" party's candidate?

I have always believed that the circumstantial evidence for this proposition was thin, and I have resisted the suggestion that *Bush v. Gore* was a nakedly political decision, though of course I have to allow for the possibility that it was. The only "evidence" for this conclusion, apart from the party affiliation of the president who nominated them (which is pertinent) was the equal protection reasoning of the decision, which is an area of my specialty. I don't wish to rehearse these arguments here, but I do know the judicial reasoning was the primary circumstantial evidence that persuaded many of my colleagues.

That brings me to the remarkable nature of the legal analysis of Chief Justice Roberts's opinion. He appears to have been the first person in the United States to have adopted this two-part legal analysis: (a) the individual insurance mandate is unconstitutional as beyond the Commerce and Necessary and Proper Clauses *and* (b) the meaning of the "individual responsibility requirement" can only be upheld if given a "saving construction" to eliminate its character as a requirement and render it an "option" to buy insurance or pay the tax, such that no one is actually bound or mandated by the requirement.

Before last week, I know of no legal authority in the United States who claimed to hold this position.

Of course, the government and many academics have made a tax power argument, but only (so far as I am aware) as an *additional basis* for upholding the mandate *as it existed in the statute*. Not one of the many federal judges who have ruled upon the case adopted the view that the mandate was unconstitutional under the Commerce and Necessary and Proper Clauses, *and* could only be saved under the tax power by a "construction" that deviated from its most obvious and most reasonable meaning. Perhaps I am mistaken, but I know of no academic supporter of the ACA who made this argument. The dissenting justices obviously did not hold this view. And, while the concurring justices did join in Chief Justice Roberts's opinion, thereby adopting its reasoning, their own view expressed in Justice Ginsburg's opinion conforms to the views held by most academic defenders of the law.

Which leaves Chief Justice Roberts alone, of all the persons who ever have opined on this case in a careful matter, to hold the view he adopts in his opinion. Apparently, after preparing for and sitting through three days of oral argument, even Chief Justice Roberts did not hold this distinctive legal position to be persuasive—if he had imagined the view at all—until weeks later.

So when focusing solely on the legal merits of the chief justice's decision, as articulated in his opinion, we are entitled to factor into our analysis that no one before him ever thought that this legal position was compelling enough to advance it as their own.

Bear in mind that what defines "circumstantial" evidence, as opposed to "direct" evidence, is that, by definition, circumstantial evidence is consistent with more than one conclusion. A fingerprint at the scene of the crime is circumstantial evidence that is consistent with it being put there during the crime, or at some point prior to the crime, or even planted later. So too with the uniqueness of Chief Justice Roberts's legal position.

Obviously, he could have been persuaded that the mandate was unconstitutional after oral argument, and sometime later he came also to be persuaded that he had a purely legal duty to give a "saving construction" of the statute, for reasons that have nothing whatsoever to do with the political implications to the Court of invalidating the president's "signature" legislation by a 5–4 vote of Republican-nominated justices. But if the strength of the legal reasoning of an opinion is relevant to assessing the motivation of its author—as has been so long and loudly been claimed about all five justices in the majority of *Bush v. Gore*—then it seems pertinent as well that Chief Justice Roberts was the only person in two years to look at this legal dispute and reach this legal conclusion.

I wonder if there has ever been another case in Supreme Court history to be decided by a single justice's legal theory that had not previously been held or advocated by any other person in the United States before he announced it. One even he had not deemed persuasive until sometime after his initial conference vote (a fact that no one seems to dispute). Whether or not it was political, the uniqueness of Chief Justice Roberts's opinion may well be unprecedented.

UPDATE: From the abstract it looks like Neil Siegel and Bob Cooter anticipated Chief Justice Roberts approach in their paper, "Not the Power to Destroy: An Effects Theory of the Tax Power"[50] and may even have provided him with the road map for his analysis. If so, they should get a share of the credit that is now flowing to Jack Balkin and Akhil Amar who contended that the whole mandate could be an exercise of the tax power. Here is the abstract:

Effective limits on the power of Congress to regulate interstate commerce require the Court's tax power jurisprudence to reinforce restrictions on the Commerce Clause. Otherwise Congress can circumvent limits on its commerce power by calling regulations backed by penalties "taxes" and justifying them under the tax power. When the Court restricted federal commerce power in the 1920s and 1930s, it distinguished between taxes, which raise revenues, and penalties, which regulate behavior. This distinction is useless because so many federal exactions do both, like the 18th century "imposts" that raised revenues from imports and suppressed foreign competition with American industry. The post-1937 Court essentially abandoned judicially enforceable limits on the Commerce Clause, so it had no need to rethink or overrule previous distinctions between regulations of interstate commerce and taxes. Since its "new federalism" decisions, the Court has yet to reconsider the constitutional scope of the tax power. As a result, judges and litigants contradict one other in current litigation over the minimum coverage provision in the Patient Protection and Affordable Care Act (ACA).

Legal theory helps to answer constitutional questions when existing doctrine does not. A person who must pay a pure penalty is condemned for wrongdoing. Moreover, she must pay more than the usual gain from the forbidden conduct, and she must pay at an increasing rate with intentional or repeated violations. Condemnation coerces expressively and relatively high rates with enhancements coerce materially. A pure penalty prevents behavior, thereby raising little revenue.

Alternatively, a person who must pay a pure tax is permitted to engage in the taxed conduct. Moreover, she must pay less than the usual gain from the taxed conduct, and intentional or repeated conduct does not enhance the rate. Permission does not coerce expressively and relative low rates without enhancements do not coerce materially. A pure tax dampens conduct but does not prevent it, thereby raising revenues.

Situated between pure taxes and pure penalties are mixed exactions whose expression sounds like a penalty and whose material characteristics look like a tax. Thus the ACA's exaction for non-insurance has a penalty's expression and a tax's materiality. Should courts interpret a mixed exaction as a tax or a penalty? Our answer depends on the exaction's effect. If an exaction dampens behavior and raises revenue, then it should be interpreted as a tax, regardless of what the statute calls it. If an exaction prevents behavior, then it should be interpreted as a penalty. The Congressional Budget Office predicts that ACA's exaction for noninsurance will dampen uninsured behavior but not prevent it, thereby raising several billion dollars in revenue each year. Accordingly, the exaction is a tax for purposes of the tax power.

There are two important differences between Chief Justice Roberts's approach and that of Siegel and Cooter: First, they do not appear to adopt the view that the individual insurance mandate exceeds the commerce power. Second, they did not feel the need to adopt the "saving construction" approach that is the heart of Roberts's analysis. So his position remains uniquely his, though maybe we now know whence he got his "out." Moreover, the novelty of their argument, relative to all other law professors underscores the novelty of his position too. But this is clearly a partial "precedent" for the view he ultimately adopts.

I thank Professor Siegel for bringing this to my attention and urge others to download his piece. It now only has 162 downloads. Which only goes to show, it only takes one, if it is the right one.

Mandate Begone! The Logic of Chief Justice
Roberts's Unique Tax Power Theory

Randy E. Barnett
July 6, 2012

In my previous post, I explained how no one other than Chief Justice Roberts ever held the legal position that he came, for whatever reason, to hold. Some may respond, "Hold on": Many law professors like Jack Balkin claimed loudly that the individual mandate was a tax. True. But that is not what Chief Justice Roberts held. Instead he rewrote the section in which the mandate appears by giving it a "saving construction" so that it was no longer a mandate, then upheld the penalty alone as a tax because it was so low that it did not coerce compliance. In other words, he did not hold that the individual insurance mandate was either a tax or that it could be upheld as written under the tax power.

In this post, I examine the text of Roberts's reasoning in some detail, so it is not for all readers. In my next post, I will provide a more layman's overview of this analysis from my column in today's *Washington Examiner*.[51]

Let's start with the fact Roberts did not uphold the mandate as written but instead changed its meaning by providing a "saving construction." This is his most crucial move to reach his desired result (emphasis added):

> The most straightforward reading of the mandate is that **it commands individuals to purchase insurance**. After all, it states that individuals "shall" maintain health insurance. 26 U.S. C. §5000A(a). Congress thought it could enact **such a command** under the Commerce Clause, and the Government primarily defended the law on that basis. But, for the reasons explained above, the Commerce Clause does not give Congress that power. Under our precedent, it is therefore necessary to ask whether the Government's alternative reading of the statute—that it only imposes a tax on those without insurance—is a reasonable one. . . .
>
> [A]ccording to the Government, . . . the mandate can be regarded as establishing a condition—not owning health insurance—that triggers a tax—the required payment to the IRS. Under that theory, **the mandate is *not* a legal command to buy insurance**. Rather, it makes going without insurance just another thing the Government taxes, like buying gasoline or earning income. And if the mandate is in effect just a tax hike on certain taxpayers who do not have health insurance, it may be within Congress's constitutional power to tax.
>
> The question is not whether that is the most natural interpretation of the mandate, but only whether it is a "fairly possible" one. *Crowell v. Benson*, 285 U.S. 22, 62 (1932). As we have explained, "every reasonable construction must be resorted to, in order to save a statute from unconstitutionality." *Hooper v. California*, 155 U.S. 648, 657 (1895). The Government asks us to interpret the mandate as imposing a tax, **if it would otherwise violate the Constitution**. Granting the Act the full measure of deference owed to federal statutes, it can be so read, for the reasons set forth below.[52]

Notice that the first two sentences in bold are the opposite of each other. The most natural interpretation of what the statute calls the "individual responsibility *requirement*" is that it *is* a command or mandate, but reading it that way would "violate the constitution." So, to "save" it, Roberts accepts the government's "alternate" view that that it is *not* a mandate or command:

> And it is only because we have a duty to construe a statute to save it, if fairly possible, that §5000A can be interpreted as a tax. Without deciding the Commerce Clause question, I would find no basis to adopt such a saving construction.[53]

Why not? Because this construction is not the legal meaning of the statute as normally read. One has to change the statute to mean the opposite of what it says to uphold it as a tax. This may be the most crucial passage of his whole opinion, which renders it unique. It also renders the Commerce Clause analysis absolutely necessary to its holding that, only as rewritten, can §5000A be upheld under the tax power. This is even conceded by the four liberal justices who, as Ilya notes previously,[54] sign onto part III-C of Roberts's opinion, which includes the following (emphasis added):

> **The Court** today **holds** that our Constitution protects us from federal regulation under the Commerce Clause so long as we abstain from the regulated activity.[55]

Let me now turn to the substance of his "saving construction" to see that he does not uphold a mandate as a tax; instead he eliminates the "requirement" or mandate from the statute. According to his reconstruction, the "penalty" included in the "individual insurance requirement" was NOT a *penalty* to compel conduct but merely a *tax* that could "affect" or "influence" conduct. He accomplishes this by (a) functionally distinguishing a tax *from* a penalty then (b) providing a "saving construction" that the "penalty" in the ACA is *not* a penalty but is *instead* a tax. Let me explain how he did this by inserting my own comments in brackets and adding some bold and italics for emphasis:

First, he started by adopting a "functional approach" to distinguish taxes from penalties (footnotes omitted):

> Our cases confirm this functional approach. For example, in *Drexel Furniture*, we focused on three practical characteristics of the so-called tax on employing child laborers that convinced us **the "tax" was *actually* a penalty** [ME: that is, it was NOT a tax but was INSTEAD a penalty, so he puts "tax" in quotation marks]. First, the tax imposed an exceedingly heavy burden—10 percent of a company's net income—on those who employed children, no matter how small their infraction. Second, it imposed that exaction only on those who knowingly employed underage laborers. Such scienter requirements are typical of **punitive statutes** [ME: what he will construe the ACA "penalty" NOT to be because punishing inactivity would be unconstitutional], because Congress often wishes to punish only those who intentionally break the law. Third, this "tax" was enforced in part by the Department of Labor, an agency responsible for punishing violations of labor laws, not collecting revenue.[56]

Next, he applies this functional approach to the "penalty" in the ACA to show that this "penalty" COULD BE construed to function as a tax and NOT as a penalty because it does not compel conduct:

The same analysis here suggests that the shared responsibility **payment** [ME: *not* the statute's own "individual responsibility *requirement*"] may for constitutional purposes be considered a tax, **not a penalty** [ME: Bingo]: First, for most Americans the amount due will be far less than the price of insurance [ME: rendering it a "choice" that is NOT compelled, like the mortgage interest deduction], and, by statute, it can never be more. It may often be a reasonable financial decision to make the payment rather than purchase insurance, unlike the "prohibitory" financial punishment in *Drexel Furniture.* 259 U.S., at 37. Second, the individual mandate contains no scienter requirement. Third, the payment is collected solely by the IRS through the normal means of taxation—except that the Service is not allowed to use those means most suggestive of a punitive sanction, such as criminal prosecution. See §5000A(g)(2). The reasons the Court in *Drexel Furniture* held that what was called a "tax" there [ME: notice he puts "tax" in quotation marks] was [ME: *really*] a penalty support the conclusion that what is called a "penalty" here may [ME: *instead*] be viewed as a tax.[57]

Let me repeat this sentence: "**the shared responsibility payment may for constitutional purposes be considered *a tax, not a penalty*.**"

He then distinguishes between the compulsion of a penalty and the "influence" of a tax:

None of this is to say that the payment is not intended to **affect** individual conduct. Although the payment will raise considerable revenue, it is plainly designed to expand health insurance coverage. But taxes that seek to **influence** conduct are nothing new. . . . Some of our earliest federal taxes sought to **deter** the purchase of imported manufactured goods in order to foster the growth of domestic industry. See W. Brownlee, Federal Taxation in America 22 (2d ed. 2004); cf. 2 J. Story, Commentaries on the Constitution of the United States §962, p. 434 (1833) ("the taxing power is often, very often, applied for other purposes, than revenue"). Today, federal and state taxes can compose more than half the retail price of cigarettes, not just to raise more money, but to **encourage** people to quit smoking. And we have upheld such obviously regulatory measures as taxes on selling marijuana and sawed-off shotguns. See *United States v. Sanchez,* 340 U.S. 42, 44–45 (1950); *Sonzinsky v. United States,* 300 U.S. 506, 513 (1937). Indeed, "[e]very tax is in some measure regulatory. To some extent it interposes an economic impediment to the activity taxed as compared with others not taxed." *Sonzinsky, supra,* at 513. That §5000A seeks to **shape decisions** about whether to buy health insurance does not mean that it cannot be a valid exercise of the taxing power.[58]

Here is another place where he clearly is denying that this tax is a penalty because this tax does not fit the constitutional (i.e., Supreme Court case law) definition of a penalty:

In **distinguishing penalties *from* taxes**, this Court has explained that "if the concept of penalty means anything, it means punishment for an unlawful act or omission." [ME: that is, compulsion] *United States v. Reorganized CF&I Fabricators of Utah, Inc.,* 518 U.S. 213, 224 (1996); see also *United States v. La Franca,* 282 U.S. 568, 572 (1931) ("[A] penalty, as the word is here used, is an exaction imposed by statute as **punishment** for an unlawful act"). While the individual mandate clearly aims to induce the purchase of health insurance, **it need not be read to declare that failing to do so is unlawful.** Neither the Act nor any other law attaches negative legal consequences to not buying health insurance, beyond requiring a payment to the IRS. The Government agrees with that reading, confirming that if someone **chooses** to pay rather than obtain health insurance, they have fully complied with the law. Brief for United States 60–61; Tr. of Oral Arg. 49–50 (Mar. 26, 2012).[59]

Indeed, it is estimated that four million people each year will **choose** to pay the IRS rather than buy insurance.

Finally, as his ruling in the Medicaid challenge establishes, there is a constitutional difference between compelling (i.e., commandeering a state) and offering an inducement to influence its conduct.

So Chief Justice Roberts clearly holds that the so-called penalty is not a penalty but is instead a tax under his "saving construction." Therefore, **he did *not* hold that Congress *may* use its tax power to penalize inactivity**.

But did he also hold that Congress *may not* penalize inactivity using its tax power? That is how I read this later portion of his opinion:

> Congress's ability to use its taxing power to influence conduct is not without limits. A few of our cases policed these limits aggressively, invalidating punitive exactions obviously designed to regulate behavior otherwise regarded at the time as beyond federal authority. See, e.g., United States v. Butler, 297 U.S. 1 (1936); Drexel Furniture, 259 U.S. 20. More often and more recently we have declined to closely examine the regulatory motive or effect of revenue-raising measures. See Kahriger, 345 U.S., at 27–31 (collecting cases). **We have nonetheless maintained that "'there comes a time in the extension of the penalizing features of the so-called tax when it loses its character as such and becomes a mere penalty with the characteristics of regulation and punishment.'"** Kurth Ranch, 511 U.S., at 779 (quoting Drexel Furniture, *supra*, at 38).
>
> We have already explained that the shared responsibility payment's practical characteristics pass muster as a tax under our narrowest interpretations of the taxing power. Supra, at 35–36. Because the tax at hand is within even those strict limits, we need not here decide **the precise point at which** an exaction becomes *so punitive* that the taxing power does not authorize it. It remains true, however, that the "'power to tax is not the power to destroy while this Court sits.'" Oklahoma Tax Comm'n v. Texas Co., 336 U.S. 342, 364 (1949) (quoting Panhandle Oil Co. v. Mississippi ex rel. Knox, 277 U.S. 218, 223 (1928) (Holmes, J., dissenting)).[60]

Two points on this part of his opinion: (1) The question he does not reach is "the precise point at which" a tax on inactivity becomes so punitive as to be beyond tax power so some penalties on inactivity are unconstitutional. (2) But he also says that the line is between when an exaction is a tax "under our narrowest interpretations of the taxing power" and when "it becomes '*so punitive*' that the taxing power does not authorize it." Could Roberts be suggesting here that *some* penalty can be imposed on inactivity but not ones that are too punitive? If so, that sentence would fuzz up, if not destroy, his entire categorical analysis. The best reading—which is the opposite of a "saving construction"—of this passage, I think, is that at some point an exaction becomes so punitive that it becomes a true penalty rather than a true tax.

In short, Roberts is not upholding the power of Congress to impose penalties on inactivity—that is, a mandate—under the tax power. To the contrary, such an economic mandate would be unconstitutional. According to Roberts, even if Congress may use its tax powers to punish conduct; it may not use them to punish inactivity. Mandates are off the table under both powers. If you don't like this argument, as the concurring liberal justices clearly do not, blame Chief Justice Roberts not me.

A final note: After reading this "saving construction" analysis, it is easy to understand why no one previously adopted this position as their own and difficult to believe that Roberts is compelled by this analysis to reach the result of upholding the Affordable Care Act. So it is correspondingly difficult to resist the conclusion that he adopted it to reach his desired result of upholding the ACA for the political reasons loudly urged upon him by defenders of the law.

Making Sense of Chief Justice Roberts's Opinion

Jonathan H. Adler
July 9, 2012

I can't speak to how the chief justice interacted with his colleagues on the Court during the deliberations in *NFIB v. Sebelius* or to whether he truly flip-flopped on the mandate or (as Mark Tushnet suggests[61]) he had been the "least persuaded" of the antimandate arguments at the initial conference and eventually concluded that it could be upheld. I do, however, think many of the chief justice's critics have failed to recognize how this opinion fits with what we've seen from the chief in his first several years of the Court. Specifically, I believe we can explain Roberts's vote in a way that is quite consistent with his behavior in other cases and that does not require ascribing political motives to him. While I am not persuaded by Chief Justice Roberts's opinion, I believe it squares with his overall jurisprudential approach for reasons I first noted before[62] and will elaborate upon in this post.

NFIB v. Sebelius was not the first case in which we saw Chief Justice Roberts embrace a strained "saving construction" of a statute in order to uphold it against a constitutional challenge. He did the exact same thing in *NAMUDNO v. Holder.* The chief's *NAMUDNO* opinion is quite unpersuasive—unless one believes there is a substantial independent value in avoiding declaring a law unconstitutional. The big difference between Roberts's opinion in *NFIB* and his opinion in *NAMUDNO* is that in the *NAMUDNO* case seven other justices were willing to go along. Both cases, however, show a justice willing to take liberties with statutory text if the alternative is to strike the statute down.

A second example can be found in Jeff Toobin's behind-the-scenes account of *Citizens United.*[63] There, Toobin reports, the chief drafted an opinion that would have stretched the statute to exclude covering Citizens United's video, thereby avoiding the larger First Amendment question. While some academics and attorneys had advocated this result, few tried to argue that this outcome was dictated by the statutory text. In *Citizens United*, as in *NFIB*, it turned out Roberts was the only one willing to accept this approach. The other conservatives were persuaded by Justice Kennedy to swing for the fences, and the Court's liberals thought a saving construction was unnecessary to uphold the statute. After reargument, Roberts joined Kennedy's opinion invalidating the restrictions, but it appears not to have been his preferred course of action.

Additional evidence of the chief justice's reluctance to overturn statutes can be found in (A) his approach to severability—excising no more of a statute than is necessary to cure the constitutional violation (see, e.g., his treatment of the Medicaid expansion and his opinion in *Free Enterprise Fund v. PCAOB*[64]); (B) his hawkish approach to Article III standing, which keeps some challenges to federal laws out of court; and (C) his preference for as-applied instead of facial constitutional challenges to statutes (see, e.g., his opinion in *Wisconsin Right-to-Life v. FEC*). Consider also that the chief is almost as reluctant to overturn court precedents as he is to void federal statutes. So, for instance, he votes to deny standing in *Hein v. Freedom from Religion Foundation*[65] but refuses to overrule *Flast v. Cohen*,[66] preserving an anomaly in the law of standing. The common thread is that he tries to avoid upsetting established legal rules and creating new law (though he is willing to do so when an issue is squarely presented and other justices will go along).

These cases show that Chief Justice Roberts would rather stretch statutory text than conclude that Congress and the executive have overstepped their constitutional bounds. Thus, it should be no surprise that the Court, under his leadership, has invalidated federal statutes and overturned precedents at a slower rate than under Chief Justices Rehnquist, Burger, or Warren. Further, the chief justice prefers to avoid splintered opinions (a phenomenon he lamented in his *Rapanos* concurrence) and is reluctant to author a controlling solo opinion.

When John Roberts was nominated to the Supreme Court, many predicted he would be a conservative judicial minimalist. That is, he would have a generally conservative outlook but would try to decide cases narrowly, avoid disturbing precedents, and defer to the other political branches. Since becoming chief justice, this is what it appears Chief Justice Roberts has tried to do. From this perspective, his opinion in *NFIB v. Sebelius* makes sense. This doesn't mean I agree with Chief Justice Roberts's approach—in *NFIB* I certainly don't—but I think we can understand it.

Chief Justice Roberts and the Window Tax

David B. Kopel
July 9, 2012

In *NFIB v. Sebelius*, Chief Justice Roberts imagined a hypothetical federal tax on windows in order to bolster his point that the Court should treat the individual mandate as a "tax," even though the Obamacare statute calls it a "penalty."

Suppose Congress enacted a statute providing that every taxpayer who owns a house without energy efficient windows must pay $50 to the IRS. The amount due is adjusted based on factors such as taxable income and joint filing status, and is paid along with the taxpayer's income tax return. Those whose income is below the filing threshold need not pay. The required payment is not called a "tax," a "penalty," or anything else. No one would doubt that this law imposed a tax, and was within Congress's power to tax. That conclusion should not change simply because Congress used the word "penalty" to describe the payment. Interpreting such a law to be a tax would hardly "[i]mpos[e] a tax through judicial legislation." Post, at 25. Rather, it would give practical effect to the Legislature's enactment.[67]

The previous language is a plausible argument for the chief justice's tax/penalty analysis. But by discussing a window tax, the Roberts opinion provides one more reminder why the individual mandate, if it is a tax, is a direct tax, not an indirect tax. Direct taxes must be apportioned by state population.[68] If the individual mandate is a direct tax, then it is unconstitutional because it is not apportioned by state population.

Pursuant to the Sixteenth Amendment, direct taxes on income need not be apportioned, but neither the individual mandate nor the hypothetical window tax are taxes on income. Constitutionally, "income" subject to the federal income tax must be "undeniable accessions to wealth."[69] A decision not to buy overpriced insurance from Congress's Big Insurance pets, like the decision not to buy a particular type of window, is not an "accession to wealth." The decision provides no additional income to the person.

So let's accept Chief Justice Roberts's theory that a window tax and the individual mandate are analytically comparable. On July 9, 1798, Congress enacted a direct tax statute, to pay for national defense preparations against France. "An Act to provide for the valuation of lands and dwelling-houses, and the enumeration of slaves, within the United States."[70] On July 14, Congress passed the "Direct Tax Act," to provide for collection of the July 9 taxes. Pursuant to the Direct Tax Act, federal assessors were to examine houses to assess them for purposes of the direct tax. In addition, the Direct Tax Act ordered the assessors make records of the number and sizes of windows in each house. The window data were to be gathered so that Congress could, in the future, decide to impose a direct tax on windows.[71]

It seems there was no dispute that a window tax was a direct tax. A fortiori, a tax on not having certain types of windows would be also be a direct tax. This is one more piece of evidence that Chief Justice Roberts was wrong in stating that the individual mandate "tax" is not a direct tax.

The Impact of the Individual Mandate Decision on the Supreme Court's Legitimacy

Ilya Somin
July 13, 2012

Various leaks suggest that Chief Justice John Roberts switched his vote in the individual mandate case in order to protect his own and the Supreme Court's reputation and enhance their legitimacy. Whether or not that was his objective, it is interesting to ask whether the goal was achieved. Did the decision enhance the Court's legitimacy more than it detracted from it?

So far, the answer seems to be "no." Postdecision polls show that the majority of the public disagrees with the mandate decision, and overall public approval of the Court has fallen substantially.[72] These results were entirely predictable based on pre-decision polls, which consistently showed that an overwhelming majority wanted the Court to strike down the mandate,[73] including even a slight plurality of Democrats.

Roberts probably did succeed in enhancing the Court's reputation among law professors and left-wing legal elites, many of whom would have been very angry if the Court had invalidated the mandate. But even among this group, the results are somewhat equivocal. Many of them probably believe or at least suspect that Roberts switched his vote out of fear for his reputation rather than because he genuinely believed in the federal government's dubious tax argument (which had been rejected by every lower court to have considered it, including several liberal judges). Those who do believe this may be happy about the result, but it is unlikely to enhance their opinion of Roberts himself, who on this account comes off as a man who cares more about his and the Court's reputation among legal elites than about enforcing the Constitution. And obviously, the reputational boost among liberal elites comes at the cost of reputational harm at the hands of their conservative and libertarian counterparts. Many will not soon forgive Roberts, especially if additional evidence comes out that reinforces the perception that he switched for reputational rather than legal reasons.

It is still possible that the mandate decision will improve the Court's reputation in the long run. If future generations endorse the liberal view that judicial enforcement of constitutional limits on federal power is always or almost always inappropriate, then Roberts will come out looking prescient. But it's at least equally likely that future opinion will move in the opposite direction, in which case Roberts's ruling will be even more unpopular than it is today. Over the last thirty years, the idea of judicial enforcement of federalism has gained an enormous amount of ground. It's possible that that trend will continue rather than be reversed.

As I have previously emphasized,[74] enhancing his own and the Court's reputation is not the real job of a Supreme Court justice. If Roberts believed that the mandate was constitutional, he had a duty to vote to uphold it even if the Court's reputation might be harmed as a result. We still don't know enough to be able to tell what his true motive was and cannot rule out the possibility that it was purely legal. But if reputational concerns really were central to his decision, it is ironic that, so far, it hasn't worked out very well.

Justices interested in enhancing their reputations could potentially learn at least two valuable lessons from this experience. First, traditional liberal legal elites are not the only important arbiters of judicial reputation. Both nonliberal elites and the general public have considerable clout of their own, at least on cases big enough to attract significant public attention. A decision popular with the former group can still diminish the Court's legitimacy if it angers the latter two. *Kelo v. City of New London* and the individual mandate case are good examples of this phenomenon. Second, in this age of leaks, a justice who casts his vote for reputational reasons may not be able to keep that fact secret for long. And when the public learns what he did, the result could well harm his reputation more than it enhances it.

Chief Justice Roberts and Legitimacy versus Popularity

Orin S. Kerr
July 13, 2012

Ilya's post on the chief justice's vote in *Sebelius* and the Supreme Court's legitimacy brings up an important tension in the popular belief that Roberts switched his vote because he caved to outside pressure. People who cave to pressure generally switch to do what is popular, not what is unpopular. But there's a way out of the conflict, and that is recognizing the important difference between the legitimacy of judicial decisions and the popularity of those decisions.

Let's start with what we know. First, public opinion strongly favored striking down the mandate. Roberts cares about public opinion, the argument runs, so he must have known that striking down the mandate was the popular thing to do by wide margins (and by a nearly unanimous position among conservatives such as himself). The second thing we know is that Roberts switched his vote at some point from the popular position of striking down the mandate to the unpopular position of upholding the mandate. We don't know exactly why Roberts switched his vote, although there is speculation that he did so because he was concerned with the legitimacy of the Court. Ilya implicitly equates this with being concerned with the popularity of the Court, so he looks to opinion polls to determine whether the health care cases made the Court more or less legitimate in the eyes of the public. And from this perspective, the chief justice's game plan backfired: Roberts tried to improve the Court's legitimacy but only hurt it.

If Roberts is thought to have been influenced by public pressure, though, wouldn't that pressure push him to strike down the mandate, not uphold it? Ilya speculates that Roberts was trying to gain the acceptance of "traditional liberal legal elites" like liberal law professors. They held the opposite view from the public, so perhaps Roberts was caving into their pressure despite public opinion as a whole. Ilya's lesson is that judges wanting to be popular should realize that there's a lot more to popularity than the views of liberal elites.

But Ilya's speculation that Roberts was trying to please "liberal legal elites" strikes me as farfetched. Until the mandate case, Roberts has been a reliable conservative vote. He has written and joined decisions that greatly enraged the "traditional liberal legal elites," such as *Citizens United* and *Parents Involved v. Seattle School District.*[75] And when given the chance, he has poked fun at law professors with a smile. Given his record, Roberts doesn't strike me as the kind of guy who frets about pleasing the *New York Times* editorial page. To the contrary, he strikes me as the type who (like most of us on the Right) sees upsetting the *Times* as a sign of a job well done.

The way out of the puzzle is to recognize the difference between legitimacy and popularity. Chief Justice Roberts cares about the legitimacy of the Supreme Court. He has a conception of the judicial role in which judges generally don't jump into the political thicket and make themselves major players on the political scene. This was the often-ignored point of his umpire analogy during his confirmation hearings: "Nobody ever went to a ball game to see the umpire." The umpire is legitimate when he is unobtrusively calling pitches, but if he makes himself the story of the game, something has gone wrong. We can agree or disagree with this conception of the judicial role. But this is a very different concept than popularity. It will often be popular for judges to jump into the political thicket. Some laws are popular at a state level but unpopular at a national level. Other laws are unpopular parts of legislation that just squeaked through Congress. The public will generally approve when a court strikes down a law that people don't like. But that's just what makes a judge popular, not what makes a judge legitimate. To go back to the baseball analogy, an umpire who wants to be popular can just make every call in favor of the home team. But that's a bad umpire, even if the fans love him.

In short, legitimacy and popularity are very different ideas. We don't know why Roberts changed his vote. But if it's true that he did so out of concerns with legitimacy, that is very different from saying that he did so because he wanted the Court to be popular.

Notes

1. Northwest Austin Municipal Utility District No. 1, v. Holder, 557 U.S. 193 (2010).
2. FEC v. Wis. Right to Life, Inc., 551 U.S. 449 (2007).
3. See Jonathan H. Adler, "Correcting Misconceptions about the Roberts Court," *supra*.
4. For more on this point, see Jonathan H. Adler, "Judicial Federalism and the Future of Federal Environmental Regulation," *Iowa Law Review* 90 (2005): 377, 433–52.
5. Jonathan Adler and Michael Cannon, "If Obamacare Survives, the Legal Battle Has Just Begun," *USA Today*, June 25, 2012, http://usatoday30.usatoday.com/news/opinion/forum/story/2012–06–24/obamacare-healthcare-supreme-court-unconstitutional/55796730/1.
6. Nat'l Fed'n of Indep. Bus. (NFIB) v. Sebelius, 132 S. Ct. 2566, 2586 (2012).
7. *Id.* at 2587.
8. *Id.*
9. *Id.* at 2588.
10. *Id.*
11. *Id.* at 2590–91.
12. *Id.* at 2592.
13. *Id.*
14. *Id.*
15. *Id.* at 2594.
16. *Id.* at 2603.
17. United States v. Darby, 312 U.S. 100, 124 (1941).
18. South Dakota v. Dole, 483 U.S. 203 (1987).
19. *Id.* at 211.
20. *NFIB*, 132 S. Ct. at 2604.
21. *Id.* at 2605–06.
22. Steward Mach. Co. v. Davis, 301 U.S. 548 (1937).
23. *NFIB*, 132 S. Ct. at 2606.
24. *Id.*

25. McCulloch v. Maryland, 17 U.S. 316 (1819).
26. Gibbons v. Ogden, 22 U.S. 1 (1824).
27. Marbury v. Madison, 5 U.S. 137 (1803).
28. United States v. Lopez, 514 U.S. 549 (1995).
29. *NFIB*, 132 S. Ct. at 2594.
30. See Hylton v. United States, 3 U.S. 171 (1796).
31. Brown v. Bd. of Educ. of Topeka, 347 U.S. 483 (1954).
32. Roe v. Wade, 410 U.S. 113 (1973).
33. David Bernstein, "A Bug or a Feature?," *supra*.
34. *NFIB*, 132 S. Ct. at 2655–57 (joint dissent).
35. Ed Whelan, "Re: Majority-Opinion-Turned-Dissent," *National Review Online*, last modified June 28, 2012, http://www.nationalreview.com/bench-memos/304341/re -majority-opinion-turned-dissent-ed-whelan#.
36. Rick Hasen, "A Few Thoughts on the Chief Justice and the Health Care Decision from SCOTUS," *ElectionLawBlog*, June 28, 2012, http://electionlawblog.org/?p=36309.
37. Ilya Somin, "A Taxing but Potentially Hopeful Decision," *supra*.
38. See, e.g., Steven D. Schwinn, "Did Chief Justice Roberts Craft a New, More Limited Commerce Clause?," *Constitutional Law Prof Blog*, June 29, 2012, http://lawprofessors. typepad.com/conlaw/2012/06/did-chief-justice-roberts-craft-a-new-more-limited -commerce-clause.html.
39. Jonathan H. Adler, "Lose the Battle, Win the War," *supra*.
40. Marks v. United States, 430 U.S. 188 (1977).
41. Ilya Somin, "A Mandate for Mandates: Is the Individual Health Insurance Mandate a Slippery Slope?," *Law and Contemporary Problems* 75 (2012): 75.
42. Brief for the Washington Legal Foundation et al., *Sebelius*, 132 S. Ct. 2566, *supra*.
43. David Bernstein, "Is This 1936?," *supra*.
44. Tom Scocca, "Obama Wins the Battle, Roberts Wins the War," Slate.com, last modified June 28, 2012, http://www.slate.com/articles/news_and_politics/scocca/2012/06/ roberts_health_care_opinion_commerce_clause_the_real_reason_the_chief_justice _upheld_obamacare_.html.
45. *NFIB*, 132 S. Ct. at 2599.
46. Ilya Somin, "Potentially Hopeful Decision." *supra*.
47. David Post, "Commerce Clause 'Holding v. Dictum Mess' Not So Simple," July 3, 2012, *Volokh Conspiracy* (blog), http://www.volokh.com/2012/07/03/commerce-clause-holding -v-dictum-mess-not-so-simple/.
48. Alexander Hamilton, *Federalist No. 78*, ed. Clinton Rossiter (1961).
49. *Id.* at 433.
50. Neil Siegel and Robert D. Cooter, "Not the Power to Destroy: An Effects Theory of the Tax Power," *Virginia Law Review* 98 (2012): 1195.
51. Randy E. Barnett, "Roberts Decision Didn't Open the Floodgates for 'Compulsion through Taxation,'" *Washington Examiner*, July 5, 2012, http://washingtonexaminer .com/roberts-decision-didnt-open-floodgates-for-compulsion-through-taxation/ article/2501386#.UO7cvKxRbgw.
52. *NFIB*, 132 S. Ct. at 2594.
53. *Id.* at 2600-01.
54. Ilya Somin, "A Simple Solution to the Holding vs. Dictum Mess," *supra*.
55. *NFIB*, 132 S. Ct. at 2599.
56. *Id.* at 2595.
57. *Id.* at 2595–96.
58. *Id.* at 2596.

59. *Id.* at 2596–97.

60. *Id.* at 2599–2600.

61. Mark Tushnet, "My View on Drafting *NFIB*," *Balkinization* (blog), July 3, 2012, http://balkin.blogspot.com/2012/07/my-view-on-drafting-nfib.html.

62. Jonathan H. Adler, "Lose the Battle, Win the War," *supra*.

63. Jeffrey Toobin, "Money Unlimited: How John Roberts Orchestrated the *Citizens United* Decision," *New Yorker*, May 21, 2012, http://www.newyorker.com/reporting/2012/05/21/120521fa_fact_toobin.

64. Free Enterprise Fund v. Pub. Co. Accounting Oversight Bd., 130 S. Ct. 3138 (2010).

65. Hein v. Freedom from Religion Found., 551 U.S. 587 (2007) (holding that taxpayers do not have standing to challenge the constitutionality of executive branch expenditures).

66. Flast v. Cohen, 392 U.S. 83 (1968) (creating limited taxpayer standing to sue for unconstitutional use of taxpayer funds).

67. *NFIB*, 132 S. Ct. at 2597–98.

68. U.S. Const. art. I, § 9, cl. 4.

69. Commissioner v. Glenshaw Glass Co., 348 U.S. 426 (1955).

70. *The Public Statutes at Large of the United States of America 1789–1845, Fifth Cong., 2d Sess., Chap. 70* (1798).

71. Paul Douglas Newman, *Fries's Rebellion: The Enduring Struggle for the American Revolution* (Philadelphia: University of Pennsylvania Press, 2004), 76–77.

72. "The Supreme Court & Health Care," Pew Research Center for People and the Press, last modified July 12, 2012, http://www.people-press.org/2012/07/12/section-2-the-supreme-court-and-health-care.

73. "The U.S. Supreme Court & the Health Care Law," CBS News, last modified June 7, 2012, http://www.cbsnews.com/htdocs/pdf/CBSNYTPoll_HealthCare_060712.pdf?tag=contentMain;contentBody.

74. Ilya Somin, "When Is It Legitimate for Judges to Base Constitutional Decisions on their Perceived Legitimacy?," *supra*.

75. 551 U.S. 701 (2007) (holding that a school's voluntary desegregation plan cannot only use race as a determining factor to achieve racial balance).

Postscript and Concluding Thoughts

Randy E. Barnett

In the aftermath of the Supreme Court's decision in *NFIB v. Sebelius*, I authored op-eds for *SCOTUSblog*, the *Washington Examiner*, the *Daily Beast / Newsweek*, and the *Washington Post*, the last of which is reproduced in previous chapters. All sounded a similar theme: although I was bitterly disappointed by the failure of our legal challenge to bring down the woefully misnamed "Patient Protection and Affordable Care Act," we were victorious in defeating the expansionist readings of the Constitution that had been offered by the government, and by many law professors, on behalf of the constitutionality of the individual insurance mandate.

Had their arguments been accepted, the theory that Congress has what amounts to a "national problems power" to address any aspect of the "national economy" by any means at its discretion—provided only that such measures are not expressly prohibited—would have become the Supreme Court's doctrine for the first time in our history. Preventing this from happening made the legal challenges well worthwhile. But we did more. We also succeeded in persuading a majority of the Court to adopt a reading of the Commerce and Necessary and Proper Clauses, as well as the spending power, that is far narrower than that held by a majority of constitutional law professors. In particular, there is the following:

- We fought this case to deny the federal government the power to compel citizens to engage in economic activity. On this, we won.
- We fought this case to prevent the Court from adopting the argument that Congress may adopt any means not expressly prohibited when it is regulating the national economy. On this, we won.
- We fought this case to prevent an end run around the limits on the Commerce and Necessary and Proper Clauses by using the tax power instead. On this, we won a partial, but significant, victory.
- We fought this case to establish that conditions on federal spending that constitute compulsion on states are unconstitutional, as Chief Justice William Rehnquist stated in dictum in *South Dakota v. Dole*. On this, we also won.

I have heard it said that because the Court has only barred economic mandates, which Congress had never before employed and was unlikely to employ in the future, this ruling is of only marginal significance. Yet, as I insisted for two years in the face of claims that a ruling invalidating Obamacare would undermine the entire edifice of federal programs, the greatest possible gain from bringing down the entire Affordable Care Act (ACA) was to prevent a future Congress from imposing economic mandates on the people, something it had never previously done.

Even where we lost on the law, we avoided a far worse ruling. The fact that the "penalty" alone was upheld as a "tax" only after the chief justice adopted a "saving construction" of the statute mitigates the potentially dangerous recognition of a new congressional power to tax the failure to purchase something. Under the Court's ruling, Congress is not free in the future to supplement the monetary penalty with punitive fines or jail time. Had the argument that the mandate was a constitutional regulation of interstate commerce under the Commerce Clause been accepted, future Congresses could jack up the amount of the penalty and add prison time to boot.

For those who may still not see the difference between the legal theories we defeated and that which was adopted by Chief Justice John Roberts, imagine that all the federal drug laws were enforced by the nonpunitive tax he allowed rather than as Commerce Clause regulations, which is how the prohibitions of the Controlled Substances Act are now justified. Under Chief Justice Roberts's tax power theory, the government would have to open the jails and release tens of thousands of prisoners. And any of you reading this could legally smoke marijuana under federal law, provided you were willing to pay a small noncoercive federal tax on this activity. Such is the difference between the Commerce Clause power Congress claimed justified the Affordable Care Act, and the new limited tax power the chief justice allowed it to exercise. That is a big difference.

In the end, therefore, the true scope of our legal victory is measured by the constitutional theories we prevented from being adopted by the Supreme Court and the unprecedented powers claimed by Congress that the Supreme Court denied it. While our failure to prevent the egregious Affordable Care Act from taking effect remains a bitter pill, this should not be allowed to detract from what we accomplished legally. We prevailed in preserving and even strengthening the enumerated powers scheme of Article I, Section 8 as a protection of individual liberty. From a constitutional perspective, this is what we were fighting so hard to achieve.

On the eve of the Supreme Court's decision, I expressed my deepest appreciation, win or lose, to all those who contributed to our effort in a blog post on the *Volokh Conspiracy*. In these concluding remarks, I again wish to thank my cobloggers for the significant contributions they made to this historic challenge. Ilya Somin, Jonathan Adler, and Dave Kopel each made vital contributions to the substance of the arguments and, with David Bernstein, responded skillfully to the manifold criticisms that were launched against our challenge.

I especially want to thank Orin Kerr for the unstinting and unflagging skepticism he expressed from the inception of this debate. His contributions truly enliven the pages of this book. His indefatigable resistance to every argument offered against the constitutionality of the individual insurance mandate was absolutely essential to the growth and improvement of these arguments, especially in the first year of their development. He was a one-man moot court, testing every claim, refusing to be browbeaten into concurring with a conclusion he simply could not accept. There is no question in my mind that our legal theories would not have developed as well as they did without his intellectual combativeness and persistence. To the extent our arguments went from "off the wall" (as Jack Balkin says) to a majority of the Supreme Court, Orin merits some share of the credit for that outcome.

Without doubt, the *Volokh Conspiracy* blog was instrumental in developing the arguments that earned us a historic six hours of oral argument spread over three days. Those who credited us with responsibility for the viability of this challenge are right to do so, but there was nothing nefarious involved. Just free speech. So thanks to Eugene Volokh for creating this forum and inviting me in. And thanks to our loyal readers for patiently returning to the scene of the *Conspiracy*. Without our readers, there would be no *Conspiracy*, so they too made an important contribution to the legal success we enjoyed.

When it comes to the lawsuit itself, I have no regrets. I believe that the many lawyers involved in this challenge litigated the case as well as it could possibly have been litigated. Virginia Attorney General Ken Cuccinelli and his excellent shop of lawyers earned the first court victory that shook the confidence of the mandate's supporters, forever changing the narrative. Lawyers for the Thomas More Law Center of Liberty University, and the American Center for Law and Justice, developed important arguments in their lawsuits and made compelling oral arguments in the Sixth, Fourth, and D.C. Circuits respectively. I was honored to work with these fine and principled attorneys.

Attorney David Rivkin, who had opposed the constitutionality of an individual mandate way back in 1993 (as is noted in our previous posts), heroically brought suit on behalf of the National Federation of Independent Business (NFIB) and a bevy of state attorneys general, each with their own opinions about how to litigate a case. He managed the lawsuit to a crucial successful outcome in the Northern District of Florida. And it was Lee Casey and David's *Wall Street Journal* op-ed in September 2009 that stimulated my first blogging on the subject on the *Politico*'s *Arena* blog and then on the *Volokh Conspiracy*. David was there for the Constitution when no other firm in town wanted the case.

Speaking of stimulation, I am also grateful to Washington and Lee law professor Timothy Jost, whose deeply skeptical post about the Rivkin and Casey op-ed first drew me into this debate. Were it not for his provocation, I might never have become involved in this challenge. And speaking of intellectual opponents, I went several rounds with my former torts professor Charles Fried, as well as former Solicitor General Walter Dellinger, an intellectual combat that generated mutual respect. And it was one of the highlights of the litigation when I debated both Charles and my constitutional law professor Laurence Tribe in the Ames Moot Court Room at Harvard Law School in an event moderated by Dean Martha Minnow. After the oral argument, Martha then agreed to interview me for a public program again held in Austin Hall.

Ilya Shapiro and Trevor Burrus at the Cato Institute performed yeoman's work on the amicus briefs filed with me as their client. These briefs allowed me to inject my theories into the litigation, well before I became a formal part of the challenge as a lawyer for the NFIB. And Trevor has done an amazing job culling our blog posts and op-eds to create this book, a narrative that I found fascinating to revisit.

I wish to thank my old friend Richard Epstein for inviting me to deliver the Hayek Lecture at the New York University School of Law in October of 2010, which provided a forum in which I could develop the legal theory underlying the challenge in a more rigorous way for publication in the *New York University Journal of Law and Liberty*. I am also grateful to my Georgetown colleagues who never uttered an unkind word in response to my efforts, even after vetting them in more than one faculty workshop, and my Georgetown and Penn law students for their enthusiasm.

And I am deeply grateful to two heroic federal district court judges: Judge Henry Hudson, for having the courage to be the first judge to invalidate the individual mandate, and Judge Roger Vinson, for having the fortitude to invalidate the entire ACA while writing a brilliant opinion that anticipated much of how Chief Justice Roberts would eventually rule. And credit needs to be given to Eleventh Circuit Court Judges Joel Dubina (a Republican nominee) and Frank Hull (a Democrat nominee) for sustaining Judge Vinson's ruling and providing a clear path for the case to proceed to the Supreme Court. As the subsequent pressure applied to the Supreme Court justices later showed, all these jurists had to put principle above politics to reach the conclusions they did.

I also thank the dozens of reporters I spoke with about the constitutionality of the ACA. The coverage of these legal challenges was consistently fair, balanced, and accurate. I was never misquoted or mischaracterized by a reporter. I never felt our side was given short shrift even as reporters accurately reported the skepticism and scorn that was heaped upon our claims by others. That scorn was a legitimate part of the story. I know some on the left fault the press for heightening the credibility of our challenge by giving us unduly respectful coverage. From this, I not-so-respectfully dissent. The press simply did its job and did it well.

Of course, everyone knows that Supreme Court cases are won and lost on the briefing, not oral argument, and the briefs written by the Jones Day law firm for the NFIB—especially Mike Carvin, Greg Katsas, and Hashim Mooppan—and by Paul Clement and Erin Murphy of Bancroft LLC for the state attorneys general were superb before receiving any input from me. They deserve every credit for our success; no legal team could have done any better.

Supreme Court advocates know what academics sometimes seem to forget: you simply cannot "mandate" a justice go where he or she does not want to go with a clever argument. All you can do is present your strongest case in the most compelling way. Mike, Greg, and Paul did that during oral argument in which the pressure could not have been more intense. I was supremely grateful it was them and not me who had to bear up under the strain of oral argument. Along with Karen Harned, director of the NFIB Small Business Legal Center, win or lose, I believe we fielded the "A Team" on behalf of the majority of the American people who objected to the Affordable Care Act and believed it to be unconstitutional.

A special thanks is due to Todd Gaziano of the Heritage Foundation for asking me in November of 2009 if I wanted to "do something" about the bill that looked like it might emerge from secret deliberations in the Senate and who recruited a young associate, Nathaniel Stewart, to compose the first draft of a legal memorandum that became the basis for the initial constitutional arguments against the challenge—arguments that convinced every Republican senator (whom I also thank) to raise a point of constitutional order on December 23, 2009, which led to a floor debate that launched the constitutional difficulties of the ACA into the public arena. Nate deserves much more credit for these arguments than he has received so far. Indeed, as a former prosecutor who never worked for a law firm, my experience working closely with associates like Joshua Greenberg in the *Raich* case, and Nate, Hash, and Erin in this case, exposed me to the incredible contributions by unsung law firm associates. Nate, Hash, and Erin are three such brilliant lawyers.

Finally, and with apologies to all those I could not single out by name, I'd like to thank my Georgetown colleague and friend Larry Solum for his unstinting support and for his brilliant insights into the complex legal and tactical issues raised by this challenge, whatever his own views of the matter might have been.

Orin Kerr

Looking back over the debate that forms this book, my chief reaction is some surprise that I participated in it. Unlike most of my cobloggers, I do not teach or write about the constitutional questions that formed the heart of the Affordable Care Act challenge. Unlike most of my cobloggers, I did not participate in the cases as either counsel for a party or as an amicus. And unlike most of my cobloggers, I had conflicting instincts on the question of how I wanted the legal challenges to come out. For those reasons, my participation was often accompanied by the guilty feeling that I was wasting time blogging when I should have been doing real work instead.

Despite these challenges, blogging about the Affordable Care Act challenges was a lot of fun. My cobloggers proved excellent sparring partners. Every post drew hundreds of comments. And to my surprise, what began as a provocative, if academic debate, ended up hashing out arguments that came very close to striking down the signature legislative achievement of President Barack Obama's first term. Readers can judge whether my contributions enlivened or muddied the discussion. I hope they provided a helpful counterpoint, adding the perspective of a more traditional restraint-oriented judicial conservatism to the libertarian constitutionalism of my colleagues. But it was an engaging trip, at least for me, and I thank my colleagues for leading the way through it.

David B. Kopel

My most direct involvement in the Obamacare cases was filing amicus briefs on the original meaning of the Necessary and Proper Clause. As with my very first post about Obamacare on VC, my Independence Institute colleague Rob Natelson was at the center. Rob, Gary Lawson (Law, Boston University) and Guy Seidman (Law, Interdisciplinary Center, Herzliya, Israel) are coauthors of the first and only book on the subject, *The Origins of the Necessary and Proper Clause* (Cambridge: Cambridge University Press, 2010).

With Rob as the lead author, the four of us wrote amicus briefs in the Supreme Court, the Eleventh Circuit, and the D.C. Circuit on the original meaning of Necessary and Proper Clause.[1] As we explained, *McCulloch v. Maryland* perfectly complied with the original meaning. In 1787, as in 1819, the Necessary and Proper clause was typical of contract clauses in which a principal delegated power to an agent. Terms such as "necessary and proper" were read to formally grant incidental, lesser powers, to be used in carrying out other principal powers that were delegated to the agent by the contract.

Chief Justice Marshall's opinion in *McCulloch* relied on and explicated the well-known doctrine of principals and incidents. Chief Justice Roberts' opinion in *NFIB* does the same, relying on *McCulloch*.

Northwestern's Andy Koppelman wrote that the Roberts opinion "relies" on the approach that we had presented, which he generously calls "the most sophisticated" of the various arguments that claimed the Necessary and Proper Clause did not legitimate the mandate.[2]

At the least, our brief helped the Court find a very important source on the meaning of *McCulloch*: newspaper essays by Chief Justice John Marshall on that very topic. Marshall's essays, written in a newspaper debate with Virginia Attorney General Spencer Roane, had never previously been cited by the Supreme Court, and our brief discussed and quoted them in depth.

Perhaps one contribution of our brief, and the case, to constitutional law is renewed attention to the full opinion in *McCulloch v. Maryland* rather than the expurgated versions in many law school textbooks. In Randy Barnett's *Constitutional Law* text, students can see John Marshall working his way through doctrine of principals and incidents, as he elucidates that Necessary and Proper Clause is for inferior, less "worthy" powers—and not for a "great, substantive and independent power."

Roberts's application of this long-standing rule took some of the pro-mandate professoriate by surprise, and the professors who were not surprised were dismayed. Andy Koppelman later wrote that the principal/incident distinction had been "ignored for nearly two centuries thereafter." Ignored by the legal academy, perhaps, but not by the Supreme Court.

Our amicus brief pointed out that the Supreme Court had strongly relied on the original doctrines in the 1981 in *Dames & Moore v. Regan*.[3] In a case involving the president's power to settle debts owed by Iran to American citizens, the Court ruled that the president had the power to do so. The Constitution explicitly authorizes him to recognize foreign governments. In the words of *McCulloch*, this is a "great, substantive and independent power." The power to settle foreign debts was "incidental" to the recognition power for two reasons, the Court explained: first, a debt-settling power is nearly indispensable to recognition of foreign governments; second, the debt-settling power is long standing. Combined, these two facts show that the debt-settling power is an incident to the principal power of recognition.

That's the approach that John Marshall used to explain the Necessary and Proper Clause, and any lawyer of the early Republic would have been familiar with similar analysis of a grant of incidental powers to a private agent or to a government.

In between *McCulloch* and *Dames & Moore*, there are about a dozen cases in which the Court engages in similar analysis of whether a contract, constitution, or other explicitly written grant of a principal power also includes a particular unwritten incidental power. To many twenty-first-century readers, this kind of analysis may not be noticed for what it is; perhaps that is because agency law is no longer part of the standard law school education. For the Supreme Court justices and most other lawyers of the 1819–1981 period, agency law was much more familiar. Here's the part of our brief that provides some of the citation history:

> In the years since the Founding, the Supreme Court has applied similar tests of incidence in many contexts. Under the law of this Court, incidents are inferior (or in the word of Justice Brandeis, "subsidiary"[4]) to their principals,[5] sometimes being referred to as "mere incidents."[6] If subsidiary, an item may qualify as an incident if it is indispensable to the principal.[7] This Court sometimes refers to indispensable incidents as "necessary incidents."[8]

I wish our brief could have elaborated on some of those cases. Any case named *Poafpybitty* naturally arouses curiosity. But the nine-thousand-word limit on the brief made this impossible, and we had to focus on the original meaning, not the post-*McCulloch* cases.

Besides that, we didn't expect the Court to think that cases such as *Wood v. Chesborough* (1913) had to control the instant case. Rather, our point was that the original meaning, including the doctrine of principals and incidents, was not only recognized and described in *McCulloch*; that doctrine has continued to be applied by the Court since then, by justices as diverse as Louis Brandeis and William Rehnquist.

After the Eleventh Circuit, but before the Supreme Court brief, the *Yale Law Journal Online* was the forum for a slugfest pitting Koppelman against Gary Lawson and me. Koppelman consolidated and revised some of his blog posts from *Balkinization* and turned them into a Yale essay arguing that the Necessary and Proper clause undeniably proved the legality of the individual mandate.

Gary and I wrote a reply disagreeing and presenting our argument on original meaning. Koppelman penned a surreply, and we came back with a sur-surreply.[9] The VC and *Balkinization* blogs had some spinoff posts related to all this.

Koppelman's new book continues the dialogue. Besides describing the principals and incidents doctrine as "ignored" (a point on which we disagree), Koppelman also takes issue with the doctrine as actually applied by Chief Justice Roberts in *NFIB v. Sebelius*.

Koppelman makes a valid point that the Roberts opinion has to squirm pretty hard to reconcile the Marshall/*McCulloch* type of analysis with the Court's 2010 decision in *United States v. Comstock*. *Comstock* makes no pretense of concern about original public understanding. Justice Breyer's five-factor *Comstock* approach to the meaning of the Necessary and Proper Clause is something else entirely. Other briefs, such as those by Ilya Somin, argued that the mandate was invalid under *Comstock*.

Chief Justice Roberts faced a choice: follow the *McCulloch* path or the *Comstock* path. In my view, he chose rightly; *McCulloch* has stood the test of time. So Koppelman is correct that *Comstock* and *NFIB* are hard to reconcile. But that's only because *Comstock* failed to properly follow *McCulloch*.

Koppelman further objects to the result of *NFIB*'s application of the *McCulloch* doctrines. Roberts said that the power to compel commerce is not merely incidental to the enumerated power to regulate commerce. Rather, compelling commerce is a "great, substantive, and independent power." Therefore, it cannot be inferred from the Necessary and Proper Clause.

I concede that when the *McCulloch* tests are applied, reasonable people can differ about the right result in a particular situation. Some people who agree that Marshall correctly employed original understanding in *McCulloch* might argue that he was wrong to find that congressional creation of a Bank of the United States was merely an incidental power that could be inferred from several of the enumerated congressional powers. In the modern context, Koppelman says that use of the doctrine of principals and incidents will be based on "the interpreter's pretheoretical intuitions about which government powers are particularly scary."

He then criticizes Chief Justice Roberts's (alleged) intuitions because imprisoning someone for a long time (upheld in *Comstock*) should be seen as much scarier than forcing someone to buy insurance (held invalid in *NFIB* as an exercise of the Necessary and Proper Clause), especially when the forced insurance is an essential part of a government program that will help many people.

But it's only Koppelman who thinks that scariness is part of the test. The Constitution grants Congress the power to declare war and the power to establish a uniform system of bankruptcy. The grants of each of these principal powers also carries with it implied, incidental powers. That is what the Necessary and Proper Clause confirms.

Lots of the incidental war powers (e.g., the power to hold people in prisoner of war camps for the duration of the war) are a lot scarier than almost all the incidental bankruptcy powers. The incidental war powers allow Congress to provide for various means and systems of killing lots of people; the incidental bankruptcy powers do not.

Koppelman quotes "the Lawson group" amicus brief as an example of use of the scariness test; we wrote that the power "to compel private citizens to purchase approved products from other designated private persons" is "a power truly awesome in scope, and one, that if granted to Congress, the Constitution surely would have enumerated separately."

Observe: neither we nor Chief Justice Roberts said anything about whether the power was dangerous or scary. We said the power was "awesome." That's a description of size and potency, not of frightfulness. The question at bar was whether an allegedly "necessary and proper" power (compelling commerce) can be an incident of some enumerated power(s). As our brief detailed, there are a variety of factors one examines in determining whether an unenumerated power is an incident of some particular principal power: Is the potential incidental power "indispensable" to the exercise of the principal power? Is there a long-established custom that the power is an incident to the principal power? Is the incidental power less than, "inferior," to the principal power?

This last question was what we were answering in the sentence quoted by Koppelman. Compelling involuntary commerce is a power that is actually larger, greater, and more "awesome" than the power to regulate existing voluntary commerce.

Besides all that, if scariness really were the test, the Cato Institute and the Independence Institute are among the think tanks whose health policy experts have authored many studies explaining the grave risks and that Obamacare will seriously harm health care in the United States. Cato, Independence Institute, and many other writers have offered alternative solutions, which they argue can greatly improve health care (especially for persons in need of a safety net), at much lower costs than Obamacare and without violating the Constitution.

Today, just as during 2009–12, skeptics of Obamacare are sometimes derided as heartless libertarians who insist on rigid constitutional meaning to the detriment of the sick and dying. Actually, we think that our safety net programs will work much better than Obamacare. At the Independence Institute, we follow John Marshall in favoring a "fair construction" of the Constitution—not the "strict construction" favored by Spencer Roane nor the "liberal sense," which Spencer Roane accused Marshall of applying and which is favored today by Koppelman and the rest of the professorial and judicial advocates for Obamacare.[10]

I. The Taxing and Spending Clause

The Independence Institute filed a second brief in the Obamacare cases, this one on the Medicaid mandate.[11] As with the Necessary and Proper brief, Rob Natelson was the principal author, and I was the attorney of record. The brief addressed the original meaning of partial "sovereignty," which all proponents of the proposed Constitution agreed would remain with the states. We brought forward structural analysis of the Constitution itself, ratification documents, and similar sources to argue that among the essential attributes of a sovereign government is the ability to determine its own spending and budget. Chief Justice Roberts's opinion striking down the Medicaid mandate garnered a 7–2 majority and was grounded in analysis of state sovereignty. Perhaps our brief helped.

II. The Future

As Speaker Nancy Pelosi promised, Americans are continuing to find out more and more of what is in Obamacare. There is still plenty of constitutional litigation ahead. Was the Independent Payment Advisory Board (IPAB; the entity in charge of deciding what kinds of care various classes of patients may receive) an unprecedented usurpation of power by the 2010 Congress? The Obamacare statute purports to forbid future Congresses from repealing IPAB or thwarting its mandates. There is a special, constricted procedure to do so that can only be used in 2017; thereafter, IPAB becomes supposedly immune to the will of any future Congress.

Does the First Amendment's Free Exercise Clause prevent Congress from ordering that religious employers (e.g., Catholic hospitals, conservative Protestant universities) provide their employees with free abortion pills? Does the congressionally enacted Restoration of Religious Freedom Act (RFRA; enacted in 1993) vindicate the rights of the employers? RFRA says it controls the interpretation of all subsequently enacted legislation, unless the new legislation expressly declares RFRA inapplicable.

As for the future of the individual mandate, my approach was set forth in a pair of June 29, 2012, articles for *National Review Online* and the *Volokh Conspiracy*: repeal the individual mandate because it is unconstitutional.[12]

Once again, *McCulloch* shows the way. Chief Justice Marshall's *McCulloch* opinion expressly stated that Congress, as part of Congress's own duty to uphold the Constitution, had to make its own decision about whether a Bank of the United States was constitutionally "proper." The *McCulloch* decision explicitly deferred to this 1816 congressional judgment creating the Second Bank of the United States; creating a bank was definitely an incidental power (the Court said), and the bank did not appear to be constitutionally improper for any other reason.

In 1832, President Andrew Jackson vetoed the recharter of the Second Bank of the United States. His veto message cited this very portion of the *McCulloch* opinion: that the Court had partially deferred to Congress on a constitutional matter did not excuse the political branches from their own duty to consider the constitutionality of their actions. President Jackson considered the bank to be unconstitutional. Among other reasons, it was special legislation, enriching a favored few at the public's expense.

Jackson's veto message on this point was the very first use of the phrase "equal protection" in an American political document. Three decades later, "equal protection" would become part of our written Constitution, as part of the Fourteenth Amendment.

After an intense political struggle over the second bank, Jackson and his fellow Democrats prevailed. No more bank.

So in the twenty-first century, American citizens acting through the political branches can continue to work toward repeal of the individual mandate on the grounds that it is unconstitutional, and legislators can vote for repeal on grounds that include a legislator's own analysis of constitutionality.

At base, this is similar to the actions of many legislators in the latter twentieth century who voted against particular gun control bills because legislators considered them to violate the Second Amendment. At the time, the Supreme Court's major precedent, *United States v. Miller* (1939),[13] was opaque, and its meaning disputed. Not until *District of Columbia v. Heller* (2008)[14] did the Court provided a clearer interpretation. Legislators only act properly when they take the Constitution into account before they vote.

A person may argue with Jack Balkin over the original understanding of various constitutional provisions.[15] But Jack Balkin is right about many things, including: (1) text and original meaning are important; (2) in the United States, the constitutional interpretations that thrive are those that embody the constitutional aspirations of the American people, as expressed over the long term. Whether or not you consider the Constitution to be a "living" document, what matters most in the long run is whether and how it lives in the hearts and minds of the American people.

The *Volokh Conspiracy* is an effort to contribute to constitutional understanding, among lay persons as well as judges, professors, and lawyers. That we were able to do so in the Obamacare debate is gratifying. Many more Americans have a better understanding of the constitutional principles of limited federal powers than when we began. Because of *NFIB*, constitutional doctrine has moved significantly closer to original understanding, to the fundamental constitutional structure for preserving liberty.

David E. Bernstein

In 2011, a law professor at Yale, defending Obamacare from constitutional challenge, claimed that only one "constitutional scholar that I know at a top 20 law school" thinks that Obamacare is "constitutionally problematic." A year later, just before oral argument in *NFIB*, the same professor stated that only one law professor at a top ten law school agreed that the Obamacare was unconstitutional.

The professor's math was almost certainly somewhat off, but he was right that the overwhelming majority of constitutional law scholars at elite law schools thought that the constitutional challenge to Obamacare was not just wrong, but obviously so.

But there is a reason for this. The faculties at elite law schools have been able to define what was "mainstream" in constitutional law simply by who they hired to join them. And Yale, to take just one example, has not hired a conservative or libertarian professor to teach constitutional law in my lifetime. According to an informed source at the law school, this is not a coincidence, as some of Yale's constitutional law professors make it their business to block any right-of-center candidates.

One can therefore interpret the professor's claim a bit differently than he intended, to wit: I, and people who think like me, find the federalism-based arguments used to challenge Obamacare to be absurd; I and people who think like me get to choose who become our faculty colleagues; we don't hire people whose ideas we find absurd; therefore, almost all of our colleagues at elite law schools find the challenge to Obamacare to be absurd. Put that way, the fact that it was difficult or impossible to find professors at schools like Harvard or Yale who supported the challenge becomes something of a tautology rather than an insight.

Twenty years ago, the virtual consensus among law professors at elite schools very well may have been the end of serious debate in the academic world. The venues for law professors getting their ideas out on controversial issues of the day were few and dominated by law professors at the top schools: the mainstream media, either through op-eds or interviews with reporters, both heavily skewed toward famous professors at places like Harvard and Yale; publications at the top law reviews, which are not reviewed blindly and therefore heavily favor the already renowned; and presentations at elite law schools, to which the overwhelming majority of invitees are professors at peer institutions.

The world of blogging has upset this cozy arrangement. Good and interesting arguments from smart people can get out to the media, other law professors, and the world at large without regard to the brand name of the author's law school. Law professors could insist that there were no legitimate constitutional arguments to be made against Obamacare, and interested parties could easily see for themselves that this wasn't true by reading the *Volokh Conspiracy*. Blogs like *Volokh*, along with other Internet sources such as ssrn.com and topical and timely online law review supplements, have broken the stranglehold of the progressive-Left elite on determining what constitutional arguments get to be taken seriously in "mainstream" constitutional discourse. And it's hard not to think that the world of constitutional law is all the better for it.

Ilya Somin

Introduction

The Supreme Court's decision in the Obamacare case was one of the most controversial judicial rulings in many years. We do not yet have enough historical perspective to reach any definitive conclusions about its impact. Scholars, jurists, and others will be debating *NFIB v. Sebelius* for a long time to come. I have written more detailed analyses of the constitutional merits of the decision elsewhere.[16] Here, I only make a few observations about the significance of the case and the role of the *Volokh Conspiracy* in the public and judicial debate leading up to it.

While the long-term effect of the ruling is difficult to predict, it is clear that opponents of the individual mandate won some important legal ground, despite the painful setback of having the mandate upheld as a "tax." More fundamentally, the deep division in the Court suggests that the constitutional scope of federal power will continue to be a hotly contested issue.

It would be arrogant to assume that the *Volokh Conspiracy* was the only or even the most important factor behind the relative success of the constitutional case against Obamacare. Many other forces—both legal and political—also played an important role. But the blog did have a substantial effect on both the legal arguments made in the case and the development of public debate.

I. The Meaning of NFIB v. Sebelius

The most immediate result of *NFIB* is that the Affordable Care Act survived largely intact. Although the Court transformed the individual mandate into a "tax,"[17] there will probably be no more than minor effects on the operation of the mandate in practice. The Court's decision to strike down the mandatory expansion of Medicaid was an important victory for federalism.[18] But many states have already accepted the expansion voluntarily and others may do so in the future. The Medicaid ruling impedes the implementation of Obamacare but surely does not prevent it completely.

But those who supported the legal case against the mandate also got a lot out of the Court's ruling. Indeed, they prevailed on almost all the major legal arguments. They came as close to winning the case as they possibly could without actually prevailing all the way. In his decisive swing vote opinion, Chief Justice John Roberts endorsed the plaintiffs' argument that the individual mandate was outside the scope of Congress's powers under the Commerce Clause and Necessary and Proper Clause.[19] Particularly gratifying to me was his conclusion that "[e]ven if the individual mandate is 'necessary' to the Act's insurance reforms, such an expansion of federal power is not a 'proper' means for making those reforms effective."[20] The argument that the mandate was improper even if "necessary" was the central focus of the amicus brief I had written on behalf of the Washington Legal Foundation and a group of constitutional law scholars,[21] though I certainly do not mean to suggest that this brief was what persuaded the five justices who ruled that the mandate was "improper."

In its ruling striking down the mandatory Medicaid expansion that the ACA sought to impose on the states, the Court set limits to Congress's powers under the spending clause for the first time since the 1930s. Surprisingly, it did so by a 7–2 margin, with Justices Elena Kagan and Stephen Breyer joining the five most conservative justices in the majority.

Even Chief Justice Roberts's decision upholding the individual mandate as a "tax" was somewhat equivocal. Roberts admitted that construing this provision as a tax was not the "most natural interpretation" of the law.[22] The text of the statute refers to the fine as a "penalty," not a tax.[23] He nonetheless chose to construe it as a tax as a "saving construction" in order to preserve it from invalidation.[24]

In my view, even the chief justice's reinterpreted version of the mandate does not truly qualify as a tax under the Constitution.[25] I also have serious doubts about the justifiability of courts deviating from the "most natural" interpretation of a law in order to save it from being invalidated as unconstitutional. Rewriting legislation to make it constitutional is the job of the legislature, not the courts. Still, Roberts's interpretation does establish four constraints that future federal mandates must work within if they are to be upheld as taxes: that the only penalty be a monetary fine, that the fine is not high enough to be "coercive," that it be collected by the IRS, and that violation of the mandate should not be considered law breaking if the fine is paid.[26] As Randy Barnett explains in his concluding essay in this volume, this prevents Congress from simply criminalizing those who violate its mandates. On the other hand, Congress can still use such "taxes" to compel almost any behavior it wants, so long as the means of compulsion are limited by Roberts's four criteria.

The Court's Commerce and Necessary and Proper rulings might nonetheless have some bite. They could forestall future mandates requiring Americans to purchase the products of politically influential industries.[27] Such mandates were more than just a theoretical possibility if the Court had endorsed the federal government's defense of the mandate.[28] Unfortunately, Congress could partially circumvent these restrictions on mandates by structuring them as taxes, so long as it follows Roberts's four guidelines. Yet those strictures at least impose constraints on the severity of the mandates they allow. And it is not clear whether future Supreme Court decisions will follow Roberts's somewhat jury-rigged approach to the tax issue.

Perhaps the most important legacy of *NFIB* is its refutation of claims that there is a broad expert consensus that the Constitution gives Congress the power to enact virtually any regulation that has some substantial effect on the economy. This belief underlay many of the early predictions that the individual mandate case would be a slam dunk for the government.

In reality, the Supreme Court's conservative justices had not accepted that theory for a long time. In the academic world, it has come under challenge from two generations of conservative and libertarian federalism scholars, including Steven Calabresi, Lynn Baker, Gary Lawson, and the *Volokh Conspiracy*'s own Randy Barnett, among others. This lack of consensus long predated the legal battle over Obamacare. But *NFIB v. Sebelius* drove the reality home to many who did not see it before.

The lack of consensus on judicial review of federalism is not entirely good news for those of us who support strong enforcement of constitutional limits on federal power. In practice, it is difficult to ensure consistent judicial enforcement of any part of the Constitution without at least some substantial bipartisan support. And if *NFIB* showed that most conservatives and libertarians do support judicial review of federalism issues, it also reinforced the reality that most liberals and Democrats do not.

Yet it is worth noting that liberal Supreme Court justices Breyer and Kagan did vote to strike down Obamacare's Medicaid expansion. In the Eleventh Circuit, Democratic-appointed Judge Frank Hull voted to strike down the individual mandate.[29] These examples of deviationism on the left are at least partially offset by Laurence Silberman of the D.C. Circuit and Jeffrey Sutton of the Sixth, prominent conservative judges who voted to uphold the mandate.[30] And it may well be a long time before a substantial proportion of liberal jurists are persuaded to support strong judicial review of federalism, if ever.

Still, we should remember the progress made by advocates of judicial review of federalism over the last several decades. In the 1970s, their position had very little support among jurists and almost none among elite legal scholars and other prominent commentators on constitutional issues. From the late 1930s to *United States v. Lopez* in 1995,[31] the Supreme Court went almost sixty years without striking down a single federal law as being beyond Congress's powers under the Commerce Clause. The change from that era to the present is striking.

II. The Role of the Volokh Conspiracy

What role did the *Volokh Conspiracy* play in the legal battle over Obamacare? It is easy to identify two polar-opposite views on the subject: that our influence was decisive and that it made no real difference at all. A March 2012 article in the *Atlantic* claimed that "[b]logs—particularly a blog of big legal ideas called *Volokh Conspiracy*—have been central to shifting the conversation about the mandate challenges."[32] On the other hand, Yale Law School Professor Jack Balkin argues that "the single most important factor in making the mandate opponents' constitutional claims plausible was strong support by the Republican Party, including its politicians, its affiliated lawyers, and its affiliated media."[33] The support of the GOP was the main factor giving credence to a position that was "in the view of most legal professionals and academics, simply crazy."[34]

In my view, the truth is somewhere in between. Balkin's emphasis on the role of the GOP has considerable validity. If Obamacare and the individual mandate had enjoyed broad bipartisan support, it is highly unlikely that the Supreme Court would have even come close to striking them down. The justices rarely invalidate major federal legislation that enjoys widespread public support. They fear the possible political backlash that would result from such action. Obamacare, however, was notable for being a rare major federal law that was generally unpopular from the time of its enactment to the present. Polls consistently showed that the law had more opponents than supporters.[35] A *New York Times* / CBS survey conducted just before the Supreme Court issued its decision in June 2012 found that 68 percent of the public wanted the Court to strike down the mandate, including even a 48–42 plurality of Democrats.[36] Even when Barack Obama was reelected in November 2012, CNN exit polls and other survey data showed a plurality of the public supporting repeal of his principal legislative achievement.[37] The combination of Obamacare's—and especially the individual mandate's—unpopularity and strong GOP opposition made it possible for the Court to strike down the law without fear of a massive political backlash.

But such political factors are only a partial explanation of what happened. We should remember that the ACA was far from the only Obama policy that was bitterly opposed by the GOP. Republicans were just as strongly united in opposition to other administration initiatives, such as the 2009 stimulus bill. At least with respect to the stimulus, there was also considerable public skepticism. Yet no major legal challenge was ever mounted against the stimulus.

Why not? Certainly not because the Republicans were unwilling to try if they thought such an effort could work. The reason is that such challenges were doomed to failure because the legal arguments underpinning them would either lack credibility with legal professionals, require the overruling of a great deal of Supreme Court precedent, or both. By contrast, the legal challenge to Obamacare gained traction precisely because it was backed by serious legal arguments that did not require extensive revision of precedent to prevail.

And that's precisely where the *Volokh Conspiracy* came in. As documented elsewhere in this book, VC posts had a significant influence on the development of the legal arguments put forward by the plaintiffs challenging the mandate. Randy Barnett's work played an especially crucial role in explaining how the Court could strike down the mandate without overturning any existing precedent. His work at the VC helped lead to his later direct involvement in the case.

Some of the rest of us also became involved with the case against the mandate because of our blogging. My own writings at the *Volokh Conspiracy* led to an invitation to write amicus briefs in several of the cases challenging the mandate, on behalf of the Washington Legal Foundation, a prominent pro–free market public interest law firm. This effort culminated in a Supreme Court amicus brief on behalf of WLF and a group of leading constitutional law scholars arguing that the mandate was not "proper" under the Necessary and Proper Clause because the government's rationale for the mandate would give Congress virtually unlimited power to impose other mandates.[38] Although there is no way to know for certain whether our brief influenced him, Justice Antonin Scalia raised this exact issue during the individual mandate oral argument.[39] Andrew Koppelman, a leading academic defender of the constitutionality of the mandate suggests that the brief may have influenced Chief Justice Roberts.[40]

The *Volokh Conspiracy's* role in developing the legal arguments against the mandate should not be overstated. Important parts of the case had been developed by prominent appellate lawyer David Rivkin as far back as 1993. Scholars such as Gary Lawson, Rob Natelson, and Steve Calabresi also emerged as prominent critics of the constitutionality of the mandate and contributed to the case against it, as of course did a number of leading lawyers working for the 28 state governments and numerous private plaintiffs challenging Obamacare. But if the VC was far from the only influence on the legal case against the mandate and other parts of the ACA, it was at least a significant one.

Perhaps the most important role of the blog was breaking down the perception that there was an expert consensus supporting the constitutionality of the mandate. From early on, many defenders of the mandate claimed that virtually all experts on constitutional law agreed that the mandate was obviously constitutional and that contrary views must be the result of either ignorance or partisan bias.[41]

The *Volokh Conspiracy* was a crucial factor in countering this meme. By constantly presenting constitutional arguments against Obamacare developed by leading legal scholars, we called into question the initially dominant narrative that the case was an easy slam dunk for the government. People like Randy Barnett, David Kopel, and Jonathan Adler were prominent constitutional federalism scholars and could not easily be dismissed as mere partisan hacks. The VC also helped highlight antimandate arguments developed by other leading scholars such as Gary Lawson and Richard Epstein.

It was never really true that the case against the mandate was "in the view of most legal professionals and academics, simply crazy."[42] From the very beginning, there was deep disagreement on the subject among experts. But the *Volokh Conspiracy* played a major role in driving this point home to legal professionals, the media, and the more attentive members of the general public. It was crucial that the VC presented these arguments in a forum that had a large audience among legal reporters, jurists, academics, and other elites. Most commentators who followed the case were at least aware of our arguments, even if they did not agree with them. The blog format also allowed us to react to events and respond to new opposing arguments "in real time," thereby making it harder for defenders of the mandate to "shape the narrative" without opposition.

The growing recognition that the constitutional case against the ACA was backed by serious arguments was an important factor in the legal battle. If lower court judges had perceived that there was an expert consensus in favor of the mandate's constitutionality, there would likely have been few if any rulings striking it down. And without lower court decisions ruling against the government, it is far less likely that the Supreme Court would have taken the case or that five justices would endorse many of the plaintiffs' arguments.

It is possible that the perception of an expert consensus in favor of the mandate would have broken down even without the *Volokh Conspiracy's* contributions. Randy Barnett and other leading critics of the mandate would surely have found alternative ways to make their views known. But—especially early on in the debate—mandate opponents had no other forum that combined all the VC's crucial assets: a large preexisting audience, commentary by leading academic experts such as Adler and Barnett, and the ability to respond to events in real time.

This combination of assets is a unique strength of the blogosphere that had a significant influence over the litigation leading up to *NFIB v. Sebelius*. The general strategy of presenting legal arguments in major cases to the court of public opinion as well as judges was far from novel. Antislavery activists pioneered that tactic in the early nineteenth century, and the NAACP used it to great effect as part of its litigation strategy leading up to *Brown v. Board of Education*. But the Obamacare case may have been the first in which blogs played a significant role in developing the arguments and presenting them to the public and the legal community. I suspect it will not be last.

Our side of the case was not the only one that used the blogosphere to its advantage. Defenders of the mandate did so as well, especially at Jack Balkin's *Balkinization* blog, where he and other academics wrote many insightful posts defending the mandate's constitutionality. At the VC itself, Orin Kerr wrote many well-written posts arguing that precedent required the Court to uphold the mandate.

The Obamacare litigation raised novel issues that the Supreme Court had never clearly addressed before. It also presented a clash of constitutional visions between those who believe that the courts should enforce serious limits on federal power and those who argue that judges should uphold almost any federal regulations that have some effect on the economy. Both sides had strong arguments to offer and neither could persuasively dismiss the other as merely ignorant or partisan.

It would therefore be wrong to conclude that the *Volokh Conspiracy* bloggers dominated the legal debate over Obamacare or that we proved our opponents' position was utterly without merit. But we did play an important role in making more people aware that there *was* a serious debate here in the first place.

Jonathan H. Adler

Shortly before the oral arguments in *NFIB v. Sebelius*, one of my colleagues came into my office with a confession: Having read the merits briefs on either side, she had concluded (however reluctantly) that the individual mandate was unconstitutional. I asked what caused her to reach this conclusion. The lack of limits, she replied. Although she supported the Patient Protection and Affordable Care Act, she was persuaded that a commerce power capable of justifying the mandate was a commerce power without meaningful limit. Put another way, the mandate could not be reconciled with the notion that, by its own terms, Article I, Section 8 was a limited source of federal power.

Like my colleague, I had originally assumed the constitutional case against the mandate was a loser. As chronicled in these pages, I was initially skeptical of anti-mandate arguments. After *Gonzales v. Raich*, it seemed there was little basis upon which to claim that an individual component of a broader regulatory scheme concerning economic matters was not, at the very least, a necessary and proper exercise of federal power. If, for instance, the mere possession of marijuana could be prohibited so as to effectuate a broader prohibition on the drug's sale and consumption, why couldn't the federal government enact regulations designed to facilitate community rating requirements for health care? If newly adopted health insurance regulations would encourage adverse selection, would it not be "necessary and proper" to enact additional regulations to counteract these effects?

Such questions are difficult to answer. Mandate defenders were more likely to elide the question than to take it on; more prone to dismissing "absurd" hypotheticals than to take seriously the need to identify the outer limits of federal authority. Most constitutional justifications offered for a requirement that individuals purchase health insurance from a private provider would not equally justify other mandates to purchase private goods or services. While health insurance could be differentiated from other products and services on policy grounds, it was difficult for its defenders to justify such distinctions in constitutional terms. Some mandate defenders, such as Harvard Law Professor Charles Fried, were undaunted by such concerns, readily accepting that other mandates would be equally constitutional. Of course the government could force you to purchase broccoli, Fried conceded, it just could not force you to *eat* it. That limit could not be found in Article I's enumeration of powers, however, but in the Due Process Clause. As modified by the New Deal Court, the enumeration of powers was not, itself, to be a real limit on what the federal government could do, particularly not when enacting a broader regulatory scheme.

As the mandate debate unfolded, I was increasingly alienated by the broad and effectively unbounded arguments made on the mandate's behalf. It was almost as if the Rehnquist Court's federalism jurisprudence was no more than a footnote and not, as then-Chief Justice Rehnquist had proclaimed in *United States v. Lopez*, a matter of "first principles." At the same time, it became clear to me that if a limiting principle could not be identified, then the case for the mandate was incompatible with the principle that the powers enumerated in Article I, Section 8 are themselves subject to judicially enforceable limits.

In the end, the question of the individual mandate's constitutionality could not be resolved without reference to a broader theory of federal power. If federal power was largely unconstrained by the enumeration in Article I, Section 8 the mandate should be upheld. If, on the other hand, political safeguards against federal overreach were insufficient, and courts retained an obligation to police Congress's construction of its own authority, the mandate rested on thin ice, and the lack of limiting principle would consign the mandate to oblivion. This was a conflict of visions, not a question of doctrine.

It remains to be seen whether the Court's federalism holdings in *NFIB* herald newfound judicial enthusiasm for policing federal power. If nothing else, *NFIB* indicates that the conflict will endure.

Notes

1. The Supreme Court brief is available at http://davekopel.org/Briefs/11–398bsacAuthors Lawsonetal.pdf.
2. Andrew Koppelman, *The Tough Luck Constitution and the Assault on Health Care Reform* (New York: Oxford University Press, 2013).
3. Dames & Moore v. Regan, 453 U.S. 654 (1981).

4. New York Life Ins. Co. v. Dodge, 246 U.S. 357, 381 (1918) (Brandeis, J., dissenting) ("It was an act contemplated by the policy and was subsidiary to it, as an incident thereof.").

5. See, e.g., Michaelson v. United States ex rel. Chicago, St. P., M. & O. Ry. Co., 266 U.S. 42, 65 (1924) ("The discretion given the court in this respect is incidental and subordinate to the dominating purpose of the proceeding."); Anderson v. Forty-Two Broadway, 239 U.S. 69, 73 (1915) (stating approvingly that "Congress deemed that corporate indebtedness is an incident only if it does not exceed the corporate capital," and if it did, "the carrying of the indebtedness should be considered as a principal object of the corporate activities"). Cf. Federal Power Comm'n v. Transcontinental Gas Pipe Line Corp., 365 U.S. 1, 36 (1961) (Harlan, J., concurring and dissenting) ("[T]he Commission can properly assert this *more limited power as an incident* of its transportation certificating powers.") (emphasis added); Int'l Union v. Russell, 356 U.S. 634, 642–43 (1958) ("The power to order affirmative relief under § 10(c) is merely incidental to the primary purpose of Congress.").

6. For example, Poafpybitty v. Skelly Oil Co., 390 U.S. 365, 368 (1968) ("mere incidents"); United States v. Sealy, 388 U.S. 350, 356 (1967) (same).

7. For example, Dames & Moore v. Regan, 453 U.S. 654, 682, 688 (1981) (holding that the president's power to settle debts is nearly indispensable to recognition of foreign governments and is long standing and therefore is incidental); Nebraska v. Wyoming, 325 U.S. 589, 636 (1945) (approvingly quoting United States v. Haga, 276 F. 41, 43 (D. Idaho 1921) that certain activities are "necessarily incident to practical irrigation"); First Nat'l Bank in St. Louis v. Missouri, 263 U.S. 640, 656 (1924) (national banks "can rightfully exercise only such [powers] as are expressly granted or such incidental powers as are necessary to carry on the business for which they are established"); Lewis Publ'g Co. v. Morgan, 229 U.S. 288, 314 (1913) ("the right to exercise that power carries with it the authority to do those things which are incidental to the power itself, or which are plainly necessary to make effective the principal authority when exerted."); Wood v. Chesborough, 228 U.S. 672, 678 (1913) ("[t]o the extent necessary to do so the power exists as a necessary incident to a decision upon the claim of denial of the Federal right."); Miller v. King, 223 U.S. 505, 510 (1912) (applying a statute permitting bank to "exercise all such incidental powers as shall be necessary to carry on banking").

8. For example, *Dames & Moore*, 453 U.S. at 688 ("But where, as here, the settlement of claims has been determined to be a necessary incident to the resolution of a major foreign policy dispute"); United States v. Barnett, 376 U.S. 681, 699–700 (1964) ("The power to fine and imprison for contempt, from the earliest history of jurisprudence, has been regarded as a necessary incident . . . of a court, without which it could no more exist than without a judge."); Wood v. Chesborough, 228 U.S. 672, 678 (1913) ("[t]o the extent necessary to do so the power exists as a necessary incident to a decision upon the claim of denial of the Federal right."); Ex Parte, In the Matter of Duncan N. Hennen, 38 U.S. 230, 259 (1839) ("[i]n the absence of all constitutional provision, or statutory regulation, it would seem to be a sound and *necessary* rule, to consider the power of removal as incident to the power of appointment."). (emphasis added)

9. Andrew Koppelman, "Bad News for Mail Robbers: The Obvious Constitutionality of Health Care Reform," *Yale Law Journal Online* 121 (2011): 1; Gary Lawson and David B. Kopel, "Bad News for Professor Koppelman: The Incidental Unconstitutionality of the Individual Mandate," *Yale Law Journal Online* 121 (2011): 267; Andrew Koppelman, "Bad News for Everybody: Lawson and Kopel on Health Care Reform and Originalism," *Yale Law Journal Online* 121 (2012): 515; Gary Lawson and David B. Kopel, "Bad News for John Marshall," *Yale Law Journal Online* 121 (2012): 529.

10. For an article written in John Marshall's voice and applying his jurisprudential rules to the individual mandate, see Robert G. Natelson and David B. Kopel, "'Health Laws of Every Description': John Marshall's Ruling on a Federal Health Care Law," *Engage* 12 (2011): 49; Gerald Gunther, ed., *John Marshall's Defense of McCulloch v. Maryland* (Palo Alto, CA: Stanford University Press, 1969), 92 (reprint of newspaper article written by Marshall).

11. Available at http://davekopel.org/Briefs/Medicaid-mandate.pdf.

12. David B. Kopel, "Next Step: Repeal the Individual Mandate Because It Is Unconstitutional," *Volokh Conspiracy* (blog), June 29, 2012, http://www.volokh.com/2012/06/29/next-step-repeal-the-individual-mandate-because-it-is-unconstitutional; David B. Kopel, "What's Next for the Opposition Symposium: Andrew Jackson Shows What We Need to Do Next," *National Review Online*, June 29, 2012, http://www.nationalreview.com/articles/304394/what-s-next-opposition-nro-symposium.

13. United States v. Miller, 307 U.S. 174 (1939).

14. District of Columbia v. Heller, 554 U.S. 570 (2008).

15. For example, Jack M. Balkin, "Commerce," *Michigan Law Review First Impressions* 109 (2010): 1; Robert G. Natelson and David B. Kopel, "Commerce in the Commerce Clause: A Response to Jack Balkin," *Michigan Law Review* 109 (2010): 55.

16. See Ilya Somin, "The Individual Mandate and the Proper Meaning of 'Proper,'" in *The Health Care Case: The Supreme Court Decision and Its Aftermath*, ed. Gillian Metzger, Trevor Morrison, and Nathaniel Persily (New York: Oxford University Press, 2013); Ilya Somin, "A Mandate for Mandates: Is the Individual Health Insurance Mandate a Slippery Slope?," *Law and Contemporary Problems* 75 (2012): 75; Ilya Somin, "Assessing the Health Care Decision," *Harvard Health Policy Review* 13 (2012): 13; Ilya Somin, "A Taxing, But Potentially Hopeful Decision," *SCOTUSblog*, June 28, 2012, *supra*.

17. NFIB v. Sebelius, 132 S. Ct. 2566, 2593–600 (2012).

18. *Id.* at 2601–8.

19. *Id.* at 2579–92 (Roberts, C.J.).

20. *Id.* at 2592.

21. Brief for the Washington Legal Foundation & Constitutional Law Scholars, U.S. Dep't of Health & Human Servs. v. Florida, 132 S. Ct. 2566 (2012) (No. 11-398), available at http://www.wlf.org/upload/litigation/briefs/11–398bsacWashingtonLegalFoundation .pdf.

22. *NFIB*, 132 S. Ct. at 2594.

23. 26 U.S.C. § 5000A(b) (2012).

24. *NFIB*, 132 S. Ct. at 2594.

25. See Ilya Somin, "A Taxing but Potentially Hopeful Decision," *supra*; and Somin, "Assessing the Health Care," *supra*.

26. *NFIB*, 132 S. Ct. 2593–99.

27. Some scholars contend that Roberts's Commerce and Necessary and Proper holdings are mere "dictum" not binding on lower courts. For my critique of that view, which has largely been rejected by lower courts so far, see Somin, "The Individual Mandate and the Proper Meaning of 'Proper,'" 160.

28. For a detailed discussion of this issue, see Somin, "Mandate for Mandates," 84–96; and Somin, "Broccoli, Slippery Slopes, and the Individual Mandate," *supra*.

29. See Florida ex rel. Atty. Gen. v. U.S. Dep't of Health & Human Servs., 648 F. 3d 1235 (11th Cir. 2011) rev'd NFIB v. Sebelius, 132 S. Ct. 2566 (2012).

30. See Seven-Sky v. Holder, 661 F. 3d 1 (D.C. Cir. 2011); Thomas More Law Ctr. v. Obama, 651 F. 3d 529 (6th Cir. 2011).

31. 549 U.S. 514 (1995).

32. Adam Teicholz, "Did Bloggers Kill the Health Care Mandate?," *Atlantic*, last modified March 28, 2012, http://www.theatlantic.com/national/archive/2012/03/did-bloggers -kill-the-health-care-mandate/255182/#bio. For my evaluation of this article, see Ilya Somin, "Crediting/Blaming the VC for the Possible Defeat of the Individual Mandate," *supra*.

33. Jack Balkin, "From off the Wall to on the Wall: How the Mandate Challenge Went Mainstream," *Atlantic*, June 4, 2012, http://www.theatlantic.com/national/archive/2012/06/ from-off-the-wall-to-on-the-wall-how-the-mandate-challenge-went-mainstream/ 258040.

34. *Id.*

35. For citations to relevant survey data, see Somin, "Mandate for Mandates," 104.

36. Ilya Somin, "New Poll Showing that 68 Percent of the Public Want the Court to Strike Down the Individual Mandate," *Volokh Conspiracy* (blog), June 7, 2012, http://www .volokh.com/2012/06/07/new-poll-showing-that-68-percent-of-the-public-want-the -court-to-strike-out-the-individual-mandate.

37. Ilya Somin, "Public Opinion on the Role of Government," *Volokh Conspiracy* (blog), November 9, 2012, http://www.volokh.com/2012/11/09/public-opinion-on -the-role-of-government.

38. Brief for the Washington Legal Foundation et al., *Sebelius*, 132 S. Ct. 2566, *supra*.

39. See Ilya Somin, "Thoughts on the Individual Mandate Oral Argument," *supra*.

40. See Andrew Koppelman, "Necessary, 'Proper,' and Health Reform," in *The Health Care Case: The Supreme Court Decision and Its Aftermath*, ed. Gillian Metzger, Trevor Morrison, and Nathaniel Persily (New York: Oxford University Press, 2013).

41. For many examples of such statements, see David Hyman, "Why Did Law Professors Misunderestimate the Lawsuits against PPACA?," *University of Illinois Law Review* (forthcoming), at: 4–7, http://papers.ssrn.com/sol3/papers.cfm?abstract_id=2224364.

42. Balkin, "From off the Wall."

About the Contributors

Randy E. Barnett is the Carmack Waterhouse Professor of Legal Theory at the Georgetown University Law Center where he teaches constitutional law and contracts. Additionally, he has been a visiting professor at the University of Pennsylvania, Northwestern University, and Harvard University law schools. Professor Barnett earned his bachelor's degree from Northwestern University in 1974 and his JD from Harvard Law School in 1977. In 2004, Professor Barnett appeared before the United States Supreme Court in the case of *Gonzalez v. Raich*, the last major case challenging the scope of Congress's commerce power before the challenge to the Affordable Care Act (ACA). In 2008, he was awarded a Guggenheim Fellowship in constitutional studies. In 2010, Professor Barnett authored the first major academic article, "Commandeering the People: Why the Individual Health Insurance Mandate is Unconstitutional," that argued the individual mandate was unconstitutional. Later, Barnett joined the National Federation of Independent Business's litigation team as the case made its way to the Supreme Court. Among his publications are over one hundred law review articles and nine books, including *Restoring the Lost Constitution: The Presumption of Liberty* and casebooks on constitutional law and contracts. He has also appeared on programs such as *CBS Evening News*, *The NBC Nightly News*, and *Parker-Spitzer* (CNN).

Ilya Somin is professor of law at the George Mason University School of Law where his research focuses on constitutional law, property law, and the study of popular political participation and its implications for constitutional democracy. Somin is the author of *Democracy and Political Ignorance: Why Smaller Government Is Smarter*. He has served as a visiting professor at the University of Pennsylvania Law School, the University of Hamburg, and the University of Torcuato Di Tella in Argentina. Somin holds bachelor's degrees in political science and history from Amherst College, a master's degree in political science from Harvard, and a JD from Yale Law School. In addition to authoring scholarly articles on the challenge to the ACA, including "A Mandate for Mandates: Is the Individual Health Insurance Mandate Case a Slippery Slope?" in *Law and Contemporary Problems* and a forthcoming article explaining why the mandate was not "proper" even if it was necessary, he also authored numerous amicus briefs during the Obamacare litigation on behalf of the Washington Legal Foundation and a group of prominent constitutional law scholars, including one before the Supreme Court that explained why the Necessary and Proper Clause does not authorize the individual mandate—an argument eventually endorsed by a majority of the Supreme Court.

He is frequently published in both the scholarly and popular press, including the *Yale Law Journal*, the *Stanford Law Review*, the *Northwestern University Law Review*, as well as *Reason*, the *LA Times*, and *USA Today*.

Orin S. Kerr is the Fred C. Stevenson Research Professor of Law at the George Washington University School of Law. He is nationally recognized for his scholarship in criminal procedure and computer crime law. Professor Kerr holds a bachelor's degree in mechanical and aerospace engineering from Princeton University, a master's degree in mechanical engineering from Stanford University, and a JD from Harvard Law School. He has served as a trial attorney in the Computer Crime and Intellectual Property Section of the Criminal Division at the U.S. Department of Justice as well as a law clerk to Justice Kennedy on the United States Supreme Court. Professor Kerr has been widely published in academic journals as well as the popular press and counts among his publications the leading casebook in criminal procedure.

David E. Bernstein is the George Mason University Foundation Professor at the George Mason University School of Law. Professor Bernstein earned his bachelor's degree in history from Brandeis University and his JD from Yale Law School. Professor Bernstein has published dozens of law review articles, been quoted in numerous publications, and has been a guest on radio and television shows. In addition, he has authored or edited five books, including *Rehabilitating* Lochner: *Defending Individual Rights against Progressive Reform* and *You Can't Say That! The Growing Threat to Civil Liberties from Antidiscrimination Laws*.

David B. Kopel is the research director of the Independence Institute in Denver, Colorado, an associate policy analyst at the Cato Institute, and an adjunct professor at the University of Denver Sturm College of Law where he teaches advanced constitutional law. Professor Kopel holds a bachelor's degree in history from Brown University and a JD from Michigan Law School. His scholarly articles on Obamacare were published in the *Yale Law Journal*, the *Michigan Law Review*, and the *American Journal of Law & Medicine*. He authored two Supreme Court briefs in the Obamacare cases, one on the Necessary and Proper Clause, the other on the Medicaid mandate and the spending power. The arguments in both briefs were accepted by a majority of the Supreme Court. He is an expert on firearms policy, juvenile crime, drug policy, antitrust, constitutional law, criminal sentencing, and environmental law. He has authored 15 books and 85 scholarly articles, including the first law school textbook on the Second Amendment and *The Samurai, the Mountie, and the Cowboy: Should America Adopt the Gun Controls of Other Democracies?*, which was named book of the year by the American Society of Criminology, Division of International Criminology. He writes frequently for the *Wall Street Journal*, *National Review Online*, and other periodicals.

Jonathan H. Adler is the Johan Verheij Memorial Professor of Law at Case Western University School of Law where his primary focus is on environmental law issues. He earned his bachelor's degree in history from Yale University and his JD from the George Mason University School of Law. A 2007 study identified Professor Adler as the most cited legal academic in environmental law under age forty. He has made countless media appearances and testified before Congress on a dozen occasions. His work has appeared in the *Harvard Environmental Law Review*, the *University of Illinois Law Review*, the *Boston College Law Review*, and many others. He is also the author or editor of five books including *Environmentalism at the Crossroads: Green Activism in America; The Costs of Kyoto: Climate Change Policy and Its Implications*; and *Ecology, Liberty and Property: A Free Market Environmental Reader*.

Trevor Burrus (Editor) is a research fellow in the Cato Institute's Center for Constitutional Studies. He received his bachelor's degree in philosophy from the University of Colorado at Boulder and his JD from the University of Denver Sturm College of Law. He was a primary author of the Cato Institute's briefs opposing the Affordable Care Act, and he assisted in coordinating the unprecedented level of amici involvement in the case. In addition to numerous popular publications, particularly as a national columnist for the *Huffington Post*, his work has also been published in the *Harvard Journal of Law and Public Policy*, the *Vermont Law Review*, the *Syracuse Law Review*, and the *Widener Law Journal*.

Index

Ackerman, Bruce, 100
Act for the Relief of Sick and Disabled
    Seamen (1798), 33–34, 39
activity. *See* activity/inactivity distinction;
    economic activity regulation;
    noneconomic activity regulation
activity/inactivity distinction, 80
    assumptions and conclusions, 74–77
    commerce power of Congress and, 60–
        61, 107, 153n21
    economic decisions and, 60–61, 62
    examples of, 68–69, 104–6
    as first impression issue, 63
    in individual mandate, 72–74, 120–21
    intuitively, 113
    judicial bafflement, 103–4, 106–8
    mandates and, 80, 118
    multiple ways of determining, 108–11
    necessity and, 86–87, 210
    NFIB in Supreme Court, 223–24, 245,
        247–48
    omission as activity, 108, 109
    regulation of, 19, 72–74, 80
    in Steeh opinion, 60–61, 62, 72
    in Sutton opinion, 118–19, 120–21
    taxability of former vs. latter, 26
act/omission distinction. *See* activity/
    inactivity distinction
actuarial risk issue, 192–93, 204–5
actus reus requirement, 108–10, 113–14
Adler, Jonathan, 22, 70, 108–9, 134, 141–
    42, 175, 184–85, 237, 239, 258, 272–73
affirmative actions. *See* activity/inactivity
    distinction
affirmative duties, 111
Affordable Care Act (2010, ACA)
    challenges rested on technicality, 232
    future litigation, 265–66
    lawsuits against, after *NFIB*, 223

loopholes, 6
nonlegal arguments for, 206–10
Obama and, 158–59
passage and signing, 9–10, 101
pillars, 2, 10
popularity, 28
public opinion about, 168, 206, 271
significance of Supreme Court decision,
    214–15, 235–37, 257–58, 268–70
trajectory to Supreme Court, vii–viii,
    65, 117
agency law, 112
Akaka, Daniel, 188
Alito, Samuel
    as activist judge, 216
    actuarial risk and, 193
    background, ix–x
    individual mandate and, 224–25
American Law Institute, 1
Anti-Injunction Act (AIA)
    as barring challenges to individual
        mandate, 179
    in court of appeals, 145
    as inapplicable, 179–80
    preemptive challenges and, 157
appellate courts. *See* courts of appeals
as-applied challenges
    Raich as, 166–67
    Roberts and facial vs., 249
    Supreme Court precedents, 170
    Sutton and facial vs., 119, 121–26, 132,
        134–35
    winning, 167
Atlantic, 184–85, 270

Bagenstos, Sam, 169
Bailey v. Drexel Furniture, 12–13, 196, 245,
    246
Balkin, Jack, 12, 26, 27, 35, 103, 266, 270

Barnes, Robert, 200
Barnett, Randy, 3, 16, 19, 22, 27–28, 33, 40–41, 43–45, 66–69, 89, 103, 113, 117, 127, 162–63, 171, 183, 185, 186, 195, 197, 262, 269, 270, 271, 272
Baucus, Max, 20, 22, 184–85
Bernstein, David E., 172, 176, 238, 258
Blackmun, Harry, 81
blog posts, 1, 184–86, 270–73
Bondi, Pam, 2
Bond v. United States, 151
Boumediene v. Bush, 128, 129–30, 184
Boy Scouts of America v. Dale, 90
Breyer, Stephen, 101–2, 128, 182, 200, 228, 269
broccoli analogy, 91–92, 105–6, 118, 225–26, 274
Buck, Stuart, 234
Buffett, Warren, 121
burden of proof, 45, 127, 130, 131
Burroughs v. United States, 51, 85
Burrus, Trevor, 139, 141, 143, 259
Bush, George W., 232, 233
Bush v. Gore, 91, 241
Butler, Stuart, 31

capitation, 19–20, 103, 250
Carvin, Michael D., 179, 193
Casey, Lee, 11–15
Cato Institute, 3, 31–32, 259
Champion v. Ames, 189
circuit courts
   due process decisions, 132, 135
   interstate commerce rulings, 43
   split and likelihood of Supreme Court decision, 65, 117
   United States v. Lopez, 100–101
circumstantial evidence, 242
Citizens United v. Federal Election Commission, 168, 203, 248–49
class of activities issue, 122–23, 124–26, 134, 154n21
Clement, Paul D., 179, 196
Clyburn, James, 188
Cohn, Jonathan, 169
collective-action theory of federalism, 210–12
commandeering, 69–70, 140, 151, 160, 161–63, 165–66

Commandeering the People: Why the Individual Health Insurance Mandate is Unconstitutional (Barnett), 66–67
Commerce Clause, 239
   economic decisions doctrine under, 60–61
   Framers and, 3–4
   individual mandate and, 2–3, 22–23, 166, 189–90
   National Labor Relations Act and, 213
   penalties and, 146
   predictions about ruling on, ix
   rational basis test, 16
   Supreme Court decision in *NFIB,* 222, 235, 245
   wording, 14
   See also commerce power of Congress
commerce power of Congress
   activity/inactivity distinction and, 60–61, 107, 153n21
   extent of, 3, 15–16, 21, 22–23, 66–67, 76, 77, 95–97, 136–37, 170–71, 212–13
   facial challenge tests to, 124–25
   individual mandate as not necessary under, 166
   intrastate activity and, 86–87, 88
   mandates and, 166
   noneconomic activity and, 11–12
   Obama view of, 199
   regulation of inactivity, 118–19
   regulation of prices, 148–49
   regulations vs. mandates, 21
   Supreme Court decision in *NFIB,* 258
   Supreme Court precedent prior to *NFIB,* 43–44, 72
common law doctrine of duties, 109, 111
community rating price controls, 2, 10, 179, 189, 193, 274
compelled speech, 140–41
Comstock, United States v.
   enumerated powers and, 51
   federalism, 67–68, 76
   five-part test, 48–50, 52, 85, 94
   means to achieve ends, 85
   rationality of means and, 47–50, 53–54, 57n44, 99
   Roberts's actions, 52–53, 101–2
conditional regulations, 105
congressional powers
   baseline, 164

extent of, 14, 95–97, 136, 176
granted by Necessary and Proper Clause,
  82–83
judicial deference, 208
power of purse, 222–23
Supreme Court decision in *NFIB*, 231,
  235–37, 257–58
See also commerce power of Congress;
  enumerated powers of Congress;
  police power, plenary; taxing power
  of Congress
constitutionality
of already approved federal programs/
  agencies, 34
arguments against, 10–12
aspirational, 35
beliefs about, and political realm, 170–
  71, 188, 270–71
Congressional consideration of
  legislation and, 21, 208
of expansion of federal powers, 13–14
of first impression issues, 64
of goal, 46–47
good ideas and, 5
of New Deal and Great Society, 34–35
originalism theory, 4, 38, 98–99, 207–9
popular will and changes, 27
predictions about, ix, 29–31, 65, 182,
  183, 195–97, 214–15
presumption of, 126–31, 145, 153n19,
  154n31
of rationality of means to achieve ends,
  47–51, 52
Supreme Court as arbiter of, 14–15,
  38–40
Supreme Court precedents as, 90
unprecedented and, 44–46
Volokh Conspiracy and perception of
  uniform consensus about, 272–73
Conyers, John, 188
Cooter, Robert, 210, 211, 242–43
"Cornhusker Kickback," 9
cost shift argument, 174, 175, 204–6
courts of appeals
Anti-Injunction Act, 145
economic activity regulation in, 133,
  153n21
individual mandate in, 117, 118–23,
  126–31, 152
limits to decisions, 135

penalties vs. taxes, 133
political realm and decisions, ix, 117
*Cruzan v. Director, Missouri Department of
  Health,* 13, 174
Cuccinelli, Ken, II, 2, 25, 259
See also *National Federation of
  Independent Business v. Sebelius,
  Supreme Court decision; National
  Federation of Independent Business
  v. Sebelius* in Supreme Court

Dames & Moore v. Regan, 262
Darby, United States v., 66, 86, 100, 165,
  227
Daschle, Nathan, 32
Davis, Andre M., 104
Dellinger, Walter, 132, 173, 174
DeMars, Jann, 120
DeMint, Jim, 22
Denniston, Lyle, 103–4, 106, 194
dictum vs. holding, 237–38, 239–41
direct evidence, 242
direct taxes, 19–20, 103, 250
district courts
decisions and trajectory to Supreme
  Court, vii–viii
economic activity, 83–84, 94
economic decisions doctrine in, 71
individual mandate in, vii–viii, 59, 71–
  72, 79, 83–85, 96–97
motions to dismiss, 59
penalties vs. taxes in, 71, 81, 84
political realm and appointments, viii, ix
political realm and decisions, 63
standing issue, 71–72
value of decisions, 63
Dubina, Joel, 117, 157, 260
Due Process Clause
circuit court decisions, 132, 135
commandeering and, 160
limiting principle and, 191
duties, common law doctrine of, 109

Easterbrook, Frank, 132, 135
Eastern Enterprises v. Apfel, 201
Eastman, John, 194–95
economic activity regulation
commandeering and, 162, 163
in courts of appeals, 133, 153n21
in district courts, 83–84, 94

economic activity regulation (*continued*)
economic decisions doctrine and, 62
forcing entrance into market, 148–50
interstate nature of health care, 46–47
Raich and, 11, 16, 136–37, 151
Supreme Court decision in *NFIB*, 269–70
Supreme Court definition of, 18
Wickard and, 73
economic decisions
under Commerce Clause, 60–61
Congressional police power and acceptance of, 62
in district courts, 71
regulation, 93–94
as slippery slope, 64–65, 73
Steeh and, 62, 64
education law argument, 172–73
Edwards, Harry, 145
effects test. *See* substantial effects rule
Eleventh Amendment, 160
emanations-and-penumbras arguments, 162–63
ends (goals)
constitutionality of means to achieve, 47–51, 55, 85
Necessary and Proper Clause, 82–83
Engel, Steve, 183
Ensign, John, 22
entitlements, repeal of, 27–28
enumerated powers of Congress
Affordable Care Act lies beyond, 10–12
collective-action theory of federalism and, 210–12
Comstock and, 51
indirect use of, 150
Lopez and *Morrison* and, 21
militia, 36
Necessary and Proper Clause, 84
New Deal and, 274
plenary powers vs., 76, 77
powers granted besides, 82–83
presumption of constitutionality and, 126–27
state sovereignty and, 37
Supreme Court decision in *NFIB*, 221–22, 258
Epstein, Richard, 22
essential to a broader regulatory scheme doctrine, 87–88, 165–66

European Union (EU), example of, 4
event taxes, 20, 228–29
Ex Parte Milligan, 90
Ex Parte Quirin, 90

facial challenges, 81
individual mandate as, 167, 170
Roberts and as-applied vs., 249
Sutton and as-applied challenges vs., 119, 121–26, 132, 134–35
Fallows, James, 216
Farr, H. Bartow, III, 179
federalism
after New Deal, 100
collective-action theory, 210–12
commandeering and, 69–70, 140, 151
federal prohibitions and, 69
individual mandate as death of, 36–37
judicial power in, 240
Kennedy on, 37, 67–68, 76
plenary powers and, 76, 77
regulations on states and, 69–70
Supreme Court decision in *NFIB as victory*, 223–25
Supreme Court make-up and, ix–x, 214
Federalist No. 78, 198, 240
Fifth Amendment, 160, 161, 191
Filburn, Wickard v. See Wickard v. Filburn
first impression issue, 61–63, 64
five-part test, 48–50, 52, 85, 94
Flast v. Cohen, 249
Florida et al. v. Department of Health and Human Services in Supreme Court, 157
See also *National Federation of Independent Business v. Sebelius*, Supreme Court decision; *National Federation of Independent Business v. Sebelius* in Supreme Court
Florida v. U.S. Department of Health and Human Services, 59
framer's intent, 4
Fried, Charles, 176, 274
Fuller, Lon, 161
Fuller, Melville, 189

Garcia v. San Antonio Metropolitan Transit Authority (SAMTA), 81, 100
Garwood, William, 100
general welfare, 81, 187, 194–95

Gibbons v. Ogden, 210
Goldberg v. Kelly, 90
Gonzales v. Raich
  activities are economic, 11, 16, 136–37,
    151
  activity/inactivity distinction and, 60–
    61, 80
  as-applied challenges and, 166–67, 170
  class of activities applied to, 125, 126
  collective-action theory of federalism
    and, 211
  extent of Congressional power, 67, 95,
    96
  individual mandate and, 15–19, 35–36,
    71
  intrastate activity, 86–87
  substantial effects, 89
  wrongly decided, 16–17, 21
Graham, James, 118, 132
Great Society, 34–35, 137–38
Greenhouse, Linda, 170, 171–72, 174
Griswold v. Connecticut, 13
"Guaranteed issue," 10
Gun-Free School Zones Act (GFSZA,
  1990). See *Lopez, United States v.*

Hall, Mark, 212
Hamilton, Alexander, 198
Hare, Phil, 188
Hasen, Rick, 234
health care
  bronze plans vs. catastrophic coverage,
    205
  Great Society, 137–38
  insurance industry, 2, 12, 92, 93
  as market, 19, 73–74
  media coverage, viii
  percent of US economy, 46
  political realm and, 139
  reform in Massachusetts, 31
  right of refusal, 174
  as special case argument, 94, 174–76,
    183, 223–24
Hein v. Freedom from Religion Foundation,
  249
Heritage Foundation, 31–32, 138
Hill, Frank, ix
holding vs. dictum, 237–38, 239–41
Hudson, Henry E., vii–viii, 45, 59, 65, 79,
  83–85, 260

Hull, Frank, 117, 157, 260

indirect taxes, 20, 228–29
individual mandate
  as Affordable Care Act pillar, 2, 10
  activity/inactivity distinction and, 72–
    74, 120–21
  arguments against constitutionality,
    10–12
  as bestowing plenary powers, 76
  as commandeering individuals, 161–63
  Commerce Clause and, 2–3, 22–23, 166,
    189–90
  cost shift argument, 174, 175
  in courts of appeals, 117, 118–23, 126–
    31, 152
  in district courts, vii–viii, 59, 71–72, 79,
    83–85, 96–97
  as economic stimulator, 92
  as facial challenge, 167, 170
  false arguments for, 173–75
  federalism and, 36–37, 136, 189–91
  health insurance companies and, 93
  as intellectually indefensible, 228
  as necessary and proper, 80, 238
  as necessary but not proper, 94, 96–97,
    181, 224
  as noneconomic activity, 137
  nonlegal arguments for, 206–9
  penalties and, 71, 84, 179–80
  political realm and, 158–59, 170–71
  precedents for, 15–19, 33–34, 35–36,
    39, 71
  predictions about constitutionality, 29–
    31, 65, 182, 183, 214–15
  public opinion about, 28, 168, 177, 271
  purpose, 83
  as rational means, 47–50, 80
  as redistributive, 144
  as Republican idea, 31–32, 138
  right to privacy and, 13
  single-pay system vs., 141–44
  as slippery slope, 91–92, 118, 225–26
  striking down as judicial activism,
    203–4
  Supreme Court decision in *NFIB,* 222,
    224, 236, 238, 239–41, 242, 244–49,
    268–69
  as tax, 39, 84, 102–3, 190–91, 225–26,
    242–43

individual mandate (*continued*)
  as unprecedented, 45
  virtually everyone argument, 173–75
interstate "hook," 42–43

Jackson, Andrew, 266
Jackson, Robert, 148–49
Jefferson, Thomas, 199
Johnson v. Eisentrager, 184
Jost, Timothy Stoltzfus, 14–15, 45
judicial activism, 201–4, 215–16, 222
judicial conservatism, 207–9
jurisdictional elements, 124, 126

Kagan, Elena, 228, 269
Katsas, Greg, 179–80
Katyal, Neal, 106–8, 112, 125
Kavanaugh, Brett, 145–46, 152
Kelo v. New London, 168, 185, 203, 206, 251
Kennedy, Anthony
  actuarial risk questions, 192–93
  on federalism, 37, 67–68, 76
  health care as special argument and, 183
  individual mandate and, 224–25
  Lochner argument and, 200–201
  Vinson and, 99
Kennedy, Ted, 9
Kerr, Orin, 29–30, 34–35, 38, 40, 48–49,
    52–55, 65–67, 69, 75–76, 84–85, 95,
    98, 110–13, 128–31, 139, 143–44, 160,
    258–59, 273
Kneedler, Edwin, 179
Kopel, David B., 3, 34, 117, 185, 258, 261–
    62, 272
Koppelman, Andrew, 91–92, 196, 212,
    263–64

Landrieu, Mary, 188
Langbein, John H., 1
Lawrence v. Texas, 200–201
law reviews, 1
Leahy, Patrick, 188
legal academia, predictions from, ix, 29–
    31, 65, 182, 183, 195–97, 214–15
legal duty, creation of, 109
Levinson, Sandy, 35
"libertarians are coming" meme, 209–10
liberty, presumption of, 37, 191
Liberty University, 71–72, 73

Liberty University v. Geithner, 59, 106–8,
    112
Lieberman, Joe, 9
limiting principles, 182–83, 189–91, 192–
    93, 196, 210–12, 274
Lincoln, Abraham, 199
Lithwick, Dahlia, 171–72
Lochner v. New York, 13, 200–201
Long, Robert A., 179
Lopez, United States v.
  absence of limiting principle, 210
  application of Sutton reasoning to, 122,
    123–24
  collective-action theory of federalism
    and, 211
  Congressional powers and, 21, 66, 76,
    95, 164, 165
  federal authority regulatory limits, 32,
    80
  history, 30
  lower court decisions and, 30, 100–101
  presumption of constitutionality and,
    128
  rationality of means and, 18, 49–50
  regulation of noneconomic activity,
    11–12, 136
  Rehnquist opinion, 3, 86, 88, 164, 210

Magliocca, Gerard, 44, 45, 46
mandates
  activity/inactivity distinction and, 80,
    118
  heightened scrutiny for, 214
  as improper means under commerce
    power of Congress, 166
  Medicare as, 140
  popular will and, 81
  prohibitions vs., 105
  regulations vs., 21, 39–40, 42, 83
  as slippery slope, 150
  on states, 69–70
  Supreme Court decision in *NFIB*, 236,
    238
  as tax, 81, 116n55
  taxes in place of, 238
  upholding of, will be unprecedented, 46
  See also individual mandate
Marbury v. Madison, 228, 229
marijuana legalization, 5
  See also *Gonzales v. Raich*

market mechanisms, 2, 19, 73–74, 138, 140, 148–50

Marshall, John, 116n55, 210, 228, 229, 262, 266

Martin, Boyce, 118–19, 132, 133, 134–35, 153n21

Maryland v. Wirtz, 12

Massachusetts health care reform, 31, 138

Mathews v. Eldridge, 90

McCain-Feingold campaign finance challenge, vii

McCollum, Bill, 25

McConnell, Michael, 33

McConnell v. FEC, vii

McCullough v. Maryland, 47–50, 86, 116n55, 228, 262, 266

McDonald v. City of Chicago, 132, 135

McMaster, Henry, 25

means to achieve goal, constitutionality of, 47–51, 52, 55, 85, 160

media coverage, viii–ix

Medicaid expansion, 3
   as coercive to states, 169–70, 194, 226
   Constitution preamble goals and, 187
   general welfare definition, 194–95
   Supreme Court decision in *NFIB,* 222–23, 226, 236, 268, 269

Medicare, 33, 39, 137–38, 140

Meyer v. Nebraska, 13

Miers, Harriet, 232

Militia powers, 36, 39

Miller, Tom, 31–32

Moon, Norman, 71–72, 73

Morrison, United States v.
   application of Sutton reasoning to, 122–23
   collective-action theory of federalism and, 211
   Congressional powers and, 21, 43, 66, 154n31, 164, 165
   failure of Supreme Court to apply rational basis test, 18
   presumption of constitutionality and, 128, 129
   regulation of noneconomic activity, 12
   Rehnquist and, 3

Most Democratic Branch: How the Courts Serve America, The (Rosen), 208

motion to dismiss, 59

Motz, Dianna, 106–8, 112

NAMUDNO v. Holder, 248

Natelson, Rob, 10–11

National Federation of Independent Business (NFIB), 2
   See also Vinson, Roger

National Federation of Independent Business v. Sebelius, Supreme Court decision
   dissenting judges, 224–25
   dissent wording, 233, 234
   health care as special, 223–24
   holding or dictum issue, 237–38, 239–41
   individual mandate, 222, 224, 236, 238, 239–41, 242, 244–49, 268–69
   legitimacy of Supreme Court and, 250–53
   limits on federal power, 221–23, 235–36
   Medicaid expansion, 268, 269
   significance, 214–15, 235–37, 257–58, 268–70
   taxing and spending power of Congress, 222, 225–26, 228–29, 245–48, 249–50, 258, 269

National Federation of Independent Business v. Sebelius in Supreme Court
   actuarial risk questions, 192–93
   agreement to hear, 157
   briefs, 261–63, 265, 271
   Kennedy and heightened scrutiny for mandates, 214
   oral arguments, 179, 271
   public attention, ix
   Roberts-Katsas dialogue, 179–80
   Scalia-Verrilli dialogue, 181
   Verrilli use of *Lochner,* 200–201

National Labor Relations Act (1935), 213

Necessary and Proper Clause, ix, 47–55
   essential to a broader regulatory scheme doctrine, 87–88, 165–66
   individual mandate and limits, 189
   individual mandate as necessary and proper, 80, 238
   individual mandate as necessary but not proper, 94, 96–97, 181, 224
   individual mandate as rational means, 47–50, 80
   Kennedy in *Comstock,* 67–68
   powers granted to Congress by, 82–83
   rationality of means and, 47–50, 53–54, 57n44, 99

Necessary and Proper Clause (*continued*)
   Scalia-Verrilli dialogue, 181
   substantial effects rule, 88, 165
   Supreme Court decision in *NFIB*, 222,
      224, 228, 235–36, 269
   wording, 14
Nelson, Ben, 9
New Deal
   constitutionality, 34–35
   enumeration of powers and, 274
   federalism after, 100
   National Labor Relations Act
      constitutionality, 213
   popular will during, 27
   substantial effects rule, 86
   Supreme Court jurists, 229, 230, 232–33
   See also specific cases
New England Journal of Medicine, 26
New Federalism, 165
New York Times, 72, 84, 216, 271
New York v. United States, 69, 140, 160, 211
Ninth Amendment, 27, 37
NLRB v. Jones & Laughlin Steel, 5, 42, 86,
      87, 100
noneconomic activity regulation, 86,
      87–88
   individual mandate as, 137
   necessity of collective solution, 210
   Raich and, 16
   rulings against Congressional power,
      11–12
   Supreme Court definition of, 18
   taxation, 26–27
"Not the Power to Destroy: An Effects
   Theory of the Tax Power" (Siegel and
   Cooter), 242–43

Obama, Barack, 2
   denial of individual mandate as tax, 39
   importance of Affordable Care Act,
      158–59
   individual mandate as penalty, 102
   legitimacy of judicial review, 197–200
   priorities, 9
   on Supreme Court decision, 236
O'Connor, Sandra Day, ix, 160, 214
omission as activity, 108, 109
oral argument, 65
   in *Comstock*, 101
   defining class of activities in, 125

   in D.C. Circuit, 145–50
   in Florida District Court, 94
   in *Liberty University v. Geithner*, 106–7,
      112
   in Supreme Court, 157, 165, 167, 179,
      180, 182, 186, 187, 189, 192, 194,
      196–97, 206, 214
originalism, 4, 38, 98–99, 207–9

Patient Protection and Affordable Care
   Act (PPACA). *See* Affordable Care Act
   (2010, ACA)
Pelosi, Nancy, 10, 44, 188
penalties vs. taxes
   Congressional powers and, 102–3
   in courts of appeals, 133
   in district courts, 71, 81, 84
   Roberts-Katsas dialogue, 179–80
   Supreme Court decision in *NFIB*, 245–
      48, 249–50, 269
   Supreme Court decisions, 84, 103,
      225–26
Pierce v. Society of Sisters, 13
Planned Parenthood v. Casey, 13
plenary powers vs. enumerated powers,
      76, 77
police power, plenary
   acceptance of economic decisions
      doctrine, 62
   Constitution withholds from Congress,
      96
   as inherent state power, 67, 150, 172
   limiting principle, 182–83
   Supreme Court in *Morrison*, 12
political realm
   Affordable Care Act passage, 9–10
   beliefs about constitutionality and, 171–
      72, 188, 270–71
   courts of appeals decisions and, ix, 117
   decisions and, 118
   district court appointments and, viii, ix
   district court decisions and, ix, 63
   health care measures and, 139
   Hudson refusal of motion to dismiss,
      59, 65
   individual mandate and, 158–59, 170–71
   judicial activism and, 201–3
   repeal of entitlements, 27–28
   reversal of presidential agenda and, 184

Supreme Court decisions and, 17, 28, 90, 91, 159, 207
Supreme Court jurists, 229–30, 232–33, 237, 238
taxing power of Congress and, 140
Posner, Richard, 132
power, granting of, 6
PrawfsBlawg, 40, 41
"precedent," legal use of word, 41
  binding nature of, 35, 97, 99
  judicial activism and, 202, 215–16, 222
  limiting principle and, 189
  originalism vs., 98–99
  use of, 90
Predictions about constitutionality, ix, 29–31, 65, 182, 183, 195–97, 214–15
preemptive challenges, 157
presumption of constitutionality, 126–31, 145, 153n19, 154n31
prices, 2, 10, 148–49
Printz v. United States
  collective-action theory of federalism and, 211
  commandeering and, 69, 140, 151, 165–66
  means to achieve goal, constitutionality of, 160
  necessary but not proper, 54–55
  novelty claim, 162
  presumption of constitutionality, 130, 131, 145
prohibitions vs. mandates, 105
"proper," use of word, 49–50, 52, 54–55, 57n44, 238
public opinion
  changes in constitutionality and, 27
  mandates and, 81
  opinion about Affordable Care Act/individual mandate, 28, 168, 177, 206, 271
  opinion about Supreme Court, 215, 251
  Supreme Court decisions and, 28, 30–31, 35, 90, 91, 168, 177, 234, 271

Rapanos v. United States, 211
Rasul v. Bush, 184
rational basis test, 16, 18, 47–51, 52
  See also substantial effects rule
regulation(s)

of activity vs. of inactivity, 19, 72–74, 80, 106–7
conditional, 105
economic decisions doctrine and, 93–94
of inactivity, 118–19
includes prescription and proscription, 121
limits on, 32, 80
mandates vs., 21, 39–40, 42, 83
of requirement of action, 183
taxes as penalties, 84
  See also economic activity regulation; noneconomic activity regulation
Rehnquist, William
  background, ix
  federalism and, 214
  Lopez and, 3, 86, 88, 164, 210
  taxing and spending, 227
Reid, Harry, 9
Reorganized CF&I Fabricators of Utah, Inc., United States v., 84
rescue, duty to, 104, 109
right to privacy and individual mandate, 13
ripeness issue, 61
Rivkin, David, 11–15, 212–13, 259, 272
Roach Motel theory, 132, 134
Roberts, John
  actuarial risk and, 193
  background, ix–x, 232
  Comstock and, 52–53, 101–2
  hints about changing *NFIB* vote, 233, 234, 241, 252–53
  as judicial minimalist, 222
  on law reviews, 1
  as leader of activist court, 215–16, 222
  questions on individual mandate as mandate, 179–80
  severability issue, 249
  taxing power upheld, 3
Roberts, John, opinion in *NFIB*
  as conservative, 231–32
  as consistent with previous behavior, 248–49
  individual mandate, 242, 244–49, 268–69
  individual mandate as necessary but not proper, 224
  limits on federal power, 221–22, 223–24, 235–36

Roberts, John, (*continued*)
  logic of, 241–48
  significance of, 237–38
  taxing and spending, 225–26, 228–29,
    245–48, 249–50, 258
Roberts v. United States Jaycees, 90
Roe v. Wade, 11, 91
Romney, Mitt, 31, 138, 230, 231
Rosen, Jeffrey, 207, 208, 210
Rosenkranz, Nick, 167
Ruger, Ted, 176

Sabri v. United States, 47–50
Sargent, Greg, 195
"Saving construction" of Roberts, 241, 242,
    243, 244–49, 269
Scalia, Antonin
  Comstock dissent, 166
  individual mandate and, 224–25
  Lochner used in *Lawrence* dissent,
    200–201
  NFIB dialogue with Verrilli, 181
  NFIB dissent, 228
  Printz opinion, 54–55, 145, 160, 162,
    165–66
  Raich concurrence, 21, 86–87, 89–90,
    165–67
Schauer, Frederick, 91–92
Schechter Poultry Corp. v. United States, 11
Seaman Act (1798). *See* Act for the Relief
    of Sick and Disabled Seamen (1798)
Sedgwick, Thomas, 26
self-financing vs. self-insurance, 134
Seven-Sky v. Holder, 145–48
severability issue, 59, 84–85, 94–95, 179,
    249
Sex Offender Registration and Notification
    Act (2006, SORNA), 42–43
Shapiro, Ilya, 126–27, 259
Siegel, Neil, 189–91, 210, 211, 242–43
Silberman, Laurence, ix, 145, 147–48
single-payer system, 2, 138, 141–44
slippery slope issues
  economic decisions doctrine, 64–65, 73
  individual mandate, 91–92, 118, 225–26
  mandates, 150
Somin, Ilya, 3, 34, 50–52, 53, 61, 74–75, 77,
    96, 97, 117, 123, 127, 129–30, 134, 245,
    252, 258, 263
Sonzinsky v. United States, 26, 35–36, 103

Sorrell v. IMS Health Care, Inc., 200
South Dakota v. Dole, 194, 222, 223, 227
spending power of Congress, ix, 14
standing issue, 61, 71–72, 249
Stark, Fortney "Pete," 188
state sovereignty
  coercion and, 169, 194
  federal prohibitions and, 69
  federal regulations and, 69–70
  individual mandate as death of, 36–37
  Kennedy in *Comstock*, 67–68, 76
  limitations presupposed by
    Amendments, 160–61
  police power and, 67, 150, 172
  Supreme Court decision in *NFIB*,
    226–27
Steeh, George C., III
  activity/inactivity distinction, 60–61,
    62, 72
  dismissal by, 59
  economic decisions doctrine, 62, 64
  first impression issue, 61–63, 64
  on health care as market, 73–74
Steward Machine Company v. Davis,
    227–28
Stone, Harlan Fiske, 227
subsidies, as Affordable Care Act pillar,
    2, 10
substantial effects rule
  limits and, 3, 15–16, 88, 89
  as misguided, 17
  Necessary and Proper Clause, 165
  qualifications on, 86–87
Supreme Court
  as arbiter of constitutionality, 14–15,
    38–40
  federalism and make-up of, 214
  legitimacy, 206–7, 250–53
  media coverage, viii–ix
  politics of jurists, 229–30, 232–33, 237,
    238
  public opinion about, 215, 251
  trajectory to, vii–viii, 65, 117
Supreme Court decisions
  authority to determine constitutionality
    of statutes, 198–99
  collective-action theory of federalism,
    211
  deference to other branches and, 43–44,
    188, 228

effect on public opinion, 215
influence of lower court opinions, 132
political realm and, 17, 28, 90, 91, 159, 207
popular will and, 28, 30–31, 35, 90, 91, 168, 177, 234, 271
presumption of constitutionality, 128
Roberts court as activist, 215–16, 222
use of word "proper" by, 49–50, 54–55, 57n44
See also specific cases
Sutton, Jeffrey
facial vs. as-applied challenges, 119, 121–26, 132, 134–35
individual mandate and, 120–21
legislative novelty, 133, 135
political realm and decision by, ix, 117
regulation of inactivity, 118–19
SWANCC v. Army Corps of Engineers, 211

Taxing and Spending Clause, 60, 71, 85, 119, 194, 225–28, 237, 265
See also taxing power of Congress
taxing power of Congress
commandeering under, 163
credits and, 39
direct taxes, 19–20, 103, 250
in district courts, 71
extent of, 26–27
form of law vs. function of law and, 231–32
individual mandate and, 2–3, 39, 84, 102–3, 190–91, 225–26, 242–43
mandates as tax, 81, 116n55
noneconomic activity, 26–27
penalty vs., 81, 84, 102–3, 133
political restraints on, 140
as power to destroy, 116n55
Seaman Act as precedent, 33, 39
spending power and, 14
as superfluous, 119
Supreme Court decision in *NFIB,* 222, 225–26, 228–29, 245–48, 249–50, 258, 269
using in place of mandates, 238
Teicholz, Adam, 184–85, 186
Tenth Amendment, 14, 151, 160, 161, 166, 227
See also state sovereignty
Third Amendment, 161

Thirteenth Amendment, 161
Thomas, Clarence, 96, 97, 166, 167, 224–25
Thomas More Law Center, 59, 61
See also Steeh, George C., III
Toobin, Jeffrey, 216, 248–49
Turley, Jonathan, 36

United Nations, jurisdiction of, 5
United States Jaycees, Roberts v., 90
United States v. Comstock. See *Comstock, United States v.*
United States v. Darby. See *Darby, United States v.*
United States v. Lopez. See *Lopez, United States v.*
United States v. Morrison. See *Morrison, United States v.*
United States v. Reorganized CF&I Fabricators of Utah, Inc., 84
unprecedented issue, 40, 41–42, 44–46, 138–39, 172

Verrilli, Donald B., Jr., 179, 187, 200–201
vertical stare decisis, 37, 97, 99
Vinson, Roger
decision, 93–99, 260
individual mandate as regulatory penalty, 71
integration of individual mandate, 59
refusal of motion to dismiss, 59
trajectory to Supreme Court and, vii–viii
Virginia v. Sebelius, 88
virtually everyone argument, 173–75
Volokh, Eugene, viii
Volokh Conspiracy (VC), viii, 1, 184–86, 270–73

Walker, Wolf, 127
Wall Street Journal, 212–13
Washington Post, 25–26, 173, 174
Washington Times, 213
Watson v. United States, 128–29
Whelan, Ed, 234
White, Ed, 147–48
Wickard v. Filburn, 152
activity/inactivity distinction and, 80, 120
as-applied challenge and, 170
collective-action theory of federalism and, 211

Wickard v. Filburn (continued)
  commodity vs. service, 12
  definition of economic activity, 73
  extent of Congressional power, 11, 96, 147–48
  individual mandate and, 35–36, 71

Jackson opinion, 148–49
  Roberts's opinion in *NFIB* and, 224
  substantial effects rule, 86
window tax, 249–50

Zywicki, Todd, 185